Frommer's®
Amsterdam

My Amsterdam

by George McDonald

WELCOME BELOW SEA LEVEL. IT ALWAYS ADDS A *FRISSON* OF EXCITEMENT to my wanderings around Europe's capital of Alternative Everything—a city more than occasionally compared to Sodom and Gomorrah—to know that given one good shove from nature, the whole place will vanish beneath the waves. Fortunately, so far the earthly and heavenly powers have been remarkably tolerant, and Amsterdam continues on its unorthodox way, its collective head still above water.

Tolerance is integral to the Dutch capital's DNA. Easygoing, disarmingly friendly, and irreverent, Amsterdammers have turned their small, flat, watery city into a hothouse for social and personal growth. Moralizers near and far may gaze disapprovingly on a permissiveness that seems to know no bounds. But Amsterdam tunes them out and chafes a little harder at what boundaries do exist, as much out of habit as from conscious choice. The canals and their glorious 17th-century Golden Age architecture are merely the scenic stage upon which daily life plays out.

When all is said, and much of it done, I think what I like best about Amsterdam is its love affair with the . . . bicycle. A city reckoned to be at the bleeding edge where lifestyle choices are concerned, yet whose transportation mode of choice is a battered pedal-bike, is not one to threaten civilization as we know it, whatever axe-grinding commentators might say to the contrary.

Amsterdam's gigantic Koninginnedag or **QUEEN'S DAY (left)** street party and free street market, every year on April 30, celebrates the Dutch queen's "official" birthday (meaning it's not her real one). Holland's royal House of Orange is a popular institution and Queen Beatrix a people-friendly monarch. Her Amsterdam "subjects" celebrate by turning the city into a sea of orange—including everything from orange tulips to orange afros—during the wild festivities.

Vincent has never had it so good. His paintings sell for stratospheric amounts and exhibits of his work draw huge crowds. Amsterdam is the world center of the Vincent cult, and the **VAN GOGH MUSEUM (above)** is its temple. Nowhere else are so many paintings by the 19th-century artist displayed, and in chronological order, allowing visitors to track his progress. These are accompanied by drawings, sketches, and voluminous correspondence with his brother Theo.

Working outward from the heart of town, Herengracht, Keizersgracht, and **PRINSENGRACHT (above)** are the Canal Belt's three 17th-century Golden Age canals. Prinsengracht, or Princes' Canal, was intended to be a residence for storekeepers and craftsmen. These workaday folks were judged not blue-blooded or wealthy enough to justify homes on Herengracht (Gentlemen's Canal) or Keizersgracht (Emperor's Canal). Today, Prinsengracht, with its moored houseboats and barges, is still the most animated of the three canals.

The bicycle is truly the way to go here, as the **MASSES OF BIKES (right)** parked throughout the city can attest. By going around on your own two rented wheels, you're not only helping the environment and your health, you're making it easy to explore the nooks and crannies of the city that would otherwise be hard to reach.

Downing a foaming pilsener beer at a traditional Dutch bar, known as a *bruine kroeg* or **BROWN CAFE,** is one of the quintessential Amsterdam experiences. Bars like Hoppe, In de Wildeman, or In 't Aepjen are most ideal, but any brown cafe will do. Though Heineken and Amstel are the most common beers here, my own favorite Dutch pilsener is Grolsch.
© *Charlie Knight/Alamy*

© Frans Lemmens/Alamy

AROUND TOWN The mile-long **ALBERT CUYPMARKT (above right)**, on Albert Cuypstraat, is the city's biggest outdoor bazaar, and a particularly great place to pick up Dutch and exotic food, cheap clothing, and more. The premier antiques quarter, **NIEUWE SPIEGELSTRAAT (below)**, is home to 100 reputable dealers. Amsterdam's canals don't freeze over in winter as often as they used to, so don't expect the sorts of scenes of **CANAL SKATERS (left)** the Dutch old masters made famous in paintings. But if ice does form, be prepared to see practically the whole city glide. More a way of life than a railway station, frenetically busy **CENTRAAL STATION (below right)** is, for many new arrivals in town, their first taste of Amsterdam. A Catholic architect designed it to be the transportation cathedral of a Protestant city, and tweaked the aesthetic sensibilities of his Calvinist 19th-century fellow citizens by slipping in Gothic motifs wherever he could get away with them.

© Peter Horree/Alamy

At the very first hint of sunshine in this damp northern city, offices, homes, and factories all around town empty out in the blink of an eye, and the streets fill with hurrying masses yearning to be free at one of Amsterdam's **SIDEWALK CAFES.** Scoring the perfect table right beside the canal or under a plane tree in the garden is an indication that you've finally arrived.

Frommer's®

Amsterdam

15th Edition

by George McDonald

Here's what the critics say about Frommer's:

"Amazingly easy to use. Very portable, very complete."
—**BOOKLIST**

"Detailed, accurate, and easy-to-read information
for all price ranges."
—**GLAMOUR MAGAZINE**

"Hotel information is close to encyclopedic."
—**DES MOINES SUNDAY REGISTER**

"Frommer's Guides have a way of giving you a real feel
for a place."
—**KNIGHT RIDDER NEWSPAPERS**

WILEY

Wiley Publishing, Inc.

ABOUT THE AUTHOR

George McDonald has lived and worked in Amsterdam, as deputy editor of KLM's in-flight magazine, *Holland Herald*. Now a freelance journalist and travel writer, he has written extensively about Amsterdam and the Netherlands for magazines and travel books, including *Frommer's Belgium, Holland & Luxembourg, Frommer's Europe, Frommer's Europe by Rail,* and *Europe For Dummies.*

Published by:

WILEY PUBLISHING, INC.

111 River St.
Hoboken, NJ 07030-5774

ISBN 978-0-470-38225-7

Editor: Jennifer Reilly
Production Editor: Eric T. Schroeder
Cartographer: Liz Puhl
Photo Editor: Richard Fox
Production by Wiley Indianapolis Composition Services

Front cover photo: Bikers in front of cafe
Back cover photo: Building facade

For information on our other products and services or to obtain technical support, please contact our Customer Care Department within the U.S. at 800/762-2974, outside the U.S. at 317/572-3993 or fax 317/572-4002.

Wiley also publishes its books in a variety of electronic formats. Some content that appears in print may not be available in electronic formats.

Manufactured in the United States of America

5 4 3 2 1

CONTENTS

8 STROLLING & BICYCLING IN AMSTERDAM   180

9 SHOPPING IN AMSTERDAM   202

10 AMSTERDAM AFTER DARK   223

11 SIDE TRIPS FROM AMSTERDAM   247

APPENDIX A: FAST FACTS, TOLL-FREE NUMBERS & WEBSITES   285

LIST OF MAPS

AN INVITATION TO THE READER

In researching this book, I discovered many wonderful places—hotels, restaurants, shops, and more. I'm sure you'll find others. Please tell me about them, so I can share the information with your fellow travelers in upcoming editions. If you were disappointed with a recommendation, I'd love to know that, too. Please write to:

Frommer's Amsterdam, 15th Edition
Wiley Publishing, Inc. • 111 River St. • Hoboken, NJ 07030-5774

AN ADDITIONAL NOTE

Please be advised that travel information is subject to change at any time—and this is especially true of prices. We therefore suggest that you write or call ahead for confirmation when making your travel plans. The authors, editors, and publisher cannot be held responsible for the experiences of readers while traveling. Your safety is important to us, however, so we encourage you to stay alert and be aware of your surroundings. Keep a close eye on cameras, purses, and wallets, all favorite targets of thieves and pickpockets.

Other Great Guides for Your Trip:

Frommer's Amsterdam Day by Day
Frommer's Brussels & Bruges Day by Day
Frommer's Belgium, Holland & Luxembourg
Frommer's Europe
Frommer's Europe by Rail

FROMMER'S STAR RATINGS, ICONS & ABBREVIATIONS

Every hotel, restaurant, and attraction listing in this guide has been ranked for quality, value, service, amenities, and special features using a star-rating system. In country, state, and regional guides, we also rate towns and regions to help you narrow down your choices and budget your time accordingly. Hotels and restaurants are rated on a scale of zero (recommended) to three stars (exceptional). Attractions, shopping, nightlife, towns, and regions are rated according to the following scale: zero stars (recommended), one star (highly recommended), two stars (very highly recommended), and three stars (must-see).

In addition to the star-rating system, we also use **seven feature icons** that point you to the great deals, in-the-know advice, and unique experiences that separate travelers from tourists. Throughout the book, look for:

(Finds)	Special finds—those places only insiders know about
(Fun Facts)	Fun facts—details that make travelers more informed and their trips more fun
(Kids)	Best bets for kids, and advice for the whole family
(Moments)	Special moments—those experiences that memories are made of
(Overrated)	Places or experiences not worth your time or money
(Tips)	Insider tips—great ways to save time and money
(Value)	Great values—where to get the best deals

The following **abbreviations** are used for credit cards:

AE	American Express	DISC	Discover	V	Visa
DC	Diners Club	MC	MasterCard		

FROMMERS.COM

Now that you have this guidebook, to help you plan a great trip, visit our website at **www.frommers.com** for additional travel information on more than 4,000 destinations. We update features regularly, to give you instant access to the most current trip-planning information available. At Frommers.com, you'll find scoops on the best airfares, lodging rates, and car rental bargains. You can even book your travel online through our reliable travel booking partners. Other popular features include:

- Online updates of our most popular guidebooks
- Vacation sweepstakes and contest giveaways
- Newsletters highlighting the hottest travel trends
- Podcasts, interactive maps, and up-to-the-minute events listings
- Opinionated blog entries by Arthur Frommer himself
- Online travel message boards with featured travel discussions

What's New in Amsterdam

The old IJ waterfront docks west, east, and north of Centraal Station now serve as a giant redevelopment zone for residential and commercial properties. This is a new kind of Amsterdam—modern, bright, shiny, often impersonal, and on a gargantuan scale that's not typical of the Dutch. Touring these areas will give you a good idea of where Amsterdam's headed.

Oosterdokseiland, just east of Centraal Station, is the latest piece in the rapidly filling harbor redevelopment jigsaw. The city's giant new **Centrale Bibliotheek (Central Library)** opened here in 2008; it has an excellent English department, good for anyone who wants to spend a rainy day browsing the bookshelves. Nearby is the shiny new **Conservatorium van Amsterdam,** the city's music school, where you can take in concerts staged by the students in their fine new concert hall.

SMOKING Secondhand smoke no longer gets in your eyes and up your nose as much as formerly, in this city where rolling one's own cigarettes from foul-smelling loose tobacco known as *shag* is almost a traditional craft. Since July 2008, smoking has been banned in restaurants, bars, cafes, clubs, and other places, and in public spaces in hotels. There are exemptions only for separate enclosed spaces where smokers are kept (and taken care of) by themselves. In a typically Dutch compromise, the tobacco ban applies to drug-selling "smoking coffeeshops," where patrons are still permitted to puff joints, but not cigarettes, cigars, or pipes. See p. 11.

GETTING AROUND An obstacle to getting around smoothly is the ongoing construction of the underground stations and tunnels for a new subway line, the Noord-Zuid (North-South) Metro line. The line will bisect the city from Amsterdam-Noord and slice south through the center city, via Centraal Station, all the way to Station Zuid/WTC (World Trade Center). The line was originally due to be completed in 2011. Then the due date got kicked back to 2013, and now to 2015.

Centraal Station itself, the hub of the city's transit net, is still in the throes of a massive construction project. The new Noord-Zuid Metro line station is being fitted out at the front, and the waterfront zone and harbor-ferry docks at the rear are being completely rebuilt. Two harbor-ferry routes have been discontinued—and wouldn't you just know they were the ones that afforded the finest harbor views? Trams and buses now serve the redeveloped islands of the Eastern Docks zone, and the ferries have been retired. See p. 42.

From the start of 2009, all Dutch public transportation will use the new national **OV-chipkaart.** This stored-value smart card is loaded up with a preselected number of euros, which get automatically deducted each time you ride. See p. 42 for more details.

LODGING There are probably a few hotel proprietors who would like to do as one of their number has done—pick up their beds and move to a new location. Of course, as a floating hotel, the **Amstel Botel,** NDSM-Werf 3 (© 020/521-0350), has some advantages when it comes to mobility, and the retired river cruise-boat made light of its voyage from the south bank of the IJ waterway to a new home on the north bank. See p. 87.

DINING Gaining a coveted Michelin star can be a mixed blessing. After all, what happens if you lose it? That was the fate of the new owners of elegant French restaurant **Christophe,** Leliegracht 46 (© 020/625-0807)—probably because they *were* new and Michelin wanted to wait and see how things turned out. If it's any consolation to them, *Frommer's Amsterdam* thinks chef Jean-Joel Bonsens and *sommelier* Ellen Mansfield are doing a standout job. See p. 119.

At a time when it seems that virtually all of Amsterdam wants to remove to the redevelopment zones along the IJ waterfront, the rigorously traditional Japanese restaurant **Osaka** has moved from its former seat atop the Harbor Building to a new home across, but well away from, the water, in Amsterdam-Noord (North), at Rode Kruisstraat 22 (© 020/638-9833). It's worth the trip. See p. 136.

WHAT TO SEE & DO In what has become a modern Amsterdam tradition, several museums have announced further delays in emerging from years-long renovation projects. The nation's top museum, the **Rijksmuseum,** Jan Luijkenstraat 1B (© 020/674-7000), is still restricted to showing off a selection of "masterpieces" in a single wing of its vast building at Museumplein, while the target date for reopening the remainder has slipped back to 2013. See p. 140 for more details.

Likewise, the city's stellar modern-art **Stedelijk Museum** has missed any number of deadlines for returning to its permanent home at Museumplein. They now say they'll get there by December 2009, when the refurbishing and partial rebuilding

there is due to be completed (don't hold your breath). Meanwhile, the museum has had to move out of its alternate base on two floors of an office tower east of Centraal Station, where it operated for several years as **Stedelijk Museum CS.** If you're a fan of modern art, look out for a series of temporary exhibits at various venues around town, aimed at keeping the "homeless" museum in the public eye until it moves back to its old digs.

These two institutions are at least faring better than that harbor landmark, the **Scheepvaartmuseum (Maritime Museum),** which has secured its hatches entirely until sometime in 2010—unless contrary winds should cause delay—while the refurbishing of its home in the former Amsterdam Admiralty Arsenal (1656) continues. In the meantime, you can still go on board the museum's full-size replica 18th-century, three-masted sailing ship, the *Amsterdam,* just across the water outside **Science Center NEMO,** Oosterdokskade 2 (© 020/531-3233). See p. 165.

AFTER DARK An, ahem, much-loved fixture of the city's platinum-card nightlife scene has vanished from these pages, having been forced to go, though not gentle, into that good night (apologies to Dylan Thomas). There are surely those who will rage, rage against the dying of the (green) light outside **Yab Yum,** which I described as "the most celebrated Amsterdam bordello." The city council concluded it was a front for the Hells Angels and pulled the plug.

Farther down the money ladder from Yab Yum's lofty heights, hard times have come to other parts of the city's flesh trade. In an assault on human trafficking and other criminal activities, the council has cut the number of red-lit rooms in the Red Light District, in favor of small fashion boutiques and other wholesome stores. There are even proposals to shutter two of the leading "live-show" operations, the **Bananenbar** and **Casa Rosso.** See p. 244.

The Best of Amsterdam

Amsterdam is a city built on human scale. Few tall buildings mar the sky's clarity, and most of the populace walks or rides bicycles. Amsterdam's Old Town recalls the city's Golden Age in the 17th century, when it was the hub of a vast trading network and colonial empire. It was then that wealthy merchants constructed gabled residences along neatly laid canals. A delicious irony is that these placid old structures now host brothels, smoke shops, and some extravagant nightlife. The city's inhabitants, proud of their pragmatic live-and-let-live attitude, have decided to control what they cannot effectively outlaw. They permit licensed prostitution in the Red Light District—as much a tourist attraction as the Rijksmuseum or the Van Gogh Museum—and the sale of hashish and marijuana in designated "coffeeshops."

But don't think Amsterdammers drift around town trailing clouds of marijuana smoke. They're too busy zipping around on bikes, in-line skating through Vondelpark, sunning on their porches, browsing arrays of ethnic dishes, or watching the parade of street life from a sidewalk cafe. A new generation of entrepreneurs has revitalized old neighborhoods like the Jordaan, turning some of its distinctive houses into offbeat stores, bustling cafes, hotels, and restaurants. Along the waterfront, old harbor installations have either been put to bold new uses, or swept away entirely in favor of architecturally intriguing modern developments.

The city will quickly capture you in its spell. At night, many of the more than 1,200 bridges spanning 160 canals are lined with tiny lights, giving them a fairy-tale appearance. Some mornings, the cityscape emerges from a slowly dispersing mist to reveal its enchanting form.

Amsterdam doesn't merely have style; it has substance too. Besides the many canals and bridges, antiquarian bookstores, brown cafes (the Dutch equivalent of neighborhood bars), gin-sampling houses, and chic cafes and nightclubs, it offers up treasures such as the Jewish Historical Museum and the Rembrandt House Museum.

Perhaps Amsterdam's greatest asset, though, is its inhabitants. Many speak English fluently and virtually all are friendly to visitors. Plop yourself down amid the nicotine-stained walls of a brown cafe to enjoy a beer or a *jenever* (gin), and you'll soon find yourself chatting with an amiable local.

Much of Amsterdam's pleasure arises from just being in it, so toss out any "miles and miles to go before I sleep" mind frame. Between dips into artistic and historic treasures, take time to simply absorb the freewheeling spirit of this vibrant city.

1 THE MOST UNFORGETTABLE TRAVEL EXPERIENCES

- **Cruising the Canals:** Hop aboard a glass-topped tour boat for a cruise on Amsterdam's storied canals. From this vantage point, you get the best possible view of all those gabled Golden Age merchants' houses. Ignore anyone who tells you it's a tourist trap—it *is* a tourist trap, but it got that way by being justifiably popular. See p. 173.

- **Biking the City:** To pass for an authentic Amsterdammer, pick up a bicycle so ancient, rusted, and worn that no self-respecting thief would waste a second of his time trying to steal it (ah, but he will). Then charge into the ruckus of trams, cars, buses, and other bikes. Better yet, rent a bicycle that's in decent condition—and go carefully. See p. 175.

- **Riding a Canal Bike:** Lifelong Amsterdammers—and even expats who ought to know better but aim to pass as natives—scoff long and loud at this. Let them. Pedal yourself through the water for an hour or two on your own private *pedalo.* Go at your own speed to view the canals in style (not much style, I'll admit). See p. 173.

- **Skating the Canals:** When the canals freeze—it doesn't happen every winter—you'll find few locals who'll argue against the proposition that God is a Dutchman. Giving Amsterdammers the chance to go around on ice is one of the few ways to pry them off their bicycles. Strap on a pair of long-bladed *Noren* skates and join them. See p. 177.

- **Walking on the Wild Side:** Stroll through De Wallen to examine the quaint 16th-century canal architecture, peruse secondhand bookstores, and observe inhabitants as they walk their dogs, ride their bikes to the shops, and take the kids to school. Oh, and since this is the Red Light District, you're bound to see certain minimally attired women watching the world go by through red-tinted windows. See p. 160.

- **Whiffing a "Coffeeshop":** It's true—smoking marijuana is officially tolerated in Amsterdam's "smoking coffeeshops." These aren't your neighborhood cafes, and they're not for everyone, but they're an established part of Amsterdam's alternative tradition. You'll be able to buy and smoke marijuana inside, and no law-enforcement agency will hassle you. See chapter 10.

2 BEST SPLURGE HOTELS

- **InterContinental Amstel Amsterdam,** Professor Tulpplein 1 (© 020/622-6060): The last word in opulence offers much more, including one of the city's best restaurants and a superb location beside the Amstel River. This is the first choice of visiting celebrities, so don't be surprised if you see famous faces. See p. 100.

- **Amsterdam American,** Leidsekade 97 (© 020/556-3000): This hotel boasts the best location in town—it's on Leidseplein, Amsterdam's most lively square, and is close to theaters, cinemas, and a casino. Location aside, this is a fine hotel, and its Art Deco–style **Café Americain** is a city institution. See p. 92.

- **Sofitel The Grand Amsterdam,** Oudezijds Voorburgwal 197 (© 020/555-3111): The Grand really is rather grand, both inside and out; it once served as the seat of the Amsterdam Admiralty and the city council, among other official municipal functions since the 15th century. Now it guards its virtue along a tranquil canal edging the Red Light District. See p. 79.

- **Pulitzer,** Prinsengracht 315–331 (© 020/523-5235): No fewer than 25 old canal houses on Prinsengracht were converted to create this hotel, which would ordinarily be considered a serious loss, except that the Pulitzer is a real prizewinner. See p. 87.

THE BEST OF AMSTERDAM

1

BEST SPLURGE HOTELS

North Sea

↑Alkmaar

A9

BEVERWIJK

IJMUIDEN

Nationaal Park
Zuid-Kennemerland
Bloemendaal
aan Zee

Zandvoort

HAARLEM A200 N200

A9

Badhoevedorp

N201

N208

Hoofddorp

Schiphol
Airport

Alkmaarder-
meer A7

E22

Zaanse Schans

ZAANSTAD

A8

Zaandam

A10

E22

A9

N200

AMSTERDAM

Hoorn↑ Edam

Volendam

PURMEREND

Monnikendam Marken

Broek in
Waterland N247

Uitdam

Durgerdam

E35

Diemen

Muiden

A1

E231

AMSTELVEEN AMSTERDAM-
ZUIDOOST

Ouderkerk
aan de Amstel

Amsterdamse
Bos

A4

E19

Westeinder-
plassen

A44

Kaager-
plassen

Brassemer-
meer

A4

E19

Alphen
aan de
Rijn

←Leiden

Amstel

A2

E35

N201

Vinkeveense-
plassen

Nieuwkoopse-
plassen

N11

Noordzee Kanaal

Amstel

IJsselmeer

Almere-Stad

Almere-
Haven

A6

Naarden

BUSSUM

Ankeveense-
plassen

Wijde
Blik N201

HILVERSUM

Loosdrechtse-
plassen

Breukelen

Amsterdam-Rijnkanaal

Maarsseveense-
plassen

N230 A27

UTRECHT

A12 E25 E30

A2

E25

←The Hague

A12 E30

Reeuwijkse-
plassen

E25

A20

←Delft

GOUDA

IJssel

Hollandse

Lek

ROTTERDAM

✈ Airport
— Railroad

0 ___ 5 mi
0 ___ 5 km

N

Area of
detail

Amsterdam ✪

Rotterdam

NETHERLANDS

0 ___ 50 mi
0 ___ 50 km

3 THE BEST MODERATELY PRICED HOTELS

- **Agora,** Singel 462 (☎ 020/627-2200): Those canal-house hotels that don't hit you over the head with opulence more than make up for it with the personal touch. This paragon of the type feels like a canalside home. See p. 88.

- **Ambassade,** Herengracht 341 (☎ 020/555-0222): Here, in 10 neighboring canal houses just off the Golden Bend (for centuries the city's most fashionable district), you'll feel like you're in the home of a rich 17th-century merchant. Most of the spacious, individually styled rooms have large windows overlooking the canal. See p. 88.

- **Arena,** 's-Gravesandestraat 51 (☎ 020/850-2410): What this unusual place has, in spades, is an action-oriented and informal temperament that's typical of Amsterdam—the kind of shared outlook that attracts many to this city in the first place. Arena combines this unpretentiousness bustle with genuine style and a judicious level of comfort. See p. 100.

- **De Filosoof,** Anna van den Vondelstraat 6 (☎ 020/683-3013): Few—if any—hotels have an operating philosophy as distinctive as this one, which takes its inspiration from the great thinkers of the past. And this is no shameless sophistry disguising a grim underlying truth. In this case, idealism has produced a more-than-acceptable reality. See p. 95.

- **Seven Bridges,** Reguliersgracht 31 (☎ 020/623-1329): In some hotels, you realize the owners aren't just running a business, but doing what they love. This is that kind of place. It's obvious that all the furniture, fixtures, and fittings have been selected with loving care, and guests receive the same conscientious attention. See p. 90.

4 THE MOST UNFORGETTABLE DINING EXPERIENCES

- **Pop a Herring:** Amsterdam folk like their herring fresh and raw from a neighborhood fish stall. The best in the business is **Zeebanket van Altena,** Stadhouderskade at Jan Luijkenstraat (☎ 020/676-9139). Eat your fish in the approved Dutch manner—whole, holding the fish by its tail, with your face to that wide Holland sky. Amsterdammers prefer theirs chopped, with onion. See p. 126.

- **Eat on the Water:** I can't say you'll never eat better than on a **Dinner Cruise.** But you'll have the music, the candlelight, the canals, and, if you're lucky, the moon over the water. Variations on this theme are cooked up by most of the canal tour-boat lines. See p. 134.

- **Feast in the Park:** Tucked away behind the trees of Vondelpark, **Vertigo,** Vondelpark 3 (☎ 020/612-3021) lends a touch of the country to a convivial venue that's backed up by some fine food. See p. 133.

- **Try a *Rijsttafel*:** Dutch settlers in the East Indies created the banquet-style "rice table." Comprising from 10 to 30 little dishes, some as fiery as rocket propellant, *rijsttafel* is a great introduction to Indonesian cuisine. See p. 106.

- **Live the Americain Dream:** Join *tout* Amsterdam for coffee and *gâteau* in the stunning Art Nouveau and Art Deco ambience of the Amsterdam American Hotel's Café Americain. You'll be pleased to learn that the service has improved since a postwar Dutch writer described the waiters as "unemployed knife throwers." See p. 124.

5 BEST FREE (OR ALMOST FREE) THINGS TO DO

- **Sail the IJ Ferry:** The short ferryboat ride across the IJ channel between Centraal Station and Amsterdam-Noord (North) is a great little cruise and affords good harbor views. Only the shortest routes are free; the others cost little more than a song. See p. 174.
- **View Golden Age Paintings:** Usually it costs a bundle to see paintings from the Old Masters period of Dutch art. An exception is the multiple images of Civic Guards (Militia) companies hanging in the **Schuttersgalerij** of the Amsterdams Historisch Museum. See p. 144.
- **Visit the Begijnhof:** Even though admission is free, there's a price to pay for stepping into the cloistered community that for centuries has been a residence for women of "sound character." You need to be tolerably quiet and comport yourself with dignity—or

you'll get tossed out by the guards. See p. 154.
- **Visit the Flower Market:** The vast array of flowers and potted plants in their "floating" home on the Singel canal comprises the city's largest and most colorful plant assortment. The flowers, however, are not free. See p. 221.
- **Take in a Lunchtime Rehearsal Concert:** If you can live with the occasional duff note and a program that doesn't always follow the script, treat your ears to classical music from 12:30 to 1pm at the Muziektheater (Tues) and the Concertgebouw (Wed), every week from October to June. See p. 228.
- **Stroll through Vondelpark:** Its 48 hectares (120 acres) of trees, ponds, flower beds, and picnic grounds comprise the city's green lung. In summer, concerts and all kinds of open-air activities take place. See p. 168.

6 THE BEST OUTDOOR ACTIVITIES

- **Cross Bridges over Untroubled Waters:** Amsterdam has more bridges, and more canals, than Venice—a city Italians are proud to call "the Amsterdam of the South." Find out what humbles Italians, by crossing as many of Amsterdam's 1,200-plus bridges as you can; the views are unparalleled. See chapter 7.
- **Tiptoe through the Tulips:** Join 4 centuries of Dutch tradition by going overboard for a flower that's become synonymous with Holland. In spring,

you'll find them everywhere. Sharp promotion (and a seed of truth) says the best place to pick up a bunch is at the Flower Market on Singel. See p. 221.
- **Beach About Zandvoort:** Come rain, hail, or shine (and often enough, all three on the same day), Amsterdammers ride the rails for a short hop out to its brassy—but not classy—coastal resort. The bracing North Sea air blows away all that marijuana smoke. See p. 252.

7 THE BEST MUSEUMS

- **Rijksmuseum:** The State Museum houses some of Holland's most important artworks: Rembrandt's world-famous *The Night Watch,* four of Vermeer's miniatures, and numerous pieces by Frans Hals. In all, this is one of the world's most impressive Old Masters collections. See p. 140.

- **Van Gogh Museum:** The world's largest collection of Vincent's works is housed here—some 200 paintings and 500 drawings—ranging from *Sunflowers* to earless self-portraits. Here, you

can trace this great, tragic painter's artistic development and psychological decline. See p. 142.

- **Anne Frankhuis:** The clear and haunting words of a young Jewish girl trying to survive and grow in unimaginable circumstances have moved millions since her diary was first published in the aftermath of World War II. It's a melancholy but unforgettable experience to spend a reflective moment in Anne Frank's stark hide-out from Nazi terror. See p. 137.

8 THE MOST INTRIGUING NEIGHBORHOODS

- **De Wallen:** Just below the low-life sin section of "The Walls"—that is, the Red Light District—is a contrast: This delightful southern district of Old Amsterdam encompasses tranquil canals lined with handsome 16th-century houses and the University of Amsterdam's bustling campus. See p. 160.

- **Het IJ:** Day by day, Amsterdam's future unfolds before your eyes along the narrow channel on which the city's old port

zone east and west of Centraal Station stood. A whirl of gargantuan redevelopment projects and modern architecture is transforming the waterway. See p. 161.

- **Jordaan:** Bounded by Brouwersgracht, Singelgracht, Prinsengracht, and Leidsestraat, this former artisan neighborhood has become gentrified. With its own small canals, street markets, and an array of minor attractions, it's a great place for random wandering. See p. 160.

Amsterdam in Depth

Prosperity, in the shape of everything from crass commercialism to genteel gentrification, has settled like a North Sea mist around Amsterdam's graceful cityscape of 17th-century canals and canalside houses. Yet "free thinking" and "anything goes" still have their place: They're the catchphrases by which Amsterdam lives its collective life. And all this free living is fueled by a successful economy, not by the combustion of semilegal exotic plants. City government has worked hard to transform Amsterdam from a hippie haven to a cosmopolitan business and cultural center—and it's succeeding.

Mostly. Amsterdam's 750,000 denizens aren't so easily poured into the restrictive molds of trade and industry. They continue to mix tolerably well in their multiracial melting pot (though there are growing signs of discontent with continued immigration).

A side effect of the city's concern with economics and image is that youthful backpackers who don't wash much, stay in cheap hostels, and think smoking hash is the high point of the city's cultural life aren't as welcome as they once were. But when they come back with a paycheck that allows them to stay at an upscale hotel, buy tickets for the Concertgebouw and the Muziektheater, eat in a Japanese restaurant, and splash out for a diamond or two, well, that's another story. Still, all is far from lost for the bohemian souls: If they want, they can smoke hash all the livelong day. And anyone can partake in Amsterdam's culture, history, and scenic cityscape, without stretching credit card limits.

So step aboard for a cruise through highlights from 800 years of history in this city of canals; a working knowledge of Amsterdam's history will add dimension to your visit. Then, go below the surface to fathom why the Dutch capital's lifestyle provokes heated debate in other countries, and to permit some of the impassioned artists and architects who helped to make Amsterdam worth visiting to take a bow from their places in the corridors of time.

1 AMSTERDAM TODAY

Amsterdam is the capital and major city of the Netherlands, a country barely half the size of the state of Maine. Today, this sophisticated international city has a multicultural population of 750,000 (and 600,000 bicycles), a busy harbor, multistory apartment communities, and elevated highways—all hallmarks of a modern urban center. The modernization process has had its pluses and minuses: Much tranquillity has been lost along the way, but has been replaced with an increased vibrancy. Despite it all, Amsterdam remains a kind of big village, retaining a human scale that at least affords the illusion of simplicity.

More and more people from Holland, Europe, and farther afield are making tracks toward the city. Footloose young Hollanders seem to have no other ambition than to live here—and who can blame them when you consider the "excitement" of growing up in a squeaky-clean Dutch village?

Young Americans and Europeans still see Amsterdam as a kind of mecca of youth rebellion to which a pilgrimage must be made. Immigrants find social support

Impressions

Amsterdam will at least give one's regular habits of thought the stimulus of a little confusion.

—Henry James, *Transatlantic Sketches*, 1875

systems and a relative absence of the discrimination they face in many other European cities, though some immigrant-heavy areas, like Amsterdam East and the Bijlmermeer housing project, are experiencing growing social problems. A 2003 survey projected that by 2010, white native Amsterdammers would for the first time be the minority.

Although flowers gleam in window boxes on gabled houses, shopkeepers keep their portals tidy, and a few homemakers still wash their steps each morning, graffiti, grime, and other problems of city life inhabit Amsterdam as much as any other urban center. (The ubiquitous mounds of dog poop on the sidewalks have become something of a symbol of the city.)

But maybe you just want to know what to expect from the person in the street and behind the shop counter. Amsterdammers can be both the most infuriating and the most endearing people in the world. One minute, they treat you like a naughty child (surely you've heard the expression about someone talking to you like a Dutch uncle), and the next, they're ready for a laugh and a beer. They can be rude or cordial (it may depend on the weather), domineering, or ready to please (it may depend on you). In a shop, they may get annoyed with you if you don't accept what they have, or get mad at themselves if they don't have what you want.

Fortunately, it's easy to overlook all these shortcomings. The city's historic heart is still there to beguile you with its tree-lined canals, gabled houses, and graceful bridges. The National Monument Care Office has exercised great foresight in working to preserve the 17th-century feel along the canals. You'll have no problem finding the legacy of the city's Golden Age, 400 years ago, in the new Amsterdam. Fuming traffic, power drills, pay phones, bicycles, tour boats, and souvenir stores have dulled some of the luster, yes, but a moment always arrives when a window in time opens and Amsterdam's radiant heritage peeks out.

WHEN IN AMSTERDAM . . .

"The Dutch Disease" is what a conservative U.S. columnist once called Holland's social liberalism. But not many of the hookers in Amsterdam's Red Light District are Dutch, and relatively few denizens of the smoking coffeeshops are Dutch. If Amsterdam's a latter-day Sodom and Gomorrah, it's one for foreigners mainly. The Dutch themselves are a moderate, conservative lot, whose stable history in a small, densely populated land has led them to seek social consensus rather than confrontation whenever possible.

For centuries, Amsterdam has been a magnet for the oppressed and persecuted, particularly in the 17th century, when it became a haven for Jews and Huguenots driven from France and other Catholic countries (though, for a time, Catholics in Holland were not allowed to practice their faith openly). That tradition of tolerance has continued into the 21st century, though there are signs it may be beginning to fray around the edges. In 2006, a law was proposed to outlaw any other language than Dutch in public. The idea never flew but seemed to be a sign of the times.

Amsterdammers aren't particularly emotional or hotheaded, but they aren't shy about speaking their minds either. They are fiercely independent, yet so tolerant of other people's problems and attitudes that their city nearly equals New York as a traditional haven for the world's exiles and émigrés.

The liberalist tradition impacts areas of personal and social morality that in other countries are still hot-button issues. Such topics are researched and debated, and perceived solutions implemented, with a surprising lack of partisan passion—indeed often without passion of any kind. In 2002, the world's first same-sex marriage with legal status identical to heterosexual matrimony took place in Amsterdam, and the Dutch parliament legalized regulated euthanasia ("mercy killing"), making the Netherlands the world's first country to do so. And then there's the easygoing approach to prostitution and drug use.

Authorities aren't duty-bound to prosecute criminal acts, which leaves a loophole for experimentation in areas that technically are illegal. It's been said the Netherlands has one of the lowest crime rates in Europe because whenever something becomes a criminal problem, the Dutch make it legal, thereby reducing crime with a stroke.

Don't laugh, at least not in Holland. The Dutch will take aim at anyone, on any issue, outside their borders. Just so long as it's understood that everything *inside* has arrived at that hallowed state of perfection. Run through any list of America's international misdemeanors and the Dutch will nod sagely and open-mindedly in agreement. Laugh to your heart's content about the soap-opera antics of Britain's House of Windsor, and they'll laugh right along with you. But refer, however obliquely, to negative aspects of the Dutch Way, and watch the air turn cool. Go so far as to openly criticize the country, or to joke about Queen Beatrix, and you'll quickly find that you have touched the natives where they are tender.

DRUG HAZE

Popular opinion notwithstanding, narcotic drugs are illegal in the Netherlands. But the Dutch treat drug use mainly as a medical problem rather than purely a crime, and there's no Dutch "war on drugs." Treatment—not arrest—of addicts is the Dutch way. Authorities distinguish between soft drugs like cannabis, considered unlikely to cause addiction or pose a serious health risk, and hard drugs like heroin and cocaine, which are addictive and significantly deleterious to users' health. Both types are illegal, but the law is tougher on hard drugs. Dealers who import and export drugs face 4 years in jail for soft drugs and 12 years for hard drugs.

Amsterdam's casual acceptance of pot-smoking and pot-smokers makes some dissidents crazy enough to make you wonder what *they* are smoking. In recent years, the Netherlands has bowed to pressure from surrounding countries regarding its drug policy and has tightened the rules for "coffeeshops"—establishments in which hashish and marijuana are sold. You used to be allowed to buy and retain 30 grams (1 oz.) of soft drugs for personal use; now, you can buy only 5 grams ($^1/_5$ oz.) at a time, though you're still allowed to possess 30 grams. Coffeeshops aren't allowed to sell hard drugs, to advertise, or to sell to minors. If they create a public nuisance, the local *burgemeester* (mayor) can shut

Thin Red Line

Prostitution is legal in Holland, and prostitutes in Amsterdam's Red Light District work in clean premises, pay taxes, receive regular medical checks, are eligible for welfare, and even have their own trade union.

2

Impressions

To understand the Dutch, you've got to start out with the word gedogen. *It basically means to permit, to live with, to be able to tolerate. A lot of what you see in terms of legislation has been subject to* gedogen *for years. By the time it's written into law, it almost doesn't make a difference.*

—K. Terry Dornbush, former U.S. ambassador to the Netherlands, 2001

them down. Yet despite these new, stricter rules, Amsterdam remains a mecca for marijuana smokers and seems likely to remain that way.

Supplying free heroin to addicts, with medical support, has helped prevent the spread of HIV and slashed the drug's street price so that addicts commit fewer crimes to feed their habit, and so that healthcare and law-enforcement costs have gone down. The Netherlands has significantly lower rates of drug use, drug-related deaths, and heroin addiction than Britain, France, Germany, and other Western European countries that criticize Holland so fiercely on this issue.

2 LOOKING BACK AT AMSTERDAM

AMSTERDAM'S ORIGINS

Amsterdam was founded at the place where two fishermen and a seasick dog jumped ashore from a small boat to escape a storm in the Zuider Zee. The dog threw up, thereby marking the spot. Sound like a shaggy-dog story? Well, the city's original coat of arms backs up the tale. In some ways, it's an appropriate metaphor for a city with a lifestyle that has about as many boosters and detractors as did Sodom and Gomorrah. Some first-time visitors want to throw up everything and live this way forever; others just want to throw up.

At any rate, fishermen, with or without a seasick dog, did play the decisive role in founding Amsterdam. Around 1200, they realized that the area at the mouth of the Amstel River allowed their wooden cog boats easy access to rich fishing on the Zuider Zee beyond. They built their huts on raised mounds of earth called *terpen.*

The low-lying marshy terrain left these early settlers at the mercy of tides and storms, and many must have perished or lost their homes as a result of flooding. In an effort to control periodic flooding, the populace dammed the Amstel (they'd likely been damning it from the beginning) at the point where today's square called the Dam stands. This is the source of the city's original name, Aemstelledamme.

Archaeological finds show that by 1204, local big wheels were moving in on what the ordinary folks had created. Count Gijsbrecht II of Aemstel made the first power play, building a castle at the settlement and lording it over the locals. In the 1990s, archaeologists uncovered the castle's foundations under Nieuwezijds Kolk, a side street off Nieuwendijk—and brought to light the earliest known clog shoe, made from alder wood and dating from the early 13th century.

There are few records of Aemstelledamme (or Amestelledame, or Amstellodame, as it was also known in an age without spelling bees) before 1275, when Count Floris V of Holland granted village locals the right to trade anywhere in the Holland and Zeeland counties without having to pay tolls along the way. This is the settlement's first official documentary record, and the year that's now celebrated as Amsterdam's foundation date.

TRADING CENTER

Amsterdam began its rise to commercial prosperity in 1323, when Count Floris VI established the city as a toll point for beer imports. Later, Amsterdam was granted toll rights on exported ale. Beer thus became a major component of the city's prosperity, and remains important to this day, as anyone who visits a traditional *bruine kroeg* (brown cafe) will see.

Always skillful merchants, Amsterdammers began to establish strong craftsman guilds and to put ships to sea to catch North Sea herring. They expanded into trading salted Baltic herring, amber, Norwegian salted or dried cod and cod-liver oil, German beer and salt, bales of linen and woolen cloth from the Low Countries and England, coal from England, Russian furs and candle wax, Polish grain and flour, Swedish timber, pitch, and iron. They opened up lucrative trade by both doing business with and competing against the trading towns of the powerful Baltic-based Hanseatic League.

The city's merchants, growing rich on the contents of the warehouses they built along the canals, trampled over the Hanseatic League in the competition for wealth, and by the 1600s, had come out head and shoulders in front.

WARS OF RELIGION

During the Middle Ages, the Netherlands was a bastion of Catholicism, with powerful bishops in the cities of Utrecht and Maastricht and a holy shrine in the upstart Aemstelledamme, which attracted its share of pilgrims. No one is sure when Amsterdam became an independent parish, but it's thought to have been around 1334, when the Oude Kerk (Old Church) is first mentioned in the city's records—though a small timber chapel on the spot dated from around 1300.

As the town grew in prosperity, churches, monasteries, convents, and cloisters called *begijnhofen* sprung up. Eventually, there were 18 *begijnhofen*, which functioned as social welfare agencies, providing care to the sick, orphaned, and poor, and hospitality to travelers and pilgrims. You can visit the main Begijnhof (see p. 154).

Protestantism emerged at the same time as the Low Countries came under the rule of Charles V, the intensely Catholic Habsburg emperor and king of Spain. Holland, and Amsterdam in particular, became

Below Sea Level

Amsterdam lies up to 5.5m (18 ft.) below mean sea level. The city's solid, timeless buildings stand, and its 750,000 inhabitants live, where waves should by all rights be lapping. If the sea-dikes should ever go down, most of the city would vanish beneath the waves. Vondelpark would become a lake, the Metro would be truly drowned, and the trams would float away. If you happened to be standing on top of Oude Kerk's tower, however, you wouldn't even get your feet wet.

Don't get too worried. The dikes are built to repel almost everything the North Sea can throw at them. Only a 1-in-10,000-years super storm could take them down (famous last words?). And because of climate change concerns, the government plans to raise that safety margin to 1-in-100,000 years.

a fulcrum for the shifting political scene the Reformation brought about everywhere in Europe. John Calvin's rigorous doctrines and his firm belief in separating church and state began to take root in Amsterdam.

In 1555, Philip II, son of Charles V and great-grandson of Emperor Maximilian I, became Spain's king and the ruler of the Low Countries. An ardent Catholic, he was determined to defeat the Reformation. The Dutch resented Philip's intrusion into their affairs and began a resistance movement. Within 10 years, William of Orange, count of Holland (known as William the Silent), formed a League of Protestant Nobles. Philip's response, in 1567, was to send the ruthless duke of Alba, Fernando Álvarez de Toledo, to the Low Countries with an army of 9,000 men (accompanied by 2,000 courtesans) to enforce the death-to-heretics policy.

The Dutch nobles fought back, though they had no army and no money. William of Orange and his brother, John of Nassau, managed to wage war on Spain despite all this, their only ally a ragtag "navy" of Protestant privateers called the *Geuzen* (Sea Beggars). When Spain levied a new tax on the Dutch, the action was so unpopular that it rallied the majority of Dutch—Protestant and Catholic alike—to the anti-Spanish cause.

Amsterdam's Calvinist merchants expelled the Catholic city council in a 1578 revolution called the *Alteratie* (Changeover). As the Protestant Reformation took hold, the city's many Catholics were forbidden to hold public office or to worship openly, a situation that continued for more than a century.

THE GOLDEN AGE

Over the first 75 years of the 17th century, the legendary Dutch entrepreneurial gift would come into its own. These years have since become known as the Golden Age. It seemed every business venture the Dutch initiated during this time turned a profit, and each of their many expeditions to the world's unknown places resulted in a new jewel in the Dutch trading empire. Colonies and brisk trade were established to provide the luxury-hungry merchants at home with new delights, such as fresh ginger from Java; jewels, spices, and silks from the Orient; foxtails from America; fine porcelain from China; and flower bulbs from Ottoman Turkey that produced big, bright, waxy flowers and grew quite readily in Holland's sandy soil—tulips. Holland was rich and Amsterdam was booming.

In 1589, Amsterdam's greatest commercial rival, Antwerp, fell to the Spanish, prompting its many industrious Protestant and Jewish merchants and craftspeople to flock to Amsterdam. Of the Jewish influx, the jurist Hugo Grotius wrote in 1614: "Plainly God desires them to live somewhere. Why not here rather than elsewhere?" These migrants brought with

---

Impressions

What other place in the world could you choose where all of life's comforts, and all novelties that man could want are so easy to obtain as here and where you can enjoy such a feeling of freedom?

—René Descartes, French philosopher (1634)

While Amsterdam may box your Puritan ears, this great, historic city is an experiment in freedom.

—ABCNEWS.com (2000)

them their merchant skills and industries—including diamond dealerships, establishing what's still a famous part of Amsterdam commerce.

Amsterdam grew into one of the world's great cities; its population reached 50,000 by the end of the 16th century. In 1602, Dutch traders set up the Vereenigde Oostindische Compagnie (V.O.C.), the United East India Company, the world's first limited-liability joint-stock corporation, which was granted a monopoly on trade in the East.

It was a runaway success—in 1611, the V.O.C. paid its shareholders a dividend of 162%—and established the Dutch presence in the Spice Islands (Indonesia), centered on their colony at Batavia (Jakarta), which was run by a company-appointed governor-general. The big V.O.C. merchant vessels could hold twice as much cargo as their English rivals. A full-size replica of one of these sailing ships, the *Amsterdam,* is tied to a wharf at the city's Science Center NEMO (p. 165).

Great wealth flowed back to Amsterdam, and the merchants used it to build the canals and the impressive 17th-century architecture along Herengracht's Golden Bend. The merchant owners of canalside mansions liked to put up a good facade, but canal frontage was expensive, so the houses behind those elegant gables were built long and narrow. Their upper floors were storerooms bulging with their owners' wares, hoisted up on loft-mounted rope and pulleys.

In 1613, work began on the three concentric waterways of the *Grachtengordel* (Canal Belt)—Herengracht, Keizersgracht, and Prinsengracht. City planners designed a system for smaller transverse canals to connect the large canals, making travel by water more convenient throughout Amsterdam. They decided the wealthy would live facing the major canals, while the connecting canals were set aside for middle and lower classes. Thus began the popular comparison with Venice—though Amsterdam has more canals than the Italian city.

Golden Age Amsterdam can be compared to Renaissance Florence and Periclean Athens for the great flowering that transformed its society. Of Amsterdam's Golden Age, historian Simon Schama wrote, "There is perhaps no other example of a complete and highly original civilization springing up in so short a time in so small a territory." Artists like Rembrandt worked overtime, cranking out paintings for newly affluent merchants obsessed with portraying themselves and filling their homes with beautiful images (see "Amsterdam's Art & Architecture," later in this chapter).

DECLINE & FALL

A long period of decline set in during the 18th century. At the Museum Willet-Holthuysen (p. 149) and the Museum Van Loon (p. 148), you get an idea of the decadent, French-influenced style in which wealthy Amsterdam families lived during the Golden Age's fading afterglow, rich

Impressions

Amsterdam did not answer our expectations. It is a kind of paltry, rubbishy Venice.
—William Hazlitt, English essayist, 1826

You lose no time, of course, in drawing the inevitable parallel between Amsterdam and Venice, and it is well worth drawing, as an illustration of the uses to which the same materials may be put by different minds.
—Henry James, *Transatlantic Sketches,* 1875

(Fun Facts Flower Power

With the profits from global trade flooding in, Amsterdam's merchants needed a visible sign of their vast disposable income to flaunt in the faces of friends and rivals. These strait-laced, parsimonious Calvinists went astonishingly overboard for tulips. Bulb prices skyrocketed from virtually zero in 1620. By 1630, single bulbs were going for 1,000 florins ($200,000 in today's U.S. dollars) and the price finally topped out at 30,000 florins ($6 million in today's U.S. dollars) for three bulbs in 1637. To give that context, that was also the going rate for the most prestigious houses along Amsterdam's canals, with the garden and coach house thrown in. When the Tulip Mania bubble burst soon afterward, more than a few fortunes vaporized with it.

with Italian majolica and Nuremberg porcelain.

By the second half of the century, revolution was in the air. The "Patriots," pro-French, antiroyalist democrats, seized control of the city on April 27, 1787. Prussian troops rescued the House of Orange, tramping into the city to put down the rebellion. In 1799, the United East India Company was liquidated, a key indicator of the nation's steep commercial decline.

Revolutionary France invaded Holland in 1794, capturing Amsterdam and establishing the Batavian Republic the following year, headed by the Patriots. Napoleon brought the republic to an end in 1806 by setting up his brother, Louis Napoleon, as king of Holland, and installing him in the town hall on the Dam in Amsterdam, which was converted into a palace. In 1810, Napoleon deposed his brother and brought Holland formally into the empire.

The French reign was short-lived, but the taste of royalty proved sweet. When the Dutch in 1814 recalled the House of Orange from exile in England, it was to fill the role of king in a constitutional monarchy.

For 2 centuries after Amsterdam's Golden Age, the city's population remained at a quarter of a million. Between 1850 and 1900, however, it jumped to half a million. As did most major cities during

the Industrial Revolution, Amsterdam began to face overpopulation issues. Housing was in short supply, and the canals were increasingly befouled with sewage.

Holland was neutral during World War I, but the city suffered from acute food shortages. During the 1930s, widespread unemployment brought on by the Great Depression convinced the government to use the army to control the unruly masses.

Amsterdam was just beginning to recover from the Depression when, on May 10, 1940, the Germans invaded. The overmatched Dutch army bravely resisted, but with Rotterdam blitzed into ruins, the end came quickly.

Hitler managed to gain a following in Amsterdam. However, Amsterdammers mostly resisted how Nazis treated Jews, Gypsies, and homosexuals. In February 1941, city workers organized a strike to protest the deportation of 400 members of the city's Jewish community. Today, in the old Jewish Quarter, stands *The Dockworker,* a statue in tribute to the February Strike. Unfortunately, the strike did little good; by 1942, the Nazis had forced all Dutch Jews to move to three isolated ghettos in Amsterdam. Between July 1942 and September 1943, most of Amsterdam's Jews were sent to death camps. Of Amsterdam's 60,000 Jews, only 6,000 survived.

Among the murdered was a girl who has come to symbolize the Holocaust's many victims: Anne Frank (1929–45). Anne is famous the world over for her diary, a moving record of a teenager's struggle to cope with coming of age amid the horrific realities of war and the Nazi occupation. When the Germans began deporting Jews, Anne and her family hid in an Amsterdam canal house, now the Anne Frankhuis (p. 137). Cut off from other outlets for her energies, she began to keep a journal telling of her thoughts, feelings, and experiences.

On May 5, 1945, the grim ordeal came to an end when German forces in the Netherlands capitulated. Canadian troops reached Amsterdam first, on May 7.

HIPPIE HAVEN

In the 1960s, the city was just as much a hotbed of political and cultural radicalism as was San Francisco. Hippies trailing clouds of marijuana smoke took over the Dam and camped out in Vondelpark and in front of Centraal Station. Radical political activity, which began with "happenings" staged by the small group known as the Provos—from *provocatie* (provocation)—continued and intensified in the 1980s. In 1966, the Provos were behind the protests that disrupted the wedding of Princess Beatrix to German Claus von Amsberg in the Westerkerk; they threw smoke bombs and fighting broke out between protesters and police.

Some radicals joined neighborhood groups to protest specific local government plans. The scheme that provoked the greatest ire was a plan to build a subway through the Nieuwmarkt area. In 1975, demonstrations aimed to defend the housing that had been condemned for the subway. The most dramatic confrontation between the police and the human barricades happened on Blue Monday, March 24. Thirty people were wounded and 47 arrested in a battle of tear gas and water cannons against paint cans and powder bombs. Despite the protests, the subway opened in 1980.

Protests similar to those against the subway were launched against proposals to build a new Stadhuis (Town Hall) and Opera (Muziektheater) side by side on Waterlooplein, a complex that became known as the Stopera. Despite an energetic and at times violent campaign to "Stop the Stopera," both buildings were completed in 1986, and the Muziektheater (p. 228) is now a star in the city's cultural firmament.

Though the turbulent events of the 1970s and 1980s seem distant today, the independent spirit and social conscience that fueled them remain—*Make Sex Not Guns,* reads a typical retro piece of graffiti—and Amsterdam is still one of Europe's most socially advanced cities.

New priorities have emerged, however, with the general aim of boosting Amsterdam's position as a global business center and the location of choice for foreign multinationals' European headquarters. The city aims to consolidate its role as one of Europe's most important transportation

---

Fun Facts   What's in a Name?

"Dutch" is a medieval misnomer on the part of the English, who couldn't distinguish between the people of the Netherlands and Germany. To describe the former, they corrupted *Deutsch* (which, in German, means "German") to "Dutch." Another misnomer is "Holland," which actually refers only to the old Holland province (today's Noord-Holland and Zuid-Holland provinces), not to the whole country. The Dutch call their country *Nederland* (Low Country), their language *Nederlands,* and themselves *Nederlanders.* But they recognize that "Dutch" and "Holland" are popular internationally, and being a practical people they use these terms.

and distribution hubs. These goals are aided by an ongoing effort to change the city's hippie-paradise image to one more in tune with the needs of commerce.

3 AMSTERDAM'S ART & ARCHITECTURE

Dutch art came into its own during the 17th-century Golden Age. Artists were blessed with wealthy patrons whose support allowed them to give free reign to their talents. The primary art patrons were Protestant merchants who commissioned pictures depicting their world: portraits, landscapes, seascapes, domestic scenes, and still lifes—not the kind of religious works commissioned by the Church in Catholic countries.

Art held a cherished place in the hearts of average Dutch citizens too, and few were the houses not adorned with paintings, as the Englishman Peter Mundy, who traveled to Amsterdam in 1640, observed: "Many times blacksmiths and cobblers will have some picture or other by their forge and in their stall."

Early-17th-century Utrecht artist **Gerrit van Honthorst** (1590–1656), who studied in Rome with Caravaggio, brought the new "realism of light and dark," or *chiaroscuro,* technique to Holland, where he influenced Dutch artists like the young Rembrandt. Best known for lively company scenes such as *The Supper Party* (ca. 1620; Uffizi, Florence), which depicted ordinary people against a plain background and set a style that continued in Dutch art for many years, Honthorst often used multiple hidden light sources to heighten the dramatic contrast of lights and darks.

Among this period's great landscape artists, **Jacob van Ruisdael** (1628–82) stands out. His *Windmill at Wijk bij Duurstede* (ca. 1665; Rijksmuseum, Amsterdam) combines characteristic elements of his style: The windmill stands in a somber landscape, containing a few small human figures, a cloud-laden sky, and a foreground of agitated water and reeds.

Antwerp-born **Frans Hals** (ca. 1580–1666), the Haarlem school's undisputed leader (schools differed from city to city), was a great portrait painter whose relaxed, informal, and naturalistic portraits contrast strikingly with the traditional formal masks typical of Renaissance portraits. Hals is best known for works like *The Laughing Cavalier* (1624) and *The Gypsy Girl* (1630)—neither of which is in the Haarlem museum dedicated to him (they're in, respectively, Madrid's Thyssen-Bornemisza Museum and Paris's Louvre). His light brushstrokes help convey immediacy and intimacy, lending his works a perceptive psychological quality. He had a genius for comic characters, showing men and women as they are and a little less than they are, as in *Malle Babbe* (ca. 1635; Gemäldegalerie, Berlin). It's worth taking a day trip to Haarlem just to visit the Frans Hals Museum (p. 250) and view such works as his *A Banquet of the Officers of the St. George Civic Guard* (ca. 1627) and *Officers and Sergeants of the St. Hadrian Civic Guard* (ca. 1633).

The period's great genius was **Rembrandt Harmenszoon van Rijn** (1606–69), one of few artists of any period to be

---

(Fun Facts Art, Anyone?

An estimated 20 million paintings were produced in Amsterdam during the Golden Age.

known simply by his first name. This painter, whose works hang in places of honor in the world's great museums, may be *the* most famous Amsterdammer. But he was born in Leiden. He earned acclaim in Amsterdam as a portraitist. Later, as he refused to compromise his artistic ideas, he began to lose popularity. One of his most famous paintings, *The Night Watch,* was refused by those who had commissioned it. In 1656, Rembrandt declared bankruptcy, a financial state from which he would never recover.

Rembrandt pushed *chiaroscuro* to unprecedented heights, blending together light and dark gradually and softly—which may have diffused some of *chiaroscuro*'s inherent drama, but helped his works achieve a more truthful appearance. The etching *Self-Portrait with Saskia* (1636; Rijksmuseum, Amsterdam) shows him with his wife at a prosperous time when he was being commissioned to do portraits of many wealthy merchants. Later self-portraits are more psychologically complex, often depicting a careworn old man whose gaze is nevertheless sharp, compassionate, and wise.

In group portraits like *The Night Watch* (1642) and *The Syndics of the Cloth Guild* (1662), both in the Rijksmuseum, it's clear that each individual portrait was done with care. The unrivaled harmony of light, color, and movement in these works is a marvel. Compare, too, these robust, masculine works with the tender *The Jewish Bride* (ca. 1665), also in the Rijksmuseum.

Jan Vermeer (1632–75) of Delft is perhaps the best known of the "little Dutch masters" who specialized in one genre of painting (Vermeer focused on portraiture). Although they confined their artistry within a narrow scope, these painters rendered subjects with exquisite care and faithfulness to actual appearance.

Vermeer's work centers on domestic life's simple pleasures—a woman pouring milk or reading a letter, for example—and all of his simple figures positively glow with color and light. A master at lighting interior scenes and rendering true colors, Vermeer was able to create an illusion of three-dimensionality in works such as *The Love Letter* (ca. 1670), in Amsterdam's Rijksmuseum. As light—usually afternoon sunshine pouring in from an open window—moves across the picture plane, it caresses and modifies all the colors.

Jan Steen (ca. 1626–79), born in Leiden, painted marvelous interior scenes, often satirical and didactic in their intent. The allusions on which much of the satire depends may escape most of us today, but any viewer can appreciate the fine drawing, subtle color shading, and warm light pervading such paintings as *Woman at Her Toilet* (1663) and *The Feast of St. Nicholas* (ca. 1665), both in the Rijksmuseum. Many of his pictures revel in bawdy tavern scenes fueled by drunken overindulgence—being an innkeeper afforded him plenty of opportunity for research. Then there are his sly *double-entendres,* like the ostensibly innocent *Girl Eating Oysters* (ca. 1660), in The Hague's Mauritshuis—oysters were considered to be an aphrodisiac, and the girl's Mona Lisa smile could easily be interpreted as a come-on.

ARCHITECTURE

Hendrick de Keyser (1565–1621), an architect who worked in Amsterdam at the height of the Renaissance, is known for using decorative, playful elements in a way that was practical to the structure. For instance, he combined hard yellow or white sandstone decorative features (like volutes, keystones, and masks) with soft red brick, creating a visually stimulating multicolored facade, while utilizing the sandstone as protection from rain erosion. **Philips and Justus Vingboons** were architects and brothers who worked in the Renaissance style; while walking along Herengracht, Keizersgracht, and Prinsengracht, you'll see many of their buildings. With them, the medieval stepped gable

A New School

Between 1900 and 1940, various Amsterdam architects purveyed many different styles of architecture. One of these styles stands out above the others: the Amsterdam School, with **Eduard Cuypers** (nephew to P. J. H. Cuypers) at the helm, and **P. L. Kramer, M. de Klerk,** and **J. M. van der Mey,** all employed by Cuypers, as contributors. These architects succeeded in creating forms of brickwork that had existed only in earlier architects' fantasies. Their buildings are massive yet fluid, and feature decorations like stained glass, wrought iron, and corner towers.

gave way to a more ornate one with scrolled sides, decorative finials, and other features.

Many other 17th-century buildings have typically classical elements, such as pilasters, entablatures, and pediments. These details give a sense of order and balance and move away from de Keyser's playful Renaissance style. The classical pediment, often used as a protective element against the rain, was typically used to shield windows and to cap gable ends. During this time, a harder brown brick also replaced the red brick used in the 16th century.

Because classical elements tend to have straight lines and don't flow like the Renaissance elements did, facades shifted to a more boxed-in, central look that eventually grew into the raised-neck gable (a tall, narrow, rectangular gable). Fruits and flowers were used as ornamentation in the scrolls. Soon, the raised-neck gable gave way to the neck gable (which looks relatively similar, only shorter) with human and animal figures carved into the scrolls. **Jacob van Campen** (1595–1657), who built the elaborate **Town Hall** at the Dam, now the Royal Palace, was probably the single most important architect of Amsterdam architecture's classical period.

Around 1665, **Adriaan Dortsman** (1625–82), best known for his classic restrained Dutch style, began building homes with balconies and attics, leaving off the pilasters and festoons that adorned earlier facades. The emphasis had once again shifted, this time from decorated ornamentation to space utility and harmonization with structure.

4 AMSTERDAM IN POPULAR CULTURE: BOOKS, FILMS & MUSIC

BOOKS
Fiction

The Booker Prize–winning short novel *Amsterdam* plays with themes of love and friendship, death and mortality, and on Amsterdam's status as a city where euthanasia laws are relatively liberal, but most of it actually takes place in England. In that sense the city is more of a city of the mind than a real place. Amsterdam is actually quite familiar with playing the role of a screen on which outsiders project both their fantasies and their fears. Far more sense of place is provided by Nicolas Freeling's *Love in Amsterdam*, the first in his series of Inspector Piet Van der Valk detective novels, and even though it's the Amsterdam of almost a half century ago, the city is easily recognizable, and something of a co-protagonist. Much the same could be said of Alistair MacLean's thriller *Puppet on a Chain*, though written at a time when the author had descended into faintly ridiculous, formulaic tales.

History

Simon Schama's *The Embarrassment of Riches: An Interpretation of Dutch Culture in the Golden Age* lets you inside Amsterdam's greatest period. Schama, adeptly, is simultaneously lighthearted and scholarly—a chapter headed "The Pretzel and the Puppy Dog" refers to a portrait by Jacob Cuyp. Most of the 700 pages feature works of art which are explained in the text. Though Schama modestly describes his essays as "more eccentric than persuasive," he succeeds in his intention "to map out the moral geography of the Dutch mind, adrift between the fear of deluge and the hope of moral salvage."

If a single individual personifies the Holocaust, that person must be Anne Frank. Her diary, compiled as a series of letters addressed "Dear Kitty," and kept for more than 2 years until her arrest on August 4, 1944, has come to symbolize the plight of millions of Jews during Nazi terror. *The Diary of a Young Girl* includes photos of Anne and the people she hid with, plus a map of the secret annex in the house on Prinsengracht. Her candid descriptions of living as a teenage girl in tragically restricted conditions, of her thoughts and dreams, hopes and fears, boredom and anguish, provide an unusually moving account of a life cut far too short.

Amsterdam, A Brief Life of the City roves through 800 years in 300-some pages during which author Geert Mak lays bare the city's soul, linking tales about ordinary folk with historical fact. Amsterdam's journey from boggy 12th-century fish-and-farm settlement to modern metropolis is populated with princes and painters, Calvinists and Catholics, Provos and rebels; in this book, it's enlivened with black-and-white illustrations. Mak's journalistic skill and historical insight amply fulfill his ambition to write a historical work readable enough that you can read it in your hotel room before going to bed.

Art

Painters of Amsterdam: Four Centuries of Cityscapes is the kind of book that makes you wonder why nobody thought of putting out something like it before. Spread by spread, the large-format book unfolds a veritable gallery of paintings depicting the grand old Maid of the Amstel in all her moods and at key periods in history, from a 1640 Rembrandt etching to Matthias Meyer's *Museumplein*. Art historian Carole Denninger-Schreuder's incisive text accompanies the reproductions, which are by artists as diverse as Pieter Saenredam, George Hendrik Breitner, Isaac Israëls, Claude Monet, Vincent van Gogh, Piet Mondrian, and many more. The book adds up to an unforgettable trip down Amsterdam's memory lane, in the company of those observers best able to illuminate the journey.

If you want to buy a book about Old Masters, make it *The Glory of the Golden Age*, by Judikje Kiers and Fieke Tissink. Published to coincide with the bicentennial of Amsterdam's Rijksmuseum (p. 140), this weighty tome comprehensively covers the painting, sculpture, and decorative art of Holland's Golden Age (1600–1700). Works by Rembrandt, Vermeer, Frans Hals, and Jacob van Ruisdael are presented along with those of artists not as famous. Roughly chronological, the book contains a wealth of description about the country's vibrant 17th-century art scene.

Maybe you'd rather not be overwhelmed by Golden Age art but would still like an idea of what the heck was going on then. In this case, a good, affordable, and tolerably portable insight is afforded by *100 Memories: Paintings from the Golden Age*, by Ronald de Leeuw—the Rijksmuseum's former director.

For a personal insight into van Gogh's life and art, read Ken Wilkie's *The van Gogh File: A Journey of Discovery*. What began as a routine magazine assignment in 1972 to coincide with the opening of the

Van Gogh Museum became exactly what the book's subtitle indicates: A journey that continued long after the article was published. Wilkie followed van Gogh's trail through the Netherlands, Belgium, England, and France. Along the way, Wilkie met some of the last surviving people to have known or met the artist. In one of many dramatic discoveries, he finds an original van Gogh drawing while rummaging through a pile of old photographs in an English attic. Equally compelling are revelations from Vincent's private life, especially descriptions of his star-crossed search for love and family.

Society

You may find yourself chuckling over *The UnDutchables*, as you learn more about Dutch attitudes to home, money, children, transport, and much more. Are all Dutch people rude, their children undisciplined, and Dutch drivers abusive? Colin White and Laurie Boucke, Anglo-American expatriates who first published this paperback in 1989, have their tongues firmly in their cheeks throughout, choosing first to amuse and only second to inform.

Cuisine

Heleen Halverhout's postcard-size *The Netherlands Cookbook* (also published as *Dutch Cooking*), might be considered unambitious, but then, the same is true of Dutch cooking—nourishing rather than rich, solid rather than subtle. What other cookbook would give recipes for boiled, mashed, and fried potatoes? Halverhout includes winter favorites like pea soup, *hachée* (beef and onion stew), and *hotch-potch* (alongside whimsical illustrations that play on Dutch stereotypes) and explains Dutch eating habits, devoting plenty of space to cakes and traditional desserts such as *Hague bluff* and *John-in-the-bag*.

Photography

The 143 pages of photographer Martin Kers's *Amsterdam* dazzle with a mix not only of subjects, but also of vantages and camera angles, panorama and detail. His graceful images depict subjects like morning mist over a canal, abandoned bicycle remains, kids playing soccer in Vondelpark, and explosions of merrymaking on Queen's Day. A master of composition, Kers infuses even demolished buildings and library books with visual magic, capturing the city's atmosphere and those in it as they pose, walk dogs, or mend a bike. The accompanying text is by Dutch poet Willem Wilmink.

Jacob Olie's evocative images of 19th-century Amsterdam have only recently been rescued from oblivion—5,000 of his negatives resurfaced in 1960. A schoolteacher with a passion for photography, Olie shot most of his pictures during the 1860s, when photography was in its infancy, and during the 1890s, when development in technique permitted him to break new ground. Though strictly documentary, the 79 black-and-white photographs in *De Verbeelding*, a small horizontal book, ooze nostalgia. They afford glimpses of recognition and show people going about their business in a semi-rural, unhurried city where canals haven't yet been filled, and where trams are powered by horses, carts by men, and trains by steam.

FILMS

Amsterdam-born film director Paul Verhoeven is probably the best-known Dutch filmmaker—but that's not saying much, and Verhoeven's Hollywood films, such as *Basic Instinct, RoboCop,* and *Starship Troopers,* don't contain much (if anything) inspired by his hometown. Closer to home is his wartime resistance drama *Soldier of Orange* (1977), starring Jeroen Krabbé and Rutger Hauer. Another wartime drama, *The Assault,* won the Oscar for best Foreign Language Film in 1986.

The city starred as the darkly atmospheric setting of the underworld thriller *Puppet on a Chain* (1972), based on the novel of the same name by Scottish writer

Alistair MacLean—which contained a memorable chase sequence on the canals. And it played a supporting roll in the James Bond movie *Diamonds Are Forever* (1971). *Girl With a Pearl Earring* (2003), starring Scarlett Johansson and Colin Firth, is an appropriately moody interpretation of the "back story" to the Vermeer painting, set and partly filmed in Delft.

MUSIC

About the only well-known song in English to feature Amsterdam in a starring role is *Tulips From Amsterdam* (1956), which was originally written in German. This dose of concentrated saccharine keeps unlikely company with pot smoking, sex tourism, and gay parades as popular images of the city. Kids might likely be more familiar with *A Windmill in Old Amsterdam* (1965), which tells a heart-warming tale of "a little mouse with clogs on, going clip-clippety-clop on the stair."

The city's homegrown music scene runs more to jazz, blues, and experimental electronic music, as can be experienced at the Muziekgebouw aan 't IJ, Bimhuis, and a slew of clubs around town. For something a little more traditional, there are schmaltzy bars and clubs around Rembrandtplein and in the Jordaan, where you can sway to songs about stolen kisses behind the windmill, if you've a mind to—but of course they'll be in Dutch. For big international stars, head out to the Heineken Music Hall, and for bigger-than-big names, to the Amsterdam ArenA stadium, both of them in Amsterdam-Zuidoost (Southeast).

5 EATING & DRINKING IN AMSTERDAM

The concept of **"Dutch cuisine"** is generally considered a contradiction in terms. Dutch national dishes tend to be ungarnished, hearty, and wholesome—solid, stick-to-your-ribs stuff. A perfect example is *erwtensoep,* a thick pork-accented pea soup that provides inner warmth against cold Dutch winters and is filling enough to be a meal by itself. Similarly, *hutspot,* a potato, carrot, and onion "hotchpotch," or stew, is no-nonsense nourishment that becomes even more so with the addition of *klapstuk* (lean beef). *Hutspot* also has an intangible ingredient—a story behind its name that's based on historical fact: Spanish troops besieging Leiden in 1574 left behind a stew pot when a Dutch relief force surprised them in the middle of dinner, and this became a national symbol of freedom for Holland.

Seafood, as you might imagine in this traditionally seafaring country, is a big deal. Common options, depending on season, are Zeeland oysters and mussels (*Zeeuwsoesters* and *Zeeuwsmosselen*), and herring pickled or "new"—fresh from the North Sea and eaten raw. In fact, if you happen to be in Holland for the beginning of the herring season in June, interrupt your sidewalk strolls for a "green" (raw) herring with onions from a fish stall, or *haringhuis.* Look for signs that say HOLLANDSE NIEUWE (HOLLAND'S NEW). Great excitement surrounds the season's first catch, part of which goes to the queen and the rest to restaurateurs amid spirited competition. At fish stalls, you can also get snacks of baked fish, smoked eel, and seafood salads, taken on the run.

Dutch explorers and traders brought back recipes and exotic spices—and the popular **Indonesian *rijsttafel*** (rice table), a feast of 15 to 30 small portions of different dishes eaten with plain rice, has been a national favorite since the 17th century (see "Secrets of the Rijsttafel," in chapter 6). If you've never experienced this minifeast, it should definitely be on your "must-eat" list for Holland. Should you part company with the Dutch and "their" Indonesian food, you'll find the cuisines of China,

France, Greece, India, Italy, Japan, Spain, Turkey, Yugoslavia, and other nations.

At the top of the restaurant scale are those posh dining rooms affiliated with the prestigious **Alliance Gastronomique Néerlandaise** or the **Relais du Centre.** They're likely to be elegant and sophisticated or atmospherically old-world and quaint. They will certainly be expensive. Then there are the numerous moderately priced restaurants and little **brown cafes.** Dutch families gravitate to the restaurants, while brown cafes are cozy social centers with simple but tasty food, often served outside on sidewalk tables. **Sidewalk vendors,** with fresh herring, the ubiquitous *broodjes* (sandwiches), and other light specialties, are as popular as the brown cafes.

For more info on dining in Amsterdam, see chapter 6.

TERMINOLOGY

The first step in getting to know Dutch gastronomy is to forget that in American restaurants, the word *entree* means a main course; in Holland, *entrees* are appetizers, also known as *voorgerechten,* and main courses, *hoofdgerechten,* are listed separately as *vis* (fish) or *vlees* (meat), and in some restaurants, as *dagschotel* (dish of the day). Other courses on Dutch menus include *soepen* (soups), *warme* or *koude voorgerechten* (warm or cold appetizers), *groenten* (vegetables), *sla* (salad), *vruchten* (fruits), *nagerechten* (desserts), *dranken* (beverages), and *wijn* (wine).

The next step is to understand that Dutch is a language of compound words, and just as Leiden Street becomes Leidsestraat— one word for two ideas—the same goes for menus: Beef steak becomes *biefstuk,* pork chop becomes *varkenscotelette,* and so on.

Similarly, you'll find listings for *gehakte biefstuk* (chopped beef) or *gebakken worst* (fried sausage). Look for the following key words as you scan menus:

- For modes of preparation: *gekookt* or *gekookte* (boiled), *gebakken* (fried),

gebraden (roasted), *geroosterd* (broiled), *gerookte* (smoked).
- For meat cooked to your taste: *niet doorgebakken* (rare), *half doorgebakken* (medium), *goed doorgebakken* (well-done).
- For cuts of meat: *-stuk* (steak or, literally, piece), *-scotelet* or *-scotelette* (chop), *-kotelet* or *-kotelette* (cutlet).

MENU CHOICES
BREAKFAST
See "Hotel Orientation," in chapter 5.

LUNCH & SNACK SPECIALTIES
Below are clarifications of dishes you may see on lunch menus:

BAMI/NASI GORENG & NASI RAMES
Miniature versions of an Indonesian *rijsttafel* (see chapter 6); they come in a bowl on either noodles or rice, with spiced meat and possibly a fried egg or satay (a grilled kabob) on top.

BITTERBALLEN
Fried potato balls, or croquettes, that usually come quite spicy.

BROODJES
Small sandwiches on round buttered rolls made with ham, cheese, roast beef, salami, or other fillings. They're often ordered in pairs and eaten standing up or perched at a narrow counter in a *broodjeswinkel,* or sandwich shop.

CROQUETTEN
Fried croquettes of meat, prawns, or cheese that may be gooey inside. They're at their best when served piping hot with a blob of mustard for dunking.

ERWTENSOEP
This pea soup is thick, creamy, and chock-full of ham, carrots, and potatoes—a meal by itself. (This is a winter dish, so it may be hard to find in summer.)

NIEUWE HARING
Chasing herring is what got this city started, and Amsterdam folk are still in hot pursuit. Vendors sell new herring—fresh-caught fish that's eaten whole (minus the head and the tail) with minced onion, or chopped if you're squeamish—at stands all over town during

summer; you can also eat them pickled as *maatjes*.

PANNEKOEKEN&POFFERTJES These Dutch pancakes are the equivalent of French crepes, and they're served flat on a dinner plate, topped with confectioners' sugar, jam, syrup, hot apples, or—typically Dutch—hot ginger sauce. Less common are *pannekoeken* with meat. *Poffertjes* are small fried-pancake "puffs" coated with confectioners' sugar and filled with syrup or liqueur.

SAUCIJZENBROOD A hot dog, except the bun's made of flaky pastry and the hot dog is a spicy Dutch *wurst,* or sausage.

TOSTIS Grilled ham-and-cheese sandwiches.

UITSMIJTER An open-faced sandwich consisting of a buttered slice of bread (or two) topped with cold cuts and fried eggs—tasty, inexpensive, and a good lunch choice. (The name, incidentally, is the same for "bouncer," the burly doorman at nightclubs.)

VLAMMETJES(LITTLEFLAMES) These belong to the same family of *borrelhapjes* (drinking snacks) as *bitterballen* (see above), but are more like diminutive spring rolls which, like Napoleon, make up in fiery aggression for what they lack in size.

DINNER SPECIALTIES

With the exception of one excellent treat— the Indonesian *rijsttafel* (see chapter 6)—the Dutch may seem to be less inventive with dinner specialties than they are with lunch and snacks. This is partly because many traditional Dutch dishes closely resemble dishes popular elsewhere in Europe and the U.S. But mostly, it's due to Holland's ongoing, ever-growing (and somewhat tiresome) love affair with French cuisine. Here, however, are a few typical Dutch options you may encounter, particularly in winter, when real Dutch cooking can be best appreciated:

ASPERGES Asparagus. The thick, white cultivated variety grows during a 7-week season beginning on April 30 until late June. Most of it comes from Limburg, so it's marketed as "the white gold of Limburg"—but most folks just call it asparagus.

CAPUCIJNERS MET SPEK Marrow beans with bacon.

GEMBER MET SLAGROOM A sweet-and-sour dessert of tangy, fresh ginger slices topped with whipped cream.

GEROOKTE PALING Smoked eel (most of which come from the IJsselmeer— though many are now imported). A typically Dutch appetizer.

HAZEPEPER Jugged hare.

HUTSPOT A stew made of beef ribs, carrots, onions, and potatoes, often mashed together. This is a dish with historic significance, particularly for the people of Leiden: It's the Dutch version of the stew found in the boiling pots left behind after the Spaniards were evicted after a long siege during the Eighty Years' War.

KRABBETJES Dutch spareribs, usually beef rather than pork.

MOSSELEN Mussels, raised in the clean waters of Zeeland's Oosterschelde (Eastern Scheldt) estuary. Mussel season begins in mid-August with great fanfare (it runs until Apr), and the first crop is eagerly awaited. The mollusks are often steamed and served in a bit of white wine–and–vegetable stock.

ROLPENS A combination of minced beef, fried apples, and red cabbage.

STAMPOT Cabbage with smoked sausage.

ZUURKOOL MET SPEK EN WURST Sauerkraut with bacon and sausage.

DESSERT

Desserts tend toward fruit with lots of fresh cream, ice cream, or *appelgebak,* a lovely and light apple pastry.

3

Planning Your Trip to Amsterdam

Amsterdam isn't hard to come to grips with even if you arrive there cold (in the preparedness sense). The local tourist organization, **VVV Amsterdam,** prides itself on being able to answer any conceivable travel question any conceivable traveler might have, excepting only those who are illegal or of doubtful moral worth (this being Amsterdam, both of these concepts have a lot of wiggle room). The city is foreign, of course, but not impossibly so; many Dutch speak English.

To really put your best foot forward, you'll want to know how much the essentials will cost; how you're going to get there; what documents, clothing, and other travel necessities you should bring; and when you should go to best take advantage of special events. This chapter provides the information you need to plan your trip before leaving home.

For additional help in planning your trip and for more on-the-ground resources in Amsterdam, please see the "Fast Facts, Toll-Free Numbers & Websites" appendix on p. 285.

---

1 VISITOR INFORMATION

BEFORE YOU GO

Before leaving for the Netherlands, obtain information on the country and its travel facilities by contacting the **Netherlands Board of Tourism & Conventions (NBTC),** which maintains offices around the world. Their Internet address is **www. holland.com**.

For the **U.S. and Canada,** they're at 355 Lexington Ave., 19th Floor, New York, NY 10017 (© **212/370-7360;** fax 212/370-9507). For **Great Britain** and **Ireland** (no walk-in service), the info is P.O. Box 30783, London WC2B 6DH (© **020/7539-7950;** fax 020/7539-7953).

Or contact the Dutch umbrella organization for the country's many local tourist information organizations (no walk-in service): **Netherlands Board of Tourism & Conventions,** Postbus 458, 2260 MG Leidschendam (© **070/370-5705;** fax 070/320-1654). In addition, for those

flying into Amsterdam's Schiphol Airport, there's the **Holland Tourist Information** office (p. 36).

IN AMSTERDAM

Amsterdam's own tourist information organization (no walk-in service) is the **Amsterdam Tourism & Convention Board,** P.O. Box 3901, 1001 AS Amsterdam (© **0900/400-4040,** or 31-20/551-2525 from outside the Netherlands; fax 020/201-8850; www.amsterdamtourist. nl). Handle the 0900 phone number with caution; it costs .40€ (65¢) per minute, which is tolerable if you get a fast response and not so good if you have to hold. Calls made from outside the Netherlands are at the usual international rate.

This organization operates three **VVV Amsterdam** tourist offices, identified by triangular blue-and-white vvv signs. The letters stand for a tongue-twisting name: **Vereniging voor Vreemdelingenverkeer**

(**Association for Visitor Travel**). Even the Dutch don't much like saying that every time so they call it simply the VVV (pronounced *vay-vay-vay,* though it'll sound more like *fay-fay-fay* when spoken in an Amsterdam accent). VVV Amsterdam tourist offices are efficient and have multilingual attendants on duty. They can help you with almost any question about the city, and provide brochures and maps, reserve last-minute hotel rooms and tours, and sell reduced-rate tickets for attractions, public transportation, theater, and concerts.

One VVV office is inside Centraal Station, on platform 2B, open Monday to Wednesday from 9am to 8pm, Thursday to Saturday from 8am to 8pm, and Sunday and holidays from 9am to 6pm. A second office is right in front of the station, at Stationsplein 10, open daily from 8am to 9pm (trams for both offices: 1, 2, 4, 5, 9, 13, 16, 17, 24, 25, and 26). The third office is an agency office in a white kiosk facing Stadhouderskade 1, at Leidseplein (tram: 1, 2, 5, 7, or 10), and is open daily from 9am to 5pm. All of these offices are extremely busy.

Be sure to pick up a copy of the VVV's *Amsterdam Day by Day,* for 1.95€ ($3.10). This monthly magazine in English is full of details about the month's art exhibits, concerts, and theater performances, and lists restaurants, bars, dance clubs, and more. Or get a free copy of the yellow *Visitors Guide,* which is like a mini–*Yellow Pages* with a wealth of addresses and phone numbers, from any tourist office and some hotels.

In addition, the free *Amsterdam Weekly* newspaper is available from cultural outlets and some hotels and restaurants. *The Times,* also free, covers Amsterdam, The Hague, and Rotterdam and is available from select outlets like the American Book Center (see chapter 9 under "Books").

STREET MAPS This book's maps depict Amsterdam's basic waterway patterns and the relationships between the major squares and landmarks with their connecting thoroughfares. Once you get the hang of the four major canals' necklace pattern and become familiar with the names of the five principal roads into the Center, all you need do as you walk along is keep track of whether you're walking toward or away from the Dam—the heart of the city—or simply circling around it.

Buying a street map will make detailed navigation easier. The most cost-effective map is Amsterdam Tourism & Congress Bureau's **Amsterdam City Map,** available from VVV Amsterdam offices for 2€ ($3.20). It shows every street and canal, museums and churches, and tram routes and stops, extending as far as the ring road. For even more meticulous coverage of the city (and its suburbs), buy the Falk **Easy City Amsterdam Professional Map** for 9.95€ ($16).

2 ENTRY REQUIREMENTS

PASSPORTS & VISAS

Citizens of the U.S., Canada, the U.K., Ireland, Australia, and New Zealand need only a valid passport if visiting the Netherlands for less than 3 months—in the case of visitors who reside in most other E.U. countries, a valid identity card is sufficient. Citizens of other countries should be sure to check travel regulations before leaving. You can get these in English from the website of the Ministry of Foreign Affairs in The Hague: **www.minbuza.nl**.

For information on how to obtain a passport, see **"Passports"** in the **"Fast Facts, Toll-Free Numbers & Websites"** appendix (p. 289).

Cut to the Front of the Airport Security Line as a Registered Traveler

In 2003, the **Transportation Security Administration** (**TSA;** www.tsa.gov) approved a pilot program to help ease the time spent in line for airport security screenings. In exchange for information and a fee, persons can be pre-screened as registered travelers, granting them a front-of-the-line position when they fly. The program is run through private firms—the largest and most well-known is Steven Brill's **Clear** (www.flyclear.com), and it works like this: Travelers complete an online application providing specific points of personal information including name, addresses for the previous five years, birth date, social security number, driver's license number, and a valid credit card (you're not charged the **$99 fee** until your application is approved). Print out the completed form and take it, along with proper ID, with you to an "enrollment station" (this can be found in over 20 participating airports and in a growing number of American Express offices around the country, for example). It's at this point where it gets seemingly sci-fi. At the enrollment station, a Clear representative will record your biometrics necessary for clearance; in this case, your fingerprints and your irises will be digitally recorded.

Once your application has been screened against no-fly lists, outstanding warrants, and other security measures, you'll be issued a clear plastic card that holds a chip containing your information. Each time you fly through participating airports (and the numbers are steadily growing), go to the Clear Pass station located next to the standard TSA screening line. Here you'll insert your card into a slot and place your finger on a scanner to read your print—when the information matches up, you're cleared to cut to the front of the security line. You'll still have to follow all the procedures of the day like removing your shoes and walking through the x-ray machine, but Clear promises to cut 30 minutes off your wait time at the airport.

On a personal note: Each time I've used my Clear Pass, my travel companions are still waiting to go through security while I'm already sitting down, reading the paper, and sipping my overpriced smoothie. Granted, registered traveler programs are not for the infrequent traveler, but for those of us who fly on a regular basis, it's a perk I'm willing to pay for.

—David A. Lytle

MEDICAL REQUIREMENTS

No health or vaccination certificates are required. You won't need travel shots either, but if you have a chronic illness, consult your doctor before your departure. Pack important prescription medications in your carry-on baggage, and carry them in their original containers, with pharmacy labels—otherwise they won't make it through airport security. Carry the generic name of prescription medicines, in case local pharmacists are unfamiliar with the brand name. Don't forget an extra pair of contact lenses or prescription eyeglasses. Also, you might want to visit **www.tsa.com** for up-to-date regulations on what is and isn't permissible to pack in carry-on baggage.

CUSTOMS
What You Can Bring into the Netherlands

Visitors 17 years and older arriving from countries that are not members of the European Union (E.U.) may bring in duty-free 200 cigarettes or 100 cigarillos or 50 cigars or 250 grams of tobacco; 1 liter of liquor or 2 liters of sparkling wine or fortified wine (such as port or sherry), and 2 liters of wine; 50 grams of perfume, and 0.25 liters of eau de toilette; 500 grams of coffee or 200 grams of coffee extracts or coffee essences; and 100 grams of tea or 40 grams of tea extracts or tea essences. Import of most other goods is unlimited, so long as import duty is paid on all dutiable goods above a combined value of 175€ ($280). Forbidden products include firearms, counterfeit goods, banned narcotic substances, protected animals and plants, and products made from these.

Duty-free shopping has been abolished in the E.U. Therefore, standard allowances do not apply to goods bought in another E.U. country and brought into the Netherlands. In essence, there is no limit on what travelers arriving from an E.U. country can take into the Netherlands, as long as the items are for personal use (this includes gifts), and you have already paid the necessary duty and tax. However, the law sets out guidance levels. If you bring in more than the following, you may be asked to prove that the goods are for your own use: 800 cigarettes, 400 cigars or cigarillos, and 1 kilogram of smoking tobacco; 10 liters of hard liquor (spirits), 90 liters of wine, 20 liters of fortified wine (such as port or sherry), and 110 liters of beer.

There are no limitations on the amount of foreign currency you can bring into the country.

For more information in English, visit the Netherlands Customs website: **www.douane.nl**.

What You Can Take Home from Amsterdam

You'll likely get no more than a raised eyebrow back home for schlepping in a pair of brightly colored souvenir clogs, but bulbs, plants, and flowers might not be so welcome. Some countries require a phytosanitary certificate, which many Dutch suppliers provide.

Note that the rules from the information sources referred to below also apply to legal residents of the countries concerned, whether they are citizens or not.

U.S. Citizens: For specifics on what you can bring back and the corresponding fees, download the invaluable free pamphlet *Know Before You Go* online at www.cbp.gov. (Click on "Travel," and then click on "Know Before You Go! Online Brochure.") Or contact the U.S. Customs & Border Protection (CBP), 1300 Pennsylvania Ave., NW, Washington, DC 20229 (✆ 877/287-8667) and request the pamphlet.

Canadian Citizens: For a clear summary of Canadian rules, write for the booklet *I Declare,* issued by the Canada Border Services Agency (✆ 800/461-9999 in Canada, or 204/983-3500; www.cbsa-asfc.gc.ca).

U.K. Citizens: For information, contact **HM Customs & Excise** at ✆ 0845/010-9000 (from outside the U.K., 020/8929-0152), or consult their website at **www.hmrc.gov.uk**.

Australian Citizens: A helpful brochure available from Australian consulates or Customs offices is *Know Before You Go.* For more information, call the **Australian Customs Service** at ✆ 1300/363-263, or log on to **www.customs.gov.au**.

New Zealand Citizens: Most questions are answered in a free pamphlet available at New Zealand consulates and Customs offices: *New Zealand Customs Guide for Travellers, Notice no. 4.* For more information, contact **New Zealand Customs,** The Customhouse, 17–21 Whitmore St., Box 2218, Wellington (℡ **04/473-6099** or 0800/428-786; **www.customs.govt.nz**).

3 WHEN TO GO

"In season" in Amsterdam means mid-April to mid-October. The tourist season peaks in July and August, when the weather's at its finest. Climate, however, is never really extreme at any time of year; if you're among the growing numbers who favor shoulder—or off-season—travel you'll find the city every bit as attractive during these months. Not only are airlines, hotels, and restaurants cheaper and less crowded (with more relaxed and personalized service), but some very appealing events also take place. The bulb fields near Amsterdam, for example, burst with color from April to mid-May.

THE WEATHER

Amsterdam is one of those "If you don't like the weather, wait for a minute" kind of places. Summertime temperatures don't often rise above 75°F (24°C), making for a pleasant, balmy climate. July and August are the best months for in-line skating in Vondelpark, soaking up rays on cafe terraces, dining alfresco in the evening, and going topless on the beach at Zandvoort. September usually has a few weeks of fine late-summer weather.

Mean precipitation—and the precipitation in Holland can be pretty mean—is high enough that rain shouldn't come as a surprise. Although the temperature rarely dips below freezing in winter, remember that Amsterdam and much of Holland is below sea level, making fog, mist, and dampness your too-frequent companions. This damp chill often seems to cut to the bone, so in colder months, layer yourself in Gore-Tex or something similar. There are, however, plenty of bright but cold days in winter, and if the temperature falls far enough, canals, rivers, and lakes freeze to become sparkling highways for skaters throughout the city and the surrounding countryside. Throughout the year, some rain can be expected. Average annual rainfall is 25 inches. Most of it falls November through January, though substantial showers can occur year-round.

Some pointers on being prepared for Amsterdam's often unpredictable weather: First, invest in a fold-up umbrella and hope you never have to use it; likewise, carry a raincoat (with a wool liner for winter). Second, pack a sweater or two (even in July) and be prepared to layer clothing at any time of year. Don't worry: You're allowed to leave space for T-shirts, skimpy tops, and sneakers.

Amsterdam's Average Monthly Temperature & Days of Rain

	Jan	Feb	Mar	Apr	May	June	July	Aug	Sept	Oct	Nov	Dec
Temp. (°F)	38	37	43	47	54	59	62	62	58	51	44	40
Temp. (°C)	3	2	6	8	12	15	16	16	14	10	6	4
Days of rain	21	17	19	20	19	17	20	20	19	20	22	23

THE BEST TIMES TO GO

There's no worst time to visit Amsterdam: The city provides year-round stimulation to the brain's pleasure center. High season is the spring tulip season (early Apr to mid-May), and school vacations are in July and August. The city is very busy at both times, which means hotel rooms are hard to find and bargains don't exist at all (but who wants to tiptoe through the fallow tulip fields in Nov, or sit on a sidewalk cafe terrace in a snowstorm?). If you're planning

Impressions

I call to mind a winter landscape in Amsterdam—a flat foreground of waste land, with here and there stacks of timber, like the huts of a camp of some very miserable tribe; the long stretch of the Handelskade; cold, stone-faced quays, with the snow-sprinkled ground and the hard, frozen water of the canal, in which were set ships one behind another with their frosty mooring-ropes hanging slack and their decks idle and deserted . . .

—Joseph Conrad, *The Mirror of the Sea* (1906)

to travel during high season, book several months in advance. Summer is also the best time for cycling, which is an essential Dutch experience; try a canal bike if you're squeamish about going on the roads.

In winter, room rates are generally cheaper, and cafes and restaurants are less crowded and more genuine feeling. You won't find such a big line to get into the Anne Frankhuis (though a line will still exist), you'll be able to stand longer in front of Rembrandt's *The Night Watch* and your favorite van Gogh, and you might get a chance to go skating on the canals. You also get a better view of the canals, because the trees bordering them shed their screens of leaves in winter. As an added bonus, the lights from all those canalside windows, whose curtains never close, glow with Japanese-lantern charm on the inky surface.

HOLIDAYS

A Dutch holiday can add a festive note to your trip, particularly if it involves a parade or special observance. But expect banks, government offices, shops, and many museums to be closed, and public transportation to operate on Sunday schedules for the following holidays: **New Year's Day** (Jan 1); **Good Friday, Easter Sunday, Easter Monday,** *Koninginnedag* (Queen's Day: Queen Beatrix's official birthday is Apr 30), **Ascension Day** (Thurs, 40 days after Easter), **Pentecost Sunday** (7th Sun after Easter), *Pinksteren* (Pentecost Mon), **Christmas Day** (Dec 25), and **December 26.**

In addition, there are two World War II "Remembrance Days," neither of which is an official holiday, though some establishments close: *Herdenkingsdag* (May 4) honors all those who died in the war; *Bevrijdingsdag* (May 5) celebrates the Liberation.

AMSTERDAM CALENDAR OF EVENTS

For an exhaustive list of events beyond those listed here, check http://events.frommers.com, where you'll find a searchable, up-to-the-minute roster of what's happening in cities all over the world. The following listing includes a few events outside Amsterdam.

JANUARY

New Year, throughout the center, but mostly at the Dam and Nieuwmarkt. This celebration is wild and not always wonderful. Youthful spirits celebrate the New Year with firecrackers, which they cheerfully—if not drunkenly— throw at the feet of passersby. This keeps hospital emergency rooms busy. January 1.

Rotterdam International Film Festival. More than 300 indie films are screened at theaters around town. Contact

(C) **010/890-9090;** www.filmfestival rotterdam.com. January 21 to February 1, 2009; similar dates in 2010.

MARCH

Windmill Days, Zaanse Schans. All five working windmills (out of eight windmills in total) are open to the public at this re-created old village and open-air museum in the Zanstreek, just north of Amsterdam. Contact **Zaanse Schans** (*(C)* **075/616-2862;** www.zaanseschans. nl). March to October.

Stille Omgang. This "silent procession" along Kalverstraat is walked by Catholics every year to celebrate the "Miracle of the Host"—this refers to a Roman Catholic communion wafer that is said to have resisted all attempts to burn it—which occurred in 1345. The procession begins at the Royal Palace on the Dam and goes from midnight to 2:30am. Contact the **Gezelschap voor de Stille Omgang** (www.stille-omgang.nl). March 21, 2009; similar date in 2010.

Opening of Keukenhof Gardens, Lisse. The greatest flower show on earth blooms with spectacular displays of tulips and narcissi, daffodils and hyacinths, bluebells, crocuses, lilies, amaryllis, and many others at this 32-hectare (80-acre) garden in the heart of the bulb country. There's said to be nearly eight million flowers, but who's counting? Contact **Keukenhof** (*(C)* **0252/ 465-555;** www.keukenhof.nl). March 19 to May 21, 2009; similar dates in 2010.

APRIL

National Museum Weekend. A weekend during which most museums in Amsterdam and many throughout the Netherlands offer free or reduced admission, and have special exhibits. April 4 and 5, 2009; similar dates in 2008.

Bloemencorso van de Bollenstreek (Bulb District Flower Parade). Floats keyed to a different floral theme each year parade from Noordwijk, through Sassenheim, Lisse, and Bennebroek, to Haarlem. Contact **Bloemencorso Bollenstreek** (*(C)* **0252/428-237;** www. bloemencorso-bollenstreek.nl). April 25, 2009; similar dates in 2010.

Koninginnedag (Queen's Day). This nationwide holiday for the House of Orange is vigorously celebrated in Amsterdam with a gigantic dawn-to-dawn street carnival, which packs the center city so densely that it's virtually impossible to move. A citywide street market features masses of stalls, run by everyone from kids selling old toys to professional market folk in town to make a killing. Orange ribbons, orange hair, and orange-painted faces are everywhere, as are Dutch flags. Street music and theater combine with probably too much drinking, but Koninginnedag remains a good-natured, boisterous affair. *Tip:* Wear something orange, even if it's just suspenders or a ribbon in your hair. Contact **VVV Amsterdam** (*(C)* **0900/400-4040;** www.amsterdam tourist.nl). Gay and lesbian celebrations convene around the city's main gay areas and the Homomonument (p. 159). There are stage performances from belly-dancing to drag, stalls publicizing various gay and lesbian organizations, and food and drink. April 30.

MAY

Herdenkingsdag (Memorial Day). Countrywide observance honoring World War II victims. Queen Beatrix places a wreath at the national Monument on the Dam, and 2 minutes of silence begin at 8pm. Contact **VVV Amsterdam** (*(C)* **0900/400-4040;** www. amsterdamtourist.nl). May 4.

Bevrijdingsdag (Liberation Day). This citywide event is a less frenetic version of Koninginnedag (see "April," above). It recalls the country's liberation from Nazi occupation at the end of World

War II and is celebrated on the anniversary of the German forces' surrender in the Netherlands. Canadian troops made it into the city first (2 days later), so Canadian flags are popular accessories. More street markets, music, and theater. Contact **VVV Amsterdam** (✆ **0900/400-4040;** www.amsterdamtourist.nl). Gay and lesbian participation includes stage performances, from belly-dancing to drag, stalls publicizing various gay and lesbian organizations, and food and drink. May 5.

National Windmill Day. Around two-thirds of the country's almost 1,000 windmills—including Amsterdam's eight—spin their sails and are open to the public. Contact **De Hollandsche Molen** (✆ **020/623-8703;** www.molens.nl). Second Saturday in May: May 9, 2009; May 8, 2010.

JUNE

Vlaggetjesdag (Flag Day), Scheveningen. The fishing fleet opens the herring season with a race to bring the first *Hollandse Nieuwe* herring back to port (the first barrel is auctioned for charity). Some 200,000 people pour into town for the celebrations, and Dutch flags fly everywhere. Contact **Stichting Vlaggetjesdag Scheveningen** (✆ **070/345-3267;** www.vlaggetjesdag.com). June 13, 2009; June 12, 2010.

Holland Festival, Amsterdam, The Hague, Rotterdam, and Utrecht. Each year, these four cities join forces to present a cultural buffet of music, opera, theater, film, and dance. The schedule includes all the major Dutch companies, plus visiting companies and soloists from around the globe. Contact **Holland Festival** (✆ **020/788-2100;** www.hollandfestival.nl). May 31 to June 29, 2009; similar dates in 2010.

Amsterdam Roots Festival. This festival features music and dance from around the world, along with workshops, films, and exhibits in various venues. One part is the open-air **Oosterpark Festival,** a multicultural feast of song and dance held at Oosterpark in Amsterdam-Oost (East). Contact **Amsterdam Roots Festival** (✆ **020/531-8181;** www.amsterdamroots.nl). June 13 to June 29, 2009; similar dates in 2010.

Open Gardens Days. If you wonder what the fancy gardens behind the gables of some of the city's houses-turned-museums look like, this is your chance to find out. Some of the best are open to the public for 3 days. Go to the website of **Grachten Musea** (✆ **020/320-3660;** www.grachtenmusea.nl). Third week in June.

From June to mid-August, catch a performance at the **Vondelpark Open-Air Theater.** Everything goes here: theater, all kinds of music (including full-scale classical concerts by the famed Royal Concertgebouw Orchestra), dance, and even operettas. Contact Vondelpark Openluchttheater (✆ **020/428-3360;** www.openluchttheater.nl).

JULY

Over Het IJ Festival. Performers stage avant-garde theater, music, and dance in Amsterdam-Noord, beside the IJ channel, at the old NDSM Wharf, TT Neveritaweg 15. Contact **Over Het IJ Festival** (✆ **020/492-2229;** www.overhetij.nl). July 2 to July 12, 2009; similar dates in 2010.

North Sea Jazz Festival, Ahoy, Rotterdam. One of the world's leading gatherings of top international jazz and blues musicians unfolds over 3 concert-packed days at the city's giant Ahoy venue. Last-minute tickets are scarce, so book as far ahead as possible. Contact **North Sea Jazz Festival** (✆ **0900/300-1250** in Holland, or 31-10/591-9000 from outside Holland; www.northseajazz.com). July 11 to July 13, 2009; similar dates in 2010.

Amsterdam Gay Pride. This is a big event in Europe's most gay-friendly city. 150,000 people turn out to watch the highlight: Boat Parade's display of 100 or so outrageously decorated boats cruising the canals. In addition, there are street discos and open-air theater performances, a sports program, and a film festival. Go to the website of **Amsterdam Gay Pride** (www.amsterdamgay pride.nl) for info. First weekend in August: August 1 to August 3, 2009 (Canal Parade Aug 2); similar dates in 2010.

Grachten Festival. This 5-day classical music festival, with a different theme each year, plays at various intimate and elegant venues along the canals and at the Muiziekgebouw aan 't IJ. There's always a performance or two designed for children. Part of the festival is the exuberant Prinsengracht Concert (see below), which plays on a pontoon in front of the hotel Pulitzer (p. 87). Contact **Stichting Grachtenfestival** (© 020/421-4542; www.grachtenfestival.nl). August 15 to August 23, 2009; similar dates in 2010.

Prinsengracht Concert. Chamber music floats up in the evening from an open pontoon moored in front of the Hotel Pulitzer Amsterdam, at Prinsengracht 315–331 (see "The Canal Belt," in chapter 5). Crowds pile in by boat, by bike, and on foot to take it in, jamming up the canal and both banks of the canal. The free concert, the highlight and culmination of the Grachten Festival (see above), usually begins at 9:30pm and lasts an hour. If it rains, there's an alternative indoor venue, which is announced at the time of the concert. Contact **Stichting Grachtenfestival** (© 020/421-4542; www.grachtenfestival.nl). August 23, 2009; similar date in 2010.

Uitmarkt. Amsterdam previews the soon-to-open cultural season with this superb 3-day "open information market," which runs alongside free performances at theaters, concert halls, and impromptu outdoor venues. Professional and amateur groups present shows that run the gamut of music, opera, dance, theater, and cabaret. Visit the website of **Uitmarkt** (www.uit markt.nl) for info. Usually the last weekend in August, but dates are not confirmed until the preceding March.

September

Jordaan Festival, Westermarkt. This loosely organized festival in the trendy Jordaan neighborhood features various genres of Dutch music played in front of the **Westerkerk** (p. 163). Contact **Stichting Jordaan Festival** (www. jordaanfestival.nl). Mid-September.

Open Monumentendag. A chance to see countrywide historical buildings and monuments usually not open to the public—and to get in free. Contact **Vereniging Open Monumentendag** (© 020/422-2118; www.open monumentendag.nl). Second Saturday and Sunday in September: September 12 and 13, 2009; September 11 and 12, 2010 (probable).

Dam tot Damloop (Dam to Dam Run). The country's most popular running event starts at the Dam in the center of Amsterdam, heads out of town through the IJ Tunnel to the center of Zaandam, and back again, for a distance of 16km (10 miles). Contact **Dam tot Damloop** (© 072/533-8136; www.damloop.nl). Third Sunday in September; starts at noon.

October

Leidens Ontzet (Relief of Leiden), Leiden. These processions and festivities commemorate the defeat of the 1574 Spanish siege that came close to starving the town into submission. Citizens distribute *haring en witte brood* (herring and white bread), just as the pirate-like band of Sea Beggars did during the siege, helping to drive the Spaniards away. Contact **VVV Leiden** (☎ **0900/ 222-2333;** www.leidenpromotie.nl). October 3 (Oct 4 when the 3rd is a Sun).

International Horti Fair, Amsterdam. The largest exhibit of autumn-blooming flowers in the Netherlands takes place at the RAI convention center. Contact ☎ **0297/344-033;** www.horti fair.nl. October 13 to October 16, 2009; similar date in 2010.

Leather Pride is a growing cluster of parties and other events for gays who are into a leather lifestyle. Contact **Leather Pride Nederland** (☎ **020/422-3737;** www.leatherpride.nl). Last weekend of October.

NOVEMBER

Sinterklaas Arrives. Holland's equivalent of Santa Claus (St. Nicholas) launches the Christmas season; he arrives by boat at the Centraal Station pier and is accompanied by black-painted assistants, called *Zwarte Pieten* (Black Petes), who hand out sweets to kids. Saint Nick goes in stately procession through Amsterdam before getting to the Dam, where the mayor hands him the keys to the city. Contact **VVV Amsterdam** (☎ **0900/400-4040**). Third Saturday in November: November 21, 2009, and November 20, 2010.

Crossing Border Festival, Den Haag (The Hague). This 5-day festival in The Hague combines literature, poetry, film, and music. Contact **Crossing Border** (☎ **070/346-2355;** www.crossing border.nl). Mid-November.

DECEMBER

Sinterklaas. Saint Nicholas's Eve is the traditional day in Holland for exchanging Christmas gifts. Join Dutch friends or a Dutch family if possible. December 5.

World Christmas Circus. The best acts from the world's circuses go into action under the big top at Koninklijk Theater Carré. Contact **Carré** (☎ **020/622-5225;** www.theatercarre.nl). December 19, 2008, to January 4, 2009; similar dates in 2009 and 2010.

Gouda bij Kaarslicht (Gouda by Candlelight). After dusk, the city of Gouda turns off its electric lights. Then, the Markt, the main square, the 15th-century town hall, and a giant Christmas tree are lit by thousands of glowing candles. Contact **VVV Gouda** (☎ **0900/ 468-3288;** www.vvvgouda.nl). Second Tuesday before Christmas.

4 GETTING THERE & GETTING AROUND

GETTING THERE

Amsterdam can be reached from around the world by plane, by boat from Britain, and by train, bus, and car from around Europe.

By Plane

Amsterdam Airport Schiphol (see below) is not only the airport of Amsterdam, but it's also the primary international airport of the Netherlands. The main airline operating into Schiphol is KLM Royal Dutch Airlines (a subsidiary of Air France), which has an alliance with U.S. carrier Northwest Airlines.

FROM THE U.S. AND CANADA Carriers with frequent flights to Amsterdam from such cities as Atlanta, Boston, Chicago, Detroit, Houston, Los Angeles, Minneapolis/St. Paul, Memphis, Montreal, Newark, New York, San Francisco, Seattle, Toronto, Vancouver, and Washington, D.C., are: **Air Canada** (☎ **888/247-2262;**

www.aircanada.ca); **Continental Airlines** (℡ **800/231-0856;** www.continental. com); **Delta Airlines** (℡ **800/221-1212;** www.delta.com); **KLM Royal Dutch Airlines** (℡ **800/225-2525;** www.klm.com); **Northwest Airlines** (℡ **800/225-2525;** www.nwa.com); and **United Airlines** (℡ **800/538-2929;** www.united.com).

FROM THE U.K. Airlines that fly to Amsterdam from a roster of cities that includes Aberdeen, Belfast, Birmingham, Bristol, Cardiff, Edinburgh, Glasgow, Leeds/Bradford, Liverpool, London, Manchester, Newcastle, Norwich, and Teesside, are **British Airways** (℡ **0844/493-0787;** www.britishairways.com); **bmi** (℡ **0870/ 607-0555;** www.flybmi.com); **easyJet** (℡ **0905/821-0905;** www.easyjet.com); and **KLM Royal Dutch Airlines** (℡ **0871/ 222-7474;** www.klm.com).

FROM IRELAND   Aer Lingus (℡ **0818/ 365-000;** www.aerlingus.com) flies from Dublin to Amsterdam.

FROM AUSTRALIA   KLM Royal Dutch Airlines (℡ **1300/392-192;** www.klm. com) and **Qantas** (℡ **131313;** www.qantas. com.au) fly from Sydney to Amsterdam.

FROM NEW ZEALAND   Air New Zealand (℡ **0800/737-000;** www.airnew zealand.com) flies from Auckland to London, where you can transfer to Amsterdam.

Arriving at Amsterdam Airport Schiphol

An airliner descending into **Amsterdam's Schiphol Airport** (℡ **0900/0141** from inside Holland, or 31-20/794-0800 from outside; www.schiphol.nl; airport code: AMS), 13km (8 miles) southwest of the center city, has to descend more than it would if it were landing at almost any other airport; the runway is 4.5m (15 ft.) below sea level. Where the runway is now was once a lake with access to the sea—the Dutch and Spanish fought a naval battle here in 1573. Schiphol (pronounced *skhip-*ol) is the main airport in the Netherlands,

handling just about all of the country's international arrivals and departures. It's easy to see why frequent travelers regularly vote Schiphol a favorite airport: for its ease of use and its massive tax-free shopping center, renowned for its vast range of merchandise—more than 100,000 items—and low prices.

After you deplane at one of three adjacent terminals (numbered 1, 2, and 3), moving walkways take you to the Arrivals Hall, where you enter either the E.U. Citizens or Non-E.U. Citizens section at Passport Control, then Baggage Claim, then one of two Customs clearance aisles, red or green, depending on whether or not you have goods to declare. ATMs, free luggage carts, currency-exchange kiosks, restaurants, bars, shops, baby rooms, and restrooms are available. If you need a shower, you'll find bathing facilities at Arrivals, in the Transit lounges, and at executive lounges.

Beyond Arrivals, in **Schiphol Plaza,** you'll find railway station access, the Sheraton Amsterdam Airport hotel (p. 101), a mall (sporting that most essential Dutch service—a flower store), bars, cafes, restaurants ranging from fast-food and self-service to posh establishments, and including a Japanese sushi bar, restrooms, a bank, post office, baggage storage and lockers, airport information desks, car-rental desks (Alamo, Avis, Budget, Europcar, Hertz, National, and Sixt), hotel-reservation desks, and more. Bus, shuttle, and taxi stops are just outside. For tourist information and to make hotel reservations, go to the **Holland Tourist Information** desk (℡ **0900/400-4040**) in Schiphol Plaza, open daily from 7am to 10pm.

PASSING THE TIME AT SCHIPHOL AIRPORT Level 2 at Schiphol Plaza is the "quiet floor," with first-class, business-class, and private lounges, meeting rooms, and a place of worship and repose. Level 3 bustles with bars, eateries, and a diamond store.

Take in an exhibit at the Zonneruiter art gallery or, if the weather is fine, stroll along the open-air promenade and observation deck, which has an excellent view of landing and departing aircrafts (this may be closed for security reasons).

If you ran out of time to visit Amsterdam's famed Rijksmuseum, or if you just can't get enough of the Dutch Old Masters, the **Rijksmuseum Amsterdam Schiphol** is for you. A dozen or so paintings are permanently displayed at this airport museum annex, amid changing exhibits of other works. The small museum is on Holland Boulevard, between Pier E and Pier F. It's open daily from 7am to 8pm, and admission is free.

GETTING INTO TOWN FROM THE AIRPORT Netherlands Railways (NS) (© **0900/9292;** www.ns.nl) trains for Amsterdam Centraal Station depart from Schiphol Station, downstairs from Schiphol Plaza, and stop at De Lelylaan and De Vlugtlaan stations in western Amsterdam along the way. Frequency ranges from six trains an hour at peak times to one an hour at night. The one-way fare is 3.80€ ($6.10); the trip takes about 20 minutes.

An alternative rail route serves both Amsterdam Zuid/WTC (World Trade Center) station and RAI station (near the RAI Convention Center). Be sure to check which route goes closest to your hotel (including any tram or bus interchange). If you're staying at a hotel near Leidseplein, Rembrandtplein, in the Museum Quarter, or in Amsterdam South, this route may be better for you than Centraal Station. The fare to RAI is 3.80€ ($6.10) one-way; the trip takes about 15 minutes. From Amsterdam Zuid/WTC, take tram no. 5 for Leidseplein and the Museum Quarter; from RAI, take tram no. 4 for Rembrandtplein.

The **Connexxion Hotel Shuttle** (© **038/339-4741;** www.schipholhotel shuttle.nl) runs daily every 10 to 30 minutes from 6am to 9pm, between the airport and some 100 Amsterdam hotels. Reservations aren't necessary, and buses depart from in front of Schiphol Plaza. Tickets can be procured from the Connexxion desk inside Schiphol Plaza or on board from the driver (or, for the return journey, from your hotel). The fare is 13.50€ ($22) one-way and 22€ ($35) round-trip; for children ages 4 to 14, it's 6.75€ ($11) one-way and 11€ ($18) round-trip. It takes only 15 minutes from the airport to the Bilderberg Garden Hotel, but almost an hour to the NH Barbizon Palace; going the opposite direction, the timing's reversed. Some hotels have their own shuttle service.

Connexxion line bus service from Schiphol is likely to be less useful for arriving travelers, since line buses are slower than both the train and the Connexxion hotel shuttle. The most useful line, no. 370, departs half-hourly to hourly Monday to Friday, and hourly on Saturdays, Sundays, and holidays from in front of Schiphol Plaza; it goes to Amsterdam's downtown Marnixstraat bus station via Museumplein and Leidseplein. Connexxion buses also serve other points; comprehensive information is available on the Connexxion website (see above) and at bus stops outside Schiphol Plaza.

Taxis are expensive, but they're the preferred choice if your luggage is burdensome or if there are multiple people to share the cost. You'll find taxis waiting at the **SchipholTaxi** (© **0900/900-6666;** www.schipholtaxi.nl) stands in front of Schiphol Plaza. All taxis from the airport are metered. Expect to pay around 40€ ($64) to the center city. Remember, a service charge is already included in the fare.

Long-Haul Flights: How to Stay Comfortable

• Your choice of airline and airplane will definitely affect your legroom. Find more details about U.S. airlines at **www.seatguru.com**. For international airlines, the research firm Skytrax has posted a list of average seat pitches at **www.airlinequality.com**.

- Emergency exit seats and bulkhead seats typically have the most legroom. Emergency exit seats are usually left unassigned until the day of a flight (to ensure that someone able-bodied fills the seats); it's worth checking in online at home (if the airline offers that option) or getting to the ticket counter early to snag one of these spots for a long flight. Many passengers find that bulkhead seating offers more legroom, but keep in mind that bulkhead seats have no storage space on the floor in front of you.

- To have two seats for yourself in a three-seat row, try for an aisle seat in a center section toward the back of coach. If you're traveling with a companion, book an aisle and a window seat. Middle seats are usually booked last, so chances are good you'll end up with three seats to yourselves. And in the event that a third passenger is assigned the middle seat, he or she will probably be more than happy to trade for a window or an aisle.

- To sleep, avoid the last row of any section or the row in front of an emergency exit, as these seats are the least likely to recline. Avoid seats near highly trafficked toilet areas. Avoid seats in the back of many jets—these can be narrower than those in the rest of coach. Or reserve a window seat so you can rest your head and avoid being bumped in the aisle.

- Get up, walk around, and stretch every 60 to 90 minutes to keep your blood flowing. This helps avoid **deep vein thrombosis**, or "economy-class syndrome."

- Drink water before, during, and after your flight to combat the lack of humidity in airplane cabins. Avoid caffeine and alcohol, which will dehydrate you.

By Boat from Britain

DFDS Seaways (© 0871/522-0955 in Britain, or 0255/546-688 in Holland; www.dfdsseaways.co.uk) has daily car-ferry service between Newcastle in northeast England and IJmuiden on the North Sea coast, 24km (15 miles) west of Amsterdam. The overnight travel time is 15 hours. From IJmuiden, you can go by special bus to Amsterdam Centraal Station.

P&O Ferries (© 0871/664-5645 in Britain, or 020/200-8333 in Holland; www.poferries.com) has daily car-ferry service between Hull in northeast England and Rotterdam (into Europoort's harbor). The overnight trip time is 10 hours. Ferry company buses shuttle between the Rotterdam Europoort terminal and Rotterdam Centraal Station, from where there are frequent trains to Amsterdam.

Stena Line (© 0870/570-7070 in Britain, or 0900/8123 in Holland; www.stenaline.co.uk) has twice-daily car-ferry service between Harwich in southeast England and Hoek van Holland (Hook of Holland) near Rotterdam. The travel time during the day is 6 hours, 15 minutes, and 7 hours overnight. Frequent trains depart from Hoek van Holland to Amsterdam.

By Cruise Ship

Annually, Amsterdam welcomes some 100 ocean cruise liners from around the world and 700 river cruise boats from Europe's inland waterways. You'll likely arrive at the cruise-liner dock, **Passenger Terminal Amsterdam,** Piet Heinkade 27 (© 020/509-1000; www.ptamsterdam.com; tram: 25 or 26), on the IJ waterway just east of Centraal Station and within easy walking distance of the center city.

By Train

Rail service to Amsterdam from elsewhere in Europe is frequent and fast. International trains arrive at Centraal Station from Brussels, Paris, Berlin, Cologne, and some cities in Austria, Switzerland, Italy, and Eastern Europe.

Nederlandse Spoorwegen (Netherlands Railways; ℂ 0900/9292; www.ns.nl) trains arrive in Amsterdam from towns and cities around Holland. Service is frequent and trains are modern, clean, and punctual.

Schedule and fare information about travel by train and other public transportation *(openbaar vervoer)* in the Netherlands is available by calling ℂ **0900/9292,** or visiting **www.9292ov.nl.** For international trains, call ℂ **0900/9296.**

Britain is connected to mainland Europe via the **Channel Tunnel** (nicknamed "The Chunnel"). On **Eurostar**'s (www.eurostar.com) high-speed train (top speed 300kmph/186 mph), travel time between London St. Pancras Station and Brussels Midi Station (the closest connecting point for Amsterdam) is around 2 hours. For Eurostar reservations, call ℂ **08705/ 186-186** in Britain.

The burgundy-colored **Thalys** (www.thalys.com) high-speed train, with a top speed of 300kmph (186 mph), connects Paris, Brussels, and Cologne to Amsterdam. Travel time from Paris to Amsterdam is 4 hours, 10 minutes; from Brussels, it's 2 hours, 45 minutes. For Thalys information and reservations in France, call ℂ **03635;** in Belgium, ℂ **020/528-2828;** in Germany, ℂ **11861;** and in Holland, ℂ **0900/9296.** Tickets are also available from main railway stations and travel agents.

Note: An improved Thalys service operating on a new high-speed rail line in Belgium and Holland is expected to be operational sometime in 2010, and will reduce the travel time from Brussels by an hour.

ARRIVING BY TRAIN AT AMSTERDAM CENTRAAL STATION If you arrive by train, you'll likely find yourself deposited at Amsterdam's Centraal Station, built in the 1880s on an artificial island in the IJ channel. The building, an ornate neo-Renaissance architectural wonder, is the bustling hub of the city's concentric rings of canals and connecting main streets, and the originating point for most of the city's trams, Metro trains, and buses.

A VVV Amsterdam **tourist information office** is inside the station's Platform 2; a similar office is right in front of the station on Stationsplein. Both have hotel reservation desks. Other facilities include a GWK Travelex currency-exchange office, ATMs, train info center, baggage office, luggage lockers, restaurants and snack bars, newsstands, and small specialty stores. The station is a departure point for Metro trains, trams (streetcars), buses, taxis, passenger ferries, water taxis, canalboat cruises, the Museum Quarter Line (p. 45), and the Canal Bus (p. 45). At the station's rear, there are docks for the ferryboats that shuttle passengers around the city's fast-developing waterfront.

Outside, on **Stationsplein,** there might be a barrel organ grinding away. The **Smits Coffee House NZH** (ℂ **020/623-3777**) has a pleasant waterside terrace overlooking the inner harbor; watch as canal boats glide by.

An array of **tram stops** are on either side of the main station exit—virtually all of Amsterdam's hotels are within a 15-minute tram ride from Centraal Station. The **Metro station** is downstairs, just outside the main exit. City **bus stops** are to the left of the main exit, and **taxi stands** are to the right. At the **GVB Tickets & Info** office on Stationsplein, you can buy cards for trams, Metros, and buses. (For more details about public transportation within the city, see "Getting Around," below.)

Note: The station will be, for some years to come, a confusing construction site. Under development right now is a new Metro station, to be the hub of the Noord-Zuid (North-South) line. It's due to enter service in 2015. At the same time, construction is underway on a new main entrance and all-around improved passenger facilities. On top of all that, the waterfront zone at the rear is being completely revamped.

Centraal Station is also a pickpocket convention that's in full swing at all times. Messages broadcast in multiple languages warn people to be on guard, but the artful dodgers still seem to do good business. Avoid becoming a victim by keeping money and valuables under wraps, especially amid crowds. You'll likely also encounter a "heroin whore" or two, a platoon of panhandlers, and more than a whiff of pot smoke.

By Bus

International buses (sometimes known in Europe as "coaches"), especially Eurolines' (www.eurolines.com), arrive at the bus terminal outside **Amstel rail station** (Metro: Amstel) in south Amsterdam. Eurolines operates bus service between London Victoria Bus Station and Amstel Station, with up to five daily departures in summer. Travel time is just over 12 hours. For reservations, contact **Eurolines** (✆ **08717/818-181** in Britain, or 020/560-8788 in Holland). From Amstel bus station, go by train and Metro to Centraal Station, and by tram no. 12 to the **Museumplein** area (p. 137), and then to connecting points for trams to the Center. For the **Leidseplein** area (p. 66), take the Metro toward Centraal Station, get out at **Weesperplein**, and go aboveground to take tram lines 7 or 10.

By Car

For listings of the major car-rental agencies in Amsterdam, please see the "Fast Facts, Toll-Free Numbers & Websites" appendix (p. 285) and the "By Car" section under "Getting Around," below.

To drive in Holland, drivers need only produce a valid driver's license from their home country. The Netherlands is crisscrossed by a network of major international highways. European expressways E19, E35, E231, and E22 converge on Amsterdam from France and Belgium to the south and from Germany to the north and east. These roads also have Dutch designations; as you approach Amsterdam they become, respectively: A4, A2, A1, and A7. The city's ring road (beltway) is A10. Traffic is invariably heavy—but distances between destinations are relatively short, road conditions are generally excellent, service stations are plentiful, and highways are plainly signposted.

To drive from Britain to Amsterdam, use the efficient **Le Shuttle** (www.eurotunnel.com) automobile transporter through the Channel Tunnel from Folkestone to Calais (a 35-min. trip), and drive up from there through Belgium and Holland. Le Shuttle has departures every 15 minutes at peak times, every 30 minutes at times of average demand, and hourly at night. For information and reservations, call ✆ **08705/35-35-35** in Britain, ✆ **0810/63-03-04** in France, or ✆ **0900/504-0540** in Holland. Reserving in advance makes sense at the busiest times, but the system is so fast, frequent, and simple that you may prefer to retain travel flexibility by just showing up, buying your ticket, waiting in line for a short while, and then driving aboard.

The best way to experience most European cities is to drive to the city, park your car, and never touch it again until you

---

Impressions

Though Amsterdammers are helpful, they're also detached, aloof, as if they themselves were from some different, parallel city.

—*Departures* (Jan/Feb 2000)

Your Passport to Amsterdam

To get the most out of your trip, avail yourself of the **I amsterdam Card.** The card, valid for 1 day for 33€ ($53), 2 days for 43€ ($69), and 3 days for 53€ ($85), affords free travel on public transportation, free admission to more than 20 museums and attractions, including the **Rijksmuseum** or the **Van Gogh Museum** (but not both). The card also provides for discounted admission to additional museums and attractions, a free canal-boat cruise, discounted excursions, including reduced rates on the **Museum Quarter Line** boat and the **Canal Bus,** and discounts in certain restaurants and stores. The card comes with a public transportation ticket and a color information booklet. Total possible savings: around 150€ ($240).

Before purchasing, though, consider carefully whether you'll get your money's worth out of this card. Remember, this is Holland, where local fondness for the coin of the realm is proverbial, and bargains are thin on the ground. You'll have to work pretty hard to come out ahead on the cost of the card, jumping on and off trams, buses, and canal boats, and running in and out of museums that fall mostly into the culture class.

Some of Amsterdam's most memorable experiences come from idle strolling, hanging out on cafe terraces, and visiting offbeat stores and attractions. But if a cram course of solid culture is what you're here for, and you're ready to work to achieve it, the card could be a sound investment.

The I amsterdam Card is available from Holland Tourist Information at Schiphol Airport and from VVV tourist information offices in the city. Note that only the person who signs the card can use it. Further details are available from **www.iamsterdamcard.com**.

leave. In Amsterdam, it's smart not to even bring a car (for reasons, see the "By Car" section under "Getting Around," below).

GETTING AROUND

Amsterdam's Centrum (Center) district is small enough for its residents to think of it as a village, but it can be one confusing village until you get the hang of it. It's easy to think you're headed in one direction along the canal belt, only to discover that you're going completely the other way. Those concentric rings of canals, along with several important squares, are the city's defining focal points. This section explains the city's layout, introduces its neighborhoods, tells you how to get around, and squeezes in other useful knowledge.

FINDING AN ADDRESS Wherever possible in this book, addresses include the name of a nearby square, major thoroughfare, adjacent canal, or well-known sight. Street numbers along the canals ascend from west to east (left to right as you look at the map); on streets leading away from Centraal Station and out from the Center, they ascend from north to south (top to bottom). Now, all you need to know is that, in Dutch, -straat means "street," -gracht means "canal," -plein means "square," -markt means "market," -dijk means "dike," and -laan means "avenue." These suffixes are attached directly to a place name: For example, Princes' Canal becomes Prinsengracht.

On Foot

Walking is the best way to appreciate the city's relaxed rhythm. When you look at an Amsterdam map, you may think the city's too large to explore on foot. Not true: It's possible to see almost every important sight on a 4-hour walk. Be sure to wear comfortable walking shoes, as those charming cobbles get under your soles and on your nerves after a time; leave thin-soled shoes and boots at home.

When walking, remember that cars have the right of way when turning. Don't step in front of one thinking it's going to stop for you. And be aware that many drivers consider road signs and red stoplights to be not much more than occasionally useful suggestions. When crossing a street, watch out for trams, buses, even bikes. Look both ways before crossing a dedicated bike lane—some pedalers get unreasonably irritated if you force them to crash into you.

Kids are irresistibly attracted to water, so watch out for them near any of Amsterdam's 160 canals. Protective fencing rarely exists and the low metal railings meant to keep cars from rolling into the water are ideally positioned for small feet to stumble over.

By Public Transportation

The central information and ticket sales point for GVB Amsterdam, the city's public transportation company, is **GVB Tickets & Info,** Stationsplein (© **0900/9292;** www.gvb.nl), in front of Centraal Station, open Monday to Friday from 7am to 9pm, Saturday and Sunday from 8am to 9pm. You can buy certain tickets here for less than from tram drivers, conductors, and bus drivers.

Most tram and bus shelters and all Metro stations display maps showing the entire urban transit network. All stops have signs listing the main stops yet to be made by trams or buses at that location. Detailed maps of the network are available free from the GVB Tickets & Info office. Daytime hours of operation for public transportation are from 6am (trams start at 7:30am on Sun) to around 12:30am. Night buses operate a limited service thereafter, with buses usually on an hourly schedule.

Note: For many of the locations featured in this book, information about the nearest public transportation stop or station is provided, with preference given to the nearest tram (streetcar) stop. The nearest Metro station or bus stop is listed in the few instances that it would be a better option.

CARDS & FARES From 2009, all public transportation in the Netherlands should be using an electronic stored-value card called the **OV-chipkaart.** This replaces the old system of tickets, "strip cards," and fare zones. "OV" is the initials for *openbaar vervoer,* which is Dutch for public transportation. Three main types of OV-chipkaart are available: re-loadable "personal" cards that can be used only by

---

(Tips) **Urban Minefield**

In a city with so many high and varied gables, there's a temptation to walk along gazing upward. Be careful: There's the possibility you'll walk straight into a canal, but that's a minor danger compared to the one underfoot. Many Amsterdammers have dogs, some of them the size of Shetland ponies. Signs on the sidewalk saying HOND IN DE GOOT (DOG IN THE GUTTER) are mostly ignored. Take your eye off the ground for so much as an instant and you might regret it.

Impressions

From afar at the end of Tsar Peter Straat, issued in the frosty air the tinkle of bells of the horse tramcars, appearing and disappearing in the opening between the buildings, like little toy carriages harnessed with toy horses and played with by people that appeared no bigger than children.

—Joseph Conrad, The Mirror of the Sea (1906)

their pictured owner; reloadable "anonymous" cards that can be used by anyone; and non-reloadable "throwaway" cards. The personal and anonymous cards, both valid for 5 years, cost 7.50€ ($12) and can be loaded and re-loaded with up to 30€ ($48). Throwaway cards, which are likely to be the card of choice for short-term visitors, cost 2.50€ ($4) for one ride and 4.80€ ($7.70) for two rides. Electronic readers on Metro and train station platforms and on board trams and buses deduct the correct fare; just hold your card up against the reader at both the start and the end of the ride. Reduced-rate cards are available for seniors and children ages 4 to 11; children 3 and under ride free.

Purchase cards from the GVB Tickets & Info office (see above), GVB and Netherlands Railways ticket booths in Metro and train stations, automats at Metro and train stations, and automats on board some trams. Not every kind of card is available from each of these sources. Note that the cards are valid throughout the Netherlands, no matter where you purchase them.

Should you plan to splash out on a 1-, 2-, or 3-day **I amsterdam Card** (see "Your Passport to Amsterdam," earlier in this chapter), remember that this affords "free" use of public transportation, so you don't need to purchase additional cards. The same applies if you purchase the **All Amsterdam Transport Pass** associated with travel on the Canal Bus (see "On the Water," below).

Teams of roving inspectors do their best to keep everyone honest. The fine for riding without a valid card is 37.40€ ($60), plus the fare for the ride, payable on the spot.

BY TRAM　Half the fun of Amsterdam is walking along the canals. The other half is riding the smooth blue-and-gray trams that roll through most major streets. There are 16 tram routes in the city. Ten of these (lines 1, 2, 4, 5, 9, 13, 16, 17, 24, and 26) begin and end at Centraal Station, and one (line 25) passes through, so you know you can always get back to that central point if you get lost and have to start over. The other tram routes are 3, 7, 10, 12, and 14.

Most trams have an access door that opens automatically. Board toward the rear following arrowed indicators outside the tram that point the way to the door. To board a tram that has no such arrowed indicators, push the button on the outside of the car beside any door. Getting off, you may need to push a button with an open-door graphic or the words DEUR OPEN. Tram doors close automatically and they do so quite quickly, so don't dawdle.

BY BUS　An extensive bus network operated by GVB (see above) complements the trams. Many bus routes begin and end at Centraal Station. It's generally faster to go by tram, but some points in the city are served only by bus. Regional and intercity bus service from Amsterdam is operated by **Connexxion** (✆ **0900/266-6399;** www.connexxion.nl), and **Arriva** (✆ **0900/202-2022;** www.arriva.nl). Information about national public transportation is available by calling ✆ **0900/9292** or visiting www.9292ov.nl.

Moments Stop and Go

A grand little bus service, the **Stop/Go,** is helping to solve one of Amsterdam's knottiest transit problems: accessing the long, narrow canalsides of the *Grachtengordel* (Canal Belt). Colorful Stop/Go minibuses go in both directions between the Oosterdok, via Centraal Station and Brouwersgracht, all the way along Prinsengracht, to the Amstel River and Waterlooplein. A bus departs every 12 minutes from each terminus, daily from 9am to 5:30pm—it makes a great mini-sightseeing tour. There are no regular stops; just hold out your hand and the bus stops for you to get on. When you want to get out, just tell the driver. A ticket valid for 1 hour, only on the Stop/Go bus, costs 1€ ($1.60).

BY METRO It can't compare to the labyrinthine subway systems of Paris, London, and New York, but Amsterdam does have its own Metro. Four lines—50, 51, 53, and 54—run partly overground and bring people in from the suburbs, but from Centraal Station you can use Metro trains to reach both Nieuwmarkt and Waterlooplein in the central zone. You may want to take them simply as a sightseeing excursion, though to be frank, few of the sights on the lines are worth going out of your way for. If you do take these lines, be sure to validate your strip card on the platform before boarding.

A new Metro line, the Metro Noord-Zuidlijn (North-South Line), is currently under construction to link Amsterdam-Noord, through the Center, to Station Zuid/WTC (World Trade Center). It's slated for completion in 2015.

BY TRAIN The rail network is not as useful within Amsterdam as are the tram, bus, and Metro—but sensitive souls might like that they get to ride in a first-class car or compartment. In addition to the Centraal Station hub, there are seven train stations in the city: Zuid/WTC, RAI (the city's main convention center), Amstel in the south, Muiderpoort in the east, and Lelylaan, De Vlugtlaan, and Sloterdijk in the west. Because the transportation network is tightly integrated, all rail stations are also served by two or more other modes of public transportation.

The excellent Dutch rail network comes into its own for longer distances. It's by far the quickest and best way to get to Schiphol Airport, Haarlem, Zandvoort, Hoorn, and most other points in Holland. Purchase international tickets from an office on platform 2 of Centraal Station, or domestic tickets from an office in the main hall (note that you save .50€/80¢ per ticket if you get domestic tickets from the station automats).

By Taxi

It used to be that you couldn't simply hail a taxi in Amsterdam, but nowadays cabbies stop for most attempts. Alternatively, find one of the taxi stands sprinkled around the city, generally near luxury hotels or at major squares such as the Dam, Stationsplein, Spui, Rembrandtplein, Westermarkt, and Leidseplein. Taxis have rooftop signs and blue license tags, and are metered.

Liberalization of the city's taxis in recent years seems to have all but eliminated those once-typical drivers: professional machines functioning as smoothly as the Mercedes they drove, who all seemed to have been spat out of the same soulless mold. To a budget traveler, their fares were little short of a mugging. And then they expected a tip. On the plus side, they spoke English and generally didn't exaggerate the

Vital Stats

Amsterdam's population is 750,000, a figure projected to reach 800,000 by 2020. By 2010, native Dutch residents will likely be outnumbered for the first time by ethnic minorities—many of whom are now considered Dutch, of course—and foreign expats. The Old City, inside Singelgracht canal's arc, covers 8 sq. km (3 sq. miles) and contains 44,000 dwellings housing 80,000 people. Residents share this central space with 8,000 historical monuments, 2,000 shops, 1,500 restaurants, and 200 hotels. Every working day, a million people pour into the heart of town by bike, car, and public transportation.

price (they didn't need to). The new breed of drivers might drive something less desirable and have varying ideas about fair fares, for better or worse. Some have poor situational awareness, so bring a map or feed directions to the driver—if they understand English.

For generally reliable service, call **Taxi Centrale Amsterdam** (© **020/777-7777;** www.tca-amsterdam.nl). TCA's base fare begins at 3.10€ ($4.95) and runs up at 1.90€ ($3.05) a kilometer, or 3.05€ ($4.90) a mile; after 25km (16 miles), the rate changes to 1.40€ ($2.25) a kilometer, or 2.25€ ($3.60) a mile. The fare includes service; you can round it up if you like, or tip for a good service, like help with your luggage, or for a helpful discourse.

On the Water

With all Amsterdam's water, it makes sense to use it for transportation. Though options for canal-based transit are limited (with the exception of cruises and excursions), they do exist, and provide unique and attractive views of the city. Given the ongoing redevelopment in the old harbor areas, where new residential projects sprout like tulips in springtime, it seems likely that water transportation will become increasingly important. See also "Organized Tours," in chapter 7.

BY WATER BUS Two separate companies operate water buses (rarely, if ever, used by locals) that bring you to, or close to, many of the city's top museums,

attractions, sights, and shopping and entertainment districts. **Canal Bus** (© **020/623-9886;** www.canal.nl) has three routes—Green Line, Red Line, and Blue Line—with stops that include Centraal Station, Westermarkt, Leidseplein, Rijksmuseum (with an extension to the RAI Convention Center when big events are on there), Waterlooplein, and East Amsterdam. Hours of operation are daily from 10am to 6:30pm, with two buses an hour at peak times. A day pass is valid until noon the next day and includes a discount on some museums and attractions. It's 18€ ($29) for adults, 12€ ($19) for children ages 4 to 12, and free for children 3 and under.

An **All Amsterdam Transport Pass,** valid on the Canal Bus, trams, buses, and the Metro, costs 24€ ($38) a day, and is available from GVB Tickets & Info, VVV tourist information offices, and the Canal Bus company. It's a good value if you make extensive use of the Canal Bus and GVB public transportation.

The **Museum Quarter Line** (© **020/530-1090;** www.lovers.nl) transports weary tourists on their pilgrimages from museum to museum. And for those with limited time, it provides some of the features of a canal-boat cruise. Boats depart from the Rederij Lovers dock in front of Centraal Station daily from 10am to 5pm, every 30 to 45 minutes. They stop at seven key spots that provide access to museums and other sights, including the Rijksmuseum, the Van Gogh Museum, Anne Frankhuis,

Leidseplein, Vondelpark, Amsterdams Historisch Museum, the Flower Market, Museum Het Rembrandthuis, the Jewish Historical Museum, Artis Zoo, Muziektheater, and Tropenmuseum. Tickets, available from the Lovers Canal Cruises counter near the dock, are 17€ ($27) for adults, 13€ ($21) for children ages 4 to 12, and free for children 3 and under. Tickets include discounted admission to some museums and attractions along the route.

BY FERRY Free ferries for passengers and two-wheeled vehicles connect the Center with Amsterdam-Noord (North), across the IJ channel. The short crossings are free, and they afford fine views of the harbor, which make them ideal microcruises for the cash-strapped. Sadly, there's little of interest in Noord, so the free trip may have to be its own attraction. Ferries depart from the Waterplein West dock on De Ruijterkade behind Centraal Station. One route goes to Buiksloterweg on the north shore, with ferries every 6 to 12 minutes round-the-clock. A second route goes to IJplein, a more easterly point on the north shore, with ferries every 8 to 15 minutes from 6:30pm to around midnight. Another ferry goes west to NDSM Island, a 20-minute trip that doesn't pass any points of particular interest but still affords a decent view of the harbor.

BY WATER TAXI Since you're in the city of canals, consider splurging on a water taxi. These do more or less the same thing as landlubber taxis, except they do it on the canals, in the harbor, and on the Amstel River. You move faster than on land and you get your very own boat tour. To order one, call **VIP Watertaxi Amsterdam**

(📞 **020/535-6363**; www.water-taxi.nl), or hail one from the dock outside Centraal Station, close to the VVV office. A water taxi for between one and eight passengers, from a dock outside Centraal Station, costs 60€ ($96) per boat per for the first half-hour, and 40€ ($64) for each subsequent half-hour.

BY SWIMMING Believe it or not, some folks (perhaps influenced by too many trips to the "coffeeshop") think this is a good way to get around. It isn't. True, the canals have been cleaned up quite a bit in recent years, and the water quality is probably the best it's ever been. Even so, the liquid filling the canals is still something of a witch's brew; swallow some, and a close encounter with a hospital stomach pump may lie in your immediate future.

Bicycles, Mopeds & More

BY BIKE Instead of renting a car, follow the Dutch example and ride a bike *(fiets)*. Sunday, when the city is quiet, is a particularly good day to pedal along sleepy, off-the-beaten-path canals or through Vondelpark, and to practice riding on cobblestones and over bridges before venturing into the fray of an Amsterdam rush hour. There are more than 600,000 bikes in the city, so you'll have plenty of company.

Navigating the city on two wheels is mostly safe—or at any rate, not as suicidal as it looks—thanks to a vast network of dedicated bike lanes. Bikes even have their own traffic lights. Amsterdam's battle-scarred bike-borne veterans make it almost a point of principle to ignore every written safety rule. Though most live to tell the tale, don't think the same necessarily

---

Fun Facts   **Feeling Flushed**

Amsterdam gets a daily purging of sorts. Between 7 and 8:30pm, 600,000 cubic meters (160 million gallons) of fresh IJsselmeer water are pumped through the canal system to prevent the water from becoming stagnant.

47

PLANNING YOUR TRIP TO AMSTERDAM

3

GETTING THERE & GETTING AROUND

A Vicious (Bi)Cycle

One endearing aspect of Amsterdam life is that, instead of whacking innocent passersby, junkies here steal battered old bicycles to fund their next fix. They sell the bikes for around 20€ ($32), and plenty of young Amsterdammers—who themselves have had a series of store-bought bikes stolen by junkies—end up sighing and stepping aboard this treadmill, knowing they're only encouraging the crooks. Make this destructive transaction at your own risk; renting will endow you with better karma.

applies to you. (See "Bicycling in Amsterdam," below.)

Bike-rental rates are around 9€ ($14) per day or 30€ ($48) per week; a deposit of around 50€ ($80) is required. **MacBike** (⌀ 020/620-0985; www.macbike.nl) rents a range of bikes, including tandems and six-speeds. The company has rental outlets at Stationsplein 12 (tram: 1, 2, 4, 5, 9, 13, 16, 17, 24, 25, or 26), Centraal Station; Mr. Visserplein 2 (tram: 9 or 14), Waterlooplein; and Weteringschans 2 (tram: 1, 2, 5, 7, or 10), at Leidseplein. **Bike City,** Bloemgracht 68–70 (⌀ 020/626-3721; www.bikecity.nl; tram: 13, 14, or 17), near the Anne Frankhuis, is another good choice. **Damstraat Rent-a-Bike,** Damstraat 20–22 (⌀ 020/625-5029; www.bikes.nl; tram: 4, 9, 14, 16, 24, or 25), is centrally located near the Dam. Feminists both male and female might want to give their business to **Zijwind Fietsen,** a women's cooperative, at Ferdinand Bolstraat 168 (⌀ 020/673-7026; www.zijwind.com; tram: 25), though it's a bit out from the Center.

Mike's Bike Tours, Kerkstraat 134 (⌀ 020/622-7970; www.mikesbiketoursamsterdam.com; tram: 1, 2, or 5), is a good bet, and in addition to renting, they run great 4-hour riding tours, for 22€ ($35) for adults, 19€ ($30) for students, and 15€ ($24) for children 11 and under; there's a discount of 5€ ($8) if you bring your own bike. Tours depart from outside the Rijksmuseum, March to mid-May,

daily 12:30pm; mid-May to the end of August, daily 11am and 4pm; September to November, daily 12:30pm; December to February, Friday to Sunday noon.

Warning: Because bicycle theft is common, always lock both your bike frame and one of the wheels to something fixed and solid.

BY TAXI-BIKE You can get driven around town on a kind of sophisticated rickshaw, courtesy of **Wielertaxi** (⌀ 06/2824-7550), which operates two-seater units from the Dam. They go in the bike lanes and, like regular taxis, can get you where public transportation doesn't reach. And they make for a pretty good touring option. The fare is 1€ ($1.60) per person for every 3 minutes, or 20€ ($32) for two for 30 minutes; children ages 2 to 12 ride for half price, and children 1 and under sitting on an adult's lap ride free.

BY OTHER MEANS If you own a pair of rollerblades or even one of those dinky self-propelled scooter things, bring them along. You can go around in the bicycle lanes while saving money and staying fit.

By Car

Don't go by car around Amsterdam. You'll likely regret the expense and the hassle. The city is a maze of one-way streets, narrow bridges, and no-parking zones. It's not unheard of for an automobile, left parked with the hand brake carelessly disengaged, to roll through a flimsy foot-high railing into a canal. To park, you need either to

Bicycling in Amsterdam

What are the rules of the road for going by bicycle in Amsterdam? Apparently, there are none. Bicycle riders can go anywhere they want, whenever they want, however they want. Or so you'd think from the antics of Amsterdam's massed legions of pedal-bikers. They're enough to scare a Hells Angel. Particularly terrifying is your standard young mother with two children (one on the steering bars and the other in a kid's seat), chatting on her phone while dicing with the Leidseplein trams. Biking is one activity during which you should disregard the maxim, "When in Amsterdam, do as the Amsterdammers do"—you might easily end up dead, which could ruin your entire vacation.

It takes a while to get used to moving smoothly and safely through the whirl of trams, cars, buses, fellow bikers, and pedestrians, particularly if you're on an ancient and much-battered *stadfiets* (city bike), also known as an *omafiets* (grandmother bike)—the only kind that makes economic sense here, since anything fancier will attract a crowd wanting to steal it.

It's better to develop street smarts slowly. The first rule: Don't argue with trams—they bite back hard. The second rule: Cross tram tracks perpendicularly so that your wheels don't get caught in the grooves, which could pitch you out of the saddle. And the third rule: Don't crash into pedestrians—the subsequent punch on the chin could be painful. That's about it. Like everyone else, you'll make up the rest of the rules as you go.

feed the parking automat, or have a parking permit prominently displayed in your car.

See "By Car" under "Getting There" above for more info on driving in Amsterdam.

PARKING Street parking in the center city costs 1.30€ to 4.80€ ($2.10–$7.70) an hour, depending on time and location, payable at nearby automats; if you're staying longer than 6 hours, it's more economical to buy a day ticket (also available from automats). Reduced-rate permits are available from many hotels. Permits valid for a day, a week, or a month are available from the **Dienst Stadstoezicht** offices (see below).

Amsterdam has become a free-fire zone for marauding parking-enforcement units. Locals have learned to keep their heads down and their automat tickets clearly displayed. If you overstay your time limit or if you park illegally, you're almost sure to fall victim to the swift and merciless patrols. The cost of transgression is high: 47€ ($75) plus an hour's parking charge, payable within 48 hours.

If the car remains illegally parked, the ticket is reinforced with a wheel-clamp, which costs at least 106€ ($170) to have removed. If the wheel-clamp fine isn't paid within 24 hours, or if the parking operatives think your car constitutes enough of an obstacle, they'll tow your car to the **Dienst Stadstoezicht** car-pound at Daniël Goedkoopstraat 7–9 (© **020/251-2121**; Metro: Spaklerweg), open 24 hours a day, way out in the boonies of the southeastern Over-Amstel district, and they'll charge you a whopping 150€ ($240) for every 24-hour period (or portion thereof) that it's out there, plus the towing cost. You can pay parking, clamp, and towing fines at the car-pound office and at a second office, De Clercqstraat 42–44 (© 020/553-0333; tram: 3, 13, or 14). To get a wheel clamp removed fast, call the **Pay & Go** service (© 020/251-2222), and pay the fine by credit card. The Dienst Stadstoezicht Web address is www.stadstoezicht.amsterdam.nl.

Additional obstacles to parking on the fly are *Amsterdammertjes* (Little Amsterdammers), those zillions of ubiquitous anti-parking posts that have lined streets and canals across the city probably since Rembrandt was a kid.

To avoid charges, or parking-garage rates, stash your car for 6€ ($9.60) a day on the edge of town at **Park+Ride lots** at some of the outer Metro and rail stations (directions are indicated by blue-and-white P+R signs along the way), and come in by Metro, train, or tram. There are parking garages throughout town; most cost 3€ to 5€ ($4.80–$8) an hour and 20€ to 40€ ($32–$64) a day, depending on the location. The largest lots are at Centraal Station, Damrak, Marnixstraat, under Waterlooplein, and adjacent to Leidseplein.

As if all the parking hassle isn't bad enough, anything left in your car is cash on wheels for every junkie and ne'er-do-well in town. They can withdraw your MP3 player, cellphone, and camera faster than you can get cash from an ATM. Cars with foreign tags are most tempting, since they're likeliest to have valuables in the trunk.

GETTING OUT OF TOWN BY CAR

Outside the city, driving is a different story—you'll want to rent a car for most excursions outside Amsterdam. Each of the major agencies has a rental desk at the airport and offices downtown: **Avis** (© 0900/235-2847; www.avis.nl); **Budget** (© 0900/1576; www.budget.nl); **Europcar** (© 0900/0540; www.europcar.nl); and **Hertz** (© 020/201-3512; www.hertz.nl). Rates vary among companies, as do types of cars, rental plans, and extras (some companies, for example, have free car delivery to your hotel). Rates begin around 50€ ($80) a day for a no-frills, subcompact auto with stick shift and unlimited mileage. A fully equipped luxury car like a BMW can cost as much as 200€ ($320) per day. If your car breaks down, call the national auto club, **ANWB Wegenwacht** (© 0800/000-888).

5 MONEY & COSTS

Amsterdam is by no means inexpensive. Clearly, whether you agree with this statement will depend on how much you can bring to bear—or bear to bring—in the way of financial resources. If you are used to the prices in New York and London, it won't seem too out of whack. But opportunities for scoring genuine bargains run a thin gamut from few-and-far-between to nonexistent. Remember, the Dutch have for centuries been consummate traders and middlemen. You need only look at how well-appointed their country is to appreciate how fair a job they've done extracting money from foreigners.

In your favor is that the Dutch themselves display an almost proverbial reluctance to unnecessarily part with a euro. A sound rule of thumb is that if you lodge, dine, and entertain yourself in the same places where "ordinary" Dutch do, you can limit financial damage.

CURRENCY

The European **euro** (€) is the currency in the Netherlands. There are 100 euro cents to each euro. Eight euro **coins** are in circulation in the "eurozone": 0.01€, 0.02€, 0.05€, 0.10€, 0.20€, 0.50€ (1, 2, 5, 10, 20, and 50 euro cents, respectively), 1€, and 2€. Holland does not produce its own

What Things Cost in Amsterdam	US$	UK£
Taxi from the airport to the center city	64.00	32.00
Tram from Centraal Station to Leidseplein	2.90	1.45
Local telephone call	0.50	0.25
Double room at the NH Grand Hotel Krasnapolsky (expensive)	320.00	160.00
Double room at the Tulip Inn Dam Square Hotel (moderate)	220.00	140.00
Double room at the Prinsenhof Hotel (inexpensive)	142.00	71.00
Dinner for one, without wine, at the Excelsior Restaurant (expensive)	120.00	60.00
Dinner for one, without wine, at Café-Restaurant Amsterdam (moderate)	48.00	24.00
Dinner for one, without wine, at Nam Kee (inexpensive)	30.00	15.00
Glass of beer	4.80	2.40
Coca-Cola	4.00	2.00
Cup of coffee	4.80	2.40
Admission to the Van Gogh Museum	20.00	10.00
Movie ticket	16.00	8.00
Cheapest ticket to the Concertgebouw	24.00	12.00

1 and 2 euro cent coins for circulation (only for commemorative issues), and prices in the country are rounded to the nearest 5 cents, thus saving businesses the trouble and cost of using these two minimal-value coins. You might still find 1 and 2 euro cent coins from other "eurozone" countries in circulation, and you can use them if you insist, but nobody will be really happy to take them.

The seven euro **notes** are 5€, 10€, 20€, 50€, 100€, 200€, and 500€. The 200€ and 500€ notes are pretty much unusable because few businesses accept them. (On the other hand, they are great for money-laundering and other nefarious activities.)

The price conversions in this book are based on an exchange rate of 1€ = US$1.60. Bear in mind that exchange rates fluctuate daily. For up-to-the-minute currency conversions, go to **www.xe.com**.

ATMS

The easiest and best way to get cash away from home is from an ATM (automated teller machine). The **Cirrus** (© 800/424-7787; www.mastercard.com) and **PLUS** (© 800/843-7587; www.visa.com) networks span the globe; look at the back of your bank card to see which network you're on, then call or check online for ATM locations in Amsterdam. Be sure you know your personal identification number (PIN) and daily withdrawal limit before you depart. *Note:* Remember that many banks impose a fee every time you use a card at another bank's ATM, and that fee can be higher for international transactions (up to $5 or more) than for domestic ones (where they're rarely more than $2). In addition, the bank from which you withdraw cash may charge its own fee. For

The Euro, the U.S. Dollar & the British Pound

€	US$	UK£	€	US$	UK£
1	1.60	0.80	9	14.40	7.20
2	3.20	1.60	10	16.00	8.00
3	4.80	2.40	20	32.00	16.00
4	6.40	3.20	30	48.00	24.00
5	8.00	4.00	40	64.00	32.00
6	9.60	4.80	50	80.00	40.00
7	11.20	5.60	75	120.00	60.00
8	12.80	6.40	100	160.00	80.00

international withdrawal fees, ask your bank.

If you have a five- or six-digit PIN, be sure to obtain a four-digit number from your bank to use in Amsterdam. Some cards with five- or six-digit PINs might work, but this depends on which bank you're with. The best advice is still to get a four-digit number from your bank.

You can withdraw euros from ATMs at many locations in the city (see appendix A for more details).

CREDIT CARDS

Credit cards are not as commonly accepted in Amsterdam as they are in the U.S. and Britain. Many restaurants and shops in the city—and some hotels—don't accept them at all. Some establishments tag on a 5% charge for card payment. **Visa** and **MasterCard** (also known as **Eurocard** in Europe) are the most widely used cards in Holland. **American Express** is often accepted, mostly in the middle- and upper-bracket category. **Diners Club** is not as commonly accepted as American Express.

TRAVELER'S CHECKS

These days, traveler's checks are less necessary because Amsterdam has plenty of 24-hour ATMs. However, since you'll be charged an ATM withdrawal fee if the

bank isn't your own, if you're withdrawing money daily, you might be better off with traveler's checks, which will be replaced if lost or stolen. You can get traveler's checks at most banks, and from **American Express, Thomas Cook, Visa,** and **MasterCard.**

Euro traveler's checks are accepted at locations where dollar and pound checks may not be, but you'll have to reconvert unused ones or keep them for a future trip to a euro-zone country.

Traveler's checks are offered in denominations of $20, $50, $100, $500, and sometimes $1,000. Generally, you'll pay a service charge ranging from 1% to 4%.

The most popular traveler's checks are offered by **American Express** (© 800/ 807-6233 or, for cardholders, 800/221-7282—this number accepts collect calls, offers service in several languages, and exempts gold and platinum cardholders from the 1% fee). AAA members can obtain **Visa** (© 800/732-1322) checks for a $9.95 fee (for checks up to $1,500) at most AAA offices or by calling © 866/ 339-3378. For **MasterCard,** call © 800/ 223-9920.

If you carry traveler's checks, keep a record of their serial numbers separate from your checks in case they're stolen or lost. You'll get a refund faster if you know the numbers.

(Tips) **Easy Money**

You'll avoid lines at airport ATMs by exchanging at least some money—just enough to cover airport incidentals and transportation to your hotel—before you leave home.

When you change money, ask for some small bills or loose change. Petty cash will come in handy for tipping and public transit. Consider keeping the change separate from your larger bills so that it's readily accessible—and your big money will be less of a target for theft.

6 HEALTH

STAYING HEALTHY

There are no particular health concerns in Amsterdam—if you don't count the "risk" of occasionally breathing in a whiff of secondhand hashish smoke. Traveling in the Netherlands poses few health problems. The tap water is safe to drink, the milk is pasteurized, blood for transfusions is HIV-screened, and you don't need to worry much about getting too much sun.

General Availability of Healthcare

The Dutch healthcare system is among the world's best. It's easy in Holland to get over-the-counter medicines and other simple remedies for minor ailments. Local brands and generic equivalents of common prescription drugs are available. Most doctors speak English (though their lingo might be a little disturbing, like when a doctor once told me he knew what "disease" I had when I reported a minor ailment).

WHAT TO DO IF YOU GET SICK IN AMSTERDAM

If a medical emergency arises, your hotel staff can usually put you in touch with a reliable doctor. If not, contact the **Central Medical Service** (© 020/592-3434) or go to the emergency room at one of the local hospitals. The U.S. and U.K. consulates in Amsterdam can provide a list of area doctors who speak English (almost every doctor in town). This book lists **hospitals, consulates and embassies, insurance info**, and **emergency numbers** under "Fast Facts: Amsterdam," in appendix A.

Most Amsterdam hospitals have walk-in clinics for emergency cases that are not life-threatening; you may not get immediate attention, but you won't pay the high price of an emergency room visit.

I list **additional emergency numbers** in the "Fast Facts, Toll-Free Numbers & Websites" appendix, p. 285.

7 SAFETY

STAYING SAFE

In Amsterdam, if it isn't bolted to the floor, somebody *will* try to steal it—and even if it *is* bolted to the floor, somebody will still try to steal it. Watch for pickpockets on trams, buses, Metro trains, and in train and Metro stations. Constant public announcements at Centraal Station and Schiphol Airport warn about pickpockets, and tram signs warn, in a multitude of languages, ATTENTION: PICKPOCKETS. Drivers often recognize a pickpocket who gets on their bus or tram, and announce over the vehicle's PA system that passengers should watch out for their belongings. It's fun to watch the miscreants getting off again at the next stop, foiled. Pickpockets and other thieves often wait until you are occupied or distracted—or act to occupy or distract you—before making their move. Consider wearing a money belt. Women, wear your purse crossed over your shoulder so that it hangs in front, with the clasp or zipper facing in. A backpack worn on the back is an open invitation to thieves, so either don't wear it like that or don't put anything valuable in it (you could consider packing it with loaded mousetraps).

Violence is not unknown to Amsterdam, but it's not at all a violent city (foreign drug dealers whacking each other don't count—unless innocents get caught in the crossfire, this usually merits only a single-sentence news blip on p. 21 of the local paper). Drug-related crime is prevalent, but most of it, like pickpocketing, is nonviolent, relatively minor, and opportunistic. Stealing bicycles is a big problem here; see the box on p. 47 for more info. Muggings and armed robberies do happen, but only rarely.

There are some risky areas, especially in and around the Red Light District. Be leery of walking alone after dark through narrow alleyways and along empty stretches of canal. Don't use ATMs at night in quiet areas. It's wise to stay out of Vondelpark at night, but there are cafes on the edge of the park that are busy until closing time.

Amsterdam has its share (more than its share, really) of weird folks, some of whom may lock onto you for one reason or another. If you can't shake them off, go into a cafe or hotel and wait until they leave or call a taxi to take you away.

Beggars are common, although the generous Dutch welfare system ensures that few, if any, locals need to resort to panhandling. Those who do this might be drug addicts, illegal migrants, young visitors trying to make their stay last longer, lazy ne'er-do-wells—and some genuine hardship cases. If you're prepared to hand out money, keep coins handy rather than rummaging through your billfold or purse, which might get grabbed by the intended recipient of your generosity.

Report any crime committed against you to the police *(politie),* most of whom speak English and are generally helpful to visitors.

See also the section on women travelers in "Specialized Travel Resources," later in this chapter.

Note: Listing some of the possible dangers together like this can give a false impression of the threat of crime in Amsterdam. There is no need to be afraid to do the things you want to do. Amsterdammers aren't. Just remember to exercise the usual rules of caution and observation that apply in any big city.

DEALING WITH DISCRIMINATION

Most Dutch would claim that they don't have the discrimination gene, and in most cases, that's probably true. U.S. visitors are welcome but *might* occasionally encounter some hostility, due primarily to current circumstances in Iraq and the Israeli-Palestinian conflict. Among other beefs could be America's refusal to sign the Kyoto Protocol on global warming or join the International Criminal Court in The Hague. Some native Dutch and some of the country's significant Muslim minority might want to take issue with you on one or more of these topics in ways ranging from open discussion to surly service, the cold shoulder, or even verbal aggression. I know of no cases of physical aggression and would guess this to be vanishingly rare.

For info on gay and lesbian travel to Amsterdam, see "Specialized Travel Resources," below.

8 SPECIALIZED TRAVEL RESOURCES

TRAVELERS WITH DISABILITIES

The old center of Amsterdam—filled with narrow cobbled streets, steep humpback bridges, zillions of little barrier pillars called *Amsterdammertjes,* and bicycles parked all over the place—can be hard going. But many hotels and restaurants provide easy access for people with disabilities, and some display the international wheelchair symbol in their brochures. It's always a good idea to call ahead to find out about accommodations before you book; bear in mind that many older hotels have steep, narrow stairways and no elevators. Many, but not all, museums and other sites are wheelchair accessible, wholly or partly, and some have adapted toilets. Call ahead to check on accessibility at sites you wish to visit.

Schiphol Airport has a service to help travelers with disabilities through the airport. Not all trams in Amsterdam are easily accessible for wheelchairs, but newer trams have low doors that are accessible, and most buses are accessible. The Metro system is fully accessible, but that's not as good as it sounds because few Metro stations are near places where visitors want to go. Taxis are also difficult, but the new minivan taxis are an improvement. Call ahead to book a wheelchair-accessible cab from **Taxi Centrale Amsterdam** (© 020/677-7777).

There's comprehensive assistance for travelers on **Netherlands Railways** trains and in stations. Call © 030/235-7822 for information, or visit www.ns.nl. Give this organization a day's notice of your journey (by visiting a station or calling ahead), and they'll arrange for assistance along the way.

A good source of travel-related information in the Netherlands is the **ANWB Disabled Department** (© 070/314-1420; www.anwb.nl).

For more on organizations that offer resources to travelers with disabilities, go to frommers.com.

GAY & LESBIAN TRAVELERS

Amsterdam is Europe's gay epicenter—in fact, it might just be the most gay-friendly city on the planet. It even has a monument, the **Homomonument** (p. 159), dedicated to gays and lesbians who have been persecuted around the world through the ages.

Get information, or just meet people, by visiting **COC,** Rozenstraat 14 (© 020/626-3087; www.cocamsterdam.nl), the Amsterdam branch of the Dutch lesbian and gay organization, open Monday to Friday from 9am to 5pm. At COC's facilities, there's a daytime cafe serving coffee and quiche, a meeting space for special-interest groups, weekend discos (mainly men on Fri, women on Sat), and a special ethnic evening called Strange Fruit on Sundays.

COC's national office is just a few doors along, at Rozenstraat 8 (© 020/623-4596; www.coc.nl), open Monday to Friday from 9am to 5pm. The **Gay and Lesbian Switchboard** (© 020/623-6565; www.switchboard.nl), open daily from 10am to 10pm, provides all kinds of information and advice. Call **AIDS Infolijn** (© 0900/204-2040) for info on AIDS.

Gay and lesbian bars and clubs are well publicized, but for a listing, see "The Gay & Lesbian Scene" under "The Bar Scene," in chapter 10. The free biweekly magazine *Shark* is an excellent source of cultural information, in particular for offbeat and alternative scenes, and has a listings section titled "Queer Fish." *Gay News Magazine,* a monthly magazine in both Dutch and English, is available for free in gay establishments around the city.

For more gay and lesbian travel resources visit frommers.com.

SENIOR TRAVELERS

Sightseeing and entertainment attractions in the Netherlands often offer senior discounts, but some places offer these reductions only to Dutch citizens. Be sure to bring along your passport or other identity document when you want to sign up for reduced-rate fares on public transportation, and other senior benefits. A group of local seniors run so-called *Mee in Mokum* guided tours on foot through the city— "Mokum" is the name Amsterdam's once-thriving Jewish community used for the city, and it's still used informally by the populace. The name means something like *Going With Amsterdam.* People of any age can go on the tours, which are not exclusively for seniors, but are more likely to be run at a slower pace than standard tours. The guides speak English and know their beloved city inside out, as you might expect from people who have lived there for decades. Tours depart Tuesday to Sunday from the **David & Goliath** restaurant, Kalverstraat 92 (at the Amsterdams Historisch Museum); they last 2 to 3 hours and cost 4€ ($6.40). Call © **020/625-1390** or visit www.gildeamsterdam.nl for info.

Frommers.com offers more information and resources on travel for seniors.

FAMILY TRAVELERS

At first glance, Amsterdam is not a great family destination. Who wants to be taking the kids into a hash-smoking den, or traipsing around the Red Light District? Or to a country that permits children from age 12 to have "non-exploitative" sexual relationships? To boot, a legal political party, the Brotherly Love, Freedom, and Diversity Party (PNVD), openly advocates pedophilia and child pornography.

A second glance is likely to be more promising. This is a largish European capital of a country in which kids are relatively highly regarded. There's also plenty of wholesome stuff for them to do.

Let's see now: pedaling a rented bicycle around town, or a water-bike around the canals; riding trams, harbor ferries, and canal boats; visiting Artis Zoo, the Anne Frank House, and one of several children's farms; exploring the beach at Zandvoort; swimming in the IJsselmeer; working off steam at adventure parks. And lots more.

Some of the city's more expensive hotels offer kids' suites, and you might even find that a suite is cheaper than booking two rooms. Many hotels allow children up to a certain age to sleep free or for a reduced rate in their parent's room, and may provide an extra bed.

Arrange ahead of time for such necessities as a crib, bottle warmer, and car seat (in the Netherlands, small children are not allowed to ride in the front seat). For information about babysitters, see appendix A, "Fast Facts, Toll-Free Numbers & Websites," p. 285.

To locate accommodations, restaurants, and attractions that are particularly kid-friendly, refer to the "Kids" icon throughout this guide. Also see some of our "Best Of" categories in chapter 1, the family-friendly hotels box on p. 79, the family-friendly restaurants box on p. 123, and the "Especially for Kids" sightseeing section in chapter 7.

For a list of even more family-friendly travel resources, turn to the experts at frommers.com.

WOMEN TRAVELERS

Although Amsterdam is generally safe, nighttime rules about not walking alone in poorly lit and unpopulated areas apply especially to women. Harassment incidents do occur, and rape is not unheard of. It's safe for groups of women to go around the famed (and notorious) Red Light District—supposing they can stomach seeing other women serving purely as sex objects—but a young woman on her own, particularly after dark, could be subject to at least verbal harassment, and be mistaken as a "working girl." Public transportation is usually busy even late at night, so you generally won't have to worry about being alone in a tram or Metro train. If you do feel nervous, sit close to the driver, if possible. Many local women go around by bicycle at night.

The Netherlands has long enjoyed what one might call a relaxed attitude to the undraped female form—a government-issued DVD, part of a mandatory "education" for would-be migrants, portrays toplessness at the beach as an integral part of Dutch culture. But if personal observation is anything to go by, I can assure you that far fewer women are actually going without at the beach or in the park these days, and those who do aren't likely to be young.

For general travel resources for women, go to frommers.com.

STUDENT TRAVELERS

Students—and young folk in general—are big in Amsterdam. There are two major universities in the city, the UA (University of Amsterdam) and the VU (Free University), and a number of colleges, schools of this and that, and other institutes of higher learning.

Check out the **International Student Travel Confederation (ISTC)** (www.istc.org) website for comprehensive travel services information and details on how to get an **International Student Identity Card (ISIC),** which qualifies students for substantial savings on rail passes, plane tickets, entrance fees, and more. It also provides students with basic health and life insurance and a 24-hour help line. The card is valid for a maximum of 18 months. You can apply for the card online or in

person at **STA Travel** (© 800/781-4040 in North America; © 132-782 in Australia; © **0871/1230-0040** in the U.K.; www.statravel.com), the biggest student travel agency in the world; check out the website to locate STA Travel offices worldwide. If you're no longer a student but are still under 26, you can get an **International Youth Travel Card (IYTC)** from the same people, which entitles you to some discounts. **Travel CUTS** (© **800/ 592-2887;** www.travelcuts.com) offers similar services for both Canadians and U.S. residents. Irish students may prefer to turn to **USIT** (© **01/602-1904;** www.usit.ie), an Ireland-based specialist in student, youth, and independent travel.

SINGLE TRAVELERS

Amsterdam is Europe's ideal singles city, because it is not that difficult of a place to get to and to navigate for a person traveling alone. Plenty of solo travelers visit here every year—you can think of Amsterdam as Europe's singles central. There are lots of hotels and restaurants in all price bands, and it's easy to meet other people around the bars and clubs, on canal-boat tours and bicycle tours, and in other ways. Companies that specialize in solo travel to Amsterdam are thin on the ground, though. One is the **Singles Travel Company,** 56 N. Santa Cruz Ave., Los Gatos, CA 95030 (© **888/286-8687** or 408/354-3871; www.singlestravelcompany.com), which takes in Amsterdam as a part of its European tour.

For more information on traveling in the city as a single, go to frommers.com.

9 SUSTAINABLE TOURISM

The Dutch take the environment seriously. Living in a small country that's so heavily populated they need to recover land from the sea, they must. More than 60% of household waste is sorted,

collected, and recycled. As a visitor, you are expected to play your part and not to just toss stuff without first checking if it's recyclable, or reusable. For instance, if the word *Statiegeld* is written on the label of a bottle, it means you've paid a deposit on it, which you get back when you return the bottle to any shop that sells it. In 2007, a wind farm in the North Sea began generating 108 megawatts of power from 36 wind turbines, enough to supply 100,000 homes. A 120-megawatt offshore wind farm is under construction. By 2010 Holland aims to produce 9% of its electricity from renewable resources.

All those bicycles you see in Amsterdam—somewhere around 600,000—may get on your nerves after a time, considering how aggressively many young Amsterdammers ride the things and how easy it is to step unsuspectingly off the sidewalk on to a dedicated bike lane, where you promptly get hit by what seems like 200,000 of them. Yet they will help you to breathe easier, as they take plenty of cars off the street. Anyone who's not riding a bike is also more likely to be walking, or getting around by tram, than driving. Visitors are encouraged to do likewise; a recent university study found that just 1% of the "ecological footprint" tourists brought with them to the city was attributable to using local public transportation.

There are many places where you can rent bikes, and the city's public transportation is both easy to use and efficient. The **Bicycle Hotel** (p. 100) is just one of the city hotels that makes it easy to get around by bicycle. If some kind of an engine sounds like a better bet, **MisterGreen,** Kerkstraat 376 (© **020/624-2579;** www.

mistergreen.nl), rents battery-powered electric scooters.

Green living extends to what people eat. Restaurants such as **Bolhoed** (p. 119), **Golden Temple** (p. 122), and **De Kas** use "bio" and vegan products and ingredients in the meals they serve. Some hotels, among them the **Radisson SAS** (p. 83), have signed up to the Sustainable Hotels Amsterdam Center Agreement, which provides for becoming more energy-efficient in all areas of operation, conserving water, decreasing the amount of unsorted waste, and more. Hotels that meet the standard are awarded Green Key certification; see reviews throughout chapter 5 for info.

Volunteer travel has become increasingly popular among those who want to venture beyond the standard group-tour experience to learn languages, interact with locals, and make a positive difference while on vacation, and there are a number of options for this type of sustainable travel in Amsterdam. Volunteer travel usually doesn't require special skills—just a willingness to work hard—and programs vary in length from a few days to a number of weeks. Some programs provide free housing and food, but many require volunteers to pay for travel expenses, which can add up quickly.

For general info on volunteer travel, visit **www.volunteerabroad.org** and **www. idealist.org**. Also see the options listed under "Special-Interest Trips" below.

10 SPECIAL-INTEREST TRIPS

ESCORTED TOURS

With a good escorted group tour, you'll know ahead of time what your trip will cost, and you won't have to worry about transportation, luggage, hotel reservations, communicating in foreign languages, and other basics—an experienced guide will

take care of all that and lead you through all the sightseeing. The downside of a guided tour is that you trade much of the freedom and personal free time independent travel grants you and often see only the canned postcard-ready side of Amsterdam through the tinted windows of a giant bus. You get to *see* Amsterdam, but

Tips **It's Easy Being Green**

Here are a few simple ways you can help conserve fuel and energy when you travel:

- Each time you take a flight or drive a car, greenhouse gases release into the atmosphere. You can help neutralize this danger to the planet through "carbon offsetting"—paying someone to invest your money in programs that reduce your greenhouse gas emissions by the same amount you've added. Before buying carbon offset credits, just make sure that you're using a reputable company, one with a proven program that invests in renewable energy. Reliable carbon offset companies include **Carbonfund** (www.carbonfund.org), **TerraPass** (www.terrapass.org), and **Carbon Neutral** (www.carbonneutral.org).

- Whenever possible, choose nonstop flights; they generally require less fuel than indirect flights that stop and take off again. Try to fly during the day—some scientists estimate that nighttime flights are twice as harmful to the environment. And pack light—each 15 pounds of luggage on a 5,000-mile flight adds up to 50 pounds of carbon dioxide emitted.

- Where you stay during your travels can have a major environmental impact. To determine the green credentials of a property, ask about trash disposal and recycling, water conservation, and energy use; also question if sustainable materials were used in the construction of the property. The website **www.greenhotels.com** recommends green-rated member hotels around the world that fulfill the company's stringent environmental requirements. Also consult **www.environmentallyfriendlyhotels.com** for more green accommodations ratings.

- At hotels, request that your sheets and towels not be changed daily. (Many hotels already have programs like this in place.) Turn off the lights and air conditioner (or heater) when you leave your room.

- Use public transport where possible—trains, buses, and even taxis are more energy-efficient forms of transport than driving. Even better is to walk or cycle; you'll produce zero emissions and stay fit and healthy on your travels.

- If renting a car is necessary, ask the rental agent for a hybrid, or rent the most fuel-efficient car available. You'll use less gas and save money at the tank.

- Eat at locally owned and operated restaurants that use produce grown in the area. This contributes to the local economy and cuts down on greenhouse gas emissions by supporting restaurants where the food is not flown or trucked in across long distances. Visit **Sustain Lane** (www.sustainlane.org) to find sustainable eating and drinking choices around the U.S.; also check out **www.eatwellguide.org** for tips on eating sustainably in the U.S. and Canada.

rarely do you get the chance to really *know* it. Consult a good travel agent for the latest offerings and advice.

Some unique escorted tour offerings exist in the city, too. **Artifex** (© 020/620-8112; www.artifex-travel.nl) offers everything from architecture walks to painting classes on canal boats in the city. Its tailor-made tours aren't exactly cheap (the price depends on what you want to do), but the multilingual guides—trained art historians—can get you into private collections, the Royal Palace even when it's closed to the public, the Amsterdam School's Scheepvaarthuis (never open to the public), and plenty more places. Some clients wind up spending half their day in a cozy brown cafe.

See "Organized Tours" in chapter 7 for more touring options in Amsterdam.

VOLUNTEER TOURS

Here's a list of companies offering educational and volunteer opportunities in Amsterdam:

- **www.jobsabroad.com:** Listings for jobs throughout Europe, as well as links to study and volunteer options.
- **www.idealist.org:** Resources and tips on volunteering abroad, along with volunteer and paid postings.
- **www.volunteerabroad.com:** Extensive list-ings for European volunteer opportunities.

LANGUAGE & COOKING CLASSES

Maybe you've always dreamed of learning Dutch, of dazzling friends with your nonchalantly correct pronunciation of van Gogh (see "Don't 'Go,'" p. 144), Schiphol

Airport, and the many other little delights of the tongue that goes by the name of *Nederlands*. Beware. You'll need to perfect a mode of delivery that will lead both friends and beloved to believe you're choking on a chicken bone. The good news is that it can be done in Amsterdam. All three of the city's universities offer Dutch courses:

- **Universiteit van Amsterdam,** Spui 21, 1012 WX Amsterdam (✆ **020/525-9111;** www.uva.nl).
- **Volksuniversiteit,** Rapenburgerstraat 73, 1011 VK Amsterdam (✆ **020/ 626-1626;** www.volksuniversiteit amsterdam.nl).
- **Vrije Universiteit Amsterdam,** De Boelelaan 1105, 1081 HV Amsterdam (✆ **020/598-9898;** www.vu.nl).

You can even learn the lingo and whip up some Dutch dishes on the same vacation. "Dutch cooking is not a widely known cuisine," admits a reviewer of *The Art of Dutch Cooking* (1997) by Corry Countess Van Limburg Stirum. This is akin to pointing out that the pope is a Catholic. Yet all is not lost, as you can discover by making contact with **De Kookfabriek,** De Flinesstraat 2–4, 1099 CB Amsterdam-Duivendrecht (✆ **020/ 463-5635;** www.kookfabriek.nl), which (among other things) organizes Dutch cookery classes.

11 STAYING CONNECTED

TELEPHONES

To call Amsterdam from outside the Netherlands:

1. Dial the international access code: **011** in the U.S., and **00** in most other countries.
2. Dial the country code for the Netherlands: **31.**
3. Dial the area code **20** and then the number. So the whole number you'd dial would be 011-31-20-000-0000.

Area Codes: The area code for Amsterdam is **020** (use just **20** when you're calling from outside the Netherlands). When making local calls in Amsterdam, you don't need to use this area code. When making local calls within other cities, you don't need to use the city's area code. You do, however, need to use an area code between towns and cities.

There are two main formats for Dutch phone numbers: For cities and large towns, a three-digit area code is followed by a seven-digit number. For smaller towns and villages, a four-digit area code is followed by a six-digit number. In addition to Amsterdam's, some other area codes used in this book are Haarlem, **023;** The Hague and Scheveningen, **070;** Rotterdam, **010;** Delft, **015;** Leiden, **071;** and Gouda, **0182.**

Operator assistance: Call ✆ **0800/ 0410.**

Information: For numbers inside the Netherlands, call ✆ **0900/8008;** for international numbers, call ✆ **0900/8418.**

Toll-free numbers: Numbers beginning with 0800 within Holland are toll-free, but calling a 1-800 number in the States from Holland is not toll-free. In fact, it costs the same as an overseas call.

Special numbers: Watch out for the special Dutch numbers that begin with 0900. Calls to these are charged at a higher rate than ordinary local calls. Depending on whom you call, it can be up to .90€ ($1.45) a minute.

International calls: To make international calls from Amsterdam, first dial **00** and then the country code. To call the United States or Canada, dial **00** (the international access code) + **1** (the country code) + the area code + the number. For example, if you wanted to call the British Embassy in Washington, D.C., you would dial 00-1-202-588-7800. Other country codes are United Kingdom, **44;** Ireland, **353;** Australia, **61;** New Zealand, **64.**

International calls, per minute, are **U.S.** and **Canada:** .30€ (50¢); **U.K.** and **Ireland:** .35€ (55¢); **Australia** and **New Zealand:** .40€ (65¢).

You can use pay phones in booths all around town with a **KPN,** and at some places with a **Telfort** *telefoonkaart* (phone card)—but note that neither company's cards work with the other company's phones. KPN cards sell for 5€ ($8), 10€ ($16), 20€ ($32), and 50€ ($80), from post offices, train-ticket counters, VVV tourist information offices, GWK Travelex currency exchange offices, and some tobacconists and newsstands. Telfort cards sell for 8€ ($13), which includes an additional 2€ ($3.20) worth of time free.

There are, however, alternatives to buying the KPN and Telfort cards: Some pay phones take credit cards, and a few take coins of .10€, .20€, .50€, 1€, and 2€.

Tip: Use smaller coins whenever possible, at least until you are connected with the right person, as no change is given from an individual coin—and once the call has begun, excess coins will not be returned when you hang up.

A busy signal sounds like a sustained dial tone, then a beep-beep sound. Should there be no answer, hang up and the coin comes back to you. On both card and coin phones, a digital reading tracks your decreasing balance so that you know when to add another card or more coins. To make additional calls when you still have a coin or card inserted, briefly break the connection; you'll get a new dial tone for another call.

Both local and long-distance calls from a pay phone cost .30€ (50¢) a minute. Note that calls placed through your hotel switchboard or dialed direct from your room phone usually cost more than twice the standard rate.

To charge a call to your calling card, call AT&T (✆ **0800/022-9111**), MCI (✆ **0800/022-9122**), Sprint (✆ **0800/ 022-9119**), Canada Direct (✆ **0800/022-9116**), British Telecom (✆ **0800/022-9944**), Australia Direct (✆ **0800/022-0061**), or Telecom New Zealand (✆ **0800/022-4295**).

Online Traveler's Toolbox

Veteran travelers usually carry some essential items to make their trips easier. Following is a selection of handy online tools to bookmark and use.

- **Airplane Food** (www.airlinemeals.net)
- **Airplane Seating** (www.seatguru.com and www.airlinequality.com)
- **Foreign Languages for Travelers** (www.travlang.com)
- **Maps** (www.mapquest.com)
- **Subway Navigator** (www.subwaynavigator.com)
- **Time and Date** (www.timeanddate.com)
- **Travel Warnings** (http://travel.state.gov, www.fco.gov.uk/travel, www.voyage. gc.ca, and www.smartraveller.gov.au)
- **Universal Currency Converter** (www.oanda.com)
- **Weather** (www.intellicast.com and www.weather.com)
- **Amsterdam Tourism & Convention Board** (www.amsterdamtourist.nl)
- **Netherlands Board of Tourism & Conventions** (www.visitholland.com)
- **Virtual Tour of Amsterdam** (www.channels.nl)
- **Public Transportation** (www.gvb.nl)
- **Hotel Reservations** (www.go-amsterdam.org)
- **Eating Out** (www.dinner-in-amsterdam.nl, www.iens.nl, and www.special bite.nl)
- **Museums** (www.hollandmuseums.nl)
- **Hip Happenings** (www.amsterdamhotspots.nl)

CELLPHONES

If your phone has GSM (Global System for Mobiles) capability and you have a world-compatible phone, you should be able to make and receive calls from Holland. Only certain phones have this capability, though, and you should check with your service operator first. Call charges can be high. Alternatively, you can rent a phone through **Cellhire** (www.cellhire. com; www.cellhire.co.uk; www.cellhire. com.au). After a simple online registration, they will ship a phone (usually with a U.K. number) to your home or office. Usage charges can be astronomical, so read the fine print.

U.K. mobiles work in Holland; call your service provider before departing your home country to ensure that the international call bar has been switched off and to check call charges, which can be extremely high. Also remember that you are charged for calls you *receive* on a U.K. mobile used abroad.

VOICE-OVER INTERNET PROTOCOL (VOIP)

If you have Web access while traveling, consider a broadband-based telephone service (in technical terms, **Voice-over Internet protocol,** or **VoIP**) such as Skype (www.skype.com) or Vonage (www.vonage. com), which allows you to make free international calls from your laptop or in a cybercafe. Neither service requires the people you're calling to also have that service (though there are fees if they do not). Check the websites for details.

Suggested Amsterdam Itineraries

When in Amsterdam, having a strategy can take you only so far. This is a hang-loose city, and objectives-based planning works against the city's very nature. Yet having no strategy leaves you to the whims and vagaries of chance, and there's no guarantee that all your surprises will be pleasant ones. What's useful is a general plan for allocating your time while leaving time for serendipity to work its magic.

CITY LAYOUT

Amsterdammers will tell you it's easy to find your way around their city. However, when each resident offers you a different pet theory of how best to maintain your sense of direction, you begin to sense that the city's layout can be confusing. Some of the natives' theories actually do work. If you try to "think in circles," "follow the canals," or "watch the way the trams go," you might be able to spend fewer minutes consulting a map or trying to figure out where you are and which way to walk to find the Rijksmuseum, a restaurant, or your hotel.

When you step out of Centraal Station's main entrance, you're facing south toward the Center. From here, the city is laid out around you along four concentric semicircles of canals: **Singel, Herengracht, Keizersgracht,** and **Prinsengracht.** Along these canals, 16th- and 17th-century merchants lived in elegant homes, most of which are still standing. The largest and most stately canal houses are along Herengracht. Connecting these canals are many smaller canals and streets radiating out from the Center, and effectively dividing the city into an archipelago of tiny islands linked by bridges. The area inside the **Singelgracht** canal, a fifth concentric waterway forming an outer rim to the canal zone, is called the Old City—and it's so compact that a fit person should be able to walk across it in around 30 minutes.

A heavily touristed street, **Damrak,** leads from Centraal Station to the main central square called the **Dam.** In the 17th century, Damrak was a canal, its quays filled with small cargo boats and lined with mapmaker stores and ships' chandlers, coopers, and ropemakers. Narrow side streets like **Haringpakkerssteeg** and **Zoutsteeg** recall the herring packers of yore (*haring* means "herring") and where ships used to unload salt (*zout* means "salt"). In the late 19th century, Damrak got lined with fancy stores and filled with elegant shoppers. Today, it's a brash thoroughfare with souvenir stores and noisy cafes. Houses on the bank stand in water, Venice-style.

To the east of the Dam, where the original Amstel River dam was, and where the Royal Palace is now, is the famous Red Light District, where government-licensed prostitutes sit behind windows, waiting for customers. A block to the west of Damrak is **Nieuwendijk** (it becomes **Kalverstraat** on the far side of the Dam), a pedestrians-only shopping street. Follow Kalverstraat to the end, and you're at **Muntplein** beside the old Mint Tower. Cross over Muntplein and continue in the same direction to reach **Rembrandtplein,** one of the city's main nightlife areas.

The other main nightlife district is **Leidseplein,** on the outer concentric canal, Singelgracht (not to be confused with Singel, the *inner* concentric canal). Leidseplein is at the end of **Leidsestraat,** a car-free (but tram-full) shopping street leading from Singel to Singelgracht.

The wide, green **Museumplein,** site of the city's three most famous museums—Rijksmuseum, Van Gogh Museum, and Stedelijk Museum—is a 5-minute walk along Singelgracht from Leidseplein (note that much of the Rijksmuseum is closed until 2013 for refurbishment, and the Stedelijk is closed until Dec 2009 or later, for the same reason).

One other area worth mentioning is the **Jordaan** (pronounced yor-*daan*), an old neighborhood filled with inexpensive restaurants, offbeat stores, and small galleries. The Jordaan lies between Brouwersgracht, Prinsengracht, Looiersgracht, and Lijnbaansgracht. To get there, turn right off Damrak at any point between Centraal Station and the Dam, then cross Prinsengracht.

Returning to Centraal Station—and *everybody* winds up back there eventually—if you exit the station at the rear you'll be standing on the city's fast-changing **Waterfront.**

THE PRINCIPAL SQUARES   There are six major squares in central Amsterdam that will be the hubs of your visit:

The **Dam** is the city's heart and the site of the original dam across the Amstel River that gave the city its name. Encircling the square are the Royal Palace, the Nieuwe Kerk national church, and several department stores, hotels, and restaurants. On the square is the Nationaal Monument of World War II.

Leidseplein and the streets around the city's signature square glitter with restaurants, nightclubs, music venues, a casino, and movie theaters. It's a fun scene even if hustle and bustle reigns over style.

Rembrandtplein is another entertainment scene, and bustles with eateries.

Museumplein is the main cultural center, with the Rijksmuseum, Concertgebouw, Van Gogh Museum, and Stedelijk Museum in close proximity.

Waterlooplein, another cultural focal point, is home to the Muziektheater and a superb flea market (p. 220).

Muntplein is a busy transportation hub, easily recognizable for its crown-topped Munttoren (Mint Tower, ca. 1620), one of the city's original fortress towers.

NEIGHBORHOODS IN BRIEF

For the purposes of locating the hotels and restaurants reviewed in this book, I've divided the city of Amsterdam into six major neighborhoods and four outlying districts. Keep in mind that some of these could have been further subdivided and there are inevitable "border disputes" about where one area begins and another ends—and in which one a particular establishment properly belongs.

The Old Center   This core area around the Dam and Centraal Station, and through the neighborhood known as De Wallen (the Walls), is the oldest part of the city, and includes the Red Light District. It's home to the main downtown shopping areas and attractions such as the Royal Palace, the Amsterdam Historical Museum, Madame Tussauds, and many canal-boat piers. Note that the Red Light District is only a small part of the

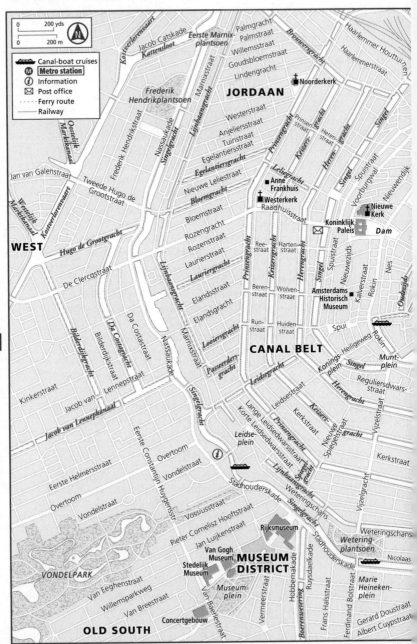

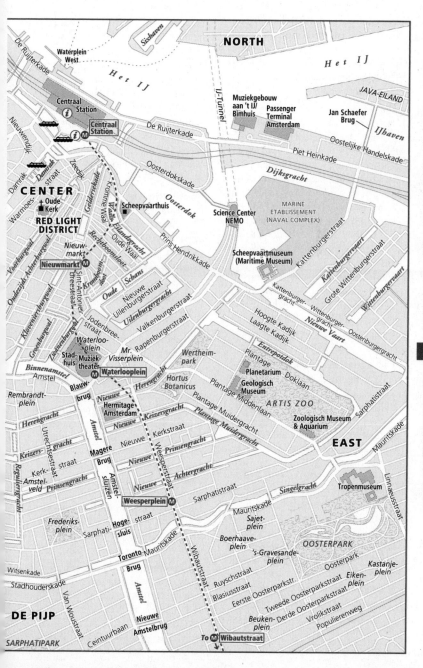

Center, so you won't be constantly tripping over hookers and dope heads. There are plenty of reasons to lodge in the Center, right in the heart of things, and a few reasons not to: It's busy, filled with traffic, noise, and social whirl. If you seek tranquillity, the Center's not the place to find it.

The Waterfront   Centered on Centraal Station and stretching east and west along both banks of the IJ channel, this fast-redeveloping area includes the artificial islands, warehouses, and other installations of Amsterdam's old harbor (the new harbor lies west of the city). A shiny new kind of Amsterdam is taking shape on parts of this waterfront where old facilities have been demolished, marked now by gentrification and vast construction sites. Across the water from Centraal Station is **Amsterdam-Noord** (Amsterdam North), a district that has been little more than a dull dormitory suburb up until now. This is changing, though, with dining and entertainment venues opening up.

The Canal Belt   The semicircular, multistrand "necklace" of man-made waterways, Herengracht, Keizersgracht, and Prinsengracht (called the *Grachtengordel* in Dutch), was built around the old heart of town during the 17th-century Golden Age. Its vista of elegant, gabled mansions fronting long, tree-lined canals forms the image most often associated with Amsterdam. This zone includes the 16th-century Singel canal, hotels of all sizes, restaurants, antiques shops, and attractions like the canal-house museums and the Anne Frankhuis (p. 137). It would be a shame to visit this watery city without staying in a canal-view hotel, particularly since those lodgings are usually in 300-year-old buildings. So to really experience Amsterdam, splurge a bit, even if it's

only for a night or two, to stay at a canal-house hotel.

Leidseplein   The city's most happening nightlife square and its immediate surroundings cover such a small area that perhaps it could have been included under "the Canal Belt." But so distinctive is Leidseplein that it demands to be highlighted on its own. In addition to performance venues, movie theaters, bars, and cafes, there are plenty of good hotels and restaurants in this frenetically busy area, which won't suit those who don't like crowds and bustle.

Rembrandtplein   Like Leidseplein but on a reduced scale, this square boasts a swatch of hotels, restaurants, cafes, and nightlife venues lively enough to justify picking it out from its surroundings.

The Jordaan   This nest of tightly packed streets and canals lies west of the Center, beyond the major canals. Once a working-class neighborhood, it's become fashionable, and is now filled with artists, students, and professionals—not to mention a growing number of upscale boutiques and restaurants. Still, its "indigenous" residents, the *Jordaaners,* are alive, well, and showing no signs of succumbing to the encroaching gentrification. In its long history, the old Jordaan has seen plenty of trends come and go; it'll still be there whether or not the trendy boutiques and restaurants prosper. Note that this book only lists a couple of Jordaan hotels; this is a great residential neighborhood but, sadly, it just doesn't have many acceptable lodging options.

Museum District & Vondelpark   Gracious and residential, this area surrounds the three major museums: the Rijksmuseum, the Van Gogh Museum, and the Stedelijk Museum. There's also the Concertgebouw (a superb concert hall), many restaurants, Amsterdam's most elegant shopping streets (Pieter Cornelisz Hooftstraat and Van Baerlestraat), and the city's best-known park, Vondelpark itself. The U.S. Consulate is here too, as is a cluster of small value-oriented hotels.

Amsterdam South This modern residential area offers a number of hotels, particularly along Apollolaan, a broad avenue the locals dubbed the "Gold Coast" for its rows of expensive houses.

Amsterdam East This residential zone on the Amstel River has attractions like the Tropical Museum (p. 150), and Artis, the city's zoo (p. 172). The East, which is rich in ethnic minority groups, also has great views along the Amstel, a

status-symbol hotel (the **InterContinental Amstel Amsterdam**) and restaurant **(La Rive)**, and a top performance venue **(Koninklijk Theater Carré).**

Amsterdam West The district west of the Singelgracht canal covers a lot of ground but doesn't have much in the way of sights and delights.

Amsterdam North Across the IJ channel from Centraal Station, this part of the city has up until now been a largely uninteresting "dormitory" district. That's beginning to change, but for now most of the interesting developments in this area are along what used to be the old harbor, and these are featured under the "Waterfront" heading.

1 THE BEST OF AMSTERDAM IN 1 DAY

You'll want to limit yourself in what you attempt to accomplish with just a day in Amsterdam. It's better to leave with a few good memories than try for quick, unsubstantial glimpses of everything. That doesn't mean you can't see a lot. The Center is a small enough neighborhood that you'll get around it without much trouble, either by foot or using public transportation. This itinerary takes you to most of the must-see attractions, and includes the two most popular museums, the **Rijksmuseum** and the **Van Gogh Museum.** Still, the route affords plenty of opportunity for diverting to sights that strike your fancy. *Start: Trams 4, 9, 14, 16, 24, or 25 to the Dam.*

❶ The Dam ★★★

Amsterdam grew up around a dam on the Amstel River that's now a monumental square. So opulent was the town hall on the Dam, royalty took it over for the **Koninklijk Paleis (Royal Palace)** ★. Teens can join the young people hanging at the World War II **Nationaal Monument,** just across the tram rails. Younger kids might want to feed the pigeons in front of the palace. See p. 151.

❷ Canal-Boat Cruise ★★

Sailing is easier on your feet than walking, and the view of this city from the water is the best one. Stroll or take any tram from the Dam south along Rokin to Spui and cross the street to get to the tour-boat dock. Catch you back here in an hour. See p. 173.

❸ The Begijnhof ★★

A once-religious cloister for women, the Begijnhof, founded in the 14th century, is now a residence for elderly women. You're allowed to stroll (quietly) through the tranquil courtyard. See p. 154.

SUGGESTED AMSTERDAM ITINERARIES

THE BEST OF AMSTERDAM IN 1 DAY

4

DAY ONE
1. The Dam
2. Canal-Boat Cruise
3. The Begijnhof
4. Café Luxembourg
5. Leidseplein
6. Café Américain
7. Rijksmuseum
8. Zeebanket Van Altena
9. Museumplein
10. Van Gogh Museum
11. The Concertgebouw
12. Bodega Keyzer
13. Vondelpark
14. Vertigo

DAY TWO
1. Anne Frankhuis
2. Westerkerk
3. Homomonument
4. De Prins
5. Houseboat Museum
6. Amsterdams Historisch Museum
7. Kantjil & de Tijger
8. Bloemenmarkt (Flower Market)
9. Muntplein
10. Rembrandtplein
11. Café Schiller
12. Magere Brug
13. Muziektheater
14. Breitner

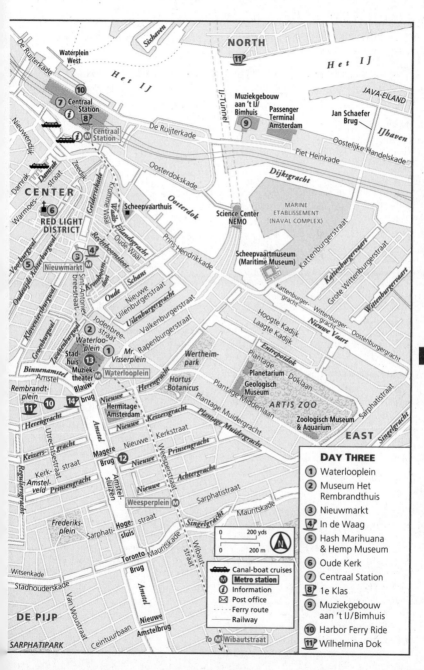

DAY THREE

1 Waterlooplein
2 Museum Het Rembrandthuis
3 Nieuwmarkt
4 In de Waag
5 Hash Marihuana & Hemp Museum
6 Oude Kerk
7 Centraal Station
8 1e Klas
9 Muziekgebouw aan 't IJ/Bimhuis
10 Harbor Ferry Ride
11 Wilhelmina Dok

Canal-boat cruises
M Metro station
(i) Information
✉ Post office
.... Ferry route
—— Railway

0   200 yds
0   200 m

4 CAFÉ LUXEMBOURG ★

The best of the "grand cafes" is a place to kick back for coffee, breakfast, lunch, or a cosmopolitan salad or snack. Dine in the dusky interior or on the sidewalk terrace. Spuistraat 24. ✆ 020/620-6264. See p. 144.

5 Leidseplein

Humpback bridges on Leidsestraat afford views of the Herengracht, Keizersgracht, and Prinsengracht canals: Amsterdam's 17th-century Golden Age *Grachtengordel* (Canal Belt). In summer, Leidseplein's sidewalks are just about filled with cafe tables. See chapter 10.

6 CAFÉ AMERICAIN ★

This Art Nouveau and Art Deco jewel dating from 1900 has lost none of its visual allure, though tourist popularity has ruined its once-exclusive cachet. Amsterdam American Hotel, Leidsekade 97. ✆ 020/556-3000. See p. 124.

7 Rijksmuseum ★★★

Renovative work at this national museum means that most of this trove of Dutch art and culture is behind impenetrable walls until 2010. Yet the vast collection's highlights alone, squeezed into the Philips Wing under the title *The Masterpieces,* is more than worth a visit. See p. 140.

8 ZEEBANKET VAN ALTENA ★

Nowhere is that Dutch specialty, fresh raw herring, better than at this *haringhuis* fish stall next to the Rijksmuseum. Stadhouderskade (at Jan Luijkenstraat). ✆ 020/676-9139. See p. 126.

9 Museumplein

The **Rijksmuseum** is at the top, the **Van Gogh Museum** and the **Stedelijk Museum**

are down one side, and the **Concertgebouw** is at the bottom of this wide open space. In warm weather, picnic under the trees or cool your feet in an oval pond. See chapter 7.

10 Van Gogh Museum ★★★

Be prepared to join the line for a museum dedicated to a no-hope 19th-century Dutch artist who sold a single painting during his lifetime and ended his life by suicide. Vincent's admirers are now legion and each of the more than 200 van Goghs is as near priceless as paintings get. See p. 142.

11 The Concertgebouw ★★★

If you've planned ahead, you'll be the one with the smug look and the ticket in your pocket for a concert by the **Royal Concertgebouw Orchestra** at Amsterdam's stellar concert hall. See p. 225.

12 BRASSERIE KEYZER ★

Dine adjacent to the Concertgebouw at this venerable, atmospheric, and moderately formal restaurant. Van Baerlestraat 96. ✆ 020/671-1441. See p. 130.

13 Vondelpark ★★

A walk in the park should be a relaxing way to end your explorations on a late afternoon or early evening when it's still light. After dark, it's not so desirable. See p. 168.

14 VERTIGO ★

With its terrace looking out on Vondelpark, the **Film Museum**'s cafe-restaurant sets the scene for some fine-dining action. Vondelpark 3. ✆ 020/612-3021. See p. 133.

Before you leave your hotel on the second day, try getting tickets to the ballet or opera at the **Muziektheater** for an evening performance. See the **Anne Frankhuis** first and go early because there's always a line (although during summer, when the museum is busiest and open until 10pm, it's better to go in the evening). *Start: Trams 13, 14, or 17 to Westermarkt.*

❶ Anne Frankhuis ★★★

The Prinsengracht canal house where Anne Frank hid from the Nazis during World War II seems haunted by tragic ghosts, yet filled with her brave spirit. See p. 137.

❷ Westerkerk ★

A bronze statue of Anne Frank graces the square outside the 17th-century Protestant church where Rembrandt was laid to rest. Head up the steeple for heavenly views of the city. See p. 163.

❸ Homomonument

The world's first ever monument to persecuted gays and lesbians takes the form of three rose-colored granite triangles, recalling the shape of the badge the Nazis forced homosexuals to wear. See page 159.

> ### ❹ DE PRINS ★★
> Though it's in a heavily touristed area, De Prins has kept the finest qualities of a quintessential Amsterdam *eetcafé*. Prinsengracht 124. ✆ **020/624-9382.** See p. 122.

❺ Houseboat Museum

Ever wondered what it would be like to own a houseboat? Find out aboard the vintage canal-barge *Hendrika Maria*. Be sure to duck when you go below. See p. 166.

❻ Amsterdams Historisch Museum ★★

Amsterdam manages to stay on the cutting edge of just about every trend even while remaining immersed in more history than is easy to digest. That's where the Historical Museum's breezy traipse through 800 years comes in handy. See p. 144.

> ### ❼ KANTJIL & DE TIJGER ★★
> Nothing is more typical of Amsterdam than its love affair with Indonesian cuisine. This elegant eatery is a master of the genre. Spuistraat 291–293. ✆ **020/620-0994.** See p. 113.

❽ Bloemenmarkt (Flower Market) ★

The famed floating flower market stands partly on barges permanently moored on Singel and partly on shore—so that "floating" tag is more marketing-driven than real. By any name, the flower market is a colorful sight. See p. 221.

❾ Muntplein

This misshaped "square" doesn't quite cut it as a visitor attraction, despite boasting the medieval **Munttoren (Mint Tower)** with its graceful spire and tinkling carillon. Most people are preoccupied with staying alive at this busy tram intersection. See p. 156.

❿ Rembrandtplein

A city square that makes up in sheer tackiness for what it lacks in sophistication. Actually, that's not quite fair. There are a few decent cafes and the determination to have a good time can be infectious, or at any rate loud. Don't miss Rembrandt's so-so statue and the cheesy bronze representation of *The Night Watch*. See chapter 10.

11 CAFÉ SCHILLER ★

While it can seem *too* cool for Rembrandt-plein—perhaps the reason it's often empty—Schiller has Art Deco style and a calm-oasis character some locals find engaging. Rembrandtplein 36. ℰ **020/624-9864.** See p. 239.

12 Magere Brug ★

The "Skinny Bridge" over the Amstel River has about as many tales associated with its creation as lights that illuminate it at night. In daylight or darkness, the view from this wooden drawbridge is memorable. See p. 158.

13 Muziektheater ★★

A synthetic-modern architecture has earned the city's opera and dance venue the biting epithet of the "False Teeth." The Amsterdam-based Netherlands Opera and National Ballet, and the regularly visiting Netherlands Dance Theater (from The Hague) do their impressive best to keep it real on the inside. See p. 228.

14 BREITNER ★

For pre- or post-Muziektheater dining, and even during the performance (if you didn't attend), Breitner puts on a pretty refined show. Amstel 212. ℰ **020/627-7879.** See p. 118.

3 THE BEST OF AMSTERDAM IN 3 DAYS

If you want to visit the Red Light District on your third day, morning is the best time. Most of its weird folk have crashed for the day and there's an air almost of innocence to the place, which occupies one of the prettiest parts of the Old Center. Only the middle segment of this itinerary goes through the Red Light District; the rest is a picture of purity—or as much purity as a smudgy city like Amsterdam ever aspires to. *Start: Metro and trams 4, 9, or 14 to Waterlooplein.*

1 Waterlooplein

The flea market here was once a fixture of the old Jodenbuurt (Jewish Quarter). Not much of the Jewish community survived the war, and neither did much of their neighborhood. There's still a flea market on the square, though, and plenty of grungy stuff to buy. See p. 220.

2 Museum Het Rembrandthuis ★★

Rembrandt painted some of the world's finest art, and put on airs and graces at this house—before bankruptcy spoiled the party and he had to leave. Be sure to view his etchings and drawings. See p. 148.

3 Nieuwmarkt

Sint-Antoniesbreestraat curves around to this lively old market square which, partly

because its only public transportation link is a Metro station, seems like a place apart from the rest of the Old Center. See chapter 9.

4 IN DE WAAG ★

Housed in a centuries-old fortified city gate and weigh house, this cafe-restaurant combines a medieval setting with sharp modern cuisine. Nieuwmarkt 4. ℰ **020/422-7772.** See p. 113.

5 Hash Marihuana & Hemp Museum ★

The hash museum goes far out of its way, or maybe just far out, to demonstrate that hemp has all manner of useful applications besides being tamped into little pipes. Yeah, right. Look for David Teniers's painting of long-ago puffing peasants. See p. 170.

⑥ Oude Kerk ★★

It's somehow symbolic of Amsterdam—a once-Catholic place of pilgrimage turned sober Calvinist—that its Old Church should sit smack in the middle of what's now the Red Light District. Surrounding the church are neat little homes once occupied by pious women. Today, many are still occupied by women, who might well be pious, if not exactly virtuous. See p. 162.

⑦ Centraal Station

Everyone ends up here sooner or later. The architecturally noteworthy station, a great place for people-watching, is the focal point of the city's public transportation by train, tram, bus, Metro, taxi, water-taxi, ferry, and canal bus. Stroll to the rear of the station for a fine harbor view. See p. 156.

> ## ⑧ 1E KLAS
> Surprising as it might seem, the station restaurant is a decent place to grab a bite, whether or not you're catching a train. Platform 2B, Centraal Station. ℰ **020/625-0131.** See p. 118.

⑨ Muziekgebouw aan 't IJ/ Bimhuis ★

East of Centraal Station, the waterfront redevelopment zone acquired one of its shiniest works of modern architecture, when the Muziekgebouw aan 't IJ concert hall for contemporary music (and the attached Bimhuis jazz club) opened to thunderous applause in 2005, even though both operations had previously occupied grungy premises that seemed to fit better with the city's rep. See p. 228.

⑩ Harbor Ferry Ride

Free ferries shuttle back and forth across Het IJ waterway from the Waterplein West dock behind Centraal Station. They make for a good way of viewing the city's old harbor. Along its shores, residential, commercial, and cultural properties are surging up in waves of redevelopment. See p. 174.

> ## ⑪ WILHELMINA-DOK ★
> Taking the free ferry across Het IJ to IJplein in Amsterdam-Noord puts you within easy walking or bicycling distance of this breezy restaurant. Nordwal 1. ℰ **020/632-3701.** See p. 117.

SUGGESTED AMSTERDAM ITINERARIES

4

THE BEST OF AMSTERDAM IN 3 DAYS

5

Where to Stay

Is your preference old-world charm combined with luxurious quarters? Glitzy modernity with every conceivable amenity? Small, intimate, family-run hotels? A historic canal house reflecting the lifestyle of centuries past? A modern, medium-size hotel on the fringe of inner-city bustle? A bare-bones dorm room that frees up scarce dollars for other purposes? Amsterdam has them all, and more. Some hotels share more than one of these characteristics: A common fusion is that of historic canal house on the outside and glitzy, amenity-laden modernity on the inside.

You probably have your own idea of what makes a great hotel. My advice is to let your choice reflect the kind of city Amsterdam is—democratic, adventurous, quirky, and always in search of that enigmatic Dutch quality, *gezelligheid,* which is the ambience that makes a place warm, cozy, and welcoming (for more, see the "In Search of *Gezelligheid*" box later in this chapter). You can find this quality at all price levels, and especially among moderately priced hotels owned by locals.

HOTEL ORIENTATION

Amsterdam is expensive, but don't despair if you need to spend less than 100€ ($160) a night for a double room. Most city hotels, whatever their cost, are clean and tidily furnished, and in many cases, they've been recently renovated. I've mostly listed hotels with rooms that have private facilities, even in the inexpensive category—and if I've included a hotel where this is not the case, I've only done so for the most compelling of reasons.

Many hotels offer significant rate reductions between November 1 and March 31, with the exception of the Christmas-to–New Year period. The city is as much a delight during this season as it is during the tourist-packed summer months; you'll enjoy a calendar full of cultural events, many traditional Dutch menu dishes not offered in warm weather, and streets, eateries, and museums filled with more locals than visitors.

If a particular hotel strikes your fancy but is out of your price range, inquire whether special off-season, weekend, specific weekday, or other packages will bring prices down to what you can afford.

You may want to avoid certain neighborhoods that harbor the haunts of drug or sex peddlers—I say "may" because many visitors head for Amsterdam precisely to experience these aspects of the city. Amsterdammers accept them as facts of life, and there are really no "no-go" areas, but it's wise to limit ventures into Amsterdam's shady corners to daylight or early-evening hours—there's no reason to spend your nights in a less-than-desirable area. The hotels described here are all decent hotels in decent neighborhoods (for the few on the fringes of dubious neighborhoods, I've mentioned this in the review).

The Netherlands adheres to the Benelux Hotel Classification System. Hotels get stars based on set criteria—having a pool, an elevator, and so on—so the hotel with the most stars isn't necessarily the most comfortable or elegant (though often, it is). Each establishment must display a sign indicating its classification, from "1" for those with minimum amenities to "5" for deluxe, full-service hotels.

Smoke Won't Get in Your Eyes

Smoking is forbidden by law in Dutch hotel public areas—such as the lobby, restaurants, and bars—except in separate designated and enclosed spaces, in which staffers are not allowed to provide waiting or other services. Few, if any, hotels plan to establish such a separate space. Each hotel can decide whether or not smoking is legally allowed in its guest rooms. Around 80% of Dutch hotels have implemented a total ban on smoking in guest rooms, and this already large percentage is likely to grow over time. Many plan to charge guests who ignore the ban for extra cleaning costs associated with smoking.

STANDARD AMENITIES   A major element in the upgrading of low-cost hotels has been squeezing bathrooms into guest rooms in the city's canal houses and older buildings. The term *bathroom,* by the way, is used whether the facilities include a tub, tub/shower combination, shower stall, or even one of those silly shower/toilets that inevitably results in lots of soggy toilet paper. If having a full bathroom is important to you, verify in advance that all you need is included.

Dutch TV channels air American and British programs in English with Dutch subtitles. Cable TV offers CNN, BBC, MTV, Sky, and others. If you're traveling with kids, be warned that some Dutch, German, and Luxembourg stations broadcast soft (and some not-so-soft) porno shows late at night.

RESERVATIONS   Should you arrive without a reservation, VVV Amsterdam tourist offices will help you for 3.50€ ($5.60), plus a refundable room deposit. They can find you something, even during the busiest periods, but it may not be exactly what, or where, you want. To reserve ahead of time, contact the **Amsterdam Tourism & Convention Board,** P.O. Box 3901, 1001 AS Amsterdam (© **020/551-2525;** fax 020/625-2869; reservations@atcb.nl; www.amsterdamtourist.nl). Online reservations are free; those made by phone, fax, and e-mail cost 15€ ($24) and it costs an additional 15€ ($24) to change a reservation.

RATES   Many moderately priced and budget hotels now copy expensive hotels by varying their rates from day to day for both online and phone reservations, according to the level of demand, and whether it's an advance-purchase or a last-minute reservation. A particular hotel reviewed in this chapter might be categorized as "Expensive" or "Very Expensive" even when its lowest possible rate would fit into the "Moderate" or even "Budget" range. If you manage to secure a room at that rate, rejoice in your luck or acumen, but be aware that plenty of your fellow guests will be paying at the higher end of the range.

TAXES   Value-added tax (BTW) of 6% and service are included in hotel bills. In addition, a 5% city tax applies to rooms at all Amsterdam hotels. Most hotels add this tax separately to the room rate; others include it in the rate. Be sure to check this when reserving.

VEXATIONS   Mosquitoes, which thrive in the damp conditions on and near the canals and on marshy reclaimed land around the city, can be a major nuisance. You can buy various plug-in devices to hold them at bay, and a fly-swatter to bring 'em down, but it's best not to let them into your room in the first place.

The lower down the price scale you go, the more likely you are to find yourself subject to "amenities" such as tiny sinks in which you can just about wash one hand at a time, no soap or shampoo in the bathroom, or a supplementary charge for orange juice at breakfast—talk about being nickel-and-dimed (or dollar-and-pounded).

GAY & LESBIAN HOTELS   Though by law no hotel is allowed to turn away same-sex couples—in Amsterdam, such a thing is unimaginable anyway—service will be better-tailored at gay-run accommodations, and Amsterdam has gay hotels aplenty. Prices and facilities are pretty unexceptional—the innkeepers' knowledge that most guests will be out enjoying themselves is probably why these hotels don't turn up the luxury level.

COMPLAINTS   Standards of service can be, aah . . . "relaxed" . . . in Amsterdam. That's doesn't mean you won't get good, friendly service—you will—but there's a subtle subtext: Dutch service providers just naturally assume they're doing you a favor, rather than their job. This attitude surfaces most clearly when you make a complaint. You may be astonished to discover that if you have a problem, you might be blamed for not being satisfied with what's provided.

If you dare to make a complaint like some, shall we say, Americans—rearing up on your hind legs and hollering until the staff person gets his or her butt into gear—your effort goes down like the *Titanic*. In big international hotels, where staffers are accustomed to the demanding "foibles" of global business travelers, the response is likely to be glacial but correct. But in a hotel farther down the financial food chain, watch out: You may have a stand-up fight on your hands.

BREAKFAST   If breakfast isn't included, expect to pay 5€ to 25€ ($8–$40) for a continental, buffet, or full breakfast, depending on the hotel category. A typical morning begins with a selection of breads—whole-grain, nutty, or rye—fresh from the *warme bakker;* rusks (crunchy toasted rounds, like Zwieback); *ontbijtkoek* (spicy gingerbread cake); a platter of cheese and sliced meats (ham, roast beef, salami); coffee (thicker and stronger than American coffee, and often served with *koffiemelk*—gunk similar to condensed milk, which does to coffee what water does to a fine malt whiskey) or tea. Some hotels throw in a boiled egg, yogurt, fruit juice, or all three.

This, at any rate, is the ideal spread, but cheap hotels may present only a few sorry-looking, curled-up-at-the-edges cheese slices, assorted cold meats of indeterminate provenance, and eggs boiled hard enough to sink an enemy sub.

A Down-to-Earth Warning

Elevators are hard to shoehorn into the cramped confines of a 17th-century canal house–turned-inn and cost more than some moderately priced and budget hotels can afford. Many simply don't have them. If lugging your old wooden sea chest up six flights of steep, narrow stairs is liable to void your life insurance, you better make sure an elevator is in place and working. Should there be no elevator and you have trouble climbing stairs, ask for a room on a low floor. Or think positively and regard the stairs as your workout for the day.

The **rack rate** is the maximum rate that a hotel charges for a room. However, hardly anybody pays this price, except in high season or on holidays. To lower your cost:

- **Ask about special rates or discounts.** You may qualify for corporate, student, military, senior, frequent-flyer, union, or other discounts.
- **Dial direct.** When booking a room in a chain hotel, you'll often get a better deal by calling the individual hotel rather than the chain's main number.
- **Book online.** Many hotels offer Internet-only discounts or deals on Priceline, Hotwire, or Expedia; these rates are much lower than those available through the hotel itself.
- **Remember the law of supply and demand.** Resort hotels are most crowded and therefore most expensive on weekends, so discounts are usually available for midweek stays. Business hotels in downtown locations are busiest during the week, so expect big discounts over the weekend. Many hotels have high- and low-season prices; booking even a day after high season ends can mean big discounts.
- **Look into group or long-stay discounts.** If you come as part of a large group, you should be able to negotiate a bargain rate. Likewise, if you're planning a long stay (at least 5 days), you may qualify for a discount. As a general rule, expect 1 night free after a 7-night stay.
- **Avoid excess charges and hidden costs.** When you book a room, ask whether the hotel charges for parking. Use your own cellphone or prepaid phone card instead of dialing direct from hotel phones, which usually charge exorbitant rates. Don't be tempted by the room's minibar offerings. Finally, ask about local taxes and service charges, which can increase a room's cost by 15% or more.
- **Book an efficiency.** A room with a kitchenette allows you to shop for groceries and cook your own meals. This is a big money saver, especially for families on long stays.
- **Enroll in hotel frequent-stay programs,** which are upping the ante lately to win repeat customers' loyalty. Frequent guests can accumulate points or credits to earn free hotel nights, airline miles, in-room amenities, merchandise, tickets to concerts and events—and even credit toward stock in the participating hotel, in the case of the Jameson Inn hotel group. It's not only the many chain hotels and motels (**Hilton HHonors, Marriott Rewards, Wyndham ByRequest,** to name a few) that award perks, but also individual inns and B&Bs. Many chain hotels partner with other hotel chains, car-rental firms, airlines, and credit card companies to give consumers additional incentive to do repeat business.

LANDING THE BEST ROOM

Somebody has to get the best room in the house, and it might as well be you. Start by joining the hotel's frequent-guest program, which may make you eligible for upgrades. A hotel-branded credit card usually gives its owner "silver" or "gold" status in frequent-guest programs for free. Always ask for a corner room—they're usually larger and quieter, with more windows and light, and they often cost the same as standard rooms. When making your reservation, ask if the hotel is renovating; if it is, request a room away from the construction. Ask about nonsmoking rooms, rooms with views, rooms with twin, queen-, or king-size beds. If you're a light sleeper, request a quiet room away from vending machines, elevators, restaurants, bars, and discos. Ask for a room that has been most recently renovated or redecorated. If you're not happy with your room when you arrive, ask for another one. Most lodgings will accommodate.

1 BEST HOTEL BETS

For additional recommendations, see "The Best Splurge Hotels," and "The Best Moderately Priced Hotels," in chapter 1.

- **Best Value:** Taking all factors into account—price, location, facilities, hospitality, Dutchness, and that indefinable element that makes a stay memorable—the **Estheréa,** Singel 303–309 (✆ 020/624-5146), is the best value in town. See p. 88.
- **Best for Tradition: Die Port van Cleve,** Nieuwezijds Voorburgwal 176–180 (✆ 020/ 718-9013), is one of Amsterdam's oldest hotels, but has entirely modernized rooms, so you can celebrate the 17th century in 21st-century comfort. See p. 82.
- **Best for Families:** The **Crowne Plaza Amsterdam City Centre,** Nieuwezijds Voorburgwal 5 (✆ 020/620-0500), provides reliable accommodations and service in a family-friendly environment close to Centraal Station and the main public transportation links. There's also an indoor swimming pool. See p. 82.
- **Best for Business Travelers:** The **NH Barbizon Palace,** Prins Hendrikkade 59–72 (✆ 020/556-4564), is modern, luxurious, stylish, efficient, and has an excellent location—opposite Centraal Station—and a full range of business facilities. See p. 86.
- **Best Unknown Hotel:** This accolade goes to **Seven Bridges,** Reguliersgracht 31 (✆ 020/ 623-1329) for its combination of location, decor, personal service, enthusiastic owners, and general all-around quality. See p. 90.
- **Best Budget Hotel:** Many cheap hotels in Amsterdam leave a lot to be desired. Not so the **Museumzicht,** Jan Luykenstraat 22 (✆ 020/671-2954), a plain, clean, and friendly hotel at a superb location across from the Rijksmuseum. See p. 98.

2 THE OLD CENTER

VERY EXPENSIVE

Hotel de l'Europe ★★   Occupying a stretch of prime waterfront where the Amstel River flows into the city's canal net, this grande dame from 1896 is small enough to seem almost homey. It retains a dignified, *fin de siècle* style behind its pastel-red and white facade. Those airs and graces come at a price, though, and to some the hotel may seem old-fashioned and a tad dull. Guest rooms and marble bathrooms are spacious and bright, furnished in classic style. Some could do with having those classics updated a notch or two, but in most this has already been done. Try for a room with a mini-balcony overlooking the river. The **Excelsior** (p. 109) is among the toniest restaurants in town. **Le Relais** is a less formal setting for a light lunch or dinner. Drinks are served in the summer on **La Terrasse,** an outdoor cafe overlooking the Amstel. *Note:* During 2009 and 2010, the hotel will be expanding and undergoing major renovations to all existing rooms and public spaces. *Note:* This hotel has been awarded a Green Key certificate for its environmental awareness and sustainable practices.

Nieuwe Doelenstraat 2–8 (facing Muntplein), 1012 CP Amsterdam. ✆ **800/223-6800** in the U.S. and Canada, or 020/531-1777. Fax 020/531-1778. www.leurope.nl. 100 units. 420€–510€ ($672–$816) double; from 560€ ($896) suite. AE, DC, MC, V. Valet and self-parking 50€ ($80). Tram: 4, 9, 14, 16, 24, or 25 to De Munt. **Amenities:** 2 restaurants; 2 bars; heated indoor pool; health club; sauna; concierge; business center (small); room service; babysitting; laundry service; same-day dry cleaning; smoke-free rooms. *In room:* A/C, TV, minibar, hair dryer, safe.

(Fun Facts   No Stomach for Art

So repelled were diners by the Karel Appel mural *Inquisitive Children* in the then–Town Hall's staff restaurant—now the Grand Hotel's elegant **Grand Restaurant**—that it was covered up for 10 years. Today, modern-art devotees visit just to view the mural.

Sofitel The Grand Amsterdam ★★   In a courtly building that was a 15th-century convent, a 16th-century royal guesthouse, the 17th-century Amsterdam Admiralty headquarters, and the city's 19th-century Town Hall, the Grand is grand indeed. To reach the lobby, walk through a courtyard with a fountain, then pass through a brass-and-wood revolving door. Enjoy afternoon tea in the lounge amid Art Deco and stained-glass windows; Oriental rugs grace black-and-white marble floors. All this elegance, and it's only a few blocks south of the Red Light District. Individually styled and furnished rooms reflect the different phases of the building's past and are the last word in plush. Most have couches and armchairs. Views are of 17th-century canals, the garden, or the courtyard. The **Grand Restaurant,** a jacket-and-tie modern French brasserie, sports an abstract expressionist mural, *Inquisitive Children* (1949), by Cobra-movement artist Karel Appel. *Note:* This hotel has been awarded a Green Key certificate for its environmental awareness and sustainable practices.

Oudezijds Voorburgwal 197 (off Damstraat), 1012 EX Amsterdam. ✆ **800/515-5679** in the U.S. and Canada, or 020/555-3111. Fax 020/555-3222. www.thegrand.nl. 178 units. 250€–400€ ($400–$640) double; from 500€ ($800) suite. AE, DC, MC, V. Valet parking 35€ ($56). Tram: 4, 9, 14, 16, 24, or 25 to Spui. **Amenities:** Restaurant; snack bar; lounge; bar; heated indoor pool; health club and spa; concierge; airport transfer; business center (self-service); room service; babysitting; laundry service; same-day dry cleaning; all rooms smoke-free. *In room:* A/C, TV, high-speed Internet, minibar, coffeemaker, hair dryer, safe.

(Kids   Family-Friendly Hotels

Amstel Botel (p. 87)   Though it is more common to find youthful spirits traveling alone or in small groups here, there's no reason it shouldn't work for families. For kids, there's the added interest of being on a ship, even if it isn't going anywhere.

Crowne Plaza Amsterdam City Centre (p. 82)   The Crowne Plaza has good reliable amenities that provide comfort and convenience for traveling families. It also has an indoor pool.

Estheréa (p. 88)   Though most rooms in this canal-house hotel are rather small, all are tastefully furnished, and a few have bunk beds.

Sint Nicolaas (p. 84)   A centrally located hotel, run by the warm Mesker family, welcomes guests into a comfortable and relaxed environment that is child-friendly.

Stayokay Amsterdam Vondelpark (p. 98)   This ideal choice for families traveling on a limited budget offers a good blend of facilities, space, easygoing atmosphere, and security. It's got a green location in the city's famous Vondelpark.

Central Amsterdam Accommodations

Acacia **23**
Agora **6**
Ambassade **9**
Amstel Botel **30**
Amsterdam American **4**
Amsterdam Wiechmann **7**
Arena **44**
Avenue Hotel **28**
Bridge Hotel **42**
Budget Hotel Clemens
  Amsterdam **15**
Canal House **21**
Crowne Plaza Amsterdam
  City Centre **27**
Die Port van Cleve **16**
Dikker & Thijs Fenice **5**
The Dylan Amsterdam **8**
Eden Hotel Amsterdam **38**
Estheréa **10**
Hegra **12**
Hoksbergen **11**
Hotel Amsterdam–
  De Roode Leeuw **18**
Hotel de l'Europe **37**
InterContinental Amstel
  Amsterdam **43**
Keizershof **2**
Lloyd Hotel **32**
Mercure Amsterdam
  Arthur Frommer **1**
NH Barbizon Palace **31**
NH Grand Hotel
  Krasnapolsky **17**
NH Schiller Hotel **39**
Orfeo **3**
Park Plaza Victoria
  Amsterdam **29**
Prinsenhof **41**
Pulitzer **14**
Radisson SAS **36**
Rembrandt Centrum **13**
Renaissance Amsterdam **25**
Rho Hotel **34**
Seven Bridges **40**
Singel Hotel **24**
Sint Nicolaas **26**
Sofitel The Grand
  Amsterdam **35**
The Toren **20**
Tulip Inn Dam Square **19**
Van Onna **22**
Winston **33**

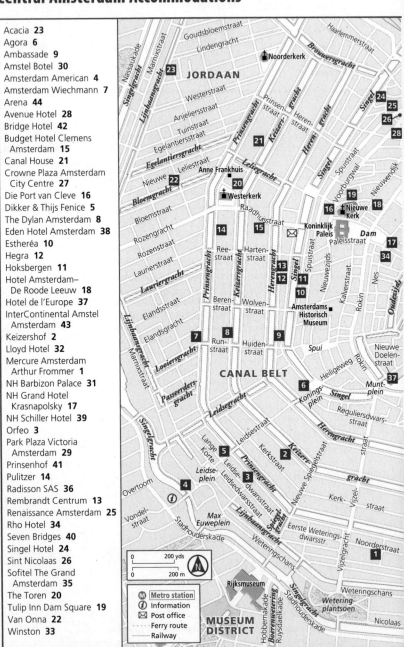

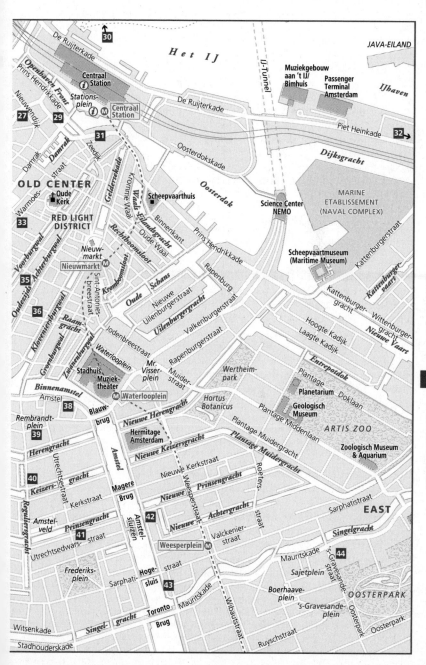

EXPENSIVE

Crowne Plaza Amsterdam City Centre ★ (Kids) A red-coated footman greets arriving visitors; he sets the tone for everything else at this fine hotel 2 blocks from Centraal Station. Relaxed luxury is perhaps the best way to describe the Crowne Plaza. Some rooms have the wooden beams typical of canalside houses in Amsterdam, and each of the accommodations comes equipped with a trouser press, comfortable armchairs, and good desks for those who want to work. This hotel is a good bet for tourists as well as expense-account travelers. An ongoing renovation program ensures that rooms and public spaces are kept up-to-date. **Dorrius Brasserie** is a decent impersonation of an Old Dutch restaurant. The **Amsterdammer Bar & Patio** has the style of a typical local cafe. *Note*: This hotel has been awarded a Green Key certificate for its environmental awareness and sustainable practices.

Nieuwezijds Voorburgwal 5 (at Hekelveld), 1012 RC Amsterdam. © **877/227-6963** in the U.S. and Canada, or 020/620-0500. Fax 020/620-1173. www.amsterdam-citycentre.crowneplaza.com. 270 units. 200€–300€ ($320–$480) double; from 400€ ($640) suite. Club Room rates include continental breakfast. AE, DC, MC, V. Valet parking 40€ ($64). Tram: 1, 2, 5, 13, or 17 to Martelaarsgracht. **Amenities:** 2 restaurants; lounge; bar; heated indoor pool; health club and spa; bikes; game room; concierge; business center; room service; in-room massage; babysitting; laundry service; same-day dry cleaning; smoke-free rooms; executive rooms. *In room:* A/C, TV, high-speed Internet, minibar, coffeemaker, hair dryer, iron, safe.

Die Port van Cleve One of the city's oldest hotels—it actually started life in 1864 as the first Heineken brewery—stands right across the street from the Royal Palace on the Dam. The ornamental facade, with its turrets and alcoves, is original and has been fully restored. Likewise, the interior was completely renovated a few years back. The guest rooms are relatively small, and in general are furnished in a plain way that doesn't quite complement the building's handsome looks. Watch out for noise from the busy (or bustling, if you prefer) street, in rooms at the front, especially in summer when you may want the windows open due to the absence of air-conditioning. You won't eat much more traditionally Dutch than in the **Brasserie de Poort,** and you can drink in the **Bodega de Blauwe Parade** watched over by a feast of Delft blue tiles.

Nieuwezijds Voorburgwal 176–180 (behind the Royal Palace), 1012 SJ Amsterdam. © **020/718-9013.** Fax 020/718-9001. www.dieportvancleve.com. 121 units. 305€–350€ ($488–$560) double; from 420€ ($672) suite. AE, DC, MC, V. No parking. Tram: 1, 2, 5, 13, or 17 to the Dam. **Amenities:** Restaurant; cafe; 2 bars; concierge; room service; babysitting; laundry service; same-day dry cleaning; smoke-free rooms; executive rooms. *In room:* TV, high-speed Internet, hair dryer, safe.

Hotel Amsterdam-De Roode Leeuw A stone's throw from the Dam, this hotel, founded in 1911 and still owned by descendants of the original proprietors, has an 18th-century facade. Its rooms are super-modern, though, with thick carpets and ample wardrobe space. Rooms at the front of the hotel tend to get more light, but are also subject to more street noise; some have balconies. The award-winning **De Roode Leeuw** restaurant serves typical Dutch cuisine. The glassed-in heated terrace overlooking the Dam is a pleasant spot for a beer (open daily 11am–11:30pm). *Note*: This hotel has been awarded a Green Key certificate for its environmental awareness and sustainable practices.

Damrak 93–94 (beside the Dam), 1012 LP Amsterdam. © **800/44-UTELL** in the U.S. and Canada, or 020/555-0666. Fax 020/620-4716. www.hotelamsterdam.nl. 79 units. 110€–325€ ($176–$520) double. AE, DC, MC, V. No parking. Tram: 4, 9, 14, 16, 24, or 25 to the Dam. **Amenities:** Restaurant; cafe; business center; room service; laundry service; same-day dry cleaning; almost all rooms smoke-free; executive rooms. *In room:* A/C, TV, high-speed Internet, minibar, coffeemaker, hair dryer, safe.

NH Grand Hotel Krasnapolsky   The "Kras," located right on the Dam, began as the Wintertuin (Winter Garden) restaurant, founded in 1866 by a Polish tailor turned entrepreneur. Victorians sipped wine and nibbled pancakes beneath the hanging plants and lofty skylight ceiling, where breakfast and lunch are now served. This was Holland's first hotel to sport parquet floors, central heating, and electric lights. Since then, it has spread amoeba-like over four buildings, including one with a Japanese garden and another with a Dutch roof garden. Some rooms are small, while others have been converted into individually decorated apartments. Their state varies from worn to tastefully renovated. Since there are so many, I advise you to have a look at one first and retain an option to change one that's not suitable. The street alongside the hotel leads into the Red Light District, which may not be everyone's idea of the perfect evening stroll. *Note*: This hotel has been awarded a Green Key certificate for its environmental awareness and sustainable practices.

Dam 9 (facing Royal Palace), 1012 JS Amsterdam. ℂ **020/554-9111.** Fax 020/622-8607. www.nh-hotels.com. 468 units. 194€–204€ ($310–$326) double; from 450€ ($720) suite. AE, DC, MC, V. Parking 35€ ($56). Tram: 4, 9, 14, 16, 24, or 25 to the Dam. **Amenities:** 2 restaurants; lounge; bar; health club; Jacuzzi; concierge; business center; salon; room service; babysitting; laundry service; same-day dry cleaning; smoke-free rooms; executive rooms. *In room:* A/C, TV, high-speed Internet, minibar, coffeemaker, hair dryer, iron, safe.

Radisson SAS ★   You can't get much closer to Old Amsterdam than at this stylish hotel in the higgledy-piggledy heart of the city. When you walk into the dazzling atrium, you face a vicarage dating from 1650. Because of Amsterdam's strict preservation laws, Radisson couldn't knock the building down, so they built around it and incorporated it into the new structure. Two 18th-century merchants' houses and a former paper factory complete the renovated ensemble. The hotel offers four types of themed rooms: Typical Dutch, with oak furnishings and orange curtains, Scandinavian, Asian, and Art Deco. All offer a standard of comfort and style that has made this hotel a firm Amsterdam favorite. Each room has a writing desk, and king-, queen-, or twin-size beds. Dine in the Dutch restaurant **De Palmboom.** The oak-beamed **De Pastoriebar** in the old vicarage handles drinks and snacks. *Note*: This hotel has been awarded a Green Key certificate for its environmental awareness and sustainable practices.

Rusland 17 (at the University of Amsterdam), 1012 CK Amsterdam. ℂ **800/333-3333** in the U.S. and Canada, or 020/623-1231. Fax 020/520-8200. www.radissonsas.com. 242 units. 150€–350€ ($240–$560) double; from 600€ ($960) suite. Buffet breakfast included in business class, executive, and suite rates. AE, DC, MC, V. Parking 48€ ($77). Tram: 4, 9, 14, 16, 24, or 25 to Spui. **Amenities:** Restaurant; bar; health club; sauna; concierge; airport transfer; secretarial services; room service; babysitting; laundry service; same-day dry cleaning; smoke-free rooms; executive rooms. *In room:* A/C, TV, high-speed Internet, minibar, hair dryer, safe.

Renaissance Amsterdam ★   Van Gogh liked this setting well enough to paint part of it in his *View of Amsterdam from Centraal Station* (1885). Built around an open central courtyard in an area of old warehouses, the six-story Renaissance blends with the gabled facades nearby. Antiquity's influence stops at the front door, however: The Renaissance is highly modern, offering big beds, color TVs with in-house movies, electronic security, and message-retrieval systems. It's a matter of opinion whether the hotel's transformation of the adjacent domed Lutheran **Koepelkerk** into an ultramodern conference center is appropriate. The restored old church, which dates from 1671 (and was painted in 1885 by Vincent van Gogh), occasionally serves as a dining room for special events. The hotel's regular restaurant was closed for rebuilding at the time of writing; in the meantime, there's still the brown-cafe–style **Koepelcafé,** which serves light meals.

Kattengat 1 (at Spuistraat), 1012 SZ Amsterdam. ℂ **888/236-2427** in the U.S. and Canada, or 020/621-2223. Fax 020/627-5254. www.renaissancehotels.com. 381 units. 285€–325€ ($456–$520) double; from 585€ ($936) suite. Club Room rates include continental breakfast. AE, DC, MC, V. Limited street parking. Tram: 1, 2, 5, 13, or 17 to Martelaarsgracht. **Amenities:** Restaurant; bar; access to nearby health club and spa; concierge; business center; room service; babysitting; laundry service; same-day dry cleaning; all rooms smoke-free; executive rooms *In room:* A/C, TV, high-speed Internet, minibar, hair dryer, iron, safe.

MODERATE

Avenue Hotel ★   Part of this hotel is a converted Golden Age warehouse that belonged to the V.O.C., the United East India Company. The rooms aren't huge, but they're bright and have clean furnishings and good-size bathrooms, some with a double sink. At the time of writing the hotel was starting with a renewal project, to add air-conditioning to the rooms and improve the bathrooms. The location is pretty central and convenient for getting to and fro by tram—the downside is the clackety-clack of outside traffic. If this is likely to disturb you, ask for a room at the back or at least not on a low floor. Or simply look for a hotel in a location with less action. The Dutch buffet breakfast is more than decent, and the St. Jacobsstreet Café, around the corner in Sint-Jacobsstraat, takes care of dinner in reasonable style.

Nieuwezijds Voorburgwal 33 (near Centraal Station), 1012 RD Amsterdam. ℂ **020/530-9530.** Fax 020/530-9599. www.emb-hotels.nl/avenue. 80 units. 112€–160€ ($179–$256) double. Rates include buffet breakfast. AE, DC, MC, V. Limited street parking. Tram: 1, 2, 5, 13, or 17 to Nieuwezijds Kolk. **Amenities:** Cafe/bar; dry cleaning; smoke-free rooms. *In room:* A/C (some rooms), TV, high-speed Internet, hair dryer.

Rho Hotel   Once you find it, you'll bless this hotel for its generally quiet-yet-central location, surely one of the best in town, and a friendly staff, which together make up for some deficiencies in other attributes. Tucked away on a side street just off the Dam's **Nationaal Monument** (p. 151), the Rho's building was once the offices of a gold company and, before that, a theater from around 1908 (which is now the reception and breakfast area). Most rooms are modern and comfortable, if not overly inspired in the looks department, and some are on the small side. This is one of those places where it pays to check out a few rooms, if you can, before committing.

Nes 5–23 (at the Dam), 1012 KC Amsterdam. ℂ **020/620-7371.** Fax 020/620-7826. www.rhohotel.com. 165 units. 115€–155€ ($184–$248) double. Rates include buffet breakfast. AE, MC, V. Parking 20€ ($32). Tram: 4, 9, 14, 16, 24, or 25 to the Dam. **Amenities:** Lounge; bikes; all rooms smoke-free. *In room:* TV, high-speed Internet, fridge, hair dryer, safe.

Sint Nicolaas ★ ⓥⓐⓛⓤⓔ   Named after Amsterdam's patron saint, this hotel is conveniently near the Centraal Station, in a prominent corner building at the apex of two converging streets. It's a typical family hotel with an easygoing atmosphere. Originally, the building was a factory that manufactured ropes and carpets from sisal imported from the then-Dutch colonies. In 1980, it became a hotel. The Mesker family has consistently upgraded their hotel's rooms year after year, taking them from once rather basic furnishings to a level of comfort rarely achieved by Amsterdam hotels in this price range. All of this is complemented by the location and a friendly staff.

Spuistraat 1A (at Nieuwendijk), 1012 SP Amsterdam. ℂ **020/626-1384.** Fax 020/623-0979. www.hotel nicolaas.nl. 24 units. 95€–115€ ($152–$184) double. Rates include continental breakfast. AE, DC, MC, V. Limited street parking. Tram: 1, 2, 5, 13, or 17 to Martelaarsgracht. **Amenities:** Bar; all rooms smoke-free. *In room:* TV, hair dryer, safe.

Tulip Inn Dam Square   This hotel is another example of putting an old building to good use. This time, the old building—and a magnificent building it is—was a distillery.

It's behind **Nieuwe Kerk** (p. 152), and its granite details accentuate the brickwork and massive curve-topped doors with elaborate hinges. The location is superb, just footsteps off the Dam. Inside, the rooms are all you'll want: modern, bright, comfortable, and attractively priced.

Gravenstraat 12–16 (at the Dam), 1012 NM Amsterdam. ✆ **800/344-1212** in the U.S. and Canada, or 020/623-3716. Fax 020/638-1156. www.tulipinndamsquare.com. 38 units. 175€–195€ ($280–$312) double; 295€ ($472) suite. Rates include continental breakfast. AE, DC, MC, V. No parking. Tram: 1, 2, 4, 5, 9, 13, 14, 16, 17, 24, or 25 to the Dam. **Amenities:** Bar; dry cleaning. *In room:* A/C, TV, coffeemaker, hair dryer.

INEXPENSIVE

Budget Hotel Clemens Amsterdam   A 2-minute walk from the **Anne Frankhuis** (p. 137), this hotel spreads over four floors in one of those typical steep-staired Dutch buildings, with the reception and breakfast room up one flight of stairs. There's no elevator. The hotel is owned and operated by a mother-and-daughter team, Dee and Emely, who keep the fairly spacious rooms in good trim and regularly bring in fresh flowers. Nos. 7 and 8 each have a balcony facing the **Westerkerk** (p. 163). Particularly good guests—those who don't misbehave—are in line to win a complimentary fruit basket.

Raadhuisstraat 39 (near the Westerkerk), 1016 DC Amsterdam. ✆ **020/624-6089.** Fax 020/626-9658. www.clemenshotel.nl. 9 units (5 with bathroom). 80€–120€ ($128–$192) double with bathroom; 60€–80€ ($96–$128) double without bathroom. AE, MC, V. Limited street parking. Tram: 13, 14, or 17 to Westerkerk. **Amenities:** Room service. *In room:* TV, high-speed Internet, minifridge, hair dryer, safe.

Winston   Maybe too close to the Red Light District for some people's taste, and on a slightly seedy street, the Winston is a step up from grungy and has a hang-loose, alternative rep. You might even hear some (fanciful) comparisons made to New York's Chelsea Hotel. Local artists created paintings, photographs, and other works of what you might call art, for the halls, rooms, doors, and bathrooms. The sparely furnished rooms vary in size, contain from two to six beds, and are tolerably clean and maintained. None of them has a view that's worth looking out the window for. Bathrooms are small, but have most of the requisite bits and pieces in them, and most rooms that don't have a bathtub do have a shower. The **Belushi's** bar is a fun meeting place and the next-door **Winston Kingdom** club has daily live music or DJs.

Warmoesstraat 129 (off Damrak), 1012 JA Amsterdam. ✆ **020/623-1380.** Fax 020/639-2308. www. winston.nl or www.st-christophers.co.uk. 69 units. 85€–105€ ($136–$168) double. Rates include buffet breakfast. AE, DC, MC, V. No parking. Tram: 4, 9, 14, 16, 24, or 25 to the Dam. **Amenities:** Restaurant; lounge; bar; high-speed Internet in lobby. *In room:* TV (some rooms), no phone.

ⓘ Tips   Summer Stays: Reserve Ahead

July and August are tough months for finding rooms in Amsterdam; you're advised to reserve as far ahead as possible. If you have problems getting a room, contact the **VVV Amsterdam** tourist office, which will find you one somewhere, though it might not be in the kind of hotel you want. It can be particularly hard to find hoteliers willing to give away rooms for a single night when that might cost them a longer booking. In this circumstance, a last-minute search might be called for, since a hotel that's had a last-minute cancellation is more likely to consider single-night occupancy. This is a *possible* exception to the rule that a last-minute search is the wrong way to go about finding a hotel room in Amsterdam.

EXPENSIVE

Lloyd Hotel ★   Located in the redevelopment zone of the old harbor east of Centraal Station, the Lloyd was an emigrants' hotel from 1921 to 1935. Each of its rooms has a different shape, style, and modern decor, and with rooms of various classes, the hotel straddles all categories except "Very Expensive." Its most expensive rooms, which are the largest, have a view of the water or a specially designed interior (or both). The mattresses are firm, but only a few rooms have king-size doubles—one does, however, have a bed that "sleeps" eight. The hotel's **Culturele Ambassade** houses art exhibits, modern artworks are scattered around the property, and there's an attic library. Two restaurants aim to make it cool to dine in a hotel: **Snel**, fast and affordable, is open 24/7; **Sloom** is leisurely and expensive, and you can order whatever you desire and the kitchen will aim to cook it.

Oostelijke Handelskade 34, 1019 BN Amsterdam (at IJhaven). ✆ **020/561-3604.** Fax 020/561-3600. www.lloydhotel.com. 117 units (106 with bathroom). 95€–295€ ($152–$472) double with bathroom; 450€ ($720) suite. AE, DC, MC, V. Parking 20€ ($32). Tram: 10 or 26 to Rietlandpark. **Amenities:** 2 restaurants; bar; bikes; secretarial services; room service; in-room massage; babysitting. *In room:* TV, high-speed Internet.

NH Barbizon Palace ★   Centrally located, within easy walking distance of Centraal Station and the Dam, this sparkling establishment meets every criterion for an ideal Amsterdam hotel. Built behind the facades of 19 traditional canal houses, it's fully modern and efficient inside, and loaded with amenities. Many rooms feature split-level designs and antique oak beams. A Roman forum may come to mind as you step into the hotel; the lobby is a long promenade of highly polished black-and-white marble floor tiles, with a massive skylight arching above. The excellent French restaurant **Vermeer** earns frequent praise from food critics. **Hudson's,** serving a la carte meals, and a late breakfast of juice, two eggs, a *broodje*, and coffee or tea from 10:30am to noon, is also good. *Note*: This hotel has been awarded a Green Key certificate for its environmental awareness and sustainable practices.

Prins Hendrikkade 59–72 (facing Centraal Station), 1012 AD Amsterdam. ✆ **020/556-4564.** Fax 020/624-3353. www.nh-hotels.com. 270 units. 149€–380€ ($238–$608) double; from 449€ ($718) suite. AE, DC, MC, V. Parking 48€ ($77). Tram: 1, 2, 4, 5, 9, 13, 16, 17, 24, 25, or 26 to Centraal Station. **Amenities:** 2 restaurants; bar; health club; Jacuzzi; sauna; concierge; business center; salon; room service; babysitting; laundry service; same-day dry cleaning. *In room:* A/C, TV, high-speed Internet, minibar, coffeemaker (some rooms), hair dryer, iron, safe.

Park Plaza Victoria Amsterdam ★   The proprietors' idea is to give guests a five-star hotel at four-star rates—and a great location. This is as close as you can be to Centraal Station, where most of Amsterdam's trams begin and end their routes, and where you can board a train to other parts of Holland. Since 1890, the elegant Victoria has been a turreted landmark at the head of the street called Damrak. It overlooks canal-boat piers and it can be noisy and tacky out on the busy, neon-lit street, but you won't notice that inside due to the double-glazed panes in the windows. The spacious rooms have been refurbished. Those in the new block inevitably lack some of the atmosphere of those in the old. Enjoy dinner at **Park Plaza Brasserie's** glassed-in terrace beside Damrak, or a quick lunch in **Seasons Garden** restaurant, with its Scandinavian decor.

Damrak 1–5 (facing Centraal Station), 1012 LG Amsterdam. ✆ **800/814-7000** in the U.S. and Canada, or 020/623-4255. Fax 020/625-2997. www.parkplaza.com. 306 units. 150€–350€ ($240–$560) double; from 500€ ($800) suite. AE, DC, MC, V. No parking. Tram: 1, 2, 4, 5, 9, 13, 16, 17, 24, 25, or 26 to Centraal Station.

Amenities: 2 restaurants; lounge; bar; small heated indoor pool; health club and spa; business center; salon; room service; massage; babysitting; laundry service; same-day dry cleaning; smoke-free rooms; executive rooms. *In room:* A/C, TV, high-speed Internet, minibar, coffeemaker, hair dryer, safe.

INEXPENSIVE

Amstel Botel (Kids)   Where better to experience a city on the water than on a boat-hotel moored permanently to a dock on the IJ waterway northwest of Centraal Station? The Botel is popular largely because that extra thrill added by sleeping on the water—its modest (for Amsterdam) rates don't hurt either. This retired inland waterways cruise boat has cabins on four decks that are connected by an elevator. The bright, modern rooms are no-nonsense but comfortable, the showers small. Be sure to ask for a room with a view on the water, to avoid the uninspiring quay. To get here, take the NDSM Ferry for foot passengers and two-wheel transportation from behind Centraal Station, to the NDSM dock and you'll see it floating in front of you. A free shuttle bus goes between the Botel and the station when the ferry's not running.

NDSM-Werf 3, 1033 RG Amsterdam. © **020/521-0350.** Fax 020/639-1952. www.amstelbotel.com. 175 units. 89€–94€ ($142–$150) double. AE, DC, MC, V. Limited free parking on quay. Boat: NDSM Ferry from Centraal Station. **Amenities:** Bar; concierge; dry cleaning. *In room:* TV, high-speed Internet, safe.

4 THE CANAL BELT

VERY EXPENSIVE

The Dylan Amsterdam ★   The Asian-influenced decor at this prestigious canalside boutique hotel is arguably the most stylish in town. Its setting started out as a 17th-century theater (Vivaldi once conducted here, and the serene **Dylan Lounge** still sports the theater's original brick floor). It later became a Catholic almshouse. All the guest rooms and suites have the usual array of luxury amenities and are individually decorated with different colors and themes. No. 5 is a blue Japanese-style room with a deep soaking tub and traditional sliding screens. Only three rooms have a canal view, so if this is important to you, specify it—and be ready to pay handsomely for the privilege. Style here occasionally trumps substance: The water fountain–style sinks in a few of the rooms look grand, but their design makes them somewhat hard to use. The superlative French restaurant **Vinkeles** (p. 119) draws admirers on its own account.

Keizersgracht 384 (at Runstraat), 1016 GB Amsterdam. © **020/530-2010.** Fax 020/530-2030. www.dylanamsterdam.com. 41 units. 455€–960€ ($728–$1,536) double; from 1,200€ ($1,920) suite. AE, DC, MC, V. Limited street parking. Tram: 1, 2, or 5 to Spui. **Amenities:** Restaurant; lounge; bar; exercise room; bikes; boat rental; concierge; room service; laundry service; same-day dry cleaning; smoke-free rooms. *In room:* A/C, TV/DVD, high-speed Internet, minibar, hair dryer, safe.

Pulitzer ★★   This hotel spreads through 25 old adjoining canal houses dating from the 17th and 18th centuries. It has frontage on the historic Prinsengracht and Keizersgracht canals. With the exception of bare beams or brick walls here and there, the Pulitzer's interior is modern, and the multiplicity of buildings means that rooms have different sizes, shapes, and desirability in terms of location, from elegant salons to attic garrets. The rooms with the best views look out over either the canals or the hotel garden. The Pulitzer maintains its own art gallery, and every August, it sponsors the classical-music **Prinsengracht Concert,** performed by musicians on canal barges (p. 34). As icing on the cake, the Pulitzer owns a restored 1909 motor launch, which awaits you at the hotel's own jetty. The international **Pulitzer's Restaurant** is both trendy and highly regarded.

Prinsengracht 315–331 (near Westermarkt), 1016 GZ Amsterdam. ✆ **800/325-3535** in the U.S. and Canada, or 020/523-5235. Fax 020/627-6753. www.starwoodhotels.com. 230 units. 250€–550€ ($400–$880) double; from 750€ ($1,200) suite. AE, DC, MC, V. Valet parking 45€ ($72). Tram: 13, 14, or 17 to Westermarkt. **Amenities:** Restaurant; cafe; bar; exercise room; bikes; concierge; business center; room service; babysitting; laundry service; same-day dry cleaning; all rooms smoke-free; executive rooms. *In room:* A/C, TV, high-speed Internet, minibar, coffeemaker, hair dryer, iron, safe.

EXPENSIVE

Estheréa ★★ (Kids) If you like to stay at elegant, not-too-big hotels, you're sure to be pleased by the Estheréa. It's been owned by the same family since its beginnings and, like many Amsterdam hotels, was built within a group of neighboring 17th-century canal houses. The family touch shows in attention to detail and a breezy yet professional approach. It has an elevator, a rarity in these old Amsterdam homes. In the 1940s, the proprietors spent a lot of money on wood paneling, crystal chandeliers, and other structural additions; younger family members who took over the management have had the good sense to leave it all in place. Wood bedsteads and dresser-desks lend warmth to the recently renovated and upgraded guest rooms, which vary considerably in size; a few are quite small. Most rooms accommodate two guests, but some rooms have more beds, which makes them ideal for families.

Singel 303–309 (near Spui), 1012 WJ Amsterdam. ✆ **800/223-9868** in the U.S. and Canada, or 020/624-5146. Fax 020/623-9001. www.estherea.nl. 71 units. 191€–314€ ($306–$502) double. AE, DC, MC, V. Limited street parking. Tram: 1, 2, or 5 to Spui. **Amenities:** Lounge; bar; motor scooters; concierge; room service; babysitting; laundry service; same-day dry cleaning; all rooms smoke-free. *In room:* TV, high-speed Internet, minibar, hair dryer, safe.

MODERATE

Agora ★ Old-fashioned friendliness is the keynote at this efficiently run and well-maintained lodging, a block from the **Flower Market** (p. 221). Proprietors Yvo Muthert and Els Bruijnse like to keep things friendly and personal. Bouquets greet you as you enter, and a distinctive color scheme creates a simultaneous effect of peacefulness and drama. Though the hotel occupies a canal house built in 1735, it's been fully restored in an eclectic style. Furniture from the 1930s and 1940s mixes with fine mahogany antiques. There's an abundance of overstuffed furniture; nearly every room has a puffy armchair you can sink into after a wearying day of sightseeing. Rooms with a canal view cost the most, but the extra euros are worth it—though the street's hustle and bustle can make them somewhat noisy by day. Rooms without a canal view look out onto a pretty garden at the back. There's no elevator.

Singel 462 (at Koningsplein), 1017 AW Amsterdam. ✆ **020/627-2200.** Fax 020/627-2202. www.hotel agora.nl. 16 units. 99€–159€ ($158–$254) double. Rates include buffet breakfast. AE, DC, MC, V. Limited street parking. Tram: 1, 2, or 5 to Koningsplein. *In room:* TV, high-speed Internet, hair dryer, safe.

Ambassade ★★ (Finds) Perhaps more than any other hotel in Amsterdam, this one, in ten 17th- and 18th-century houses on the Herengracht and Singel canals, re-creates what it must have felt like to live in an elegant canal house. The pastel-toned rooms are individually styled, and their size and shape vary according to the individual houses' characters. Everyone who stays here can enjoy the view each morning with breakfast in the bi-level chandeliered breakfast room, or each evening in the adjoining parlor, amid Persian rugs and a stately grandfather clock. To get to some guest rooms, you cope with a steep and skinny staircase, though other rooms are accessible by elevator. For the nimble-footed who can handle the stairs, the reward is a spacious room with large windows overlooking the canal. There's a hushed Empire-style library room and a free-to-use Internet room.

Herengracht 341 (near Spui), 1016 AZ Amsterdam. ℂ **020/555-0222.** Fax 020/555-0277. www.ambassade-hotel.nl. 59 units. 195€–275€ ($312–$440) double; 325€–375€ ($520–$600) suite. AE, DC, MC, V. Limited street parking. Tram: 1, 2, or 5 to Spui. **Amenities:** Lounge; access to nearby spa; secretarial services; room service; bikes; babysitting; laundry service; same-day dry cleaning; smoke-free rooms. *In room:* TV, high-speed Internet, hair dryer, safe.

Amsterdam Wiechmann   It takes only a moment to feel at home in the antiques-adorned Wiechmann, a classic, comfortable sort of place, despite the suit of armor you encounter just inside the front door. Its location is one of the best you'll find in this or any price range: 5 minutes in one direction is the Kalverstraat shopping street; 5 minutes in the other, Leidseplein. Most of the rooms—all of them nonsmoking—are standard, with twin or double beds, and some have big bay windows. Furnishings are elegant, and Oriental rugs grace many of the floors in public spaces. The higher-priced doubles have antique furnishings, and many have a view of the Prinsengracht canal. The breakfast room has hardwood floors, lots of greenery, and white linens. There's no elevator.

Prinsengracht 328–332 (at Looiersgracht), 1016 HX Amsterdam. ℂ **020/626-3321.** Fax 020/626-8962. www.hotelwiechmann.nl. 37 units. 140€–160€ ($224–$256) double. Rates include continental breakfast. MC, V. Limited street parking. Tram: 1, 2, or 5 to Prinsengracht. **Amenities:** Lounge; all rooms smoke-free. *In room:* TV, high-speed Internet, safe.

Canal House ★★   This small hotel's proprietors have taken a contemporary approach to reestablishing the elegant canal-house atmosphere; though it's in three adjoining houses that date from 1630, these were gutted and rebuilt to provide private bathrooms and rooms filled with antiques, quilts, and Chinese rugs. It has an elevator (though it doesn't stop at every floor, so you may still have to walk a short distance up or down stairs), along with a steep staircase that still has its carved old balustrade. Overlooking the back garden, which is illuminated at night, is a magnificent breakfast room that seems not to have been touched since the 17th century. On the parlor floor is a cozy Victorian-era saloon, and if you can get it, room no. 26 has a panoramic view of the canal. *Note:* The hotel is fully closed for renovations until spring 2009.

Keizersgracht 148 (near Leliegracht), 1015 CX Amsterdam. ℂ **020/622-5182.** Fax 020/624-1317. www.canalhouse.nl. 26 units. 150€–190€ ($240–$304) double. Rates include continental breakfast. DC, MC, V. Limited street parking. Tram: 13, 14, or 17 to Westermarkt. **Amenities:** Lounge; room service. *In room:* Hair dryer.

Dikker & Thijs Fenice   On the Prinsengracht, where it intersects lively Leidsestraat, is this small, homey hotel whose smart but cozy character emanates from the marble-rich lobby and stylish facade. Upstairs, spacious and tasteful rooms cluster in groups of two or four around small lobbies, which makes the Dikker & Thijs feel more like an apartment building than a hotel. Welcoming touches are flowers in the rooms, a subtle but elegantly modern Art Deco decor, and double-glazed windows to eliminate the noise rising up from Leidsestraat. But this hotel has existed since 1921, and some rooms clearly need renovation. Those at the front have a super view of classy Prinsengracht.

Prinsengracht 444 (at Leidsestraat), 1017 KE Amsterdam. ℂ **020/620-1212.** Fax 020/625-8986. www.dtfh.nl. 42 units. 125€–275€ ($200–$440) double. Rates include buffet breakfast. AE, DC, MC, V. Limited street parking. Tram: 1, 2, or 5 to Prinsengracht. **Amenities:** Lounge; bar; bikes; concierge; secretarial services; room service; in-room massage; babysitting; laundry service; same-day dry cleaning; smoke-free rooms. *In room:* TV, high-speed Internet, minibar, hair dryer.

Mercure Amsterdam Arthur Frommer The Mercure, once owned by Arthur Frommer, is tucked away in the canal area off Vijzelgracht. Its entrance opens onto a small courtyard off a side street that runs behind Prinsengracht; someone painted a canalside mural along the facing wall. The hotel, though not easy to find, is well worth finding. A top-to-bottom renovation has transformed its rooms, giving them a stylish decor in a soft pastel palette. All rooms have big double or single beds. There's a small, cozy bar. The **Golden Age Bar** is a pretty decent re-creation of an olde-worlde Dutch bar.

Noorderstraat 46 (off Vijzelgracht), 1017 TV Amsterdam. ℂ **800/515-5679** in the U.S. and Canada, or 020/622-0328. Fax 020/620-3208. www.accorhotels.com. 92 units. 125€–170€ ($200–$272) double. AE, DC, MC, V. Limited private parking 20€ ($32). Tram: 16, 24, or 25 to Weteringcircuit. **Amenities:** Bar; laundry service; dry cleaning; all rooms smoke-free. *In room:* A/C, TV, minibar, hair dryer, safe.

Rembrandt Centrum Built anew within a wide 18th-century building on a canal above Raadhuisstraat and four small 16th-century houses directly behind it on the Singel canal, this hotel is best described as basic. But rooms (which come in a variety of sizes and shapes) tend to be large. Some still have their old fireplaces adorned with elegant wood or marble mantels, though these furnaces no longer function. As you walk around, you'll occasionally pass through a former foyer on the way to your room, or glimpse an old beam.

Herengracht 255 (at Hartenstraat), 1016 BJ Amsterdam. ℂ **020/622-1727.** Fax 020/625-0630. www.rembrandtcentrum.com. 111 units. 100€–205€ ($160–$328) double. AE, DC, MC, V. Limited street parking. Tram: 1, 2, 5, 13, 14, or 17 to the Dam. **Amenities:** Bar; room service; dry cleaning; smoke-free rooms. *In room:* TV.

Seven Bridges ★★ Ⓕⓘⓝⓓⓢ Proprietors Pierre Keulers and Günter Glaner have made the Seven Bridges, named for its view of seven arched bridges, one of Amsterdam's canalhouse gems. Each room is individual, but furnished with antiques from the 17th to the 20th centuries, plush carpets, handmade Italian drapes, hand-painted tiles, wood-tiled floors, and Impressionist art reproductions. The biggest room, a quad on the first landing, has high ceilings, a big mirror over the fireplace, an Empire onyx table, antique leather armchairs, an array of potted plants, and a huge marble-floored bathroom (the sink and shower even have gold-plated taps). Attic rooms have sloped ceilings and exposed wood beams, and basement rooms are big and bright. Rooms at the front overlook a canal, and those at the rear overlook a garden. One or two are refurbished each year, so you may want to ask for the most recently updated. There's no elevator.

Reguliersgracht 31 (at Keizersgracht), 1017 LK Amsterdam. ℂ **020/623-1329.** Fax 020/624-7652. www.sevenbridgeshotel.nl. 11 units. 110€–260€ ($176–$416) double. Rates for most rooms include full breakfast served in room. AE, MC, V. Limited street parking. Tram: 4 to Keizersgracht. *In room:* TV, hair dryer.

Singel Hotel Style marries tradition in the elegant little Singel, near the Brouwersgracht's head in one of Amsterdam's most pleasant and central locations. Three renovated canal houses were harmoniously united to create this hotel. Decor is bright and welcoming, and the modern rooms are spacious for a small hotel; some have an attractive view of the Singel canal. An elevator services the building's four floors.

Singel 13–17 (near Centraal Station), 1012 VC Amsterdam. ℂ **020/626-3108.** Fax 020/620-3777. www.singelhotel.nl. 32 units. 90€–160€ ($144–$256) double. Rates include continental breakfast. AE, DC, MC, V. Limited street parking. Tram: 1, 2, 5, 13, or 17 to Martelaarsgracht. **Amenities:** Bar (small); high-speed Internet in lobby; babysitting; laundry service; smoke-free rooms. *In room:* TV, hair dryer, safe.

The Toren ★ Encompassing two buildings, separated by neighboring houses, the opulent boutique-hotel Toren is a clean, attractive, and well maintained canalside property. It promises private facilities with every room, though in a few cases that means a bathroom located off the public hall (with your own key, however). There's a bridal suite here, complete with a blue canopy and a Jacuzzi (some of the doubles also have a Jacuzzi). A private guesthouse off the garden is done up in Laura Ashley prints.

Keizersgracht 164 (near Leliegracht), 1015 CZ Amsterdam. ✆ 020/662-6033. Fax 020/626-9705. www. thetoren.nl. 38 units. 130€–250€ ($208–$400) double; 275€–375€ ($440–$600) suite. AE, DC, MC, V. Limited street parking. Tram: 13, 14, or 17 to Westermarkt. **Amenities:** Bar; room service; babysitting; laundry service; dry cleaning. *In room:* A/C, TV, high-speed Internet, minibar, coffeemaker, hair dryer, safe.

INEXPENSIVE

Hegra   Housed in a narrow 17th-century canal house a 5-minute walk from the Dam, this cozy little hotel has been under the same management for two generations. Robert de Vries, the proprietor, is extremely helpful and friendly. Rooms are small but tastefully furnished and have beamed ceilings. There's no elevator, so you have to climb four stories if you get a room on the top. Breakfast is served in a cozy space.

Herengracht 269 (near Hartenstraat), 1016 BJ Amsterdam. ✆ 020/623-7877. Fax 020/623-8159. www. hotelhegra.nl. 11 units, 9 with bathroom. 85€ ($136) double with bathroom; 70€ ($112) double without bathroom. Rates include Dutch breakfast. MC, V. Limited street parking. Tram: 1, 2, 5, 13, 14, or 17 to the Dam. **Amenities:** High-speed Internet in lobby; bikes. *In room:* No phone.

Hoksbergen   At a tranquil point on the historic Singel canal, this inexpensive hotel in a 300-year-old canal house isn't flashy or elegant, but it is bright and fresh, which makes it appealing to budget-conscious travelers who don't want to give up creature comforts. Its central location makes for easy access to all the surrounding sights and attractions. Rooms at the front have a canal view. There's no elevator.

Singel 301 (near Spui), 1012 WH Amsterdam. ✆ 020/626-6043. Fax 020/638-3479. www.hotelhoksbergen. nl. 19 units. 72€–129€ ($115–$206) double. Rates include buffet breakfast. AE, DC, MC, V. Limited street parking. Tram: 1, 2, or 5 to Spui. *In room:* TV.

Keizershof ★ Ⓥalue   Owned by the genial de Vries family, this hotel in a four-story canal house from 1672 has just four beamed rooms named after old Hollywood stars—though a greater claim to fame is that members of the Dutch royal family were regular visitors in its pre-hotel days. Several other touches make a stay at this nonsmoking hotel memorable: From the street-level entrance, a steep wooden spiral staircase built from a ship's mast leads to guest rooms—there's no elevator. There are, however, a television and a grand piano in the cozy lounge. In good weather, take breakfast, which includes excellent omelets and pancakes, in the flower-bedecked courtyard. Because the hotel has so few rooms, you need to book well ahead.

Keizersgracht 618 (at Nieuwe Spiegelstraat), 1017 ER Amsterdam. ✆ 020/622-2855. Fax 020/624-8412. www.hotelkeizershof.nl. 4 units. 90€–110€ ($144–$176) double with bathroom; 80€ ($128) double without bathroom. Rates include Dutch breakfast. MC, V. Limited street parking. Tram: 16, 24, or 25 to Keizersgracht. *In room:* Coffeemaker, hair dryer, safe, no phone.

Prinsenhof ★   This modernized canal house near the Amstel River offers rooms with beamed ceilings and basic—yet tolerably comfortable—beds. The place was recently refurbished with, among other additions, new showers and carpets. Front rooms look out onto Prinsengracht, where colorful houseboats are moored. Breakfast takes place in an attractive blue-and-white dining room. The proprietors, Rik and André van Houten, take pride in their hotel and will make you feel welcome. There's no elevator, but a pulley hauls your luggage up and down the stairs.

5

(Moments) In Search of Gezelligheid

When in Amsterdam, do as the Dutch do: Look for someplace *gezellig,* and treasure it if you find it.

So what is *gezellig,* or *gezelligheid* (the state of being *gezellig*)?

Ah . . . it's a simple idea, yet one that underlines everyday life. Indeed, it's one of those imprecise, enigmatic, and finally untranslatable-in-a-single-word concepts for a mood and attitude that you'll recognize right away when you find it, and then you'll say with quiet satisfaction, "This looks *gezellig.*"

So what *is* it then?

The special something that makes a place comfortable, congenial, cozy, familiar, friendly, intimate, memorable, tolerant, warm, and welcoming. Dutch, in short. You find it in abundance in brown cafes, in candlelit restaurants where the atmosphere is unforced and there's a view of a softly illuminated canal, in a Dutch home where you're made to feel like one of the family, even on a packed-to-bursting tram where everyone is in good humor and sees the funny side of the situation.

The great thing about *gezelligheid* is that it's free. Box some up and take it home with you.

Prinsengracht 810 (at Utrechtsestraat), 1017 JL Amsterdam. (C) **020/623-1772.** Fax 020/638-3368. www. hotelprinsenhof.com. 11 units, 6 with bathroom. 89€ ($142) double with bathroom; 69€ ($110) double without bathroom. Rates include buffet breakfast. AE, MC, V. Limited street parking. Tram: 4 to Prinsengracht. *In room:* No phone.

5 LEIDSEPLEIN

EXPENSIVE

Amsterdam American ★★ One of the most fanciful buildings on Amsterdam's long list of monuments, this castle-like mix of Venetian Gothic and Art Nouveau has been a prominent landmark and a popular meeting place for Amsterdammers since 1900. While the exterior must always remain an architectural treasure curiosity of turrets, arches, and balconies, the interior (except that of the cafe, which is also protected) is modern and chic. Rooms are subdued and refined, superbly furnished, and gifted with great vistas: Some have a view of the Singelgracht, while others overlook kaleidoscopic Leidseplein. The location, in the thick of the action and near many major attractions, is one of the best in town. Famous **Café Americain** is one of Europe's most elegant eateries (p. 124). There is also the **Bar Americain,** which has a closed-in terrace looking out on Leidseplein.

Leidsekade 97 (at Leidseplein), 1017 PN Amsterdam. (C) **020/556-3000.** Fax 020/556-3001. www.amsterdam american.com. 175 units. 120€–280€ ($192–$448) double; from 395€ ($632) suite. AE, DC, MC, V. No parking. Tram: 1, 2, 5, 7, or 10 to Leidseplein. **Amenities:** Restaurant; bar; exercise room; sauna; electric scooters; concierge; room service; laundry service; same-day dry cleaning; all rooms smoke-free. *In room:* A/C, TV, high-speed Internet, minibar, coffeemaker, hair dryer, iron, safe.

Paper Ploy

Cheeky but true: If you are on a very tight budget, or can't pass up a chance to save a buck, go to a top hotel's lobby to read the daily papers for free and in comfort. Many elite hotels have giveaway or lobby-only copies of the *International Herald Tribune,* the *Wall Street Journal Europe,* and the *Financial Times.* On second thought, if you're reading to check the health of your financial instruments, you can likely afford to buy your own paper.

MODERATE

Orfeo   One of the city's longest-standing gay lodgings has for more than 30 years been providing basic, practical facilities and friendly, helpful service at low rates. The front desk is in a cozy and sociable lounge, and the breakfast room has marble flooring. Only three guest rooms have a full bathroom; others share a shower or toilet or both. A perk is the small in-house Finnish sauna; it doesn't hurt either that the largest concentration of city-center restaurants is right on the doorstep.

Leidsekruisstraat 12–14 (off Leidseplein), 1017 RH Amsterdam. ✆ **020/623-1347.** Fax 020/620-2348. www. hotelorfeo.com. 19 units, 3 with bathroom. 120€–150€ ($192–$240) double with bathroom; 55€–95€ ($88–$152) double without bathroom. Rates include continental breakfast. AE, MC, V. Limited street parking. Tram: 1, 2, or 5 to Prinsengracht. **Amenities:** Restaurant; bar. *In room:* TV, minibar, hair dryer, safe.

6 REMBRANDTPLEIN

EXPENSIVE

NH Schiller Hotel ★   An Amsterdam gem from 1912, this hotel, now fully restored, blends Art Nouveau and Art Deco in public spaces and in guest rooms' tasteful decor and furnishings. Its sculpted facade, wrought-iron balconies, and stained-glass windows stand out on the often brash Rembrandtplein. **Café Schiller,** next door to the hotel, is one of Amsterdam's trendiest watering holes. The hotel is named for the painter Frits Schiller, who built it in 1912. His outpourings of artistic expression, in the form of 600 portraits, landscapes, and still lifes, are displayed in halls, rooms, stairwells, and public areas; their presence fills this hotel with a unique sense of vitality and creativity. Experience classic French and Dutch cuisine and the hotel's own beer, Frisse Frits, in the Art Nouveau **Brasserie Schiller** (p. 126), or join the in-crowd next door for a drink amid the Art Deco splendor of **Café Schiller** (p. 239). *Note*: This hotel has been awarded a Green Key certificate for its environmental awareness and sustainable practices.

Rembrandtplein 26–36, 1017 CV Amsterdam. ✆ **020/554-0700.** Fax 020/624-0098. www.nh-hotels. com. 92 units. 139€–203€ ($222–$325) double. AE, DC, MC, V. Limited street parking. Tram: 4, 9, or 14 to Rembrandtplein. **Amenities:** Restaurant; lounge; 2 bars; room service; in-room massage; babysitting; laundry service; same-day dry cleaning; executive rooms. *In room:* TV, high-speed Internet, minibar, coffeemaker, hair dryer, iron, safe.

MODERATE

Eden Hotel Amsterdam   The biggest center-city hotel in its class has a great setting in several converted 17th-century merchants' houses (and a chocolate factory) beside the

Amstel River, just behind Rembrandtplein. Rooms vary quite a lot in size, with some of them on the small side. Still, they're all well cared-for and have bright, modern furnishings. Many have a fine view of the river, and these are the most desirable—and most expensive. The **Pipa's** bar, overlooking the river, is a good place to kick back after a day's sightseeing. *Note*: This hotel has been awarded a Green Key certificate for its environmental awareness and sustainable practices.

Amstel 144 (across the river from the Muziektheater), 1017 AE Amsterdam. © **020/530-7888.** Fax 020/623-3267. www.edenhotelgroup.com. 218 units. 175€–200€ ($280–$320) double. AE, DC, MC, V. Limited street parking. Tram: 4 or 9 to Rembrandtplein. **Amenities:** Bar; bikes and motor scooters; concierge; laundry service; dry cleaning. *In room:* A/C, TV, high-speed Internet, hair dryer, safe.

7 THE JORDAAN

INEXPENSIVE

Acacia Though it's not on one of the major canals, Acacia is in the Jordaan and faces a small canal just a block from Prinsengracht. Hans and Marlene van Vliet run this pie-slice-shaped hotel; they're a friendly couple who have worked hard to make their hotel welcoming and clean, and they're justifiably proud of the result. The simple, well-kept, and comfortable rooms, all of which have canal views, were recently equipped with new beds, writing tables, and chairs. The large front-corner rooms sleep as many as five and have windows on three sides. A couple of studios have tiny kitchenettes. Breakfast (of cold cuts, cheese, a boiled egg, and a choice of coffee or tea) is served in a cozy Old Dutch room with windows on two sides and a nice canal view. There's no elevator. Two houseboats available for guests on nearby Lijnbaansgracht add an authentic local touch.

Lindengracht 251 (at Lijnbaansgracht), 1015 KH, Amsterdam. © **020/622-1460.** Fax 020/638-0748. www.hotelacacia.nl. 16 units (including 2 houseboats). 80€–90€ ($128–$144) double; 95€–110€ ($152–$176) houseboat double. Rates include continental breakfast. MC, V (5% charge). Limited street parking. Tram: 3 or 10 to Marnixplein. *In room:* TV.

Van Onna (Value) Consisting of three canal houses, the center one dating from 1644, this hotel has grown over the years, but genial owner Loek van Onna continues to keep prices reasonable. Mr. van Onna has lived here since he was a boy and will gladly regale you with tales about the building's history. Accommodations vary considerably, with the best rooms in the newest building. However, even the oldest, plainest rooms have character, and all are both neatly furnished and clean. Whichever building you wind up in, request a front room overlooking the canal. There's no elevator.

Bloemgracht 102–104 and 108 (off Prinsengracht), 1015 TN Amsterdam. © **020/626-5801.** www.hotel vanonna.com. 41 units. 90€ ($144) double. Rates include continental breakfast. No credit cards. Limited street parking. Tram: 13, 14, or 17 to Westermarkt. **Amenities:** All rooms smoke-free. *In room:* No phone.

(Tips) Booking a B&B

B&B accommodations are available by contacting **Bed & Breakfast Holland** (© 020/615-7527; www.bedandbreakfastholland.nl). Rates per person range from 30€ to 240€ ($48–$384), depending on amenities, location, and season. There's generally a 2-night minimum stay.

EXPENSIVE

Bilderberg Hotel Jan Luyken   One block from the Van Gogh Museum and from the elegant Pieter Cornelisz Hooftstraat shopping street, the Jan Luyken is a small boutique hotel with many of the amenities and facilities of a large one—though without the large rooms. Everything here is done with perfect attention to detail; there's a balance between sophisticated facilities (double sinks and bidets, an elevator, a lobby bar with fireplace, and meeting rooms for business) and an intimate and personalized approach that's apropos for this 19th-century residential neighborhood. That residential feel extends to the rooms, which look much more like they belong in a well-designed home than a hotel. The proprietors are proud of the atmosphere they've created, and are constantly improving the hotel's appearance.

Jan Luijkenstraat 58 (near the Rijksmuseum), 1071 CS Amsterdam. ℂ **020/573-0730.** Fax 020/676-3841. www.janluyken.nl. 62 units. 129€–179€ ($206–$286) double. AE, DC, MC, V. Limited street parking. Tram: 2 or 5 to Hobbemastraat. **Amenities:** Wine bar; lounge; spa (small); bikes; concierge; room service; in-room massage; babysitting; laundry service; same-day dry cleaning; all rooms smoke-free. *In room:* A/C, TV, minibar, hair dryer, iron, safe.

MODERATE

Acro ★   The Acro, in a town house on a fairly quiet street near Vondelpark and close to the main museums, appeals especially to young travelers. The hotel is modern on the inside, with crisp-and-clean bedspreads and light-blue-gray walls. Most rooms have twin beds—some have three and some four. The hotel bar has more ambience than many street cafes. The Acro definitely offers value for your money.

Jan Luijkenstraat 44 (near the Rijksmuseum), 1071 CR Amsterdam. ℂ **020/662-0526.** Fax 020/675-0811. www.acro-hotel.nl. 65 units. 80€–160€ ($128–$256) double. Rates include buffet breakfast. AE, DC, MC, V. Limited street parking. Tram: 2 or 5 to Hobbemastraat. **Amenities:** Bar; bikes. *In room:* TV, high-speed Internet, hair dryer.

Atlas   Off van Baerlestraat, the Atlas is a converted Art Nouveau house with a convenient location for shoppers, concertgoers, and museum lovers. Staffers back up the homey feel with attentive service. Guest rooms are small but tidy, decorated attractively in gray with blue comforters and a welcoming fruit basket on the desk. Leather chairs fill the front lounge, where a grandfather clock ticks away in the corner. A small bar/restaurant provides 24-hour room service.

Van Eeghenstraat 64 (near Vondelpark), 1071 GK Amsterdam. ℂ **020/676-6336.** Fax 020/671-7633. www.hotelatlas.nl. 23 units. 90€–180€ ($144–$288) double. Rates include continental breakfast. AE, DC, MC, V. Limited street parking. Tram: 2, 3, 5, or 12 to van Baerlestraat. **Amenities:** Bar; dry cleaning (Mon–Fri). *In room:* TV, high-speed Internet, hair dryer.

De Filosoof ★ (Finds)   On a quiet street facing Vondelpark, this hotel might be your place if you fancy yourself something of a philosopher. One of the proprietors, a philosophy professor, has chosen posters, painted ceilings, framed quotes, and unusual objects to represent philosophical and cultural themes; the garden is a grove of academe. Each room is dedicated to a mental maestro—Aristotle, Plato, Goethe, Wittgenstein, Nietzsche, Marx, and Einstein among them—or is based on motifs like Eros, the Renaissance, astrology, or femininity. To join the intellectual melee, consult your private bookshelf or join in a weekly philosophy debate. Rooms in an annex across the street are larger, and some open onto a private terrace. Regular improvements keep the property up-to-date.

Anna van den Vondelstraat 6 (off Overtoom, at Vondelpark), 1054 GZ Amsterdam. © **020/683-3013.** Fax 020/685-3750. www.hotelfilosoof.nl. 38 units. 105€–180€ ($168–$288) double. Rates include buffet breakfast. AE, MC, V. Limited street parking. Tram: 1 to Jan Pieter Heijestraat. **Amenities:** Lounge. *In room:* TV, safe.

Owl Hotel   If small but chic and reasonably priced describes the sort of hotel you prefer, you'll be pleased at the Owl, in the pleasant residential area around Vondelpark, behind the Marriott. One of Amsterdam's best values, the Owl has been owned by the same family since 1972 and is bright, tidy, and well kept. Rooms aren't very big, but they're not cramped either, and they've all been recently renovated. Bathrooms are tiled floor to ceiling, and there's a pleasant lounge bar overlooking a small garden.

Roemer Visscherstraat 1 (off Stadhouderskade), 1054 EV Amsterdam. © **020/618-9484.** Fax 020/618-9441. www.owl-hotel.nl. 34 units. 130€ ($208) double. Rates include buffet breakfast. AE, DC, MC, V. Limited street parking. Tram: 1 to Stadhouderskade. **Amenities:** Lounge; bar; room service; babysitting; laundry service; dry cleaning. *In room:* TV, high-speed Internet, hair dryer.

Piet Hein   Facing Vondelpark, and close to Amsterdam's important museums, this appealing, well-kept Art Nouveau villa hotel is named after a 17th-century Dutch admiral who captured a Spanish silver shipment. Its spacious rooms have all been modernized recently and are furnished with a subtle nautical theme. Half the rooms overlook the park; two second-floor double rooms have semicircular balconies. Lower-priced rooms are in an annex behind the main hotel. In summer the bar sets tables and chairs out on the garden terrace.

Vossiusstraat 53 (off van Baerlestraat), 1071 AK Amsterdam. © **020/662-7205.** Fax 020/662-1526. www.hotelpiethein.nl. 65 units. 120€–225€ ($192–$360) double; 295€–325€ ($472–$520) suite. Rates include continental breakfast. AE, DC, MC, V. Limited street parking. Tram: 3, 5, or 12 to Van Baerlestraat. **Amenities:** Bar; room service; dry cleaning; all rooms smoke-free. *In room:* TV, high-speed Internet, hair dryer, safe.

Toro ★   On Vondelpark's edge in a quiet residential district, this hotel in a renovated Art Nouveau mansion (ca. 1900) is a good choice. Both inside and out, it's as near as you can get in Amsterdam to staying in a country villa. Furnishings and decor are tasteful, and combine Louis XIV and Liberty styles while featuring stained-glass windows and Murano chandeliers. The house also has a private garden and terrace. It's about a 10-minute walk through Vondelpark to Leidseplein.

Koningslaan 64 (off Oranje Nassaulaan), 1075 AG Amsterdam. © **020/673-7223.** Fax 020/675-0031. www.hoteltoro.nl. 22 units. 120€–240€ ($192–$384) double. AE, MC, V. Limited street parking. Tram: 2 to Valeriusplein. **Amenities:** Laundry service; dry cleaning; smoke-free rooms. *In room:* A/C, TV/DVD, high-speed Internet, minibar, coffeemaker, hair dryer, safe.

Van de Kasteelen   On a quiet side street not far from the **Van Gogh Museum** (p. 142), this hotel is owned by a gracious Indonesian family. The smallish guest rooms are outfitted with a minor-key classic elegance. Wood furnishings, bright and adjustable lighting, firm mattresses, and fine drapes all indicate that the proprietors have taken great care to create a comfort zone. Bathrooms, which have a combination tub/shower, are large in relation to room size; there's space enough for two at morning *toilette,* provided neither has sharp elbows. A small patio-garden out back is a pleasant place to relax in fine weather. Van de Kasteelen lies between tram stops, but isn't too far from them.

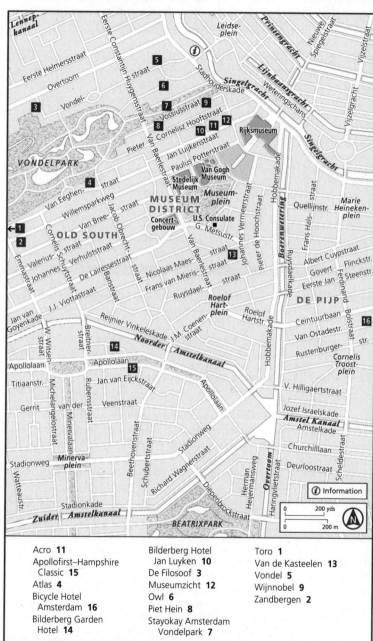

Acro **11**

Apollofirst–Hampshire
Classic **15**

Atlas **4**

Bicycle Hotel
Amsterdam **16**

Bilderberg Garden
Hotel **14**

Bilderberg Hotel
Jan Luyken **10**

De Filosoof **3**

Museumzicht **12**

Owl **6**

Piet Hein **8**

Stayokay Amsterdam
Vondelpark **7**

Toro **1**

Van de Kasteelen **13**

Vondel **5**

Wijnnobel **9**

Zandbergen **2**

Frans van Mierisstraat 34 (off van Baerlestraat), 1071 RT Amsterdam. ℂ **020/679-8995.** Fax 020/670-6604. www.hotelvandekasteelen.com. 14 units. 120€–250€ ($192–$400) double. Rates include continental breakfast. AE, MC, V. Limited street parking. Tram: 16 to Johannes Vermeerplein. **Amenities:** Lounge; laundry service; all rooms smoke-free. *In room:* TV, high-speed Internet, minibar (except in 1 single room), hair dryer, safe.

Vondel ★   Named after the famous 17th-century Dutch poet Joost van den Vondel, this hotel in six connected town houses has become one of Amsterdam's leading four-star hotels since its 1993 opening. Each room is named after one of Vondel's poems, like *Lucifer* and *Solomon*. Three of the first-floor rooms are ideal for travelers with disabilities. The furniture is solid, the rooms are spacious, the windows are soundproof, and the service is good. Vondel is comfortable, and it's in a quiet and popular area close to the museum area and Leidseplein.

Vondelstraat 26 (off Stadhouderskade), 1054 GE Amsterdam. ℂ **020/515-0455.** Fax 020/505-0451. www.hotelvondel.nl. 85 units. 170€–205€ ($272–$328) double; 295€ ($184) suite. Rates include buffet breakfast. AE, DC, MC, V. Limited street parking. Tram: 1 to Eerste Constantijn Huygensstraat; 3 or 12 to Overtoom. **Amenities:** Bar; bikes; room service; babysitting; all rooms smoke-free. *In room:* TV, high-speed Internet, minibar, hair dryer.

Zandbergen   Beside Vondelpark, this place nearly outdoes the InterContinental Amstel Amsterdam (p. 100) in its use of shiny brass handrails and door handles. Rebuilt in 1979, and modernized since then, the Hotel Zandbergen is efficiently divided into a variety of room types and sizes with simple but attractive brick-wall dividers between rooms. Wall-to-wall carpets and a bright-toned color scheme make the rooms seem more spacious and inviting; all are outfitted with some flair and have comfortable beds. There's also a great family-size room with a garden patio for up to four guests. Recent improvements include new bathrooms and air-conditioning in reception and breakfast areas.

Willemsparkweg 205 (at Vondelpark), 1071 HB Amsterdam. ℂ **020/676-9321.** Fax 020/676-1860. www.hotel-zandbergen.com. 18 units. 115€–160€ ($184–$256) double. Rates include buffet breakfast. AE, DC, MC, V. Limited street parking. Tram: 2 to Emmastraat. **Amenities:** Secretarial services; laundry service; dry cleaning; all rooms smoke-free. *In room:* TV, minibar (most rooms), hair dryer.

INEXPENSIVE

Museumzicht ★   This hotel, in a town house that dates from 1890 across from the Rijksmuseum's rear, is ideal for museumgoers on a budget. The breakfast room, which has numerous stained-glass windows, commands an excellent view of the museum. Proprietor Robin de Jong filled guest rooms with eclectic furniture that spans from the 1930s (think English wicker) to the 1950s. Note that there's no elevator and the staircase up to reception is quite steep.

Jan Luijkenstraat 22 (facing the Rijksmuseum), 1071 CN Amsterdam. ℂ **020/671-2954.** Fax 020/671-3597. www.hotelmuseumzicht.nl. 14 units, 3 with bathroom. 98€ ($157) double with bathroom; 78€ ($125) double without bathroom. Rates include continental breakfast. AE, DC, MC, V. Limited street parking. Tram: 2 or 5 to Hobbemastraat. **Amenities:** Lounge; room service (coffee and tea). *In room:* No phone.

Stayokay Amsterdam Vondelpark (Kids)   "The new generation of city hostel" is how the Dutch youth hostel organization NJHC describes this marvelous budget lodging just inside Vondelpark. The location, facing Leidseplein, could hardly be better for youthful spirits who want to be near the action. At the hostel's core is a former girls' school that's now a protected monument. All of the simple-but-modern rooms are brightly furnished, clean, and have an en suite bathroom. The four- and six-bed rooms are ideal for families traveling on a limited budget and for groups of friends. Some rooms are suitable for people with disabilities. Although the hostel is open 24 hours a day, security is taken seriously, and all guests have key cards. Internet stations are available for those who must surf, and the **Backpacker's Lounge** is a pleasant place to meet fellow travelers. In summer, a low-cost Schiphol Airport shuttle is available.

Zandpad 5 (in Vondelpark), 1054 GA Amsterdam. ✆ 020/589-8996. Fax 020/589-8955. www.stayokay.com/vondelpark. 105 units (536 beds). 22€–31€ ($35–$50) dorm bed; 24€–31€ ($38–$50) per person in 4- to 8-bed rooms; 70€–195€ ($112–$312) per room for 2- to 8-bed rooms; 2.50€ ($4) reduction for IYHF members. Rates include buffet breakfast. AE, MC, V. No parking. Tram: 1, 2, 5, 7, or 10 to Leidseplein. **Amenities:** Restaurant; lounge/bar; high-speed Internet in lobby; bikes; coin-op washers and dryers; smoke-free rooms. *In room:* No phone.

Wijnnobel   Just around the corner from the boutiques on Pieter Cornelisz Hooftstraat and only a few minutes' walk from the Rijksmuseum, this hotel overlooks a corner of Vondelpark. One way they make their guests happy is by serving in-room breakfast (there's no breakfast lounge). In addition, elderly proprietor Pierre Wijnnobel plays some perfectly acceptable Gershwin, Cole Porter, and Chopin on the piano in his private lounge. The large rooms are furnished with old-fashioned or antique pieces; the smaller ones are very small. A steep but striking central stairway leads to the hotel's four floors. Note that each floor has only one bathroom, and one shower room, so you might have to share.

Vossiusstraat 9 (at Hobbemastraat), 1071 AB Amsterdam. ✆ 020/662-2298. www.hotelwijnnobel.com. 12 units, none with bathroom. 50€–75€ ($80–$120) double. Rates include continental breakfast. No credit cards. Limited street parking. Tram: 2 or 5 to Hobbemastraat. *In room:* No phone.

---

9 AMSTERDAM SOUTH

EXPENSIVE

Bilderberg Garden Hotel ★   Amsterdam's most personal five-star hotel is set in a leafy corner along the Amstelkanaal. Because of its excellent restaurant, the Garden considers itself a "culinary hotel," an idea that extends to the rooms, whose color schemes are salad-green, salmon-pink, cherry-red, and grape-blue—you can choose whichever suits you best. The rooms themselves are furnished and equipped to a high standard and with refined taste. Bathrooms are marble, and each executive room has a Jacuzzi tub. The spectacular lobby has a wall-to-wall fireplace with a copper-sheathed chimney. A deserved international reputation attaches to the superb French-Mediterranean **Mangerie de Kersentuin (Cherry Orchard)** restaurant (p. ###); all things considered, its menu is reasonably priced. The **Kersepit (Cherry Pit)** is a cozy bar with an open fireplace and a vast range of Scotch whiskeys.

Dijsselhofplantsoen 7 (at Apollolaan), 1077 BJ Amsterdam. ✆ 020/570-5600. Fax 020/570-5654. www.gardenhotel.nl. 124 units. 325€–375€ ($520–$600) double. AE, DC, MC, V. Limited street parking. Tram: 5 or 24 to Apollolaan. **Amenities:** Restaurant; bar; concierge; secretarial services; room service; babysitting; laundry service; same-day dry cleaning; all rooms smoke-free; executive rooms. *In room:* A/C, TV, high-speed Internet, minibar, coffeemaker, hair dryer, safe.

MODERATE

Apollofirst – Hampshire Classic   The small and elegant Apollofirst, a family-owned hotel set amid the Amsterdam-school architecture of Apollolaan, advertises itself as the "best quarters in town in the town's best quarter." Their claim may be debatable, but the Venman family's justifiable pride in their intimate establishment is not. All accommodations are quiet, spacious, and grandly furnished. Bathrooms are fully tiled, and rooms at the hotel's rear overlook well-kept gardens and the summer terrace where guests have cocktails and snacks. The hotel's elegant **Restaurant Chambertin** is a French *fin de siècle* affair.

Apollolaan 123 (off Minervalaan), 1077 AP Amsterdam. © **020/577-3800.** Fax 020/675-0348. www. hampshire-hotels.com. 40 units. 135€–185€ ($216–$296) double; 275€ ($440) suite. Rates include continental breakfast. AE, DC, MC, V. Limited street parking. Tram: 5 or 24 to Apollolaan. **Amenities:** Bar; room service; babysitting; laundry service; dry cleaning; all rooms smoke-free. *In room:* TV, high-speed Internet, hair dryer, safe.

INEXPENSIVE

Bicycle Hotel Amsterdam ★ This establishment's young owners hit on a cool idea: Cater to visitors who wish to explore Amsterdam by bike. They're helpful in planning biking routes through and around the city. You can rent bikes for 7.50€ ($12) daily, no deposit, and stable your trusty steed indoors. The recently renovated rooms have new carpets and plain but comfortable modern furnishings; some have kitchenettes and small balconies, and there are large rooms for families. The hotel is a few blocks from the popular **Albert Cuyp street market** (p. 221), in the hip De Pijp neighborhood. Two old bicycles hang 6m (20 ft.) high on the hotel's facade, and there are always bikes parked in front. There's no elevator.

Van Ostadestraat 123 (off Ferdinand Bolstraat), Amsterdam 1072 SV. © **020/679-3452.** Fax 020/671-5213. www.bicyclehotel.com. 16 units, 8 with bathroom. 80€–120€ ($128–$192) double with bathroom; 50€–85€ ($80–$136) double without bathroom. Rates include Dutch breakfast. AE, MC, V. Parking 20€ ($32). Tram: 3, 12, or 25 to Ceintuurbaan/Ferdinand Bolstraat. **Amenities:** Lounge; bikes. *In room:* TV.

10 AMSTERDAM EAST

VERY EXPENSIVE

InterContinental Amstel Amsterdam ★★★ The stately Amstel has been the grande dame of Amsterdam hotels since its 1867 opening. It offers the ultimate in luxury, which is why you might spy visiting royalty and superstars hiding from eager fans here. The Amstel's only possible fault is that it may seem to run a bit *too* smoothly, with a level of perfection that's almost creepy. The hotel sports a mansard roof and wrought-iron window guards, a graceful Grand Hall, and rooms that boast all the elegance of a country manor, complete with antiques and genuine Delft blue porcelain. The Italian marble bathrooms have separate toilets and showers, and staffers note each guest's personal preferences for his or her next visit. The French **La Rive** restaurant is one of the hallowed temples of Amsterdam cuisine (p. 134). The **Amstel Bar & Brasserie** and terraces overlooking the river are more informal.

Prof. Tulpplein 1 (at the Torontobrug over the Amstel River), 1018 GX Amsterdam. © **800/327-0200** in the U.S. and Canada, or 020/622-6060. Fax 020/622-5808. www.interconti.com. 79 units. 510€–620€ ($816–$992) double; from 840€ ($1,344) suite. AE, DC, MC, V. Tram: 7 or 10 to Weesperplein. **Amenities:** Restaurant; lounge; bar-brasserie; heated indoor pool; health club and spa; concierge; business center; room service; laundry service; same-day dry cleaning; smoke-free rooms; executive rooms. *In room:* A/C, TV/DVD/VCR, high-speed Internet, CD player, minibar, hair dryer, safe.

MODERATE

Arena ★ A converted Roman Catholic orphanage from 1890 houses a friendly, stylish, youth-oriented hotel. Although the exterior bears a passing resemblance to Dracula's castle,

Impressions

I had in my mind's eye a perfect bed in a perfect hostelry hard by the Amstel River.
—Erskine Childers, *The Riddle of the Sands* (1903)

the interior proves they really knew how to do orphanages in those days. Monumental marble staircases, cast-iron banisters, stained-glass windows, marble columns, and original murals have all been faithfully restored. The rambling spaces where the dormitories once were now house stylish doubles and twins. Spare modern rooms, some that are split-level, and some that sport timber roof beams and wooden floors, are individually decorated by young up-and-coming Dutch designers. The Continental cafe-restaurant **To Dine** looks a little like an upgraded cafeteria, but has a great alfresco terrace in the garden and an attached bar, **To Drink.** Hotel guests get discounted admission to the nightclub **To Night,** which spins music from the 1960s onward in the old orphanage chapel.

's-Gravesandestraat 51 (at Mauritskade), 1092 AA Amsterdam. ✆ **020/850-2410.** Fax 020/850-2415. www.hotelarena.nl. 127 units. 100€–160€ ($160–$256) double; 195€–295€ ($312–$472) suite. Rates include buffet breakfast. AE, DC, MC, V. Free parking. Tram: 7 or 10 to Korte 's-Gravesandestraat. **Amenities:** Restaurant; bar; executive rooms. *In room:* TV.

Bridge Hotel ★   The bridge in question is the famous **Magere Brug (Skinny Bridge)** over the Amstel River (p. 158). This small, tastefully decorated hotel likely provides guests with more space per euro than any other hotel in town. Its pine-furnished rooms seem like studio apartments, with couches, coffee tables, and easy chairs arranged in lounge areas in such a way that there's plenty of room left between them and the beds for you to do your morning exercises. There's no elevator.

Amstel 107–111 (near Koninklijk Theater Carré), 1018 EM Amsterdam. ✆ **020/623-7068.** Fax 020/624-1565. www.thebridgehotel.nl. 46 units. 115€–170€ ($184–$272); double; 180€–295€ ($288–$472) apt. Rates include continental breakfast. AE, DC, MC, V. Limited street parking. Tram: 7 or 10 to Weesperplein. **Amenities:** Lounge; laundry service; all rooms smoke-free. *In room:* TV, high-speed Internet.

11 AT & NEAR THE AIRPORT

EXPENSIVE

Ibis Amsterdam Airport   A more reasonably priced alternative to the Sheraton (see below), and still close to the airport, is the Ibis, a standard modern chain hotel housed in a tinted-glass cube. It may have little in the way of character—none at all, really—but this French-run property provides perfectly good facilities for travelers in transit, and is comfortable in an efficient kind of way. Relax over a drink in the **Red Baron Bar.**

Schipholweg 181, 1171 PK Badhoevedorp. ✆ **800/515-5679** in the U.S. and Canada, or 020/502-5100. Fax 020/657-0199. www.ibishotel.com. 644 units. 195€–250€ ($312–$400) double. AE, DC, MC, V. Free parking. **Amenities:** Restaurant; heated indoor pool; indoor and outdoor tennis courts; health club; sauna; concierge; free airport transfers; business center; room service; laundry service; dry cleaning; all rooms smoke-free. *In room:* A/C, TV, high-speed Internet, minibar, coffeemaker, hair dryer.

Sheraton Amsterdam Airport ★   You could only be more convenient to the airport by lodging on the runway. All the comfort you would expect of a top-flight Sheraton is here, including soundproof rooms with big, comfortable beds, marble bathrooms with

(Fun Facts   **Bed Rest**

In 1969, John Lennon and Yoko Ono "drove from Paris to the Amsterdam Hilton" to do their famous Bed-In For Peace, from March 15 to March 31, in the hotel's room no. 902. This is now the expensive John and Yoko Suite. The Hilton is at Apollolaan 138 in Amsterdam South ((C) **020/710-6000**).

separate shower, and the well-equipped Oasis health club with pool. That said, the Sheraton is no fount of Dutch tradition. Blocky and modern is the kindest description I can muster about the exterior, which is what you'd expect of a hotel at this location. The inside story is better, with rooms that bring a touch of style to their mission of lodging itinerant businesspeople. Room styles range from modern and functional to unashamed luxury in the suites. The **Voyager** restaurant has an international a la carte menu. The Dutch-style **Runway Café** serves drinks and snacks.

Schiphol Blvd. 101 (outside Schiphol Plaza), 1118 BG Amsterdam. (C) **800/325-3535** in the U.S. and Canada, or 020/316-4300. Fax 020/316-4399. www.starwoodhotels.com. 406 units. 160€–330€ ($256–$528) double; from 930€ ($1,488) suite. AE, DC, MC, V. Parking 35€ ($56). **Amenities:** 2 restaurants; 2 bars; heated indoor pool; health club; concierge; business center; room service; babysitting; laundry service; same-day dry cleaning; smoke-free rooms; executive rooms. *In room:* A/C, TV, high-speed Internet, mini-bar, coffeemaker, hair dryer, safe.

INEXPENSIVE

Etap   A worthwhile option for budget travelers, this bare-bones facility, one of a French-owned chain, misses no opportunity to leave luxury at the door. Etap hotels used to sport a front-door notice (or warning): "You are now entering a luxury-free zone." And what Benjamin was told in *The Graduate*—that plastics are the future—could have been taken from the Etap manual. But the rooms can accommodate three people, in twin beds and a bunk bed, making them ideal for a one-kid family. The hotel is just 7 minutes from Schiphol by way of a free hotel shuttle.

Schipholweg 185, 1171 PK Badhoevedorp ((C) **800/515-5679** in the U.S. and Canada, or 020/348-3533. www.etaphotel.com. 118 units. 65€ ($104) double. AE, DC, MC, V. Free parking. **Amenities:** Free airport transfers. *In room:* TV.

Where to Dine

If cities get the cuisine they deserve, Amsterdam's ought to be liberal, multiethnic, and adventurous. Guess what? It is. A port and trading city with a true melting-pot character, this city has absorbed culinary influences from far, wide, and yonder, and rustled them all up to its own satisfaction. Just about every international cuisine type can be found on the city's restaurant roster. In Amsterdam, they say, you can eat in any language. More than 50 national cuisines are represented in restaurants here—and many of these eateries satisfy the sturdy Dutch insistence on getting maximum value out of every euro.

From elegant 17th-century dining rooms to cozy canalside bistros, to boisterous taverns with exuberant Greek waitstaff to exotic Indonesian rooms attended by turbaned waiters, to the *bruine kroegjes* (brown cafes) with smoke-stained walls and friendly table conversations, Amsterdam's eateries confront the tourist with the exquisite agony of being able to choose only one or two from their vast numbers (in all price ranges) each day. Dutch cooking, of course, is part of all this, but you won't be stuck with *biefstuk* (beefsteak) and *kip* (chicken) every night.

A relatively recent and popular trend is the **grand cafe** scene. These are cafes in the, well, grand tradition of Paris, Vienna, and Rome, with lots of style, ambience, and balconies or terraces—see-and-be-seen places. Grand cafes are distinguished by their emphasis on food and drink, architecture, production values, and style. The definition is an elusive one: The grand cafes listed below truly are grand, but be aware that others use the name even though they may not be particularly impressive.

RESTAURANT ORIENTATION

DINING HOURS Most restaurants are open from noon to 2:30pm for lunch, and from 6 or 7 to 10 or 11pm. Many kitchens are closed by 10pm. It's wise not to make reservations for 8pm or after, if you want to enjoy a relaxed, unhurried meal. Even if a restaurant is open until 11pm or midnight, you won't get served unless you arrive well before then—how much before varies with the restaurant, and maybe with the mood of the staff, but it should be at least 30 minutes in moderate and budget places, and at least an hour in more upscale venues. Recently, restaurants have been staying open later.

RESERVATIONS On weekends, unless you eat especially early or late, reservations are recommended at top restaurants and at those on the high end of the moderate price range. Call ahead to check; restaurants are often small and may be crowded with neighborhood devotees. Note that restaurants with outside terraces are always in big demand on pleasant summer evenings and fill up fast; make a reservation, if the restaurant will let you—if not, get there early or forget it.

INFORMATION Good eating-out info is available online at www.specialbite.com, www.iens.nl, www.diningcity.nl, and www.dinnersite.nl.

TIPPING A 15% service charge *and* taxes (BTW) are included in all prices. For more, see appendix A, "Fast Facts, Toll-Free Numbers & Websites," p. 285.

> ### ⓘ Tips   Good-Eats Cafes
>
> For decent, low-cost food, look for examples of that Dutch dining institution, the *eetcafé* (pronounced *ayt*-caff-ay). Many of these—some of which are reviewed below—are essentially brown cafes (bars) with a hardworking kitchen attached. The food is unpretentious, mainstream Dutch (though some are more adventurous). The *dagschotel* (plate of the day), which might come with meat, vegetable, and salad on one plate, is usually 10€ to 15€ ($16–$24).

BUDGET DINING   Eating cheaply in Amsterdam is not an impossible dream. And, happily, in some cases you can even eat cheaply in style, with candles on the table, flowers in the window, and music in the air. And though there's no such thing as a free lunch, there might be a *dagschotel* (plate of the day) and a *dagmenu* (menu of the day), for usually decent food at a bargain rate. The practical Dutch don't like to spend unnecessary euros, so almost every neighborhood has a modestly priced restaurant or two, and new budget places are popping up all over town. Another way to combat high dinner tabs is to take advantage of the tourist menu that many restaurants offer.

LUNCH & SNACK COSTS   Lunch doesn't have to be an elaborate affair (save that for evening). Typical Dutch lunches are light, quick, and cheap (see "Eating & Drinking in Amsterdam," in chapter 2). A quick midday meal can cost 6€ to 12€ ($9.60–$19). An afternoon pit stop for a pastry and coffee will set you back 4€ to 6€ ($6.40–$9.60).

WINE   Estate-bottled imported wines are expensive in Holland, and even a bottle of modest French wine can add 12€ to 20€ ($19–$32) to a dinner tab. House wine, on the other hand—which may be a carefully selected French estate-bottled wine—will be a more economical choice in restaurants of any price level. Wine by the glass costs anywhere from 3€ to 10€ ($4.80–$16).

SMOKING   Since July 2008, smoking is no longer permitted in restaurants and cafes, except in a separate room or partitioned enclosure where staff will not serve customers.

1 BEST DINING BETS

- **Best for Opulence:** Royalty eats at **La Rive,** in the InterContinental Amstel Hotel, Professor Tulpplein 1 (⟨ⓒ⟩ **020/520-3264**), as do movie stars, rockers, opera divas, tennis standouts, and even ordinary folks with well-padded pocketbooks. It's highly opulent, the location is great, and the food is outstanding. See p. 134.
- **Best Value:** It breaks my heart to write this, because I know it will only make it harder to find a seat at **De Prins,** Prinsengracht 124 (⟨ⓒ⟩ **020/624-9382**). But duty calls. When you eat in this handsome, friendly, cozy, warm—in a Dutch word, *gezellig*—brown cafe–restaurant, you'll wonder why you paid twice as much for food half as good in that other place last night. See p. 122.
- **Best Grand Cafe:** A *New York Times* reviewer went so far as to call **Café Luxembourg,** Spuistraat 24 (⟨ⓒ⟩ **020/620-6264**), "one of the world's great cafes." But Luxembourg is great on an Amsterdam scale. That is to say, it's cozy and kind of intimate, with

WHERE TO DINE

6

BEST DINING BETS

little, if any, of the pretension that would normally go along with world-class status. See p. 114.

- **Best Traditional Dutch:** It sounds contradictory to say that **D'Vijff Vlieghen** ("The Five Flies"), Spuistraat 294–302 (© 020/530-4060), is touristy and still traditionally Dutch, but somehow it manages to be both. See p. 109.

- **Best Mexican: Rose's Cantina,** Reguliersdwarsstraat 38–40 (© 020/625-9797), is more a popular institution than truly great eatery, though the food can be quite good. There will probably be a wait for a table, during which Rose's deploys its secret weapon—marvelous margaritas. See p. 116.

- **Best Vegetarian: Bolhoed,** Prinsengracht 60–62 (© 020/626-1803), takes this title for its *joie de vivre,* romantic atmosphere, and excellent, imaginative vegetarian cuisine. See p. 119.

- **Best Sandwich:** The only problem with **Sal Meijer,** Scheldestraat 45 (© 020/673-1313), is that it's a bit removed from the action. They deliver, but their delicious authentic kosher sandwiches are well worth a tram ride. See p. 126.

- **Best Indonesian:** Every Amsterdammer has his or her own favorite place for that "traditional" Dutch dinner treat: Indonesian food. With so many Indonesian restaurants in the city, it's hard to pick just one. Still, **Kantjil & de Tijger,** Spuistraat 291–293 (© 020/620-0994), has a restrained, refined character and consistently good food. See p. 113.

- **Best Brunch:** At **Café Luxembourg,** Spuistraat 24 (© 020/620-6264), you can read international newspapers while drinking coffee that actually tastes like coffee and munching your way through an extensive range of breakfast plates, sandwiches, and snacks. See p. 114.

- **Best Business Lunch:** If it's a casual affair, many Amsterdam businesspeople will be perfectly happy with a snack from a seafood stall, but if you aim to impress, try the **Mangerie de Kersentuin,** in the Bilderberg Garden Hotel, Dijsselhofplantsoen 7 (© 020/570-5600). The cuisine perfectly complements the elegant, yet unstuffy surroundings. See p. 135.

- **Best Kids' Spot:** For small diners with big appetites, there can be no better experience than the **Kinderkookkafé,** Vondelpark 6B (© 020/625-3257), where kids (carefully supervised) even get to cook their own meals. See p. 115.

- **Best Late-Night Dinner:** You can't help feeling a little sorry for the staff at **De Knijp,** Van Baerlestraat 134 (© 020/671-4248), when you saunter in around midnight. They've been going hard for hours, but are ready, willing, and just about able to do it one more time. See p. 132.

(Tips) What's in a Name

There's Chinese food and there's Indonesian food. In Holland, there's Chinees-Indisch (Chinese-Indonesian) food, too. Watch out for this not-here-and-not-there genre. Chinees-Indisch restaurants are rarely, if ever, any good (there are plenty of these restaurants in Amsterdam, and I can't think of a single one worth recommending). Places that attempt this crossover style can't get either one right.

(Moments) Secrets of the Rijsttafel

The Indonesian *rijsttafel* is Holland's favorite feast; it has been ever since the United East India Company sea captains introduced it to the wealthy Amsterdam burghers in the 17th century. The *rijsttafel* (literally, "rice table") originated with Dutch plantation overseers in Indonesia, who liked to sample selectively from Indonesian cuisine. It became a tradition upheld by Indonesian migrants to Holland who opened restaurants and, knowing the Dutch fondness for *rijsttafel,* made it a standard menu item. *Rijsttafels* are only a small part of an Indonesian restaurant's menu, and there's a trend among the Dutch to look down on them as "just for tourists"; the Dutch generally have a good understanding of Indonesian cuisine and prefer to order an individual dish rather than the mixed hash of a *rijsttafel*. However, *rijsttafels* remain popular, and many Chinese, Japanese, Vietnamese, and Thai restaurants have copied the idea.

The basic concept of a *rijsttafel* is to eat a bit of this and a bit of that, blending flavors and textures. A simple, unadorned bed of rice is the base and mediator between spicy meats and bland vegetables or fruits, between sweet-and-sour tastes and soft-and-crunchy textures. Although a *rijsttafel* for one is possible, it's better shared by two or more people. In the case of a solitary diner or a couple, a 17-dish *rijsttafel* will be enough; with four or more, order a 24- or 30-dish *rijsttafel* and experience the total taste treat.

Before you begin to imagine 30 dinner-size plates of food, it's important to note that the dishes are small and the portions served are gauged by the number of people expected to share them. Remember, the idea is to taste many things rather than hunker down with any single item. Also, an Indonesian *rijsttafel* has no separate courses. Once your table has been set with a row of low, Sterno-powered plate warmers, all 17, 24, or 30 dishes arrive all at once, like a culinary avalanche. The sweets come alongside the sours and the spicy, so you're left to plot your own course through the extravaganza.

Among the customary dishes and ingredients of a *rijsttafel* are *loempia* (Chinese-style egg rolls); *satay,* or *sateh* (small pork kabobs, grilled and served with spicy peanut sauce); *perkedel* (meatballs); *gado-gado* (vegetables in peanut sauce); *daging smoor* (beef in soy sauce); *babi ketjap* (pork in soy sauce); *kroepoek* (crunchy, puffy shrimp toast); *serundeng* (fried coconut); *roedjak manis* (fruit in sweet sauce); and *pisang goreng* (fried banana).

Caution: When something on the menu is described as *pedis,* meaning spicy, that's exactly what it is. Beware in particular of one very appealing-looking dish of sauce with small chunks of what looks to be bright-red onion—that's *sambal badjak,* or just *sambal,* and it's hotter than hot. A fire extinguisher would be a useful table accessory; for an equally effective (and better-tasting) alternative, order a *witbier* (white beer).

2 RESTAURANTS BY CUISINE

Bakery
Pancake Bakery (The Canal Belt, $, p. 123)

Chinese
Dynasty (The Old Center, $$$, p. 112)
Nam Kee ★ (The Old Center, $, p. 115)
Treasure (The Old Center, $$, p. 114)

Continental
Amsterdam ★ (Amsterdam West, $$, p. 135)
Brasserie Keyzer ★ (Museum District & Vondelpark, $$$, p. 130)
Café Americain ★ (Leidseplein, $$, p. 124)
Café-Restaurant Van Puffelen (The Canal Belt, $$, p. 120)
De Belhamel ★★ (The Canal Belt, $$, p. 120)
De Jaren (The Old Center, $, p. 115)
De Kas ★★ (Amsterdam South, $$$, p. 134)
Excelsior ★★ (The Old Center, $$$$, p. 109)
In de Waag ★ (The Old Center, $$, p. 113)
Lof ★ (The Old Center, $$, p. 113)
1e Klas (Eerste Klas) (The Waterfront, $, p. 118)
Sluizer (The Canal Belt, $$, p. 121)
Spanjer & Van Twist ★ (The Canal Belt, $$, p. 121)
't Blaauwhooft (The Waterfront, $, p. 118)
Walem (The Canal Belt, $$, p. 122)
Wildschut (Museum District & Vondelpark, $$, p. 133)
Wilhelmina-Dok ★ (The Waterfront, $$, p. 117)

Dutch
Atrium (The Old Center, $, p. 114)

Brasserie De Poort ★ (The Old Center, $$, p. 112)
Brasserie Schiller (Rembrandtplein, $$, p. 126)
Café-Restaurant Van Puffelen (The Canal Belt, $$, p. 120)
De Knijp (Museum District & Vondelpark, $$, p. 132)
De Prins ★★ (The Canal Belt, $, p. 122)
De Silveren Spiegel (The Old Center, $$$, p. 109)
D'Vijff Vlieghen ★ (The Old Center, $$$, p. 109)
Haesje Claes ★ (The Old Center, $$, p. 112)
Het Stuivertje (The Jordaan, $$, p. 128)
Piet de Leeuw (The Canal Belt, $, p. 124)
't Blaauwhooft (The Waterfront, $, p. 118)

French
Brasserie Schiller (Rembrandtplein, $$, p. 126)
Bordewijk ★★ (The Jordaan, $$$, p. 128)
Christophe ★★ (The Canal Belt, $$$, p. 119)
De Knijp (Museum District & Vondelpark, $$, p. 132)
De Prins ★★ (The Canal Belt, $, p. 122)
De Silveren Spiegel (The Old Center, $$$, p. 109)
Excelsior ★★ (The Old Center, $$$$, p. 109)
Gare de l'Est ★★ (The Waterfront, $$, p. 116)
La Rive ★★★ (Amsterdam East, $$$$, p. 134)
Mangerie de Kersentuin ★ (Amsterdam South, $$$, p. 135)
Pier 10 ★ (The Waterfront, $$, p. 116)

Key to Abbreviations: $$$$ = Very Expensive $$$ = Expensive $$ = Moderate $ = Inexpensive

Proeflokaal Janvier (The Canal Belt, $$, p. 120)

Vinkeles ★ (The Canal Belt, $$$, p. 119)

Fusion

De Luwte ★★ (The Canal Belt, $$, p. 120)

Fifteen Amsterdam ★ (The Waterfront, $$$, p. 116)

Le Garage ★★ (Museum District & Vondelpark, $$$, p. 132)

Greek

Aphrodite (Leidseplein, $$, p. 124)

Grekas Greek Deli ★ (The Canal Belt, $, p. 123)

Indian

Akbar (Leidseplein, $, p. 125)

Memories of India (Rembrandtplein, $$, p. 128)

Indonesian

Bojo (Leidseplein, $, p. 125)

Kantjil & de Tijger ★★ (The Old Center, $$, p. 113)

Sama Sebo ★ (Museum District & Vondelpark, $$, p. 132)

Tempo Doeloe ★★ (The Canal Belt, $$, p. 121)

International

Atrium (The Old Center, $, p. 114)

Brasserie De Poort ★ (The Old Center, $$, p. 112)

Breitner ★ (The Canal Belt, $$$, p. 118)

Café Luxembourg ★ (The Old Center, $, p. 114)

De Balie (Leidseplein, $$, p. 125)

Grand Café l'Opera (Rembrandtplein, $$, p. 127)

Pier 10 ★ (The Waterfront, $$, p. 116)

Italian

Fifteen Amsterdam ★ (The Waterfront, $$$, p. 116)

Hostaria ★ (The Jordaan, $$, p. 129)

Toscanini ★ (The Jordaan, $$, p. 129)

Japanese

Osaka ★ (Amsterdam North, $$$, p. 136)

Umeno ★ (Amsterdam South, $$, p. 135)

Mediterranean

Christophe ★★ (The Canal Belt, $$$, p. 119)

Gare de l'Est ★★ (The Waterfront, $$, p. 116)

La Rive ★★★ (Amsterdam East, $$$$, p. 134)

Mangerie De Kersentuin ★ (Amsterdam South, $$$, p. 135)

Vertigo ★ (Museum District & Vondelpark, $$, p. 133)

Mexican

Rose's Cantina (The Old Center, $, p. 116)

Nepalese

Sherpa (Leidseplein, $, p. 125)

Seafood

Sluizer (The Canal Belt, $$, p. 121)

Vis Restaurant Le Pêcheur ★ (The Old Center, $$, p. 114)

Visrestaurant Lucius (The Old Center, $$$, p. 112)

Southeast Asian

Dynasty (The Old Center, $$$, p. 112)

Spanish

Duende (The Jordaan, $, p. 130)

Thai

Rakang (The Jordaan, $$, p. 129)

Tibetan

Sherpa (Leidseplein, $, p. 125)

Vegetarian

Bolhoed ★ (The Canal Belt, $$, p. 119)

Golden Temple (The Canal Belt, $, p. 122)

3 THE OLD CENTER

VERY EXPENSIVE

Excelsior ★★ FRENCH/CONTINENTAL   Located in the tony Hotel de l'Europe (p. 78), one of Amsterdam's finest restaurants derives its reputation from French chef Jean-Jacques Menanteau's Michelin-starred cuisine coupled with superb service. It's quite formal, especially by Amsterdam standards. Crystal chandeliers, elaborate moldings, crisp linens, fresh flower bouquets, and picture-frame windows with Amstel River views typify this classically grand establishment. A meal here is an exercise in refinement, aided by diligent and discreet waitstaff. Respectable attire (jackets for men) is required. If your budget can't quite compete with that of the royalty and showbiz stars who dine here, try the three-course *middagmenu* (lunch menu), or the evening *menu du théâtre* (theater menu), both of which make fine dining more affordable. The appetizer menu includes foie gras, smoked eel with dill, and marinated sweetbreads of lamb with salad. Choices for main courses include halibut filet with caper sauce or filet of veal with leek sauce. There's a grand piano, the source of the soft music that plays every evening.

In the Hotel de l'Europe, Nieuwe Doelenstraat 2–8 (facing Muntplein). ⓒ **020/531-1705.** www.leurope. nl. Reservations recommended on weekends. Main courses 32€–44€ ($51–$70); fixed-price menus 49€– 95€ ($78–$152). AE, DC, MC, V. Mon–Fri 7–11am, 12:30–2:30pm, and 7–10:30pm; Sat–Sun 7–11am and 7–10:30pm. Tram: 4, 9, 14, 16, 24, or 25 to Muntplein.

EXPENSIVE

De Silveren Spiegel DUTCH/FRENCH   The owner of this traditional old restaurant, one of the best known in Amsterdam, has introduced a fresh approach. The two houses that form the premises were built in 1614 for a wealthy soap maker, Laurens Jansz Spieghel. It's typical Old Dutch inside, with a bar downstairs and dining rooms where bedrooms used to be. The whole place emanates a traditional Dutch tidiness that's very welcoming. There's a garden in back, and adjacent is the 17th-century, domed Ronde Lutherse Kerk (Round Lutheran Church). The menu has been updated and now offers finely prepared seafood and meat dishes such as baked sole filets with wild spinach, and trilogy of lamb with ratatouille—but just as in the old days, the lamb, from Texel, is still Holland's finest. Be sure to try the traditional Zaanse mustard.

Kattengat 4–6 (off Singel). ⓒ **020/624-6589.** www.desilverenspiegel.com. Main courses 22€–36€ ($35–$58). AE, MC, V. Mon–Sat 5:30–10:30pm. Tram: 1, 2, 5, 13, or 17 to Martelaarsgracht.

D'Vijff Vlieghen ★ MODERN DUTCH   The "Five Flies" is a kind of Old Dutch theme park, with nine separate dining rooms spread over five canal houses decorated with objects from Holland's Golden Age—among them four original Rembrandt etchings. Each dining room has a different character. There's the Rembrandt Room; the Glass Room, with a collection of antique handmade glassware; and the Knight's Room, adorned with 16th-century armor and accoutrements, to name just three. Chef René Cramer is passionate about what he calls "New Dutch" cuisine, which aims to convey the culinary excellence inherent in many traditional Dutch recipes and products, but in an updated, French-influenced form, employing organic ingredients as often as possible. The menu offers a seasonal selection of fish and game marinated with fresh herbs and served with unusual vegetables like chard, wild spinach, and Brussels sprouts. Enjoy quite a mouthful by choosing the *geroosteerde tamme eend op een bedje van appeltjes en*

1e Klas **39**
Akbar **6**
Amsterdam **30**
Aphrodite **1**
Atrium **45**
Bojo **4**
Bolhoed **29**
Bordewijk **34**
Brasserie De Poort **21**
Brasserie Schiller **51**
Breitner **52**
Café Americain **5**
Café Luxembourg **11**
Café-Restaurant
  Van Puffelen **20**
Christophe **24**
De Balie **3**
De Belhamel **36**
De Jaren **46**
De Luwte **23**
De Prins **26**
De Silveren Spiegel **37**
Duende **32**
D'Vijff Vlieghen **15**
Dynasty **7**
Excelsior **47**
Fifteen Amsterdam **41**
Gare de l'Est **44**
Golden Temple **56**
Grand Café l'Opera **50**
Grekas Greek Deli **17**
Haesje Claes **14**
Het Stuivertje **19**
Hostaria **27**
In de Waag **42**
Kantjil & de Tijger **12**
La Rive **57**
Le Pêcheur **9**
Lof **35**
Memories of India **48**
Nam Kee **43**
Osaka **40**
Pancake Bakery **28**
Pier 10 **38**
Piet de Leeuw **49**
Proeflokaal Janvier **55**
Rakang **18**
Rose's Cantina **8**
Sherpa **2**
Sluizer **53**
Spanjer & Van Twist **25**
't Blaauwhooft **33**
Tempo Doeloe **54**
Toscanini **31**
Treasure **22**
Vinkeles **13**
Visrestaurant Lucius **16**
Walem **10**
Wilhelmina-Dok **40**

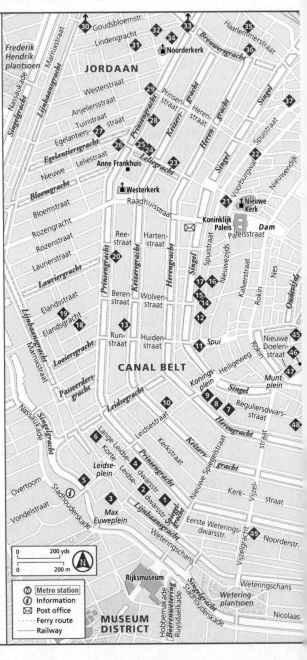

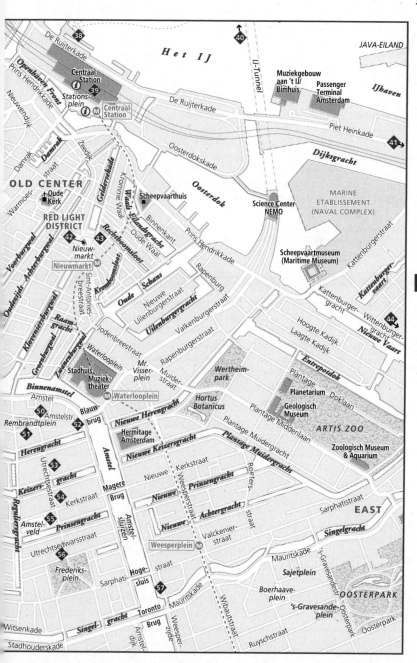

tuinboontjes overgroten met een vinaigrette van rode en groene pepers (roasted tame duck on a layer of apples and broad beans drizzled with a vinaigrette of red and green peppers).

Spuistraat 294–302 (at Spui; entrance at Vliegendesteeg 1). ℂ 020/530-4060. www.d-vijffvlieghen.com. Main courses 22€–39€ ($35–$62); seasonal menu 36€–53€ ($58–$101). AE, DC, MC, V. Daily 5:30pm–midnight. Tram: 1, 2, or 5 to Spui.

Dynasty CHINESE/SOUTHEAST ASIAN   It's an unlikely mix: tropical Asia at a formal Louis XV–style canal house. But it works. Dining in this cozy cavern of exotic colors, cushioned rattan chairs, fine table settings, and upturned Chinese paper umbrellas won't disappoint. In fine weather, enjoy your meal outdoors in the courtyard garden. Dynasty offers an array of dishes, an extravaganza of flavors—Cantonese, Thai, Malay, Filipino, and Vietnamese—that take you on a culinary tour through Southeast Asia. Among the intriguing possibilities is Promise of Spring, an appetizer of crisp pancakes filled with bamboo shoots and minced meat, and the delightfully named "drunken prawn," which is jumbo shrimp marinated in shoashing wine and Chinese herbs. Recommended main courses include the lobster lightly seasoned with ginger and scallions, and the Szechuan beef.

Reguliersdwarsstraat 30 (off Leidsestraat). ℂ 020/626-8400. www.fer.nl. Main courses 15€–36€ ($24–$58); fixed-price menus 33€–52€ ($53–$83). AE, DC, MC, V. Wed–Mon 5:30–11pm. Tram: 1, 2, or 5 to Koningsplein.

Visrestaurant Lucius SEAFOOD   Lucius, which means "pike" in Latin, has earned a reputation for fine seafood at fairly reasonable prices. Oysters and lobsters imported from Norway and Canada are the specialties. The three-course menu is also very popular. Among the six or so choices featured on the chalkboard menu, you might find fish soup to start, followed by grilled plaice, Dover sole, bass, or John Dory. The spectacular seafood plate includes six oysters, 10 mussels, clams, shrimp, and half a lobster. The long, narrow dining room features an aquarium. In summer, you can dine out on the sidewalk.

Spuistraat 247 (near Spui). ℂ 020/624-1831. www.lucius.nl. Main courses 19€–27€ ($30–$43); fixed-price menu 38€ ($61). AE, DC, MC, V. Daily 5pm–midnight. Tram: 1, 2, or 5 to Spui.

MODERATE

Brasserie De Poort ★ DUTCH/INTERNATIONAL   In a former beer hall across from the Royal Palace, this restaurant has been serving up the stolid virtues of its steaks and typically Dutch fare—though now backed by a cast of international dishes—for more than 100 years. Beamed and tiled with Delft blue from Koninklijke Porcelyne Fles, the Dutch-tavern dining room has been fully restored along with its parent hotel, called Die Port van Cleve (p. 82). De Poort maintains a tradition that's become legendary among regular patrons: Each steak is numbered, and if the number on yours is a round thousand, you win a bottle of wine. They've already served more than 6 million steaks! The restaurant is equally known for its Dutch pea soup.

In the Hotel Die Port van Cleve, Nieuwezijds Voorburgwal 176–180 (behind the Dam). ℂ 020/622-6429. www.dieportvancleve.com. Main courses 16€–28€ ($26–$45). AE, DC, MC, V. Daily 7am–10:30pm. Tram: 1, 2, 5, 13, 14, or 17 to the Dam.

Haesje Claes ★ DUTCH   If you're yearning for a cozy Old Dutch environment and hearty Dutch food at moderate prices, try this inviting place. Lots of nooks and crannies decorated with wood-paneling, Delftware, wooden barrels, brocaded benches, and traditional Dutch hanging lamps with fringed covers create an intimate, comfortable setting. The menu covers a lot of ground, from canapés to caviar, but you'll have the most luck with Dutch stalwarts ranging from omelets to tournedos. Take in *hutspot* (stew), *stampot* (mashed potatoes and cabbage), and various fish stews, including those with IJsselmeer *paling* (eel), along the way.

Spuistraat 273–275 (at Spui). ℂ 020/624-9998. www.haesjeclaes.nl. Main courses 15€–30€ ($24–$48); Neerlands Dis menu 29€ ($46). AE, DC, MC, V. Daily noon–10pm. Tram: 1, 2, or 5 to Spui.

In de Waag ★ CONTINENTAL   This cafe-restaurant is called In de Waag because it's in the Waag (see, you *can* speak Dutch). And what is the Waag? In the 14th-century, this was the Sint-Antoniespoort Gate in the city walls; by the Golden Age, a couple of centuries later, it had become a public weigh house: De Waag, where large loads of produce and other foodstuff would be officially weighed. Dissections were once carried out on the top-floor Theatrum Anatomicum. Nowadays, any dissection that occurs is of a culinary nature; this castle-like structure holds one of Amsterdam's most stylish and social eateries, and it's in an area that's becoming hipper by the day. It's romantic, with long banquet-style tables that are, in the evenings, lit with hundreds of candles, and it serves organic food. The breast of Barbary duck with sesame-cracker and sherry dressing is quite good, as is the vegetarian Kashmir bread with braised vegetables and coriander-yogurt sauce. You can also just drop by for coffee or a drink and to peruse the international newspapers and magazines available.

Nieuwmarkt 4. ℂ 020/422-7772. www.indewaag.nl. Main courses 20€–24€ ($32–$38). AE, DC, MC, V. Daily 10am–1am. Metro: Nieuwmarkt.

Kantjil & de Tijger ★★ INDONESIAN   Unlike Holland's many Indonesian restaurants that wear their ethnic origins on their sleeves, with staffers decked out in traditional costume, the Antelope and the Tiger is popular, chic, and modern. Moreover, it attracts customers who like their Indonesian food not only chic and modern, but also prepared well. Two bestsellers in this popular place are *nasi goreng Kantjil* (fried rice with pork kabobs, stewed beef, pickled cucumbers, and mixed vegetables), and the 20-item *rijsttafel* for two. Other choices include stewed chicken in *soja* sauce, tofu omelet, shrimp with coconut dressing, Indonesian pumpkin, and mixed steamed vegetables with peanut-butter sauce. Finish your meal with multilayered cinnamon cake or (try this at least once) coffee with ginger liqueur and whipped cream.

Spuistraat 291–293 (beside Spui). ℂ 020/620-0994. www.kantjil.nl. Reservations recommended on weekends. Main courses 11€–16€ ($18–$26); *rijsttafels* 40€–50€ ($64–$80) for 2. AE, DC, MC, V. Mon–Fri 4:30–11pm; Sat–Sun noon–11pm. Tram: 1, 2, or 5 to Spui.

Lof ★ (Finds CONTINENTAL   It's hard to pin down this fashionable, vaguely French-Italian eatery. For one thing, there's no menu. Its youthful chefs describe their creations as *cuisine spontane*—they go to the markets, spontaneously pick out whatever's fresh and catches their fancy, and equally spontaneously figure out what to do with it back at base. But *lof* means "praise" in Dutch, and it's an apt name, since the results are invariably admirable. The choice is deliberately limited, not quite take-it-or-leave-it, yet not far from that. Oysters are a regular feature among two or three starters; then choose from three main courses: meat, fish, or vegetarian and finish with a *torte*. You dine on one of two levels, at plain tables in a cozy setting with bare brick walls, or with a view of proceedings in the open kitchen.

Haarlemmerstraat 62 (near Centraal Station). ℂ 020/620-2997. Main course 22€ ($35); fixed-price menu 35€ ($56). AE, DC, MC, V. Tues–Sat 7–11pm (or later). Tram: 1, 2, 5, 13, or 17 to Maartelaarsgracht.

Treasure CHINESE   In a city with a passion for Indonesian food, it can be difficult to find traditional Chinese cuisine, let alone *good* traditional Chinese cuisine. Don't despair—make a beeline for this legendary restaurant. It offers a wide array of classic Chinese choices in a classic Chinese setting: lots of lanterns, watercolor paintings, and Chinese scripts adorn the place. You can eat dishes from any of the four main styles of Chinese cooking—Beijing, Shanghai, Cantonese, and Szechuan. Look for specialties such as Beijing duck, Szechuan-style prawns (very spicy), and steamed dumplings.

Nieuwezijds Voorburgwal 115–117 (near the Dam). (*©* **020/623-4061.** Main courses 9€–15€ ($14–$24); fixed-price menus 16€–39€ ($26–$62). AE, MC, V. Daily noon–11pm. Tram: 1, 2, 5, 13, 14, or 17 to the Dam.

Vis Restaurant Le Pêcheur ★ SEAFOOD   Popular and appealing, and in a frenetic neighborhood where establishments are more commonly either one or the other, Le Pêcheur has long combined elegant simplicity of presentation with a steely focus on freshness and taste. Flowers adorn tables set on a marble floor in the airy, tranquil dining room. There's also a mural ceiling, and enough space between tables to stretch a little. A romantic courtyard garden is perfect for summer dining. Dishes are prepared in Dutch, continental, and international styles. In season, come for the *coquilles Saint-Jacques* scallops, the mussels and oysters from the southern Dutch province of Zeeland, and the house-smoked salmon. You could also try poached brill with onion sauce, the fried wolffish with light mustard sauce, or sashimi. Beef tournedos are available as an alternative to seafood, and the wine list is extensive.

Reguliersdwarsstraat 32 (behind the Flower Market). (*©* **020/624-3121.** www.lepecheur.nl. Main courses 22€–36€ ($35–$58). AE, MC, V. Mon–Fri noon–midnight; Sat 5pm–midnight. Tram: 1, 2, or 5 to Koningsplein.

INEXPENSIVE

Atrium (Finds) DUTCH/INTERNATIONAL   Students, professors, and regular humans in search of cheap, sustaining nosh congregate in the casual self-service *mensa* (student restaurant) at the University of Amsterdam. A courtyard between restored buildings has been covered with a glass roof that lets in plenty of light. To reach the food lines, walk up the stairs and, just inside the door, cross over the pedestrian bridge. The menu mixes standard Dutch fare like salads and pea-and-ham soup with exotic influences like filled Indonesian *bami* (noodle) and *nasi* (rice) croquettes that have themselves become Dutch standards. None of these, it must be stated, are produced to any unforgettable effect, but they're all perfectly edible, and the knowledge that they're costing close to nothing goes a long way toward compensating for any culinary shortcomings. An added value is the nature of the place, which makes it easy to share tables and strike up conversations.

Oudezijds Achterburgwal 237 (at Grimburgwal). (*©* **020/525-3999.** Most items under 6€ ($9.60). No credit cards. Mon–Fri noon–2pm and 5–7pm. Tram: 4, 9, 14, 16, 24, or 25 to Spui.

Café Luxembourg ★ INTERNATIONAL   "One of the world's great cafes," the *New York Times* called this bohemian, see-and-be-seen grand cafe, where waitstaff wear starched white aprons. Unlike other Amsterdam cafes, which often draw distinctive clientele, Luxembourg attracts all kinds of people because it offers amazingly large portions of food at reasonable prices. Soups, sandwiches, and dishes such as meatloaf are available. Especially appealing are specials like the Chinese dim sum and the *satay ajam* (Indonesian grilled chicken in peanut sauce). Sundays in particular, but also on other days, it's a relaxing place to do breakfast with one of the many international papers available here and a cup of strong coffee; diners are encouraged to linger. In summer, there's sidewalk dining.

Spuistraat 24 (at Spui). ℂ **020/620-6264.** www.cafeluxembourg.nl. Salads and specials 7.50€–12€ ($12–$19); lunch 4.50€–9.75€ ($7.20–$16); main courses 8.50€–15€ ($14–$24). AE, DC, MC, V. Sun–Thurs 9am–1am; Fri–Sat 9am–2am. Tram: 1, 2, or 5 to Spui.

De Jaren CONTINENTAL   This cafe-restaurant with picturesque surroundings is fashionable without being pretentious. It occupies a solid-looking former bank; ceilings are unusually high and flooring is multicolored tiled mosaic. Students from the nearby University of Amsterdam lunch here, and it's popular with the media crowd. De Jaren's unique selling point is not so much the arty set that hangs out here, but its two marvelous open-air patios beside the Amstel River, sunny spots that, in fine weather, are much in demand. Occupants of those prime seats settle into them with a firmness of purpose, but it's worth checking out the outdoor decks, in case one of these permanent-seeming patrons might have fallen—or been pushed—into the river. Enjoy ham and eggs for breakfast, a salad from the extensive salad bar for lunch, or spaghetti Bolognese, couscous, or rib-eye steak for dinner. Sip on coffee, beer, or *jenever* (gin) while perusing the English-language newspapers.

Nieuwe Doelenstraat 20–22 (near Muntplein). ℂ **020/625-5771.** www.cafe-de-jaren.nl. Main courses 14€–18€ ($22–$29); lunch menu 9.50€ ($15). V. Sun–Thurs 10am–1am; Fri–Sat 10am–2am. Tram: 4, 9, 14, 16, 24, or 25 to Muntplein.

Nam Kee ★ CHINESE   Not many Amsterdam eateries have made a name for themselves in the movies, but this one played a notable role in the 2002 red-hot romance flick *De Oesters van Nam Kee* (*The Oysters of Nam Kee*). In the heart of Amsterdam's small but growing Chinatown, Nam Kee has a long interior with few obvious graces and little in the way of decor. Still, people come for authentic, excellent, modestly priced food from a 140-item menu. Those steamed oysters with black bean sauce and the duck with plum sauce are to die for. The Peking duck—always an indicator of quality in a Chinese restaurant—is satisfyingly crisp-skinned. Service is fast, so you won't have long to wait for a table.

Zeedijk 111–113 at Nieuwmarkt. ℂ **020/624-3470.** www.namkee.nl. Main courses 5.75€–16€ ($9.20–$26). AE, DC, MC, V. Daily 11:30am–midnight. Metro: Nieuwmarkt.

ⓕFinds   Chef Child

Children are both the chefs and the waiters at the **Kinderkookkafé,** Vondelpark 6B (ℂ **020/625-3257;** www.kinderkookkafe.nl; tram: 4, 9, 14, 16, 24, or 25), at Het Kattenlaantje, across the street from Overtoom 325. With the help and supervision of two adults, and a reservation, kids can prepare dinner on Saturday, and bake cookies and pies for high tea on Sunday. If they want to, they can join the kitchen brigade (though there might be a language barrier with other kids) or families can just relax and enjoy the meal. Children can do everything here—cook, wait tables, wash up, serve behind the bar (soft drinks only), and write checks. Kids must be at least 8 years old to help with the Saturday dinner, and 5 for the Sunday bake. Numbers are limited to around 8 children, but together with guests and helpers, there might be as many as 30 diners. Reserve seats on Saturday from noon to 2pm. For eating, the cafe is open Saturday from 3:30 to 8pm, and Sunday from 2:30 to 6pm. Meals are 5€ ($8) for children ages 2 to 4, 10€ ($16) for children ages 5 to 12, and 15€ ($24) from age 13.

Rose's Cantina MEXICAN   A meal starting with tortilla chips and salsa, followed by a *plato mixto* or fried *gallinas* (roast hen with fries and red peppers), and accompanied by a Mexican beer should hit the spot. The tables are oak, the service is decent but slow—the basic rate of continental drift is a good comparison—and the atmosphere is Latin American and buzzing with cheer. Beware of long waiting times for a table that'll have you at the bar downing one after another of Rose's deadly margaritas. There's a small sidewalk terrace on feverish Reguliersdwarsstraat for summer dining.

Reguliersdwarsstraat 38–40 (off Leidsestraat). ℂ 020/625-9797. www.rosescantina.com. Main courses 9.50€–17€ ($15–$27). AE, DC, MC, V. Mon–Sat 5–11:30pm; Sun 3–11:30pm. Tram: 1, 2, or 5 to Koningsplein.

4 THE WATERFRONT

EXPENSIVE
Fifteen Amsterdam ★ FUSION/ITALIAN   British celeb-chef Jamie Oliver has brought his unique restaurant concept from London to the old Brazilië building in harbor redevelopment zone east of Centraal Station. His Amsterdam hotspot has both a full-menu restaurant and an adjoining trattoria serving less-elaborate fare. Drop-dead gorgeous staff serve the equally gorgeous clientele dishes like a salad of the day with figs, prosciutto, Gorgonzola, and toasted almonds on field greens; seafood risotto; linguini with horse mushrooms and thyme; and pan-fried calves' liver with balsamic figs and pancetta. Though Oliver doesn't often preside in person, you can try his eclectic-fun cooking concept in the vast main dining room. In the more intimate trattoria, where prices are more moderate, try risottos, pasta dishes, and other Italian fare. You can also dine outdoors on a waterside terrace.

Pakhuis Amsterdam, Jollemanhof 9 (at Oostelijke Handelskade). ℂ **0900/343-8336.** www.fifteen.nl. Reservations required for restaurant. Restaurant: fixed-price menu 46€ ($74); trattoria: main courses 23€–29€ ($37–$46). AE, MC, V. Restaurant: daily 6pm–1am (closed Sun July–Aug); trattoria: Sun–Thurs 5:30pm–1am. Tram: 10 or 26 to Rietlandpark.

MODERATE
Gare de l'Est ★★ FRENCH/MEDITERRANEAN   This distinctive detached house with a conservatory extension and a large sidewalk terrace was built in 1901 as a coffee-house for longshoremen (dockworkers). A meal at this restaurant is an altogether good reason to make a trip to a part of town that's becoming ever more fashionable. As the restaurant's name indicates (it means "East Station"), the cuisine is traditional French—but its chefs do incorporate Mediterranean touches. Service is relaxed and knowledgeable, and the fixed-price menu is an excellent value: Surprises appear on your plate rather than on the check. The strict five-course formula (starter, salad, main course of meat or fish, cheese, and dessert) leaves no room for choice—except for the main course—but plenty for market-fresh ingredients and culinary creativity. Try *pulpo estofado et risotto nero* (octopus stew and black rice) as a starter, and roast lamb with gazpacho and farfalle as a main course.

Cruquiusweg 9 (at the Oosterdok/Eastern Harbor). ℂ **020/463-0620.** www.garedelest.nl. Reservations recommended on weekends. Fixed-price menu 30€ ($48). No credit cards. Daily 6–11pm. Tram: 7 or 10 to Zeeburgerdijk.

Pier 10 ★ FRENCH/INTERNATIONAL   Perched as it is on an old pier on Het IJ behind Centraal Station, this restaurant can hardly help being romantic. It has great views of the IJ waterway from its big outdoor terrace and from the *serre* (glassed-in room)

Frommer's Favorite Local Spots

- I've made my choice for **Zeebanket van Altena** (p. 126) as the top fish stand in town. But I can't resist adding an honorable mention for **Stubbe's Haring,** Haarlemmersluis Bridge ((*C* 020/623-3212; tram: 1, 2, 5, 13, or 17), at Singel, a great, centrally located stand for "new herring" and other seafood.

- There aren't many better outdoor terraces in Amsterdam than that of **Klein Kalfje,** Amsteldijk 355 ((*C* 020/644-5338; www.restaurantkleinkalfje.nl; bus: 62). This atmospheric little Dutch cafe-restaurant's waterside terrace is at a tranquil spot along the Amstel River, just outside the city limits. It's easier to get here by car or by bike.

- Sabrina and Denise of **Basilico,** Willemsstraat 29A ((*C* 020/627-2685; www.basilico.nl; tram: 3), in the Jordaan, rustle up some ace homemade Italian food, but only for takeout. If you have somewhere to eat an Italian meal, or are looking for picnic makings, go for it.

- Founded in 1870 as a soup kitchen to provide meals for poor people, **De Keuken van 1870,** Spuistraat 4 ((*C* 020/620-4018; www.keukenvan1870.nl; tram: 1, 2, 5, 13, or 17), has kept a budget outlook at heart while adapting to meet contemporary food trends. In a plain but far from downtrodden setting in the heart of town, it serves traditional Dutch fare supported by some more exotic dishes.

at the end of the pier. If the views of Waterplein-West, the ferry dock next door, are not quite as fantastic, then at least the ferries' comings and goings add a dash of nautical bustle to the scene. When cruise liners head to sea and workaday barges make for the inland waterways, they sail down the ship channel within view, making this one of only a few restaurants where you can see the sea and port traffic that was once Amsterdam's lifeblood. Candlelight softens the funky diner decor, and the food is fanciful international-eclectic—there are salads of all sorts, steak, and fish (including new herring), among other offerings.

De Ruyterkade, Steiger 10 (behind Centraal Station). (*C* 020/427-2310. www.pier10.nl. Reservations recommended on weekends. Main courses 19€–20€ ($30–$32). AE, DC, MC, V. Daily noon–3pm and 6:30pm–1am. Tram: 1, 2, 4, 5, 9, 16, 17, 24, 25, or 26 to Centraal Station.

Wilhelmina-Dok ★ (Kids) (Finds) CONTINENTAL   Just across the IJ waterway from Centraal Station, this restaurant is more than worth a short, free ferryboat ride followed by a 5-minute walk. It's on three floors (the chandeliered top floor is for groups only), and plain wood, candlelit tables, wood floors, and oak cabinets give the interior an old-fashioned maritime look. Large windows serve up views across the narrow channel. Breezy is one way to describe the impact of the prevailing westerlies, but most tables on the outdoor terrace are sheltered from the wind in a glass-walled enclosure. The menu favors plain cooking and organic products; good choices include the *zwaardvis van de grill met saffranrisotto* (grilled swordfish with saffron rice) and the *kalfslende van de grill met gemarineerde aubergine en flageolottensalade en pesto* (grilled veal cutlets with marinated eggplants, flageolet salad, and pesto). Or settle back with just a beer and a snack. On Monday evenings in August, an outdoor screen shows movies.

Nordwal 1 (at IJplein). ⓒ **020/632-3701.** www.wilhelmina-dok.nl. Reservations recommended on weekends. Main courses 17€–21€ ($27–$34); buffet 18€–35€ ($29–$56). AE, DC, MC, V. Daily 11am–midnight. Ferry: IJveer from Waterplein-West behind Centraal Station to the dock at IJplein, then go right, along the dike-top path.

INEXPENSIVE

1e Klas (Eerste Klas) Ⓥalue CONTINENTAL   Should you have both a train to catch and some eating to get done, Centraal Station's brasserie is a good choice; it's no run-of-the-mill buffet, though it is a tad overpriced. The dining room, in the station's first-class waiting room (ca. 1881), has been restored close to its original Art Nouveau elegance. Despite high ceilings, wood paneling, tall windows, chandeliers, painted pilaster columns, and potted plants, le Klas is rather gloomy. Drop by for just a coffee or a beer, and you'll sit at a table along the wall; for a meal, you get a table in the central dining area. The soup of the day is usually good and quick, as is the club sandwich. To squelch more substantial hunger pangs, there are Caesar salad, Dover sole with salad and fries, beef stroganoff, and more.

Platform 2B, Centraal Station. ⓒ **020/625-0131.** www.restaurant1eklas.nl. Main courses 7.50€–14€ ($12–$22); dish of the day 11€ ($18). No credit cards. Daily 8:30am–11pm. Tram: 1, 2, 4, 5, 9, 13, 16, 17, 24, 25, or 26 to Centraal Station.

't Blaauwhooft Ⓕinds DUTCH/CONTINENTAL   A plain neighborhood brown cafe in the gentrified Westelijke Eilanden (Western Islands) district has been transformed into a great *eetcafé* by the simple expedient of adding a kitchen and a menu. It partakes of the villagey setting on these tranquil islands—which feel isolated despite a location just west of Centraal Station—and brings its own cozy atmosphere to the party. The clientele is drawn mainly from locals who can afford to occupy one of the bijou apartments in transformed old warehouses, yet who don't want to look like it or to lose touch with their roots. There's a nice sidewalk terrace on the square, though with an uninspiring view of trains coming and going into Centraal Station on the adjacent elevated rail line. The kitchen finds its comfort zone in Dutch standbys like Zeeland mussels, but runs to ostrich steak and some adventurous salads.

Hendrik Jonkerplein 1 (Bickerseiland, off Haarlemmerhouttuinen). ⓒ **020/623-8721.** www.blaauwhooft. nl. Main courses 9€–18€ ($14–$29); *dagschotel* 12€ ($19). No credit cards. Daily 3–10pm. Bus: 18 or 22 to Haarlemmerhouttuinen.

5 THE CANAL BELT

EXPENSIVE

Breitner ★ INTERNATIONAL   A fast, last-minute dash from here should get you to the Muziektheater or **Koninklijk Theater Carré** just in time for the evening curtain rise, but that would involve dining in unseemly haste (the expression "wolfing down" comes to mind), and undervalues the performance of the excellent kitchen and knowledgeable waitstaff. The plush red carpet, chandelier, and wine cupboard suggest classical timelessness, yet modern decor and paintings tell a different story. Named after Amsterdam's Impressionist painter George Hendrik Breitner, this restaurant finds a way to fuse a classic French foundation with this city's cosmopolitan spirit. The smoked rib-eye starter with Szechuan pepper, and turbot stew with Indonesian vegetables are just two examples. Light floods in from big riverside and canalside windows, so a window seat guarantees fine views on the water. Ordering from the strong wine list will enhance your dining experience.

Amstel 212 (at Herengracht). © 020/627-7879. www.restaurant-breitner.nl. Reservations recommended at theater time. Main courses 24€–36€ ($38–$58); fixed-price menus 44€–58€ ($70–$93). AE, DC, MC, V. Mon–Sat 6–10:30pm. Tram: 9 or 14 to Waterlooplein.

Christophe ★★ MODERN FRENCH/MEDITERRANEAN   French chef Jean-Joel Bonsens has a penchant for wielding tangy Mediterranean flourishes to create a version of classic French cuisine. His ultra refined food, served in a main dining room of modern flair, employs traditional Mediterranean ingredients—figs, truffles, olives, anchovies, peppers, saffron, and more—in exciting new ways. North African *tajine* and Italian *pata negra* ham have a place on the menu, alongside French "staples" like roast Vendée duck. Bonsen rings the changes seasonally, so what you might get depends on when you visit. You get a flavor of what's on offer from dishes like the tuna carpaccio with salted lemon, the roasted pheasant in a crust of green peppers and cardamom, and the roasted turbot with turnip and a tartare of oysters, spinach, and samphire in a Noilly Prat sauce. Sommelier Ellen Mansfield has a nose for intriguing finds from French vineyards.

Leliegracht 46 (btw. Prinsengracht and Keizersgracht). © 020/625-0807. www.restaurantchristophe.nl. Main courses 29€–36€ ($46–$58); fixed-price menus 45€–65€ ($72–$104). AE, DC, MC, V. Tues–Sat 6:30–10:30pm. Tram: 13, 14, or 17 to Westermarkt.

Vinkeles ★ CONTEMPORARY FRENCH   If you dress up in black to celebrate (and I don't mean a tux) then head for this ultrahip restaurant in an unlikely setting: the converted bakery of a 17th-century almshouse. Named after Amsterdam engraver Reinier Vinkeles (1741–1816), who made an etching of the building's monumental gateway, its restrained tones soften some of the harsher edges of the über-chic designer hotel the Dylan Amsterdam (p. 87), where neo-millionaires, jetsetters, and media tycoons go to check out each other's *noir* duds. The decor includes a bare section of the bakery's brick wall, along with ovens and other fittings, all of which adds to the sense of dining in an old Amsterdam canal house. Top chef Dennis Kuipers, who has an instinct for the right taste combinations and the know-how to put them together so they hit the spot, whips up dishes such as roasted Anjou pigeon with five spices and dried apricots. Dining outside in fine weather in the tree-shaded courtyard is an added plus.

In the Dylan Amsterdam Hotel, Keizersgracht 384 (at Runstraat). © 020/530-2010. www.dylanamsterdam. com. Reservations required. Main courses 29€–44€ ($46–$70); fixed-price menu 45€ ($72). AE, DC, MC, V. Mon–Fri 7–11am, noon–2pm, and 6:30–11pm; Sat 7–11am and 6:30–11pm. Tram: 13, 14, or 17 to Westermarkt.

MODERATE

Bolhoed ★ VEGETARIAN   Forget the corn-and-brown-rice image affected by some vegetarian restaurants, that worthy but dull message: "This stuff is good for you." Instead, garnish your healthful habits with tangy flavors and a dash of zest. This former hat store—*bolhoed* is Dutch for bowler hat—has Latin style, aboriginal art, world music, ethnic exhibits, evening candlelight, and a fine canal view from each of the two plant-bedecked, cheerful rooms. Service is delivered with equal helpings of gusto and attention. Try pumpkin soup, *ragout croissant* (pastry filled with leeks, tofu, seaweed, and curry sauce), a variety of salads, and *zarzuela* (a cold Spanish soup). Even the entrees with brown rice and tofu taste good. If you want to go whole hog, so to speak, and eat vegan, most dishes can be prepared that way upon request. Ingredients and wine are organic, and in fine weather, you can dine at tiny tables on a small sliver of sidewalk right beside the canal.

Prinsengracht 60–62 (near Noordermarkt). ✆ **020/626-1803.** Main courses 11€–16€ ($18–$26); *dagschotel* 13€ ($21); 3-course menu 19€ ($30). No credit cards. Sun–Fri noon–11pm; Sat 11am–11pm. Tram: 13, 14, or 17 to Westermarkt.

Café-Restaurant Van Puffelen DUTCH/CONTINENTAL   A young professional crowd gets to choose here between brown-cafe–style eating and drinking, and a slightly more sophisticated experience in a separate dining room. Some menu dishes don't add up to much more than regular steak with accompaniments. Others, like the baked seawolf wrapped in Serrano ham and served with olive risotto and a lime sauce, display greater, Mediterranean-inspired flair. Save room for the handmade chocolates that are house specialties. The sidewalk terrace with a view of the Prinsengracht is—like most similar canalside assets—much in demand when the weather's fine.

Prinsengracht 377 (facing Lauriergracht). ✆ **020/624-6270.** www.goodfoodgroup.nl. Main courses 15€–19€ ($24–$30); fixed-price menu 19€ ($30). AE, DC, MC, V. Mon–Wed 3pm–1am; Fri–Sat noon–2am; Sun noon–1am. Tram: 13, 14, or 17 to Westermarkt.

De Belhamel ★★ (Finds) CONTINENTAL   Soft classical music complements a graceful Art Nouveau setting at this bi-level restaurant overlooking the photogenic junction of the Herengracht and Brouwersgracht canals. Tables fill up quickly most evenings, so make reservations or go early. The menu changes seasonally (game is a big deal here in the fall). Look for these—or something as good as these—on the list: puffed pastries layered with salmon, shellfish, and crayfish tails to start; and, for a main course, beef tenderloin in Madeira sauce with zucchini rösti and puffed garlic. You can also order vegetarian dishes. Try for a window table and take in the superb canal views. Although generally excellent, De Belhamel does have two potential deal-breakers: The waitstaff can be too relaxed on occasion, and when the restaurant's full, as it often is, the place's acoustic peculiarities mean that it can get noisy.

Brouwersgracht 60 (at Herengracht). ✆ **020/622-1095.** www.belhamel.nl. Main courses 22€–25€ ($35–$40); fixed-price menus 35€–45€ ($56–$72). AE, MC, V. Sun–Thurs 6–10pm; Fri–Sat 6–10:30pm. Tram: 1, 2, 5, 13, or 17 to Martelaarsgracht.

De Luwte ★★ FUSION   *Graceful* is the word that seems best to sum up this fine restaurant, though that quality never descends into stiffness. Grace comes from Florentine wall murals, floor-to-ceiling Art Deco lamps, drapes, hangings, ceiling mirrors painted with flowers and vines, a candle on each table, and not least of all, from its elegant canalside location. And it avoids being starchy by a characteristically Amsterdam exuberance and buzz. In either of the twin rooms, try for a window table looking out on the handsome little Leliegracht canal. The menu ranges across the globe; look to items such as the vegetarian coconut curry crepes filled with spinach, lentils, and nuts; and stir-fried guinea fowl with nuts and *bok choy.*

Leliegracht 26–28 (btw. Keizersgracht and Herengracht). ✆ **020/625-8548.** www.restaurantdeluwte.nl. Main courses 16€–20€ ($26–$32); fixed-price menu 32€ ($51). AE, MC, V. Daily 6–11pm. Tram: 13, 14, or 17 to Westermarkt.

Proeflokaal Janvier MODERN FRENCH   It's hard to keep up with the comings and goings at the prime Amstelveld canalside dining site just off of Prinsengracht, in a reconverted white 17th-century church, the Amstelkerk. There are many—count me among them—who still miss the superb restaurant Kort that was there until 2001. We were partly persuaded by the adventurous (if overpricey), South Seas–influenced eatery Moko that the proprietors brought in as a replacement. Now Moko has departed too, vanished like a too-brief Pacific sunset. Janvier is a worthy successor, with an adventurous chef (Patrick Kelder) who takes his classical French training and goes out on a modern limb with it, while not bulking up the tab. On warm summer evenings, try to get a table outdoors on the wide-open square beside the Prinsengracht canal.

Amstelveld 12 (at Prinsengracht). © **020/626-1199.** Reservations recommended on weekends. www. proeflokaaljanvier.nl. AE, DC, MC, V. Main courses 29€–30€ ($46–$48). Daily noon–10pm. Tram: 4 to Prinsengracht.

Sluizer CONTINENTAL/SEAFOOD Two notable restaurants (sadly, not for the price of one), both called Sluizer, stand side by side in convivial harmony. No. 45 is an old-fashioned brasserie with an eclectic, slightly French-biased menu. Try such items as *entrecôte Dijon* (steak with mustard sauce) and *poulet à la Provençal* (chicken with olives, sage, rosemary, and tomato). Next door, at nos. 41–43, the vaguely Art Deco *visrestaurant* (fish restaurant), with ceiling fans and fringed table-lamps, has at least 10 daily specials, ranging from simple cod or eel to *coquille Saint-Jacques* (scallops), crab casserole, Dover sole, halibut, and octopus. Meat dishes, such as beef stroganoff and chicken supreme, also appear on the menu. With kitchens open until midnight, both these places qualify as late-dining restaurants.

Utrechtsestraat 41–45 (btw. Herengracht and Keizersgracht). © **020/622-6376.** www.sluizer.nl. Main courses 15€–25€ ($24–$40); fixed-price menu 22€ ($35). AE, DC, MC, V. Daily 5–11pm. Tram: 4 to Utrechtsestraat.

Spanjer & Van Twist ★ ⓕⓘⓝⓓⓢ CONTINENTAL This place would almost be worth a visit for its unusual name alone, so it's doubly gratifying that the food is good, too. The interior is typical neighborhood-*eetcafé* style, with the day's specials chalked on a blackboard, a long table with newspapers at the front, and the kitchen visible in back. High cooking standards, however, put this place above others of its kind. The eclectic menu changes seasonally, but its range has included Thai fish curry and *pandan* rice; *saltimbocca* of trout in white-wine sauce; and artichoke mousseline with tarragon sauce and green asparagus. In fine weather, eat under the trees on an outdoor terrace beside the tranquil Leliegracht canal.

Leliegracht 60 (off Keizersgracht). © **020/639-0109.** www.spanjerenvantwist.nl. Main courses 14€–16€ ($22–$26). MC, V. Sun–Thurs 10am–1am; Fri–Sat 10am–2am (only light snacks after 10pm). Tram: 13, 14, or 17 to Westermarkt.

Tempo Doeloe ★★ INDONESIAN For authentic Indonesian cuisine (the name means "The Old Days" in Javanese) from Java, Sumatra, and Bali, this place is hard to beat. It's got a *batik* ambience that's Indonesian, but restrained, and is a long way from being kitschy. Attractive decor and fine china are unexpected pluses. Try the many little meat, fish, and vegetable dishes of the three different *rijsttafel* (rice table) options: the 15-plate vegetarian *rijsttafel sayoeran,* the 15-plate *rijsttafel stimoelan,* or the sumptuous 25-plate *rijsttafel istemewa.* In the big one, you get dishes like *gadon dari sapi* (beef in mild coconut sauce and fresh coriander), *ajam roedjak* (chicken in a strongly seasoned chili-pepper-and-coconut sauce), *sambal goreng oedang* (small shrimps with Indonesian spices), and *atjar* (sweet-and-sour Indonesian salad). For great individual dishes, go for *udang raksasa* (a large grilled shrimp bathed in coconut-curry sauce), the *nasi koening* (spiced yellow rice), or any of the vegetarian options. Finish with the *spekkoek,* a layered spice cake.

Utrechtsestraat 75 (btw. Prinsengracht and Keizersgracht). © **020/625-6718.** www.tempodoeloerestaurant. nl. Reservations required. Main courses 14€–25€ ($22–$40); rijsttafel 27€–35€ ($43–$56); fixed-price menu 27€–43€ ($43–$69). AE, DC, MC, V. Daily 6–11:30pm. Tram: 4 to Keizersgracht.

> (Tips) **All in Good Taste**
>
> As the waitperson removes your plate, he or she may ask: *Heeft het gesmaakt?* (Did it taste good?). If it did, the appropriate answer is: *Ja, lekker* (Yes, tasty), or *heel lekker* (very tasty). And if you had an unparalleled experience of gustatory pleasure, you can roll your eyes, pat your stomach contentedly, and purr: *Mmmm, ja, heerlijk* (wonderful). If you didn't enjoy your experience, however, you won't likely be able to, or need to, explain it in Dutch. Still, if you're adamant about expressing your displeasure, you could say: *Nee, het heeft niet gesmaakt* (No, it didn't taste good).

Walem CONTINENTAL   Walem may have lost a few of its brownie points since a few years ago when it was one of the hottest addresses in town, but that only means it's easier to get a seat on one of its two wonderful terraces: one outside beside the canal and the other at the rear in a sheltered, quiet garden patio. The space between them isn't bad either; it was designed by Philippe Starck, with small tables in front of and beside the long bar, where daily newspapers are provided. This cafe-restaurant's standards have not slipped at all, so don't worry about being seen in yesterday's in-place. Menu items include pasta specialties, steak, chicken, and salads.

Keizersgracht 449 (at Leidsestraat). © **020/625-3544.** www.diningcity.nl/walem. Main courses 17€–19€ ($27–$30). AE, DC, MC, V. Sun–Thurs 10am–1am; Fri–Sat 10am–2am. Tram: 1, 2, or 5 to Leidsestraat.

INEXPENSIVE

De Prins ★★ (Value) DUTCH/FRENCH   This friendly restaurant in a 17th-century canal house across the canal from the Anne Frankhuis, has a smoke-stained, brown-cafe style and food that could easily grace a much more expensive place. De Prins offers an unbeatable price-to-quality ratio for Dutch-French menu items, and long may it continue to do so. The youthful clientele is loyal and enthusiastic, so the relatively few tables fill up quickly. This is a quiet neighborhood place—nothing fancy or trendy, but very appealing in a human way. There's a bar on a lower level, and from March to September, you can eat on the canalside terrace.

Prinsengracht 124 (at Egelantiersgracht). © **020/624-9382.** www.deprins.nl. Main courses 10€–16€ ($16–$26); *dagschotel* 11€ ($18); specials 12€–16€ ($19–$26). AE, DC, MC, V. Daily 10am–1 or 2am (kitchen to 10pm). Tram: 13, 14, or 17 to Westermarkt.

Golden Temple VEGETARIAN   In its fourth decade of tickling meat-shunning palates, this temple of organic taste is still one of the best vegetarian (and vegan) options in town. If anything, the atmosphere is a tad too hallowed, an effect enhanced by a minimalist absence of decorative flourishes. The menu livens things up, though, with its unlikely roster of Indian, Middle Eastern, and Mexican dishes. This could make for a rewarding mix-and-match game if only the small print didn't all but instruct you to keep flavors apart. The food is delicately spiced, and evidently prepared by loving hands. Multiple-choice platters are a good way to go. For the Indian *thali,* you select from constituents like *sag paneer* (homemade cheese), vegetable *korma,* and *raita* (cucumber and yogurt dip); the Middle Eastern platter has stalwarts like falafel, chickpea-and-vegetable stew, and *dolmas* (stuffed grape leaves). A variety of side dishes range from guacamole to couscous to *pakora* (deep-fried fritters). The homemade ice cream is a finger-licking-good finish.

Grekas Greek Deli ★ Ⓕⓘⓝⓓⓢ GREEK   With just five tables and a small sidewalk terrace for summertime, Grekas would be more of a frustration than anything else, except that its main business is takeout service. If you're staying at one of the hotels in this neighborhood (particularly next door at the Estheréa, to which Grekas provides room service), this place can become your local diner. The food is fresh and authentic, and you can choose your meal like you would in Mykonos, by pointing to the dishes you want. If there are no free tables, you can always take your choices back to your room, or eat alfresco on the canalside. Menu items are standard Greek but with freshness and taste that's hard to beat. The moussaka and pasticcio are heavenly; the roast lamb with wine, herbs, olive oil, and bouillon is excellent; the seafood in the calamari salad seems to have come straight out of Homer's wine-dark sea; and there's a good Greek wine list, too. Takeout dishes cost a euro or two less.

Singel 311 (near Spui). ℂ **020/620-3590.** No reservations. Main courses 10€–15€ ($16–$24). No credit cards. Wed–Sun 5–10pm. Tram: 1, 2, or 5 to Spui.

Pancake Bakery Ⓚⓘⓓⓢ BAKERY   Located in a 17th-century canal warehouse, this two-story restaurant with winding staircases and exposed beams is a firm local favorite that serves some of the most delicious and unusual pancakes you'll ever taste. There are several dozen varieties, almost all of which make for a full meal. The satisfyingly large— you might even find them heavy—pancakes come adorned with all sorts of toppings, both sweet and spicy. Choices include salami and cheese, cheese and ginger, curried turkey with pineapple and raisins, honey nuts and whipped cream, and ice cream and

---

Ⓚⓘⓓⓢ   **Family-Friendly Restaurants**

Kinderkookkafé (p. 115)   Amsterdam's only place where children not only get to do the eating, but the cooking and the serving too. Since young Dutch children don't speak much English, you may want to query the organizers about any possible language issues before reserving.

Pancake Bakery (p. 123)   I have yet to meet a kid who doesn't love pancakes, and this is *the* best pancake source in town. Pancakes come with various inventive toppings, both sweet and savory. Suitably colorful ornaments such as umbrellas and clowns accompany child-oriented meals and desserts. Toys, children's chairs, and special menus complete the picture.

Wilhelmina-Dok (p. 117)   Though not conceived as a kid-friendly place, this waterside cafe-restaurant does have a few things going for it. You get there and return by harbor ferry, which ought to add some interest to the proceedings. Once there, either outside on the breezy terrace or snug and warm inside, young folks can see barges, ferries, yachts, and other vessels coming and going on the IJ ship channel, and maybe even spot a cruise liner docked at Passenger Terminal Amsterdam. If you have young kids in tow, this is likely a better jaunt at lunchtime.

advokaat (a Dutch eggnog-like cocktail). A bestseller is the American pancake: It comes topped with fried chicken, sweet corn, peppers, carrots, Cajun sauce, and salad. In summer, there's outdoor seating overlooking the canal, but beware: All the syrup, honey, and sugar tend to attract bees and hornets.

Prinsengracht 191 (at Prinsenstraat). ✆ **020/625-1333.** www.pancake.nl. Reservations required for large groups. Pancakes 5.35€–12€ ($8.55–$19), 3.95€–5.40€ ($6.30–$8.65) for kids. AE, MC, V. Daily noon–9:30pm. Tram: 13, 14, or 17 to Westermarkt.

Piet de Leeuw (Value) DUTCH   Think of it as "Piet's Place," the kind of joint where you feel right at home. Its dark, cozy interior, in a residential street a block behind Prinsengracht, smells slightly of beer and was probably last decorated around 1955. The famous, cholesterol-rich, artery-clogging killer beefsteaks, pan-fried in margarine with onions, come with a slice of white bread and are fantastic. Waiters check you out before bringing you toothpicks with tiny national flags to spear your raw herring, sweet pickles, and triangles of toast. On weekends, you can get a pan-fried steak or a plate of herring until midnight.

Noorderstraat 11 (at Vijzelgracht). ✆ **020/623-7181.** www.pietdeleeuw.nl. Main courses 13€–19€ ($21–$30). AE, MC, V. Mon–Fri noon–11pm; Sat–Sun 5–11pm. AE, MC, V. Tram: 16, 24, or 25 to Prinsengracht.

6 LEIDSEPLEIN

MODERATE

Aphrodite GREEK   In an area awash with Greek restaurants that do a pretty routine island-taverna impersonation, Aphrodite stands out for putting more emphasis on taste and less on dazzling Aegean colors, fishing nets, and Olympian deities. Its single room is modern, restrained in its decor, and softly lit. The specialties—*afelia* (lamb cubes in coriander-and-wine sauce), moussaka, *kleftiko* (oven-baked lamb), and others—are not much different in principle from those of other local Greek restaurants, but are generally better prepared and served—which, after all, is difference enough.

Lange Leidsedwarsstraat 91 (off Leidseplein). ✆ **020/622-7382.** Main courses 10€–19€ ($16–$30). No credit cards. Daily 5pm–midnight. Tram: 1, 2, 5, 7, or 10 to Leidseplein.

Café Americain ★ CONTINENTAL   The lofty dining room is a national monument to Art Nouveau and Art Deco. Since its opening in 1900, this has been a hangout for Dutch and international artists, writers, dancers, and actors. Seductress/spy Mata Hari held her wedding reception here in her pre-espionage days. *Tout* Amsterdam once liked to be seen here (some of it still does), but now it's mostly for tourists. Don't let that worry you, though: It's still great. Leaded stained-glass windows, newspaper-littered reading tables, bargello-patterned velvet upholstery, frosted-glass Tiffany chandeliers from the 1920s, and tall carved columns are all part of the dusky sit-and-chat atmosphere. Seafood specialties include monkfish, perch, salmon, and king prawns; meat dishes include rack of Irish lamb and rosé breast of duck with creamed potatoes. Jazz lovers can stock up on good music and food at the Sunday jazz brunch, from 12:30 to 3:30pm (reservations needed), and if you're starved for news, settle down at a long reading desk with the international press.

In the Amsterdam American Hotel, Leidsekade 97 (at Leidseplein). ✆ **020/556-3000.** www.amsterdam american.com. Main courses 16€–22€ ($26–$35). AE, DC, MC, V. Daily 10:30am–midnight. Tram: 1, 2, 5, 7, or 10 to Leidseplein.

Fun Facts   The Knives Are Out

In the 1960s, satirist Gerrit Komrij described Café Americain's famously brusque waiters as "unemployed knife-throwers."

De Balie INTERNATIONAL   In what was once a jail, this chic theater cafe-restaurant pulls in an arty, theatergoing crowd and serves them an inexpensive lunch and some great snacks along with beers, wines, and coffee, in a stylish, high-ceilinged, ground-floor cafe. Simple but fine meals are served in a restaurant upstairs, which has an ever-changing menu that's short on choice but long enough on taste. A Dutch option might be a zippy variation on something traditional, like *lamsfilet met mierikswortelsaus* (lamb filet with a horseradish sauce). There's invariably a vegetarian plate, maybe something like the Mediterranean-style *mozarellataartje met gedroogde tomaten, broccoli en olijvensaus* (mozzarella pie with dried tomatoes, broccoli, and an olive sauce). De Balie is well placed for a dinner before or after a visit to its own theater, the nearby Stadsschouwburg (p. 229), or one of the multiscreen movie theaters around Leidseplein.

Kleine-Gartmanplantsoen 10 (off Leidseplein). ℂ 020/553-5131. www.debalie.nl. Main courses 14€–17€ ($22–$27); fixed-price menus 20€ ($32). AE, MC, V. Cafe daily 11:30am–10pm. Restaurant daily 6–10pm. Tram: 1, 2, 5, 7, or 10 to Leidseplein.

INEXPENSIVE

Akbar INDIAN   The best Indian restaurant in the Leidseplein area has been here (though not always at this address) since 1981, as one of the city's first Indian restaurants. It's a consistently good performer across the range of Punjabi cuisine—tandoori, curry, balti, vegetarian, and seafood—without being exactly outstanding in any category. The set meals are a good value, and service is friendly and prompt. There's also a takeout service.

Korte Leidsedwarsstraat 15 (off Leidseplein). ℂ 020/624-2211. www.akbar.nl. Main courses 12€–22€ ($19–$35); set menus 20€–25€ ($32–$40) per person. AE, DC, MC, V. Daily 4:30pm–12:30am. Tram: 1, 2, 5, 7, or 10 to Leidseplein.

Bojo Value INDONESIAN   For quick, cheap, and tasty dishes served until the wee hours, head for long-established Bojo, a cheap and cheery eatery near Leidseplein. If hunger strikes after a late night on the town, drop in for a flavorful *longtong rames* (special boiled rice served with chewy rice cakes). If it looks too crowded, be sure to check the adjoining dining room, which has a separate entrance.

Lange Leidsedwarsstraat 49–51 (off Leidsestraat). ℂ 020/622-7434. www.bojo.nl. Main courses 6€–14€ ($9.60–$22); *rijsttafels* 12€–22€ ($19–$35). No credit cards. Mon–Thurs 4pm–2am; Fri–Sat noon–4am; Sun noon–2am. Tram: 1, 2, 5, 7, or 10 to Leidseplein.

Sherpa NEPALESE/TIBETAN   Sherpa may be a little short on the mystical tranquillity that characterizes its Himalayan homeland, but that's to be expected—it's hard for tranquillity to survive in this brash restaurants-and-bars district. Anyway, Sherpa adds a bit of culinary diversity to the area and its prices are reasonable. What's more, it's the only restaurant of its kind in Holland. You can eat "Yeti's food" (fried noodles with fried chicken and sautéed vegetables) or sample various other Nepalese and Tibetan favorites, including traditional grills.

Korte Leidsedwarsstraat 58 (off Leidseplein). ℂ 020/623-9495. www.sherpa-restaurant.nl. Main courses 9€–17€ ($14–$27). AE, DC, MC, V. Daily 4–11pm. Tram: 1, 2, 5, 7, or 10 to Leidseplein.

Quick Bites

Raw herring is a Dutch specialty, and there are dozens of *haringhuis* fish stands in town. The best of all is **Zeebanket van Altena** ★, Stadhouderskade at Jan Luijkenstraat (✆ **020/676-9139**; tram: 7 or 10), a class-act operation across from the Rijksmuseum. Connoisseurs stock up on Pieter van Altena's raw or pickled herring (peppered with Piet's acerbic observations), and lunch on salmon or crab salad, or a dozen other fishy delights, on warm whole-grain buns. You'll use proper stainless-steel flatware and drink chilled white wine from a stemmed glass. It is basically a stand, but a few lucky diners can even sit down to dine at a couple of tiny tables (though local style is to eat standing). It's open Tuesday to Sunday from 11am to 7pm.

To eat a genuine Dutch *broodje* (sandwich) in a real *broodjeswinkel* (sandwich shop), go to the ever-crowded **Eetsalon Van Dobben,** Korte Reguliersdwarsstraat 5–9 (✆ **020/624-4200**; www.vandobben.nl; tram: 4, 9, or 14), off Rembrandtplein, where you might try a smoked-eel sandwich. It's open Monday to Saturday from 9:30am to 1am (Sat to 2am), and Sunday from 11:30am to 8pm.

Popular with Amsterdammers on the go, another good choice is **Broodje van Kootje,** Spui 28 (✆ **020/626-9620**; tram: 1, 2, or 5). A specialty is the creamy *kroket broodje*. *Broodjes* and snacks cost under 6€ ($9.60). It's open Monday to Thursday from 10am to 1:30am, and Friday to Saturday from 10am to 2am.

Should Amsterdam's shortage of good pastrami on rye get to you, head out to Amsterdam South, to the great kosher sandwich shop **Sal Meijer** ★, Scheldestraat 45 (✆ **020/673-1313**; www.sal-meijer.com; tram: 12 or 25), off Churchill-laan. The sandwiches go for under 2.75€ ($4.40); the plate of the day begins at 13€ ($20). Sal's is open Sunday to Thursday from 10am to 7:30pm, and Friday from 10am to 2pm.

If you thought Amsterdam was a bagel-free zone, think again. Some of the best bagels come from **Gary's Deli,** Kinkerstraat 140 (✆ **020/412-3025**;

---

7 REMBRANDTPLEIN

MODERATE

Brasserie Schiller CLASSIC FRENCH/DUTCH   Beamed and paneled in well-aged oak and graced with etched-glass panels and stained-glass skylights, this 100-plus-year-old Art Nouveau landmark (not to be mistaken for the equally notable Café Schiller next door) is a splendid sight. Paintings by the artist who built the hotel, Frits Schiller, adorn the walls. Former chefs supplied the restaurant with the exact recipes and techniques used in the old days. On the classic menu, you'll find everything from stewed eel and potato-and-cabbage casserole to T-bone steak, roast leg of lamb with mint sauce, and

www.garysdeli.nl; tram: 7 or 17). Choose from plain, sesame, whole-wheat, poppy-seed, pumpernickel, cinnamon raisin, onion, and garlic bagels, which range from 2.75€ to 4.50€ ($4.40–$7.20). The 20 different kinds of toppings include pesto, cream cheese, goat cheese, guacamole, tomato, smoked salmon, and honey and walnuts. Gary's—which uses organic ingredients whenever possible, brews a range of herbal teas, and offers takeout service—is open Monday to Friday from 8:30am to 7pm, Saturday from 9am to 7pm, and Sunday from 10am to 7pm.

Homesick Brits and admirers of traditional British fish and chips should head straight for **Al's Plaice** (get it?), Korte Nieuwendijk 10 (© **020/427-4192;** www.fishnchips.nl; tram: 1, 2, 5, 13, 14, or 17), where business gets done with the requisite amounts of salt and vinegar. The pickled onions are big and juicy, and the paper wrappers all you could hope for. There's takeout service and seats inside. Al's is open daily from noon to 10pm.

As in most European cities, you find the best meal bargains are the offerings of the most recent immigrants. In Amsterdam's case, the Middle Eastern snack bars and Surinamese fast-food restaurants have the cheapest meals. The former specialize in shwarma and falafel, and can be found in high concentrations around Leidseplein and Rembrandtplein; the latter are known for their chicken roti, mildly curried pieces of chicken served with a pancake-like bread, and can be found in the vicinity of Albert Cuypstraat, the site of a popular daily market. About 3€ to 7€ ($4.80–$11) gets you a filling meal in either type of place.

Another quick-bite alternative, particularly for seriously cash-strapped budget travelers, are the branches of **Febo Automatiek** that you'll find all around town. They open directly on the sidewalk and look like giant street-side vending machines. Drop a few euro coins in the appropriate slots and—*voilà!*—you have a lunch of Indonesian *nasi goreng* or *bami goreng,* hamburger, fries, and a milkshake. Be prepared to order a few things.

spaghetti Bolognese. A Breton crustacean and shellfish buffet is served daily, featuring lobster, oysters, crab, mussels, and more.

In the NH Schiller Hotel, Rembrandtplein 26–36. © **020/554-0723.** www.brasserieschiller.nl. Main courses 15€–21€ ($24–$34). AE, DC, MC, V. Daily 7am–10:30pm. Tram: 4, 9, or 14 to Rembrandtplein.

Grand Café l'Opera INTERNATIONAL   The main advantage of l'Opera is that beyond its Art Nouveau facade is probably the best, most restrained terrace on Rembrandtplein (though others are more centrally located). On busy days in good weather, the Art Deco interior is a cool and quiet brasserie-style retreat, but of course on such days, no one wants to go inside. The food in this cafe-restaurant is fine, if nothing to write home about. Menu items include such standards as salads, steak and mushrooms, croquettes, and mussels, and even Thai chicken curry for variation. Service, though friendly, is at times a bit erratic.

Tips **Late-Night Eateries**

Since the majority of restaurant kitchens in Amsterdam are closed by 10:30pm, it's good to keep these late-night addresses handy in case the munchies strike: **Fifteen** and **Pier 10** (see "The Waterfront," earlier in this chapter); **Sluizer** (see "The Canal Belt," earlier in this chapter); **Bojo** (see "Leidseplein," above); and **De Knijp** (see "Museum District & Vondelpark," below).

Rembrandtplein 27–29. ⓒ **020/620-4754.** www.l-opera.nl. Main courses 13€–18€ ($21–$29). AE, DC, MC, V. Sun–Thurs 10am–1am; Fri–Sat 10am–2am. Tram: 4, 9, or 14 to Rembrandtplein.

Memories of India INDIAN   The proprietor Khan family earned their spurs in the crowded and intensely competitive London market for Indian cuisine and then brought their award-winning formula to Amsterdam. That formula is simple, really: Serve top-flight Indian cuisine in a setting that gives traditional Indian motifs a modern slant, charge moderate prices, and employ attentive waitstaff. The menu is pretty straightforward, too, and contains the usual tandoori and curry dishes, but pushes the boat out a bit with some fish items, like the Indian Ocean pomfret in roasted coriander-seed sauce. The restaurant somehow manages to combine the hallowed silence of diners intent on their plates with a buzz of friendly conversation. Takeout service is available.

Reguliersdwarsstraat 88 (at Vijzelstraat). ⓒ **020/623-5710.** www.memoriesofindia.nl. Main courses 12€–23€ ($19–$37); fixed-price menus 18€–28€ ($29–$45) a head. AE, DC, MC, V. Daily 5–11:30pm. Tram: 4, 9, or 14 to Rembrandtplein.

8 THE JORDAAN

EXPENSIVE

Bordewijk ★★ FRENCH   This pleasantly located restaurant is often regarded as one of the best in the city. The decor is tasteful, with green potted plants offsetting the severity of the white walls and metallic black tables. Service is relaxed yet attentive, and on mild summer evenings you can't beat dining alfresco on the canalside terrace. But the real treat is the food. An innovative chef accents French standards with Mediterranean and Asian flourishes to create an elegant fusion of flavors. The menu changes often, but a typical expression of this mix is found in the Bresse pigeon with fresh morel mushrooms and polenta. In the *bouillabaisse Marseillaise,* you can just about scent the Provençe coast's heady air, and the *geroosterde coquilles Saint-Jacques* (roasted scallops) are divine. Dinner is followed by a fine selection of cheeses, and the wine list is superb.

Noordermarkt 7 (at Prinsengracht). ⓒ **020/624-3899.** www.bordewijk.nl. Reservations required. Main courses 24€–29€ ($38–$46); fixed-price menu 39€–72€ ($62–$115). AE, MC, V. Tues–Sun 6:30–10:30pm. Tram: 1, 2, 5, 13, or 17 to Martelaarsgracht.

MODERATE

Het Stuivertje MODERN DUTCH   Tucked down a narrow Jordaan side street, this small and personable neighborhood eatery is invariably filled with locals. Meals come from an open kitchen in an agreeably plain, intimate room, with wood chairs and tables, and a small bar. Black-and-white photographs of American stars, like Ol' Blue Eyes, combine unusually on the walls with Old Dutch prints. The limited menu reflects the restaurant's authentic Amsterdam style, featuring classic Dutch dishes with that extra tasty little something, as in the *gegrilde varkensfilet met een cantherellen-roomsaus* (grilled pork filet in a chanterelles-cream sauce) and the *red snapper in pikante kokoskerriesaus geserveerd met rijst, groente en salade* (red snapper in a hot coconut-curry sauce, served with rice, vegetable and salad). There are vegetarian choices, daily specials, and a seasonal menu.

Hazenstraat 58 (off Lauriergracht). (C) **020/623-1349.** www.hetstuivertje.nl. Main courses 11€–19€ ($18–$30); fixed-price menu 23€ ($37). AE, MC, V. Tues–Sun 5:30–11pm. Tram: 7 or 10 to Marnixstraat.

Hostaria ★ ITALIAN Owners Marjolein and Massimo Pasquinoli have transformed this tiny space on a lively cafe-lined Jordaan street into a little piece of authentic Italy, and a showcase for the kind of cuisine Italian mothers only wish they could equal. When you sit down, Marjolein brings garlicky *tapenade* and warm bread. As an appetizer, you might select a perfectly balanced fish soup with a slice of salmon or lightly grilled eggplant slices with fresh herbs. The *zuppa di gamberone con l'acquetta,* a plate of prawns and shellfish from the market, is terrific, and there's also a choice of wonderful homemade pastas—the tagliatelle with arugula and truffles is a particular treat—and *secondi piatti* such as sausage-stuffed veal or Roman-style duck.

Tweede Egelantiersdwarsstraat 9 (off Egelantiersgracht). (C) **020/626-0028.** Reservations recommended on weekends. Main courses 15€–19€ ($24–$30); fixed-price menu 24€ ($38). No credit cards. Tues–Sun 7–10pm. Tram: 13, 14, or 17 to Westermarkt.

Rakang THAI A meal here is a delight to more than just the sense of taste. The dishes, many of them authentic regional specialties, come in generous portions and are seasoned with Thai spices, carefully blending fierce chili peppers with delicate flavors like ginger, coriander, and Thai basil, to suit any palate, whether the preference is for fiery or mild. Bowls of lightly perfumed pandang rice, yellow curry, light-textured sauces, and pad Thai noodles are just some accompaniments. A variety of sorbets is on hand to draw the sting from the sharpest flavors. In the dining room's fragrant cocoon, colorful silk fabrics drape along pastel-toned walls, and chairs are swathed in cool, soft cottons. Takeout service is available.

Elandsgracht 29–31 (off Prinsengracht). (C) **020/627-5012.** www.rakang.nl. Main courses 15€–24€ ($24–$38); fixed-price menus 30€–40€ ($48–$64). AE, DC, MC, V. Daily 6–11:30pm. Tram: 7, 10, or 17 to Marnixstraat.

Toscanini ★ SOUTH ITALIAN This small restaurant has a warm, welcoming ambience and excellent southern Italian food (at least that's the point of emphasis, but most regional Italian dishes are available—though not pizza). Popular with the artists and bohemians who inhabit the neighborhood, Toscanini has unembellished country-style decor, and an open kitchen, that speak of authenticity. Cooking is home-style and there's a long-as-your-arm list of Italian wines. Service is congenial and chatty but can be slow, though that doesn't deter loyal regulars, who clamor for specialties like the delicious veal lasagna and *fazzoletti* (green pasta stuffed with ricotta, mozzarella, and mortadella). Fish, risottos, and pastas in wondrous shapes and sizes all deserve consideration. For dessert, the Italian ice cream is as good as it looks, and the cheeses run a close second.

Lindengracht 75 (off Brouwersgracht). (C) **020/623-2813.** www.toscanini.nu. Main courses 17€–21€ ($27–$34); fixed-price menu 45€ ($72). AE, DC, MC, V. Mon–Sat 6–10:30pm. Tram: 3 to Nieuwe Willemsstraat.

(Finds) **Feeling Like Something Sweet?**

Near the Town Hall-Muziektheater complex, **Puccini,** Staalstraat 17 (© **020/ 626-5474;** www.puccinibomboni.com; tram: 9 or 14), is renowned for its coffee and homemade fruit pies, cakes, and pastries; there's a second outlet at Singel 184 (© **020/427-8341;** tram: 1, 2, 5, 13, 14, or 17 to the Dam).

A crowded Saturday-morning spot is **Kwekkeboom,** Reguliersbreestraat 36 (© **020/623-1205;** www.kwekkeboombanket.nl; tram: 4, 9, 14, 16, 24, or 25), between Muntplein and Rembrandtplein. It's a coffeeshop/candy store/pastry shop/ice-cream stand, where everything's freshly made and management proudly displays awards won for everything from fruit pies, bonbons, and butter cookies to "fantasy cakes." Two other Kwekkeboom outlets in the city are at Ferdinand Bolstraat 119 (© **020/673-7114;** tram: 3, 12, or 25), and Linnaeusstraat 80 (© **020/665-0443;** tram: 9).

You may have to push your way to the back and wait for a table at **Greenwoods,** Singel 103 (© **020/623-7071;** tram: 1, 2, 5, 13, or 17), which brings English flavor to its tea, homemade scones with jam and clotted cream, and lemon meringue pie.

Notable ice cream is created at **Gelateria Jordino,** Haarlemmerdijk 25 (© **020/420-3225;** tram: 1, 2, 5, 13, or 17), where 30 flavors of Italian ice cream, plus chocolate cake and desserts, appeal to anyone with a sweet tooth.

See also **La Ruche,** in De Bijenkorf and **Metz,** in Metz & Co, both under "Department Stores," and **Patisserie Pompadour,** under "Food & Drink," in chapter 9.

INEXPENSIVE

Duende SPANISH Dark, atmospheric, friendly—there's no better place than Duende to experience the varied palette of small plates that are Spanish tapas. Take just one or two and you have a nice accompaniment to a few drinks; put five, six, or more together and you have a full-scale meal. Pick from dozens of choices, including *tortilla española, champiñones al ajillo* (garlic mushrooms), and *calabacín a la marmera* (eggplant with seafood). Accompany them with sangria, jump into the arena of friendly conversation, and you'll be clapping your hands rhythmically and stamping your feet before long—and if not, you might want to sign up for Duende's *flamenco* lessons. Bear in mind that though tapas are cheap individually, their cost soon adds up.

Lindengracht 62 (off Brouwersgracht). © **020/420-6692.** www.cafeduende.nl. Tapas 3.30€–16€ ($5.30–$26). No credit cards. Mon–Fri 5pm–1am; Sat–Sun 4pm–1am. Tram: 1, 2, 5, 13, or 17 to Martelaarsgracht.

---

9 MUSEUM DISTRICT & VONDELPARK

EXPENSIVE

Brasserie Keyzer ★ CONTINENTAL Whether or not you attend a concert at the Concertgebouw, visit its next-door neighbor, Brasserie Keyzer. An Amsterdam landmark

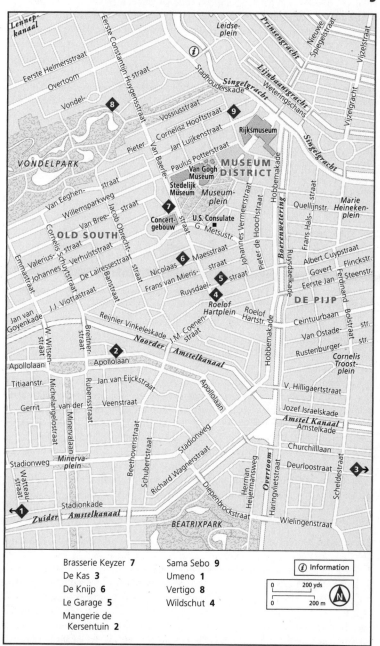

Brasserie Keyzer **7**
De Kas **3**
De Knijp **6**
Le Garage **5**
Mangerie de
 Kersentuin **2**

Sama Sebo **9**
Umeno **1**
Vertigo **8**
Wildschut **4**

ⓘ Information

0   200 yds
0   200 m

since 1903—old-timers say it hasn't changed a whit through the years—the Keyzer has enjoyed a colorful joint heritage with the world-famous concert hall. Among the many stories still told here is the one about the night a customer mistook a concert soloist for a waiter and tried to order whiskey from him. The musician, not missing a beat, lifted his violin case and said graciously, "Would a little Paganini do?" The traditional dark, dusky decor and starched pink linens add elegance, while the menu leans heavily to fish from Dutch waters and, in season, to game specialties such as hare and venison.

Van Baerlestraat 96 (beside the Concertgebouw). ℂ 020/675-1866. www.brasseriekeyzer.nl. Main courses 24€–35€ ($38–$56). AE, DC, MC, V. Mon–Sat 9am–midnight; Sun 11am–midnight. Tram: 3, 5, 12, 16, or 24 to Museumplein.

Le Garage ★★ FUSION Even local VIPs have to beg for a reservation here, one of the hottest restaurants in town. Flamboyant restaurateur Joop Braakhekke is a TV celeb. The service is a circus act, but the fusion fare is worth it. Think cubed tuna tartare with curry and a crisp spinach pancake, or flaming-hot Thai chicken with green chili sauce. The decor would be a hit in Vegas—bright lights, big mirrors, red vinyl banquettes, and black wrap-around wooden chairs. Nonetheless, the wildly creative food is virtuoso stuff. The menu shuttles between a Parisian brasserie and a Tuscan trattoria with stopovers in Tokyo, Mumbai, and Vegetariania. You'll be thankful for the basket of garlic bread because the atmosphere is so festive that it can take an hour to get food on the table (except for the 1-hr. "power lunch"). Le Garage is not a late-night place per se, but the kitchen will serve until about midnight, and the tables are still crowded well after the witching hour.

Ruysdaelstraat 54–56 (at Van Baerlestraat). ℂ 020/679-7176. www.restaurantlegarage.nl. Reservations required. Main courses 22€–40€ ($35–$64); fixed-price menu 45€ ($72). AE, DC, MC, V. Mon–Fri noon–2pm and 6–11pm; Sat–Sun 6–11pm. Tram: 3, 5, 12, or 24 to Roelof Hartplein.

MODERATE

De Knijp DUTCH/FRENCH One of this fine restaurant's advantages is that it's open late—its kitchen still takes orders when chefs at many other Amsterdam restaurants are sound asleep. This would not count for much, of course, if the food weren't good, but De Knijp is definitely worth staying up for, or worth stopping by for after a performance at the nearby Concertgebouw; many concertgoers and assorted other late-nighters do so. The menu is not wildly inventive, the standard offerings being something like oysters, grilled lamb, or roast duck, but you might find a few adventurous items, such as carpaccio with pesto, poached salmon with tarragon sauce, and goose breast with pink pepper sauce. Service is friendly, if sometimes a tad worn-out (this is a hardworking place) in this intimate bi-level bistro with lots of wood furnishings. In summer, a sidewalk terrace is available.

Van Baerlestraat 134 (near the Concertgebouw). ℂ 020/671-4248. www.deknijp.nl. Reservations required for lunch and for more than 5 people. Main courses 15€–22€ ($24–$35). AE, DC, MC, V. Mon–Fri noon–3pm and 5:30pm–12:30am; Sat–Sun 5:30pm–12:30am. Tram: 3, 5, 12, 16, or 24 to Museumplein.

Sama Sebo ★ INDONESIAN Many Amsterdammers consider Sama Sebo the city's best Indonesian restaurant, which means the place is often packed with locals. Its 23-plate *rijsttafel* sets a standard others try to match, and environs are very Indonesian, with rush mats and *batik*. Some items are hot and spicy, but in general, the memorable end result comes from effectively blending spices and sauces rather than adding rocket fuel. You can make your own mini-*rijsttafel* by selecting from the a la carte menu, or take one big menu dish, like the superb *nasi goreng* or *bami goreng*. When you order either of the two lunch specials, you get a heaping mound of food. The restaurant has two sections: the main dining room with its Indonesian motif and the bar area for more casual

dining. If the restaurant's busy (it often is), you can either think of the quarters as con- **133**
vivial or cramped. A sidewalk terrace is equally area-challenged.

Pieter Cornelisz Hooftstraat 27 (close to the Rijksmuseum). ℭ **020/662-8146.** www.samasebo.nl. Main courses 3.75€–6.75€ ($6–$11); lunch menu 15€ ($24); *rijsttafel* 28€ ($45). AE, DC, MC, V. Mon–Sat noon–2pm and 6–10pm. Tram: 2 or 5 to Hobbemastraat.

Vertigo ★ MEDITERRANEAN   If the name of this tree-shaded, animated cafe-restaurant on Vondelpark's edge suggests a high location, the reality is far less giddy—in terms of altitude, at least. The reference is to Hitchcock's classic movie. In the vaulted basement of a monumental, late-19th-century villa, Vertigo shares premises with the Film Museum. Hence the portraits of screen legends on the walls and the classic scenes of movie dining on the menu. On summer days, the terrace is a favored time-out spot for in-line skaters and joggers; a restricted menu is served here, where you can expect to share your table and make instant acquaintance of just about everyone within earshot. On summer evenings, you might even be able to take in an open-air movie. At other times, enjoy the south-Europe cuisine in an intimate indoor candlelit setting. The menu, which changes every 6 to 8 weeks, lists fish, meat, and vegetarian options, plus some fresh pasta varieties. If you see grilled breast of guinea fowl on the menu, go for it!

Vondelpark 3 (at the Film Museum). ℭ **020/612-3021.** www.vertigo.nl. Reservations recommended on weekends. Main courses 15€–18€ ($24–$29); fixed-price menu 28€ ($45). AE, MC, V. Daily 10am–1am. Tram: 1 to Eerste Constantijn Huygensstraat; 2, 3, 5, or 12 to Van Baerlestraat.

Wildschut CONTINENTAL   One of those places that keeps its chic reputation through thick and thin, Wildschut occupies a curved dining room at the junction of van Baerlestraat and Roelof Hartstraat, not far from the Concertgebouw. Amsterdam's bold and beautiful from the arts and media crowd like to see and be seen on the fine terrace, particularly on a summer evening as the setting sun lights all those carefully presented faces. In winter, the crowd congregates inside the Art Deco brasserie. Friday and Saturday evenings get crowded here, so be prepared to join the standing throng while waiting for a table. The food is straightforward but good, ranging from BLTs to vegetarian lasagna to American rib-eye with green pepper sauce. If possible, try to wear something that gets you noticed—but not *too* noticed, if you get the idea.

Roelof Hartplein 1–3 (off Van Baerlestraat). ℭ **020/676-8220.** www.goodfoodgroup.nl. Main courses 15€–24€ ($24–$38). MC, V. Mon–Thurs 9am–1am; Fri 9am–3am; Sat 10:30am–3am; Sun 9:30am–midnight. Tram: 3, 5, 12, or 24 to Roelof Hartplein.

 Picnic Picks

You can pick up almost anything you might want for a picnic, from Dutch cheeses like Edam and Gouda to cold cuts to freshly packed sandwiches at **AH (Albert Heijn)** supermarkets around town. From the AH supermarket at the corner of Leidsestraat and Koningsplein (tram: 1, 2, 5), you can head over to Vondelpark, only a 10-minute walk. At AH's Museumplein supermarket, across the street from the Concertgebouw (Tram: 2, 3, 5, 12, or 16), you can haul your brown bag right up onto the sloping, grass-covered roof, a prime spot for sunbathing, hanging out, and picnicking. Don't forget a bottle of wine.

10 AMSTERDAM EAST

VERY EXPENSIVE

La Rive ★★★ MODERN FRENCH/MEDITERRANEAN   Embedded in the stellar Amstel Hotel and cradling a Michelin star, La Rive is Amsterdam's high temple of culinary art. Ace chef Rogér Rassin combines French cuisine with influences from around the Mediterranean and farther afield. Royalty, leading politicians, showbiz stars, and captains of industry dine here—and you need not even rub shoulders with them, so discretely spaced are the tables. The dining room overlooks the Amstel River through tall French windows, and in summer it opens onto a waterside terrace. Cherry-paneled walls punctuated with tall book-filled cabinets suggest a private library called into service for a dinner party. The menu changes seasonally, so I can't guarantee the presence of palate-pleasers like the grilled baby abalone with citrus-pickled onion purée and garlic juice, the turbot and truffles with trimmings, or the grill-roasted rack of lamb with dates and Zaanse mustard, but no doubt something appropriate will replace them. The service, while impeccable, manages to keep on the right side of stuffy. The wine list is formidable, dessert pastries are luscious, and a chef's table caters to passionate foodies.

In the Amstel InterContinental Amsterdam Hotel, Professor Tulpplein 1 (off Weesperstraat). ✆ **020/520-3264.** www.restaurantlarive.com. Main courses 48€–75€ ($77–$120); fixed-price menu 112€ ($179). AE, DC, MC, V. Mon–Fri noon–2pm and 6:30–10:30pm; Sat 6:30–10:30pm. Tram: 7 or 10 to Sarphatistraat.

11 AMSTERDAM SOUTH

EXPENSIVE

De Kas ★★ CONTINENTAL   Despite its pretentious see-and-be-seen attitude, a traipse out to this hip restaurant in a reconverted hothouse on the edge of town is well merited. The 1926 edifice with a brick smokestack stands on open green ground; it's light and spacious beneath a tented glass ceiling. You get just a couple of variations on a three-course fixed menu that changes daily (it costs extra with cheeseboard). Organic, Mediterranean-style greens and herbs come fresh from an adjacent working hothouse and garden and from the restaurant's own farm. Meat is sourced daily from nearby animal-friendly eco-producers. The seafood comes from the sea, I guess. In the kitchen, persnickety attention to detail is the norm, and service is attentive enough that the waitstaff seem to be personally acquainted with every item

---

Moments   **A Dinner Cruise**

A delightful way to combine sightseeing and leisurely dining is on a dinner cruise. During these 2¹/₂-hour canal cruises, you enjoy a five-course dinner that includes a cocktail and wine with dinner, coffee with bonbons, and a glass of cognac or liqueur to finish. Reservations are required. These cruises cost around 60€–70€ ($96–$112) for adults, and 35€–45€ ($56–$72) for children ages 4 to 12. See "Organized Tours," in chapter 7, for details on tour-boat lines.

on your plate—those who dine in glass houses shouldn't throw stones, but you might want to bring along a few rocks to chase waiters away.

Kamerlingh Onneslaan 3 (close to Amstel Station). ☎ **020/462-4562**. www.restaurantdekas.nl. Reservations required. Fixed-price lunch 35€ ($56); fixed-price dinner 48€ ($77); chef's table 125€ ($200). AE, DC, MC, V. Mon–Fri noon–2pm and 6:30–10pm; Sat 6:30–10pm. Tram: 9 to Hogeweg.

Mangerie de Kersentuin ★ FRENCH/MEDITERRANEAN　All cherry red and gleaming brass, the "Cherry Orchard" has floor-to-ceiling windows looking onto the residential street outside and partly screened interior windows looking into the glimmering kitchen inside. Attention to detail (think Christofle silver-plated flatware) has made this restaurant a mecca for visiting stars. From nouvelle cuisine and a strictly French approach, Mangerie has progressed to its own unique culinary concept, based on a French foundation with Mediterranean influences. The menu changes every 2 months, but these samples should give you some idea of what to expect: lamb filet prepared in goose fat with creamy salsify and coriander-scented vanilla sauce; and sea bass sautéed with peppers, garlic, sea salt, and sesame seeds, served on stir-fried bok choy and tofu, with lemon-grass butter.

In the Bilderberg Garden Hotel, Dijsselhofplantsoen 7 (at Apollolaan). ☎ **020/570-5600**. www.mangerie dekersentuin.nl. Reservations recommended on weekends. Main courses 25€–30€ ($40–$48); fixed-price menu 45€–52€ ($72–$83). AE, DC, MC, V. Mon–Fri noon–2pm and 6–10pm; Sat 6–10pm. Tram: 5 or 24 to Apollolaan.

MODERATE

Umeno ★ JAPANESE　This intimate eatery, somewhat off the beaten track near Olympic Stadium, is popular with local Japanese residents—you get only chopsticks to eat with. Both the food and the service make the tram ride out here worthwhile. Decor is traditional and delicate, with rice-paper windows and a menu that comes in a wooden box. It's generally no problem to find a seat, but as the restaurant sits only 32, it makes sense to call ahead. The sushi and sashimi are always fresh, and their quality is high. Other traditional dishes include *shabu-shabu, sukiyaki, yakitori,* and *tonkatsu.*

Agamemnonstraat 27 (off Olympiaplein). ☎ **020/676-6089**. www.umeno.nl. Main courses 15€–35€ ($24–$56). No credit cards. Tues–Sun noon–2pm and 6–11pm. Tram: 24 to Olympiaplein.

12 AMSTERDAM WEST

MODERATE

Amsterdam ★ (Finds CONTINENTAL　Think of it as *Amsterdam: The Restaurant,* because it's quite a performance. Based in a century-old water-pumping station, complete with diesel-powered engine, the Amsterdam has taken this monument of Victorian industrial good taste and made of it a model of contemporary good eats. You dine amid a buzz of conviviality in the large, brightly lit former pumping hall, which had been so carefully tended by the water workers that some of its elegant decoration didn't even need repainting. Service is friendly and food is good. If you're feeling flush, spring for a double starter of half lobster with six Zeeland oysters. For dessert, the fried sweetbreads are popular. The Amsterdam is a little bit out from the Center, but easily worth the tram ride.

Watertorenplein 6 (off Haarlemmerweg). ☎ **020/682-2666**. www.cradam.nl. Reservations recommended on weekends. Main courses 12€–23€ ($19–$37). AE, DC, MC, V. Sun–Thurs 11am–1am; Fri–Sat 11am–2am (meals served to 11:30pm). Tram: 10 to Van Hallstraat.

EXPENSIVE

Osaka ★ JAPANESE   By moving from an antiseptic perch atop the steel-and-glass Havengebouw (Harbor Bldg.) tower and settling down across the IJ waterway, this authentic restaurant gained a user-friendly setting even as it lost its harbor views. Traditional Japanese food and *teppanyaki* are served. No matter which you choose, the food's both excellent and modestly priced, as Japanese restaurants go—which together make the somewhat onerous trip to undistinguished Amsterdam North worthwhile. Osaka has borrowed the Indonesian *rijsttafel* concept. Order one (menus are named after various Japanese cities), and you get a little of this, a little of that. Otherwise, the menu is standard Japanese, with sushi among extensive seafood listings. In the *teppanyaki* section, chefs are fast on the draw with carving knives and salt and pepper shakers.

Rode Kruisstraat 22 (off Waddenweg in Amsterdam-Noord). © **020/638-9833.** www.osaka-amsterdam. nl. Fixed-price menus 34€–77€ ($54–$123); *teppanyaki* buffet 21€–24€ ($34–$38). AE, DC, MC, V. Mon–Fri noon–midnight; Sat–Sun 6pm–midnight. Bus: 32, 33, 38, 105, 109, 336, 361, 362, 611, 614, or 693 to Rode Kruisstraat.

7

Exploring Amsterdam

Amsterdam affords sightseers an embarrassment of riches. There are miles and miles of canals to cruise, hundreds of narrow streets to wander, 7,000 historical buildings to see in the heart of town, around 40 museums of all types to visit, and diamond cutters and craftspeople to watch as they practice generations-old skills. The list is as long as every tourist's individual interests, and then some.

The city has 160 canals—more than Venice—with a combined length of 76km (47 miles), spanned by 1,281 bridges—also more than Venice. The first thing you should do is join the 2.5 million people every year who take a canal ride on a tour boat. Why? Because the water-level view

of those gabled canalside houses and the picturesque bridges lends meaning and color to everything else you do in Amsterdam.

Yet most of Amsterdam's attractions are hidden, and they're not even attractions in any conventional sense. They're part of a fabric of life, a special but elusive atmosphere that's been slowly evolving for centuries. There are few open vistas or bombastic buildings; rather, the city is enclosed within itself. You'll need to dig a certain amount to get at these hidden-in-plain-sight features. Above all, maintain that certain attitude: a willingness to slow down, open up, and mentally unbutton.

1 THE BIG THREE

Two of Amsterdam's big three attractions—the Rijksmuseum and the Van Gogh Museum—are around **Museumplein,** a big square just south of the oldest part of town (see the "Museum District & Amsterdam South Attractions" map, later in this chapter). Most of the square consists of open green areas bordered by avenues of linden trees and gardens and crisscrossed by walking and bike paths. At Museumplein's north end is a long pond that serves as a handy foot-cooler in summer and has served as a skating rink in winter. The third attraction of the top trio, the Anne Frankhuis, is in the historic Center, on Prinsengracht.

By no means should you hit all three in a single day. You'll wind up emotionally battered by the Anne Frankhuis, bedazzled by the Van Gogh Museum, and, well, Rijksmuseum-ed by the Rijksmuseum. One per day's enough.

Anne Frankhuis ★★★ You shouldn't miss seeing and experiencing this typical Amsterdam canal house, with steep interior stairs, where eight people from three separate Jewish families lived together in silence for more than 2 years during World War II. The hiding place Otto Frank found for his family, the van Pels family, and Fritz Pfeffer kept them safe until tragically close to the end of the war, when it was raided by Nazi forces and its occupants deported to concentration camps. It was in this house that Anne, whose ambition was to be a writer, kept her famous diary as a way to deal with both the boredom and her youthful array of thoughts, which had as much to do with personal relationships as with the war and the Nazi terror raging outside. Visiting the rooms in which she found refuge is a moving experience.

Allard-Pierson Museum **5**

Amsterdams Historisch Museum **8**

Anne Frankhuis **18**

Athenaeum Illustre **33**

Begijnhof **6**

Beurs van Berlage **25**

Bijbels Museum (Biblical Museum) **7**

Blauwbrug **36**

Bloemenmarkt (Flower Market) **2**

De Waag **30**

Erotic Museum **28**

Hash Marihuana & Hemp Museum **29**

Homomonument **16**

Koninklijk Paleis (Royal Palace) **11**

Madame Tussauds **10**

Magere Brug **38**

Magna Plaza **14**

Montelbaanstoren **31**

Munttoren **3**

Museum Van Loon **1**

Museum Willet-Holthuysen **37**

Muziekgebouw aan 't IJ/Bimhuis **40**

Nationaal Monument **12**

Nieuwe Kerk **13**

Noorderkerk **19**

Ons' Lieve Heer op Solder **26**

Oost Indisch Huis **32**

Oude Kerk **27**

Poppenhuis **35**

Schreierstoren **24**

Science Center NEMO **39**

Sexmuseum Amsterdam **22**

Singel 7 (narrowest house) **21**

Sint-Nicolaas Church **23**

Theatermuseum **15**

Torture Museum **4**

Westerkerk **17**

West Indisch Huis **20**

Woonbootmuseum (Houseboat Museum) **9**

Zuiderkerk **34**

JORDAAN

OLD CENTER

CANAL BELT

MUSEUM DISTRICT

Noorderkerk

Westerkerk

Nieuwe Kerk

Koninklijk Paleis

Dam

Spui

Munt plein

Max Euweplein

Leidse-plein

Rijksmuseum

Van Gogh Museum

Stedelijk Museum

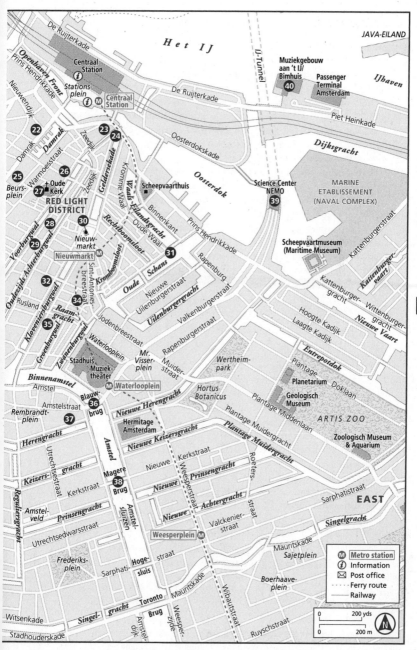

The Canals

Amsterdam would not be the same without its canals. There might still be Golden Age architecture, trams, "brown cafes," and museums, and maybe locals would retain their iconoclastic outlook on life—but without a mirror of water to reflect its soul, the city would be a shrunken glory.

I once lived aside an Amsterdam canal. Not one of the Golden Age canals, but still an honest-to-goodness Amsterdam canal. Barges, powerboats, Frisian *skûtsjes*, and rowboats all glided past my window. In winter, I could step out my front door, jump down onto the frozen water, strap on long-bladed *Noren*, and skate all the way to the North Sea if I wanted to.

I've happily played captain of my own water bike while Amsterdam friends I had lured aboard hid their faces for shame at being seen on such a "tourist trap." I even love the glass-topped canal boats, with their view of Amsterdam from the finest vantage point of all—you just sit back and let the city flow around and through you. I never tire of seeing what is, to me, quite simply the finest cityscape in the world.

To get up close and personal with Amsterdam's canals, you could start out by taking the **Golden Age Canals** tour in chapter 8, which guides you along parts of the *Grachtengordel* (Canal Belt): Herengracht, Prinsengracht, and Keizersgracht. Or stroll along the canals after dark, when they're lit up. For details of canal-boat cruises and more, see "Organized Tours," later in this chapter.

During the war, the building was an office and warehouse, and its rooms are still as bare as they were when Anne's father returned, the only survivor of the eight *onderduikers* (divers, or hiders). Nothing has been changed, except that Plexiglas panels now protect the wall on which Anne pinned up photos of her favorite actress, Deanna Durbin, and of the little English princesses Elizabeth and Margaret. As you tour the building, it's possible to imagine Anne's experience growing up in this place, awakening as a young woman, and writing down her secret thoughts.

In summer, you may have to wait an hour or more to get in. To avoid lines, get there as early as possible—and while this advice isn't as useful as it used to be, it should still save you some waiting time. A better strategy if you're in town from mid-March to mid-September, when the museum is open until 9 or 10pm, is to go in the evening; it's usually quiet then. You won't need, or get, much time inside, but a half-hour should be enough to see what little there is to see—and to pause for a moment to feel Anne's spirit in the rooms. Next door, at no. 265–267, is a modern wing for temporary exhibits.

Prinsengracht 263 (at Westermarkt). © 020/556-7105. www.annefrank.org. Admission 7.50€ ($12) adults, 3.50€ ($5.60) children 10–17, free for children 9 and under. Mid-Mar to June and 1st 2 weeks Sept Mon–Fri 9am–9pm, Sat 9am–10pm; July–Aug daily 9am–10pm; mid-Sept to mid-Mar daily 9am–7pm (Jan 1 noon–7pm; Dec 25 noon–5pm, Dec 31 9am–5pm). Closed Yom Kippur. Tram: 13, 14, or 17 to Westermarkt.

Rijksmuseum De Meesterwerken ★★★ The country's premier museum, the Rijksmuseum, is still working through a decade-long refurbishment project process that's due to be completed in 2013. Most of it is closed, but key paintings and other works

Impressions

From my favorite spot on the floor I look up at the blue sky and the bare chestnut tree, on whose branches little raindrops glisten like silver, and at the seagulls and other birds as they glide on the wind.

—Anne Frank, February 25, 1944

from the 17th-century Dutch Golden Age can be viewed in the museum's Philips Wing, under the banner of "The Masterpieces." Even in its drastically reduced circumstances, the State Museum is still one of the leading museums in the land. The three-star rating given here is justified for the Golden Age highlights alone, but remember that most of the museum's collection, which totals some 7 million objects (only a fraction of which is displayed at any given time), will be invisible to visitors for some time to come. Still, you'll need to allocate a half-day to get around everything.

Architect Petrus Josephus Hubertus Cuypers (1827–1921), the grandfather of modern Dutch architecture, designed the brick museum in a monumental, gabled Dutch neo-Renaissance style. Cuypers, a Catholic, slipped in more than a dab of neo-Gothic, too, causing the country's thoroughly Protestant King William III to scorn "that cathedral." The building opened in 1885 to a less-than-enthusiastic public reception. Since then, much has been added to both the building and the collection.

The Rijksmuseum contains the world's largest collection of paintings by the Dutch masters, including the most famous of all, a single work that all but defines Holland's Golden Age. That painting is Rembrandt's *The Militia Company of Captain Frans Banning Cocq and Lieutenant Willem van Ruytenburch, 1642,* better known as **The Night Watch.** The scene it so dramatically depicts is surely alien to most of the people who flock to see it: gaily uniformed, but not exactly warrior-looking militiamen checking their weapons and accoutrements before moving out on patrol. Captain Cocq (once described as the stupidest man in the city, and whose house at Singel 140–142 still stands), Lieutenant van Ruytenburch, the troopers, and observers (including Rembrandt himself) gaze out at us along the corridor of time, and we're left wondering what's going on underneath the paint, inside their minds. One sentiment might be irritation with this upstart artist, who painted some of their faces in profile or partly hidden, yet charged the full-face fee per man—the militiamen hated the artistic freedom Rembrandt had exercised on their group portrait. In 1975, the masterpiece was restored after having been attacked and slashed.

Vermeer, Frans Hals, Jan Steen, Jacob van Ruisdael, Maarten van Heemskerck, Paulus Potter, Pieter de Hooch, Gerard ter Borch, and Gerard Dou are among many other artists represented at the Rijksmuseum. The range is impressive—individual portraits, guild paintings, landscapes, seascapes, domestic scenes, religious subjects, allegories, and the incredible (and nearly photographic) Dutch still lifes.

In addition, the museum exhibits fine pieces of antique Delftware and silver. Two rare furnished 17th-century dollhouses should be a highlight for children, by bringing the Dutch Golden Age to life for them in a way no amount of "real" stuff could. The dollhouses' owners commissioned craftsmen to copy objects and ornaments, and the contents are exactly as they were in those days, only in miniature. Tiny seashells occupy a display cabinet. The tapestry room walls are covered with silk, the ceiling and the fireplace mantel

(Tips) **Following Anne's Footsteps**

From 1933, when the Frank family left their home in Frankfurt am Main, Germany, to escape the Nazis, until they entered their Prinsengracht refuge in 1942, Anne lived at Merwedeplein 37 (Tram: 4, 12, or 25), in the south Amsterdam Rivierenbuurt (River District). A bronze statue of Anne was unveiled on the square in 2005. Her father Otto bought Anne's diary as a present for her 13th birthday around the corner in a shop at Rooseveltlaan 62 (the street was known as Zuider Amstellaan at the time).

are painstakingly painted, and Italian marble paves the hall floor. Silver spoons rest on the dining table and the family initials are embroidered on the napkins. Look carefully, and you'll even see pins stuck in pincushions.

In the Rijksmuseum Garden, you can breathe scented air and view interesting sculptural elements and other fragments from old buildings.

Philips Wing, Jan Luijkenstraat 1B (at Museumplein). (℃) **020/674-7000.** www.rijksmuseum.nl. Admission 10€ ($16) adults, free for children 18 and under. Sat–Thurs 9am–6pm; Fri 9am–8:30pm. Closed Jan 1. Tram: 2 or 5 to Hobbemastraat.

Van Gogh Museum ★★★   More than 200 paintings by Vincent van Gogh (1853–90), along with nearly every sketch, print, etching, and piece of correspondence the artist ever produced have been housed here since the museum opened in 1973. Van Gogh's sister-in-law and a namesake nephew presented the collection to Holland with the provision that the canvases not leave Vincent's native land. To the further consternation of van Gogh admirers and scholars elsewhere in the world, all but a few of the artist's works that aren't in this museum hang at the Kröller-Müller Museum in the Hoge Veluwe National Park near Arnhem.

You can trace this great artist's artistic development and psychological decline by viewing the paintings displayed in chronological order according to the seven distinct periods and places of residence that defined his short career. (He painted for only 10 years and was on the threshold of success when he committed suicide at age 37.) Only one of van Gogh's paintings sold during his lifetime (his brother Theo sold it), but he did give others out to pay for food, drink, and lodgings—some perhaps went for little more than a song.

The Potato Eaters (1885) was van Gogh's anxious and sensitive first masterpiece. Dark and crudely painted, it depicts a group of Dutch peasants gathered around the table for their evening meal after a long day of manual labor, impressing upon the viewer a sense of the hard, rough conditions of their lives. Gone are the beauty and serenity of traditional Dutch genre painting.

After his father died, van Gogh traveled first to Antwerp and then to Paris to join Theo. In Paris, he discovered and adopted the Impressionists' brilliant color palette. Theo, an art dealer, introduced him to Gauguin, and the two artists often conversed about the expressive power of pure color. Van Gogh developed a thick, highly textured brushwork style to complement his intense color schemes.

In 1888, van Gogh traveled to Arles in Provence. He was dazzled by the Mediterranean sun, and his favorite color, yellow (it signified love to him), dominated such landscapes as *Wheatfield with a Reaper* (1889). Until his death 2 years later, van Gogh remained in the south of France painting at a frenetic pace, between bouts of madness. In *The Night Café* (1888), a billiards hall's red walls and green ceiling combine with a sickly yellow lamplight to charge the scene with an oppressive, almost nightmarish air. (With red and green, Vincent wrote, he tried to represent "those terrible things, men's passions.") We see the halos around the lights swirl as if we, like some of the patrons slumped over their tables, have had too much to drink.

One particularly splendid wall on the second floor has 18 paintings produced during that 2-year period in the south of France, generally considered to be his artistic high point. It's a symphony of colors and contrasts that includes *Gauguin's Chair, The Yellow House, Self-Portrait with Pipe and Straw Hat, Vincent's Bedroom at Arles, Wheatfield with Reaper, Bugler of the Zouave Regiment,* and the very famous *Still Life Vase with Fourteen Sunflowers,* best known simply as *Sunflowers.* By the time you reach the vaguely threatening painting of black crows rising from a waving cornfield, you can almost feel the mounting inner pain the artist was finally unable to bear.

Works by some of van Gogh's friends and contemporaries, including Toulouse-Lautrec, Gauguin, and Monet, bolster this collection. A new wing (1999), elliptical and partly underground, designed by Japanese architect Kisho Kurokawa, houses temporary exhibits of works by van Gogh and other artists.

Note: Lines at the museum can be very long, especially in summer—try going on a weekday morning. Once inside, allow 2 to 4 hours to see everything.

Paulus Potterstraat 7 (at Museumplein). *©* **020/570-5200.** www.vangoghmuseum.nl. Admission 13€ ($20) adults, 2.50€ ($4) children 13–17, free for children 12 and under. Sat–Thurs 10am–6pm; Fri 10am–10pm. Closed Jan 1. Tram: 2, 3, 5, or 12 to Van Baerlestraat.

2 MORE TOP MUSEUMS & GALLERIES

With more than 40 museums, Amsterdam suffers from no lack of cultural institutions, several of which are just a shade less worthy than the big three listed above.

Allard-Pierson Museum The University of Amsterdam's archaeological collection is permanently on view here, though the frequent temporary exhibits are more likely to have truly memorable pieces. In the Egyptian department is a model of the pyramids at Giza, along with mummies, funerary and ritual objects—and a computer that prints your name in hieroglyphics. Of other cultures, ancient Greece, Rome, Etruria, and Cyprus are among the best represented, through their pottery, sculpture, glassware, jewelry, coins, household objects, and more. A touching Greek funerary stela from 420 B.C.

> **Tips Don't "Go"**
>
> Gogh is not pronounced *go*, as Americans incorrectly say it, nor is it *goff*, as other
> English speakers would have it, but *khokh* (the *kh* sound is like *ch* in the Scottish
> pronunciation of *loch*—a kind of clearing-your-throat sound). If you can pro-
> nounce van Gogh (*vahn khokh*) correctly, you should be able to handle Schiphol
> (*skhip*-ol), Scheveningen (*skheven*-ingen), and 's-Gravenhage (ss-*khraven*-hakhe;
> the full name of Den Haag/The Hague).

depicts a young woman who likely died during childbirth reaching out toward a baby in
the arms of a maid. You can see most of the museum in an hour or two.

Oude Turfmarkt 127 (facing Muntplein). © 020/525-2556. www.uba.uva.nl/apm. Admission 5€ ($8)
adults; 2.50€ ($4) seniors, students, and children 4–16; free for children 3 and under. Tues–Fri 10am–5pm;
Sat–Sun and holidays 1–5pm. Closed Jan 1, Easter Sunday, Apr 30, May 5, Pentecost Sunday, Dec 25.
Tram: 4, 9, 14, 16, 24, or 25 to Spui.

Amsterdams Historisch Museum (Amsterdam Historical Museum) ★★ For
a better understanding of everything you'll see while exploring the city on your own, a
visit of 3 to 4 hours to this brilliantly executed museum is more than worthwhile. Its
location, the restored 17th-century former Burger Weeshuis (City Orphanage), is already
notable. Gallery by gallery, century by century, you'll learn how a small fishing village
founded around 1200 became a major sea power and trading center. The focus is on the
city's 17th-century Golden Age, when Amsterdam was the world's wealthiest city, and
some of the most interesting exhibits are of the trades that made it rich. You can also view
famous paintings by the Dutch Old Masters in context.

There are plenty of hands-on exhibits and some interesting video displays. A scale
model from around 1677 shows a then-new Stadhuis (Town Hall) on the Dam, now the
Royal Palace. It's displayed without some outer walls and the roof to allow a bird's-eye
look inside, which makes a later visit to the palace that much more enjoyable. One small
room is given over to local hero Jan Carel Josephus van Speyk, a Dutch naval officer
during the 1830 rebellion by Belgium against Dutch rule. Belgian patriots who aimed to
commandeer his warship at Antwerp didn't account for van Speyk's "Don't give up the
ship" disposition. He dropped his lit cigar into the gunpowder magazine, blowing up the
vessel, the rebel boarders, and himself.

Pop into Café 't Mandje, a typical, if tiny, Amsterdam neighborhood bar. Sadly, you
can't order a beer or a *jenever* from this museum exhibit. For real-life alimentation, visit
the museum's **David & Goliath** restaurant. It has a high-beamed ceiling and a wooden
sculpture (ca. 1650) of David and Goliath that's 5m (16 ft.) high, and salvaged from a
local amusement garden that was a feature of Amsterdam's landscape for more than 200
years until 1862. In summer, you can dine outdoors under the shade of courtyard trees.

If you don't feel like visiting the museum yet and are craving some historic art and
architecture, stroll through the **Schuttersgalerij (Civic Guards Gallery).** It's not easy to
find this narrow, two-story sky-lit passageway linking Kalverstraat to the hidden Begijnhof courtyard (p. 154), even though it is just outside the museum and is signed at various
points around it. Under the walkway's glass roof, you'll see 15 bigger-is-better, 17th-
century paintings showing the city's heroic musketeers, the Civic Guards. Elegantly
uniformed and of doubtful military effectiveness, these militia companies once played an

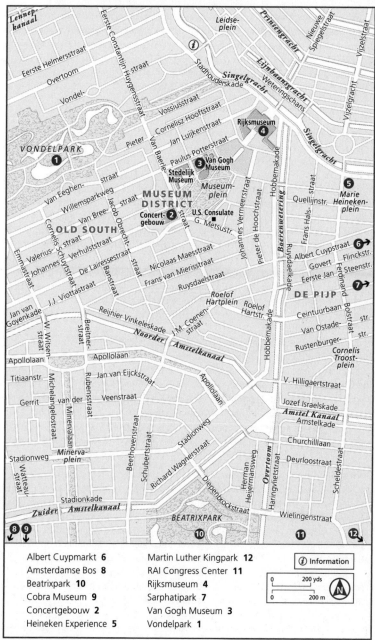

Albert Cuypmarkt **6**
Amsterdamse Bos **8**
Beatrixpark **10**
Cobra Museum **9**
Concertgebouw **2**
Heineken Experience **5**

Martin Luther Kingpark **12**
RAI Congress Center **11**
Rijksmuseum **4**
Sarphatipark **7**
Van Gogh Museum **3**
Vondelpark **1**

ⓘ Information

0   200 yds
0   200 m

important role in the city's defense but degenerated into little more than banqueting societies. The paintings are in the same tradition, if not quite the same league, as Rembrandt's *The Night Watch,* but you don't have to line up and pay to view them. And seen in this relaxed context, without crowds, they are well worth the detour. One of the best is *Captain Joan Huydecoper's Company Celebrating the Peace of Münster* (1648), by Govert Flinck. Admission is free, and hours are the same as for the museum.

Kalverstraat 92, Nieuwezijds Voorburgwal 357, and Sint-Luciënsteeg 27 (next to the Begijnhof). ℭ **020/ 523-1822.** www.ahm.nl. Admission 8€ ($13) adults, 6€ ($9.60) seniors, 4€ ($6.40) children 6–18, free for children 5 and under. Mon–Fri 10am–5pm; Sat–Sun and holidays 11am–5pm. Closed Jan 1, Apr 30, and Dec 25. Tram: 1, 2, 4, 5, 9, 14, 16, 24, or 25 to Spui.

Bijbels Museum (Biblical Museum)

Taking the Good Book as a starting point, visitors here move on to explore biblical history and geography in objects, images, and installations. The setting—twin patrician canal houses from 1662, designed by noted architect Philips Vingboons for timber merchant Jacob Cromhout—is well worth visiting for a couple of hours, both for historical interest and for the rare opportunity to tour a 17th-century canal house (though most of its decor dates from later periods). There are elegant stucco reliefs, and a dizzying elliptical grand staircase. Two ground-floor rooms have magnificent (and neck-stressing) painted ceilings depicting the four seasons, ancient mythological scenes, Greco-Roman gods, and the zodiac signs—all painted by Jacob de Wit in 1718 and 1750. There are fine views of the lovely courtyard garden from some upper-floor windows; stroll through the garden to see a pond and sculptures.

The museum collection includes a superb set of dioramas representing historical and religious scenes. One from the mid-1800s, made from wood, fabric, and gold leaf, depicts the Tabernacle—a desert tent containing the Ark of the Covenant (which holds the Ten Commandments). A model from 1725 is of the Temple of Solomon; another from 1879 evokes the Temple Mount/Haram-al-Sharîf in Jerusalem with the Dome of the Rock. There's one showing how Jerusalem looked in the 1st century A.D., and another that's a Temple of Herod. Replica archaeological finds from Israel, Palestine, and Egypt also feature Jerusalem prominently, as do paintings of biblical scenes. Among the Bibles on display are the first Bible printed in the Low Countries, dating from 1477, and the first edition of the authorized Dutch translation, from 1637.

Herengracht 366–368 (near Spui). ℭ **020/624-2436.** www.bijbelsmuseum.nl. Admission 7.50€ ($12) adults, 4.50 ($7.20) students, 3.75€ ($6) children 13–17, free for children 12 and under. Mon–Sat 10am– 5pm; Sun and holidays 11am–5pm. Closed Jan 1 and Apr 30. Tram: 1, 2, or 5 to Spui.

Cobra Museum

You have to head out to dull suburban Amstelveen south of Amsterdam to find this exciting museum—exciting, that is, if you admire the Cobra group's post–World War II, abstract-expressionist art. The group took its name from the initials of the original players' home cities: Copenhagen, Brussels, and Amsterdam. Folks like **Karel Appel,** Asger Jorn, and Lucebert weren't instantly popular in their day, and it's probably still a stretch to describe them as such today, but they undoubtedly changed the face of art. Appel (1921–2006) was the Dutchman, a controversial painter, sculptor, and graphic artist who in 1950 co-founded the experimental movement. His work, including *Child and Beast II* (1951), has a childlike quality, employing bright colors and abstract shapes. He once said, "I paint like a barbarian in a barbarous age."

Sandbergplein 1–3, Amstelveen. ℭ **020/547-5050.** www.cobra-museum.nl. Admission 9.50€ ($15) adults, 6.50€ ($10) seniors, 5€ ($8) students and children 6–18, free for children 5 and under. Tues–Sun 11am–5pm. Closed Jan 1, Apr 30, and Dec 25. Tram: 5 to Binnenhof; Metro: Beneluxbaan.

> ### ⓘ Tips   Money Savers
>
> One way to save money on museums, attractions, and more is to buy the VVV Amsterdam tourist office's **I amsterdam Card** (p. 41). If you're under 26, purchasing a **Cultureel Jongeren Pas/CJP (Cultural Youth Passport)** for 15€ ($24) gets you a year's worth of discounts at many museums, theaters, cinemas, concerts, record stores, and more around the Netherlands. Visit www.cjp.nl for full details. Serious museum-hoppers might want to purchase a **Museumjaarkaart (Museum Year Card),** which gives free access to most Dutch museums for a year—you might easily recover the card's full value in just a few days, if you visit enough museums. It costs 35€ ($56) for adults, and 15€ ($24) for those 24 and under, and it's available from most museums, or, for a 4.95€ ($7.90) charge, via www.museumjaarkaart.nl.

Hermitage Amsterdam   A visit to Amsterdam can now offer you some of the experiences of a trip to St. Petersburg. Opened in 2004 in the neoclassical Amstelhof, the Amsterdam branch of Russia's renowned State Hermitage museum recalls links between the two canal-threaded cities that date back centuries. During a visit to Amsterdam in 1697, Czar Peter the Great, an admirer of Holland, visited the Amstelhof, which dates from 1681 to 1683 and was built as a home for seniors (at first only for Protestant women). Surrounding a central courtyard, it's flanked on two sides by canals, and on a third by the Amstel River. Exhibits change twice a year, currently in the modernized Neerlandia Building, which was built next to the Amstelhof in 1888 as a home for indigent married couples. Holland even gets some of its own cultural patrimony back again, if only on loan, since the Hermitage has 600 paintings by Dutch and Flemish Old Masters. The full Amstelhof complex is expected to open in 2009, with the Neerlandia section transformed to a "Children's Hermitage."

Nieuwe Herengracht 14 (at the Amstel River). ⓒ **020/530-8751.** www.hermitage.nl. Admission 7€ ($11) adults, free for children 16 and under. Daily 10am–5pm. Closed Jan 1 and Dec 25. Tram: 9 or 14 to Waterlooplein.

Joods Historisch Museum (Jewish Historical Museum) ★   In the heart of what was once Amsterdam's thriving Jewish Quarter (see later in this chapter), this museum occupies a restored Ashkenazi synagogue complex. Its cluster of four synagogues—the **Grote Synagoge** (1671), **Obbene Sjoel** (1685), **Dritt Sjoel** (1700–78), and **Nieuwe Synagoge** (1752)—survived the Nazi occupation of Amsterdam during World War II more or less intact. In 1987, they became home to a collection of paintings and decorative ceremonial objects, including magnificent gold and silver ritual vessels. Through these objects, along with photographs, artworks—including paintings by Amsterdam artist Jozef Israëls (1824–1911)—interactive displays, and a study room with a library of books, the museum tells the intertwining stories of Jewish identity, Jewish religion and culture, and Jewish history in the Netherlands. Extended in 2006, it provides insights into the Jewish way of life over the centuries, incorporating both good times and bad. Take a morning or an afternoon, and leave time to appreciate the beauty and size of the buildings themselves, which include Europe's oldest public synagogue. This is a museum for everyone, Jewish or otherwise, and there are frequent temporary exhibits of international interest.

Tip: The museum cafe is a great place to have a cup of coffee and a pastry, or a light kosher meal. It's quiet, inexpensive, and the food is good. You don't need to visit the museum to dine at the cafe.

Nieuwe Amstelstraat 1 (at Waterlooplein). © **020/531-0310.** www.jhm.nl. Admission 7.50€ ($12) adults, 4.50€ ($7.20) seniors, 3€ ($4.80) children 13–17, free for children 12 and under. Combined admission with the Portuguese Synagogue (see later in this chapter): 10€ ($16) adults, 5€ ($8) children 13–17, free for children 12 and under. Daily 11am–5pm (Jan 1 noon–5pm). Closed Jewish New Year (2 days) and Yom Kippur. Tram: 9 or 14 to Waterlooplein.

Museum Het Rembrandthuis (Rembrandt House Museum) ★★ To view the greatest masterpieces by Rembrandt van Rijn, you must visit the Rijksmuseum, but in this house (ca. 1606), you get a more intimate sense of Rembrandt—it's a shrine to one of the greatest artists the world has ever known. Rembrandt bought the three-story, 10-room house in 1639 when he was Amsterdam's most fashionable portrait painter. In this house, his son Titus was born and his wife Saskia died. Due to his extravagant life-style, the artist was bankrupt when he left it in 1658 and moved with his son Titus and his mistress Hendrickje to a plain house (that no longer exists) on Rozengracht.

Not until 1906 was the building rescued from a succession of subsequent owners and restored as a museum. More recent restoration has returned the old house to the way it looked when Rembrandt lived and worked here, complete with the artist's art-and-curi-osities cabinet, his combined living room and bedroom, the upstairs studio in which he created, among other famous works, *The Night Watch,* a ground-floor kitchen, and the maid's bedroom.

The rooms are furnished with 17th-century objects and furniture that, as closely as possible, match the descriptions in Rembrandt's 1656 petition for bankruptcy. His print-ing press is back in place, and you can view 250 of his etchings and drawings on the walls, along with works by some of his contemporaries, like Jan Lievens, and his teacher, Pieter Lastman. These include self-portraits and landscapes, and several that relate to the neigh-borhood's traditionally Jewish character—like the portrait of Rabbi Menassah ben Israel, who lived across the street and was an early teacher of another illustrious Amsterdammer, Baruch Spinoza. Temporary exhibits are mounted in a modern wing next door, and you'll need at least 2 hours to get around the two places. Opposite the Rembrandthuis, appro-priately, is the Amsterdam High School for the Arts.

Jodenbreestraat 4–6 (at Waterlooplein). © **020/520-0400.** www.rembrandthuis.nl. Admission 8€ ($13) adults, 5.50€ ($8.80) students, 1.50€ ($2.40) children 6–15, free for children 5 and under. Daily 10am–5pm. Closed Jan 1. Tram: 9 or 14 to Waterlooplein.

Museum Van Loon ★ The van Loon family owned this magnificent patrician house between 1884 and 1945. One of a matched pair dating from 1672, its first occupant was the artist Ferdinand Bol, a student of Rembrandt. On its walls hang more than 80 family portraits, including those of Willem van Loon, one of the founders of the Dutch East India Company; Nicolaes Ruychaver, who liberated Amsterdam from the Spanish in 1578; and another, later, Willem van Loon, who became mayor in 1686. Among many other treasures you'll see on a visit, which should last an hour or two, are a family album

A Familiar Face

Rembrandt painted about 100 self-portraits, more than any other great artist.

⓪ **Tips   Don't Miss the Boat**

The tour boats of the Museum Quarter Line carry weary tourists on their pilgrimages from museum to museum (see p. 45). It's a convenient way to do the rounds. For those with limited time, it also provides some of the advantages of a canal-boat cruise.

EXPLORING AMSTERDAM

containing tempera portraits of van Loons living in the 1600s, and commemorative coins struck to honor seven different golden wedding anniversaries celebrated between 1621 and 1722. A marble staircase with an ornately curlicued brass balustrade leads up through the house, connecting restored period rooms filled with richly decorated paneling, stuccowork, mirrors, fireplaces, furnishings, porcelain, medallions, chandeliers, rugs, and more. The garden boasts carefully tended hedges and a coach house modeled on a Greek temple.

Keizersgracht 672 (near Vijzelstraat). ⓒ 020/624-5255. www.museumvanloon.nl. Admission 6€ ($9.60) adults, 4€ ($6.40) students and children 6–18, free for children 5 and under. Wed–Mon 11am–5pm. Tram: 16, 24, or 25 to Keizersgracht.

Museum Willet-Holthuysen ★   Take advantage of another rare opportunity to visit an elegant 17th-century canal house with an ornamental garden. This house, built in 1687, was renovated several times before its last owner, Mrs. Willet-Holthuysen, willed her mansion and all its contents, including a fine-arts collection, to the city in 1885. Its various owner and servant quarters allow you to compare the glittering lifestyles of the wealthy and those of the ordinary folk who took care of them. Among the most interesting rooms: a Victorian-era bedroom on the second floor, a large reception room with tapestry wall panels, and an 18th-century basement kitchen that's still so completely furnished and functional you could swear the cook had merely stepped out to go shopping. You'll easily tour this museum in 1 or 2 hours.

Herengracht 605 (near the Amstel River). ⓒ 020/523-1822. www.willetholthuysen.nl. Admission 5€ ($8) adults, 3.75€ ($6) seniors, 2.50€ ($4) children 6–18, free for children 5 and under. Mon–Fri 10am–5pm; Sat–Sun and holidays 11am–5pm. Closed Jan 1, Apr 30, and Dec 25. Tram: 4, 9, or 14 to Rembrandtplein.

Ons' Lieve Heer op Solder (Our Lord in the Attic) ★   Though Amsterdam's been known as a tolerant city for many centuries, after the 1578 Protestant *Alteratie* (Changeover), Roman Catholics fell into disfavor. Forced to worship in secret, they devised ingenious ways of gathering for Sunday services. This museum in the middle of the Red Light District incorporates the most amazing and best preserved of these clandestine places of worship. The church is in the attic of one of the oldest canal houses you can visit, which was transformed in 1661–63 by wealthy Catholic merchant Jan Hartman to house a church. Worshipers entered by a door on a side street and climbed a narrow flight of stairs to the hidden third-floor church. Seeing a rambling old canal house furnished much as it would have been in the mid–18th century, with heavy oak furniture, Delft tiles, and period paintings, makes a visit of an hour or two here worthwhile by itself.

After Hartman died in 1668, Jan Reynst, a Protestant merchant, bought the house. Reynst planned to rent the attic as storage space, but realized he could make more money charging Catholic worshipers for continued use of their secret church. An 18th-century redecoration created the chapel-size church you see now, with its large baroque altar,

7
MORE TOP MUSEUMS & GALLERIES

religious statuary, pews to seat 150, an 18th-century spinet-size pipe organ, and two narrow upper balconies. It's still used for services and concerts. Other rooms contain a trove of magnificent religious vessels, like 17th-century monstrances in gold and silver.

See also **De Rode Hoed,** under "More Historical Sights," later in this chapter.

Oudezijds Voorburgwal 40 (near the Oude Kerk). ℭ **020/624-6604.** www.opsolder.nl. Admission 7€ ($11) adults, 5€ ($8) students, 1€ ($1.60) children 5–18, free for children 4 and under. Mon–Sat 10am–5pm; Sun and holidays 1–5pm. Closed Jan 1 and Apr 30. Tram: 1, 2, 4, 5, 9, 13, 16, 17, 24, 25, or 26 to Centraal Station.

Theatermuseum (Kids) The Netherlands Theater Institute occupies a group of adjoining 17th-century canal houses, two of which house this imaginative museum. No. 168, known as Het Witte Huis (the White House) for its whitish-gray, neoclassical sandstone facade from 1617, was designed by Hendrick and Pieter Vingboons; it sports the city's first neck gable. Dazzling interior ornamentation from around 1730 includes a spiral staircase, intricate stuccowork, and painted ceilings by Jacob de Wit. Next door at no. 170–172, the lavish Bartolotti House, dating from 1618 and designed by Hendrick de Keyser, is famous for its ornate redbrick gable and Dutch Renaissance facade. Its illuminated ceilings and other interior decoration are also by Jacob de Wit. The museum houses costumes, maquettes, masks, puppets, photographs, paintings, miniature theaters, and theatrical backdrops covering all forms of theater, including opera and children's theater. Hands-on exhibits let you create your own stage and sound effects. A couple of hours should be enough here.

Herengracht 168 (at Leliegracht). ℭ **020/551-3300.** www.theaterinstituut.nl. Admission 4.50€ ($7.20) adults, 2.25€ ($3.60) seniors and children 7–16, free for children 6 and under. Mon–Fri 11am–5pm; Sat–Sun 1–5pm. Closed Jan 1, Apr 30, and Dec 25. Tram: 13, 14, or 17 to Westermarkt.

Tropenmuseum (Tropical Museum) ★ (Kids) One of the city's most intriguing museums belongs to the Royal Institute for the Tropics, a foundation devoted to studying the cultures of tropical areas around the world. Its focus reflects Holland's centuries as a landlord in areas such as Indonesia, Surinam (on South America's northern coast), and the Caribbean islands of St. Maarten, Saba, St. Eustatius, Aruba, Bonaire, and Curaçao. The Tropical Institute building complex alone is worth the tram ride to Amsterdam East; its heavily ornamented 19th-century facade is an amalgam of Dutch architectural styles: turrets, stepped gables, arched windows, delicate spires, and the monumental galleried interior court—a popular spot for concerts.

The museum's approach to its subject has matured considerably from its original 19th-century colonial pride and condescension—indeed, it's become an antidote to those kinds of views. Its representation of contemporary issues such as the causes of poverty in the developing world and the depletion of the world's tropical rainforests is both considered and balanced. The most interesting exhibits are the walk-through model villages and city-street scenes that, except for the lack of genuine inhabitants, capture daily-life moments. Stroll through a Nigerian village, wander an Arab *souk,* sit in a Mexico City bar or in a traditional *yurt* home of central Asian nomads. Examine the tools and techniques used to produce *batik* (distinctively dyed Indonesian fabrics) and the instruments and ornaments that comprise a tropical residence.

Part of the premises is given over to the children-only Kindermuseum TM Junior (see "Especially for Kids," later in this chapter). Before leaving the Tropenmuseum—and you could easily spend a full day here—take a snack or a drink at its tropically inspired cafe, Ekeko. The museum shop sells products from the Tropics and developing countries.

Impressions

This city seems to be double: One can also see it in the water; and the reflection of these distinguished houses in these canals makes this spot a fairyland.

—Jean-François Regnard, French writer, 1681

Linnaeusstraat 2 (at Mauritskade). ✆ **020/568-8200.** www.tropenmuseum.nl. Admission 7.50€ ($12) adults, 6€ ($9.60) seniors and students, 4€ ($6.40) children 6–17, free for children 5 and under, 20€ ($32) family. Daily 10am–5pm (3pm Dec 5, 24, 31). Closed Jan 1, Apr 30, May 5, Dec 25. Tram: 9, 10, or 14 to Alexanderplein.

Verzetsmuseum (Resistance Museum) Amsterdam   Take a trip back in time to Holland's dark World War II days, during the Nazi occupation (1940–45). With authentic photographs, documents, weapons, communications equipment, spy gadgets, and other materials actually used by the Dutch Resistance, exhibits show the ingenuity—along with courage—the freedom-fighters brought to bear on German occupation forces. A pedal-powered printing press is a good example of items that evoke the period and bring it to life. The fate of Amsterdam's Jewish community, herded into a ghetto, then rounded up for deportation to concentration camps, has a prominent place, as do the actions of workers who in 1941 went on strike to protest the first deportation of 400 Jewish Amsterdammers. Yet the museum doesn't shrink from less palatable aspects of Holland's wartime record, like the actions of collaborators, including those who joined Dutch Nazi SS units. The museum, which has a cafe, is in the 1876 neoclassical Plancius Building, which once housed a Jewish social club. A changing program of exhibits takes the story beyond Holland's foreign occupation to feature resistance struggles of recent times.

Plantage Kerklaan 61 (opposite Artis Zoo). ✆ **020/620-2535.** www.verzetsmuseum.org. Admission 6.50€ ($10) adults, 3.50€ ($5.60) children 7–15, free for children 6 and under. Tues–Fri 10am–5pm; Sat-Mon and holidays noon–5pm. Closed Jan 1, Apr 30, and Dec 25. Tram: 9 or 14 to Plantage Kerklaan.

3 THE DAM ★★★

In English, the city's monumental main square is generally referred to as "Dam Square." Amsterdammers call it just de Dam (the Dam)—some even find it amusing to direct hapless foreigners to "the Dam Square": by taking "this damn street and then crossing over at that damn canal." You'll look in vain for any sign of a dam on the Dam, but this is the likely site of the original dam built around 1200 on the Amstel River, which allowed Amsterdam to begin the growth trajectory that took it from backwater village to world-class watering hole.

Dedicated in 1956 to honor the World War II dead, the **Nationaal Monument,** a 22m (72-ft.) obelisk on the square's east side, is embedded with three sculptures: *War,* symbolized by four male figures; *Peace,* represented by a woman and child; and *Resistance,* signified by two men with howling dogs, all flanked by two stone lions symbolizing the Netherlands. In the base are 12 urns, containing soil from the 11 Dutch provinces (before the 12th, Flevoland, was established), and the former Dutch East Indies (Indonesia). A memorial ceremony happens here every May 4, when the queen places a wreath on the spot. For the rest of the year, it's a hangout for teens.

See also the descriptions of **NH Grand Hotel Krasnapolsky** in chapter 5 (p. 83), and **De Bijenkorf** department store in chapter 9 (p. 213).

Koninklijk Paleis (Royal Palace) ★ *Note:* The palace is closed for renovations until sometime in 2009; until then, you can view only its exterior. One of the Dam's heavier features is the solid, neoclassical facade of the Royal Palace (1648–55). Jacob van Campen designed it as a *stadhuis* (town hall) to replace the decayed old Gothic one that in 1652 did everyone a favor by going up in flames. Van Campen intended to showcase the city's burgeoning prosperity, so the interior is replete with white Italian marble, sculptures, and painted ceilings. Poet Constantijn Huygens called it the eighth world wonder, and indeed it was among Europe's largest secular buildings at the time, built on a precisely tabulated foundation of 13,659 timber pilings—a figure taught to all Dutch schoolchildren.

Not until 1808, when Napoleon Bonaparte's younger brother Louis reigned as king of the Netherlands, did it become a palace, filled with imperial furniture courtesy of the French ruler. Since the Dutch House of Orange's return to the throne in 1813, this has been the official palace of the reigning king or queen of the Netherlands. Few of them, however, have used it for more than their *pied-à-terre* in the capital or an occasional state celebration, such as Queen Beatrix's inauguration reception—she prefers living at Huis ten Bosch in The Hague, but can on occasion be seen waving from the balcony here to crowds of onlookers below on the Dam.

In the **Vierschaar (Court of Justice),** until the 18th century, magistrates pronounced death sentences under images of Justice, Wisdom, and Mercy. Atlas holds up the globe in the high-ceilinged **Burgerzaal (Citizens Chamber)** and maps inlaid on the marble floor show Amsterdam as the center of the world. Ferdinand Bol's painting *Moses with the Tablets of the Law* (1664) hangs in the **Schepenzaal (Council Chamber),** where aldermen met. On the pediment overlooking the Dam, Flemish sculptor Artus Quellinus carved a stone tribute to Amsterdam's maritime preeminence; it depicts the *Maid of Amsterdam* and figures symbolizing the oceans paying the city homage. The weathervane on the cupola is shaped like a Dutch sailing ship. Every now and then, the 17th-century Hemony carillon tinkles out a melody.

Tip: When the palace opens again to visitors, don't miss the excellent video presentation (in English) that's shown continuously, usually in the second-floor Magistrate's Court.

Dam. ☎ **020/620-4060.** www.koninklijkhuis.nl. Tram: 1, 2, 4, 5, 9, 13, 14, 16, 17, 24, or 25 to the Dam.

Nieuwe Kerk (New Church)   Many of this originally Catholic church's priceless treasures were removed and its colorful frescoes painted over in 1578 when it passed into Protestant hands, but since 1814 (when the king first took the oath of office and was inaugurated here—Dutch royalty are not crowned; Queen Beatrix, too, was inaugurated here in 1980), much of its original grandeur has been restored. The church boasts a stately arched nave, an elaborately carved altar, a great pipe organ by Jacob van Campen dating from 1645—still in regular use for concerts—and several noteworthy stained-glass windows. Look for the carved, gilded ceiling above the choir, which survived a disastrous fire in 1645. The church also holds sepulchral monuments for many of Holland's most revered poets, among them Joost van den Vondel, and naval heroes. A sculpture depicts the 17th-century Admiral Michiel de Ruyter amid seabattle wreckage. After your tour, dine on 't Nieuwe Kafé's sidewalk terrace, which has a fine Dam view. You might make it in and out of here in as little as a half-hour.

Dam (next to the Royal Palace). ☎ **020/638-6909.** www.nieuwekerk.nl. Admission varies with different events; free when there's no exhibit. Daily 10am–6pm (Thurs to 10pm during exhibits). Tram: 1, 2, 4, 5, 9, 13, 14, 16, 17, 24, or 25 to the Dam.

THE DAM'S LIGHTER SIDE

Madame Tussauds **Kids**   If you like your celebrities with a waxen stare, don't miss the Amsterdam version of the famous London attraction. It has its own cast of Dutch characters (Rembrandt, Queen Beatrix, Mata Hari), among a parade of international favorites (Churchill, Kennedy, Gandhi). Exhibits bring you face to face with waxwork images of the powerful and famous and allow you to step into the times, events, and moments that made them so. The Dutch 17th-century display is magnificent. Cannons roar in the war of liberation against Spain, Rembrandt and Vermeer get busy with their paints, and you can stroll through the streets of Golden Age Amsterdam. More recent Dutch figures get a nod, too, like van Gogh with his sunflowers and Piet Mondrian and a red-yellow-and-blue canvas. Among the characters portrayed—and often brought to life with memorabilia such as paintings or a smoking cigarette—are world leaders, religious leaders, stars, artists, and writers: Nelson Mandela, the Dalai Lama, Michael Jackson, Madonna, David Bowie, Kylie Minogue, Aretha Franklin, Bob Marley, Arnold Schwarzenegger, Sean Connery, Harrison Ford, and many more.

The Music Zone has a disco floor and video footage, music, and pictures illustrating music history since the 1950s. Then comes the Sport Gallery and its athletic heroes, and the TV Studio Backstage, where you get to "meet" TV personalities. In the Hall of Fame, movie stars shine as though it were premiere night. A video projected on a large screen illustrates how wax portraits are created at the Tussauds Studio in London. Finally, don't miss the great view of the Dam from the building's enormous "round window." Having paid the steep admission, you might want to spend a good part of the day here.

Dam 20. ✆ **020/523-0623.** www.madametussauds.nl. Admission 21€ ($34) adults, 16€ ($26) children 5–15, free for children 4 and under, family 60€–70€ ($96–$112). Generally from 10 or 11am to btw. 4.30 and 8:30pm, depending on the season and the day. Closed Apr 30. Tram: 4, 9, 14, 16, 24, or 25 to the Dam.

Special Events

April 30 is *Koninginnedag* **(Queen's Day);** locals and out-of-towners crowd the streets to enjoy performances, parades, markets, and general merrymaking. The area around the Homomonument becomes a huge outdoor dance club.

June to August, Vondelpark hosts **open-air concerts**—check at the VVV Amsterdam tourist office for dates and times. June also has the **Holland Festival,** an extravaganza of music, dance, and other cultural activities that take place all over the city. There's a different theme each year.

The **August Gay Pride Festival** in Europe's gay-friendliest city is a big event. A crowd of 150,000 turns out to watch its highlight: the Boat Parade's display of 100 or so outrageously decorated boats cruising the canals. Other draws are street discos, open-air theater performances, a sports program, and a film festival.

In September, the **Jordaan Festival** showcases this old neighborhood peppered with small inexpensive restaurants, secondhand stores, and unusual boutiques and galleries.

The single most important event in the Netherlands, however, is the **flowering of the bulb fields** each spring from March to mid-May. Two-thirds of all the cut flowers sold in the world come from the Netherlands. The best flower-viewing areas are between Haarlem and Leiden and between Haarlem and Den Helder.

4 HISTORICAL BUILDINGS & MONUMENTS

In a city with almost 7,000 officially recognized historical buildings and monuments, you'll find you're just about tripping over them. That Amsterdam has such a great mass of historical structures gives the city its overall character, but a few stand out head and gables above the crowd. See also the **Koninklijk Paleis (Royal Palace),** above.

Beurs van Berlage (Berlage Exchange)   A massive edifice of colored brick and stone enclosing three arcades with glass-and-iron roofs, the Koopmansbeurs (Merchants' Exchange, or Stock Exchange), as it was originally known, represented a revolutionary break with 19th-century Dutch architecture. Designed by Hendrik Petrus Berlage (1856–1934), the father of modern Dutch architecture and a Frank Lloyd Wright admirer, the old exchange's refined style illustrates Berlage's theories advocating a return to simplicity of form and clarity of line and structure. Now retired as an exchange, the refurbished building, constructed between 1896 and 1903, is used as a space for concerts, conferences, and exhibits. It's well worth visiting as an architectural masterpiece and a prime inspiration for the Amsterdam School of Architecture, but unless you're a fan of this period you won't need to spend much time getting the general idea.

Climb the 156 steps (there's no elevator) of the Beurs tower for a fine view of Old Amsterdam. On a corner of the facade facing Beursplein is a modern sculpture of Count Gijsbrecht II van Aemstel, who in 1204 built Amsterdam's first castle. Beursplein is dotted with plane trees and 19th-century cast-iron streetlamps. The modern **Effectenbeurs (Stock Exchange)** is on the square's east side. Amsterdam's *first* stock exchange, which opened in 1611, was on nearby Rokin.

Beursplein 1 and Damrak 243 (at the Dam). ✆ **020/530-4141.** www.beursvanberlage.nl. Admission and hours vary for exhibits, concerts, and other events. Tram: 4, 9, 14, 16, 24, or 25 to the Dam.

A PIOUS RETREAT

A cluster of small homes around a garden courtyard, the **Begijnhof** ★★, Spui (www.begijnhofamsterdam.nl; tram: 1, 2, or 5), dates from the 14th century and is one of the best places to appreciate the city's earliest history, when Amsterdam was a destination for religious pilgrims and an important Catholic center. The Begijnhof was not a convent, but a cloister founded in 1346 for pious lay women—*begijnen*—involved in religious and charitable work. These kinds of institutions gave options for women who wanted to live without a husband and children, but didn't want to become a nun, at a time when there were few alternatives. Originally, the Begijnhof was surrounded by water, with access via a bridge over what was then called the Begijnensloot canal. Even after the city's 1578 changeover from Catholicism to Protestantism, the Begijnhof remained in operation. The last *begijn* died in 1971, but you can still pay homage to these pious women by pausing a moment at the small flower-planted mound that lies at the center garden's edge and across from the **Engelse Kerk (English Church).** Despite its name, this church, built in 1607 and enlarged in 1665, was actually used by Scottish Presbyterians.

Opposite the church, at no. 30, is the **Begijnhofkapel,** a "secret" Catholic chapel from 1671. It's still in use, and dedicated to the Begijnhof's patron saints, John and Ursula. It wasn't all that much of a secret, since the city's Protestant fathers authorized its construction. It just couldn't be visible as a church from the outside, and the noted Catholic architect Philips Vingboons (1607–78) drew up the plans accordingly. The interior

Behind the Gables

You might think all canal houses look similar. Many do, so far as basic shape goes. Look closer, though, and you'll notice a wonderful mix of architectural detail ranging from classical to Renaissance to modern.

Most of Amsterdam's 6,800 landmark buildings have gables. These hide the pitched roofs and demonstrate the architect's vertical showmanship in a city where hefty property taxes and expensive canalfront land encouraged pencil-thin buildings. If you can pick out Amsterdam's various gable styles without developing Sistine Chapel neck syndrome, you can date the buildings fairly accurately.

Of the earliest, triangular wood gables (1250–1550), only two remain, at no. 34 in the Begijnhof and at Zeedijk 1. Later developments in stone on this theme (1600–50) were the pointy spout gable and the step gable, which as the name suggests, looks like a series of steps. The graceful neck gable (1640–1790) looks like a headless neck with curlicues on the shoulders; look for the first one at Herengracht 168. These were complemented by the less-elaborate bell gable, which looks like a church bell's cross section.

Daniel Marot, a French architect who lived in Amsterdam from 1705 to 1717, introduced the Louis styles, common to 18th-century buildings. The heavy baroque Louis XIV–style suited neck gables; the asymmetrical, rococo Louis XV was better for bell gables.

Among the most lavish gables is one with tritons blowing horns at Herengracht 508. Next door at no. 510, a pair of stone sea gods ride leaping dolphins.

Around 600 old *gevelstenen* (gable stones)—ornamental tiles, sculptures, or reliefs that often play on the original owner's name or profession—still exist (they even have a society of admirers). Walls in the Begijnhof and on Sint-Luciënsteeg at the Amsterdam Historical Museum have some good gable stones, including the oldest known, from 1603, showing a milkmaid balancing her buckets.

Incidentally, the *hijsbalk*—the hook you see on many gables—might look to be ideal for a hanging (the kids maybe), but is actually used with rope and pulley for hauling large, heavy items in and out of homes that have steep, narrow staircases.

stained-glass windows depict scenes from the Miracle of the Host in 1345, a religious event that led to Amsterdam becoming a place of pilgrimage. Only one of the old (ca. 1425) timber houses, Het Houten Huys, at no. 34, remains.

Visit the Begijnhof daily from 9am to 5pm—but take note that senior citizens now reside in the 47 homes, most of which date from the 17th and 18th centuries, and their privacy and tranquillity must be respected. Access is on Gedempte Begijnensloot, an alleyway off Spui. Admission is free. In fine weather, you might easily want to let a couple of hours slip by here.

You may be starting to get the impression that Amsterdam is one big historical monument. Still, some buildings are more historic and monumental than others and therefore more worth going out of your way for. You won't have to go far out of your way to see **Centraal Station.** Designed by architect Petrus Josephus Hubertus Cuypers, the city's main railway station was built between 1884 and 1889 on three artificial islands (supported on 30,000 pilings) in the IJ channel. Amsterdammers thoroughly disliked it at the time. Now it's an attraction, partly for its extravagant Dutch neo-Renaissance facade, partly for the permanent liveliness that surrounds it. The left one of the two central towers has a gilded weathervane; on the right one, there's a clock. Take time to soak up the buzz that swirls around the station in a blur of people, backpacks, bikes, trams, buses, vendors, pickpockets, and junkies. There should be a busker or two, maybe even a full-blown jazz or rock combo, and perhaps a street organ—if you're fortunate, it'll be a century-old Perlee hand-ground barrel-organ, made from richly carved and painted wood.

Not far away, across Prins Hendrikkade at the corner of Geldersekade, stands the **Schreierstoren (Tower of Tears),** built in 1480, once a strong point in the city wall bristling with cannon. Its name comes from the tears allegedly shed by wives as their men sailed away on voyages from which they might never return. A stone tablet on the wall shows a woman with her hand to her face. She might be weeping, but who knows what emotion that hand is really covering? Another tablet, placed in 1945, records the 350th anniversary of the *Eerste Schipvaart Naar Oostindië 1595* (First Ocean Voyage to the East Indies, 1595). The tower's ground floor now houses a cozy traditional bar, the **V.O.C. Café,** Prins Hendrikkade 94–95 (© **020/428-8291**), named for the Dutch initials of the United East India Company.

The **Munttoren (Mint Tower)** on Muntplein sits at a busy traffic intersection at the Rokin and Singel canals. In 1487, the tower's base was part of the Reguliers Gate in the city wall. In 1620, Hendrick de Keyser topped it with an ornate, lead-covered tower, from which a carillon of Hemony brothers bells sing out gaily every hour and play a 1-hour concert on Fridays at noon. The tower got its present name in 1672, when it housed the city mint.

The tilting **Montelbaanstoren,** the "leaning tower of Amsterdam," a fortification at the juncture of the Oude Schans and Waalseilandsgracht canals, dates from 1512. It's one of few surviving elements of the city's once-powerful defensive works. In 1606, Hendrick de Keyser added an octagonal tower and spire. The building now houses local Water Authority offices.

(Fun Facts **New York Loves Ya, Henry**

In 1609, English navigator Henry Hudson set sail from the Tower of Tears aboard the *Halve Maen*. He was under contract to the United East India Company to find a Northeast Passage to Asia. Instead, he sailed west and "discovered" Long Island, the Hudson River, and the future Nieuw Amsterdam, which would later become New York. The Greenwich Village Historical Society attached a memorial marker to the tower in 1927.

The 14th-century **De Waag (Weigh House)** Nieuwmarkt (℃ 020/557-9898; www. waag.org; Metro: Nieuwmarkt) is the city's only surviving medieval fortified gate. It later became a guild house; among the guilds lodged here was the Surgeon's Guild, immortalized in Rembrandt's painting *The Anatomy Lesson of Dr. Nicolaes Tulp* (1632), which depicts a dissection underway in the upper-floor Theatrum Anatomicum (the painting's on display at the **Mauritshuis** in The Hague). Most of De Waag now houses a specialized educational and cultural institute, and is rarely open; admission (when possible) is free, except in the case of occasional special exhibits. You can, however, visit the exceptional cafe-restaurant **In de Waag** on the ground floor (see p. 113).

Most of Golden Age Amsterdam's wealth was generated by trade, and most of that trade was organized by the Vereenigde Oostindische Compagnie (V.O.C.), based at **Oost-Indisch Huis (East India House)** on Oude Hoogstraat, off Kloveniersburgwal. Dating from 1606, the former headquarters of the first multinational corporation now belongs to the University of Amsterdam. Stroll into the courtyard and there's no problem with going inside, where corridors are hung with paintings depicting the 17th-century Dutch trading settlement of Batavia—today's Jakarta, Indonesia.

West-Indisch Huis (West India House), at Herenmarkt 93–99, off Brouwersgracht, is also interesting. On the north side of this little square is a redbrick building, built as a meat-trading hall in 1615. In 1623, it became the headquarters of the Dutch West India Company, which controlled trade with the Americas. A current tenant is the **John Adams Institute** (℃ 020/624-7280; www.john-adams.nl), a U.S.-oriented philosophical and literary society that has hosted lectures by guest speakers like J. K. Galbraith, Gore Vidal, and Norman Mailer. In the courtyard is a bronze statue of Peter Stuyvesant, the one-legged governor of Nieuw Amsterdam (later New York) from 1647 until the British took over in 1664. A wall sculpture depicts the Dutch settlement on Manhattan Island.

Not far from East India House is Amsterdam's first university, the **Athenaeum Illustre,** at Oudezijds Voorburgwal 231. Founded in 1631, the Athenaeum moved here in 1632 to occupy the 1470 Gothic **Agnietenkapel (Church of St. Agnes).** The building now houses the underwhelming University of Amsterdam Museum. In a 17th-century lecture room are portraits of the Dutch humanist and theologian Erasmus and of the Florentine strongman Lorenzo de' Medici. Across the Kloveniersburgwal canal from the university, at Kloveniersburgwal 95, is the opulent **Poppenhuis** (1642), designed by that indefatigable Golden Age architect Philips Vingboons in an Italianate style for Joan Poppen, a wealthy merchant's grandson and heir. It has a classically influenced triangular pediment and ornamental pilasters.

A monument of a far different temper is the forlorn remnant of the **Hollandsche Schouwburg (Dutch Theater),** Plantage Middenlaan 24 (℃ 020/626-9945; www. hollandscheschouwburg.nl; tram: 9 or 14), not far from the Jewish Historical Museum and the Portuguese Synagogue. All that remains of this former Yiddish theater is its facade, behind which is a memorial plaza of grass and walkways. Nazis used the theater as an assembly point for Dutch Jews—60,000–80,000 of whom passed through here on their way to death camps. A granite column rising out of a Star of David emblem commemorates "those deported from here 1940–45." On a marble memorial, watched over by an eternal flame, are inscribed 6,700 family names of the 104,000 Dutch Jews who perished in the Holocaust. An educational exhibit shows how the Nazis gradually isolated Amsterdam's Jewish community before beginning to exterminate its members. The site is open daily from 11am to 4pm. Admission is free.

For more than 2 centuries after Amsterdam's 1578 Protestant revolution, the *Alteratie,* other Christian denominations were forbidden to worship openly. Clandestine places of worship sprang up around the city. The best known of these was the Catholic **Ons' Lieve Heer op Solder** (see "More Museums & Galleries," earlier in this chapter). Another, which is in fact Holland's oldest and largest, is the **Remonstrant Church** in a one-time hat store called **De Rode Hoed (the Red Hat),** Keizersgracht 102 (© **020/638-5606;** tram: 13, 14, or 17), in a fine canalside building—look for the little red hat on the gable stone. The chapel in back, with a balcony and an impressive organ, dates from 1630 and is now a venue for classical music concerts and debates.

The **Seven Countries Houses** at Roemer Visscherstraat 20–30 were built in 1894 in architectural styles from Germany, France, Spain, Italy, Russia, Holland, and England. While these aren't really worth going far out of your way for, drop by if you're in the area, or are lodging at a hotel close to Roemer Visscherstraat.

Magna Plaza, behind the Dam and the Royal Palace, was formerly Amsterdam's main post office. The elegant, arcaded building constructed with red-and-cream bricks opened in 1899. Amsterdammers immediately dubbed it *Perenberg* (Pear Mountain) because of its pear-shaped towers. It's been transformed into a mall with an icky Latin name.

THE SMALLEST HOUSES

The narrowest house in Amsterdam (and who knows, maybe even the world) is at **Singel 7.** It's just a meter (3^1/$_2$ ft.) wide, barely wider than the front door. It is, however, a cheat. Only the front facade is really so narrow; behind that, it broadens out to more normal proportions. The real narrowest house is at **Oude Hoogstraat 22,** between the Dam and Nieuwmarkt. It has a typical Amsterdam bell gable and is 2.02m (6^2/$_3$ ft.) wide.and 6m (20 ft.) deep. A close rival, at 2.4m (7^3/$_4$ ft.) wide, is nearby at **Kloveniersburgwal 26;** this is the cornice-gabled **Klein Trippenhuis,** also known as Mr. Trip's Coachman's House. It faces the elegant **Trippenhuis** at no. 29, which, at 22m (72 ft.), is the widest Old Amsterdam house. The wealthy merchant Trip brothers had it built for themselves in 1660, and the story goes that the coachman exclaimed one day: "Oh, if only I could be so lucky as to have a house as wide as my master's door!" His master overheard this, and the coachman's wish was granted. The small house is now a fashion boutique.

NOTABLE BRIDGES

Made of African azobe wood, the famous **Magere Brug (Skinny Bridge)** ★, a double drawbridge, spans the Amstel between Kerkstraat and Nieuwe Kerkstraat. This is the latest successor, dating from 1969, to the 1672 original, which legend says was built to make it easier for the two wealthy Mager sisters, who lived on opposite banks of the river, to visit each other. The footbridge, one of the city's 60 drawbridges, is a big draw, especially after dark, when it's illuminated by hundreds of lights. A bridge master raises it to let boats through.

Though most of the **Blauwbrug (Blue Bridge)** over the Amstel at Waterlooplein looks gray, renovation reinstated blue lanterns. Now Blauwbrug, at least at night, is once

---

(Fun Facts)   Floating Cat House

The Poezenboot (Cat Boat), on the Singel canal facing no. 16 (© **020/625-8794;** www.poezenboot.nl), is a temporary home to dozens of stray cats.

again as blue as when the city's great Impressionist artist George Hendrik Breitner (1857–1923) painted it in the 1880s. The cast-iron bridge (1884), inspired by Paris's Pont Alexandre III, is named after a 16th-century timber bridge painted Nassau blue after the 1578 Protestant takeover. The columns that bear the lamps are surmounted by sculpted copies of the Habsburg imperial crown.

The widest bridge in the old town, the **Torensluis,** Singel (at Oude Leliestraat; tram: 1, 2, 5, 13, or 17), stands on the site of a 17th-century sluice gate flanked by twin towers that were demolished in 1829. Its foundations were used for what must have been a particularly damp and gloomy prison. Sidewalk terraces from nearby cafes encroach onto the span, and the bronze statue on the bridge is of Multatuli, a 19th-century author.

From the bridge over Reguliersgracht at Keizersgracht, you get a view of seven parallel bridges, which are floodlit at night.

MODERN SIGHTS & MONUMENTS

On Westermarkt is the world's first-ever monument to the gays and lesbians killed during World War II and persecuted through the ages. The **Homomonument,** by sculptor Karin Daan and formally titled *To Friendship* (1987), consists of three pink triangular granite blocks (the color and shape of the badge the Nazis forced homosexuals to wear), that together form a larger triangular outline. One block, symbolizing the future, points to the Keizersgracht canal; a second, at ground level, points toward the nearby Anne Frank House—a bronze sculpture of Anne stands on the square; the third, a kind of plinth, points toward the offices of COC, a gay cultural organization.

An equally thought-provoking memorial honors another group of persecuted individuals—black African slaves, of whom the Dutch did their share of abducting, transporting to the Americas, and setting to unrequited labor. The pleasant but undistinguished surroundings of the **Oosterpark** (Tram: 3 or 7), a 19th-century park in the English landscape style in Amsterdam-Oost (East), experienced quite a jolt in 2002 with the installation of the spectacular **Slavernijmonument (Slavery Monument).** The lengthy sculpture recounts in bronze a journey toward freedom. At the rear, a group of African men, women, and children trudge along, roped together. In the center, one of them passes under a winged arch and enters freedom. At the front, a large figure with outstretched arms greets those emerging from the arch.

Amsterdam hasn't been resting on its laurels when it comes to creating places that future generations might think of as historic. Back in the 1980s, in fact, pitched street battles took place at—ironic, this—Waterlooplein (Waterloo Square) between police and protesters whose respective views on the merits of the city's new combined opera-and-ballet hall and city hall evidently differed. (If the idea of Dutch police cracking skulls, drawing blood, and belching out clouds of tear-gas seems at odds with their laid-back image, let me assure you that a steel fist lurks within that Euro-softie kid glove.) In any case, the **Muziektheater** and **Stadhuis** (1986) on Waterlooplein are paragons of postmodern architecture, which means nobody loves them much. At least what goes on *inside* the Muziektheater is generally appreciated, something you couldn't say about the Stadhuis. (Another worthy stop for music is the 19th-century concert hall **Concertgebouw** at Concertgebouwplein 2–6; see p. 225 for info.)

Way down in south Amsterdam, the **RAI Convention Center** has been spreading like an amoeba for decades, until now it is the largest single institution inside the city limits and a big money spinner. Many visitors to the city come for no other reason than to take part in or visit a trade show, convention, or congress here—okay, they might also visit a dope den, a raunchy club, or a red-light haunt.

5 NEIGHBORHOODS TO EXPLORE

All of Amsterdam is worth exploring. Naturally, some parts more than others.

THE JORDAAN ★

Few traditional sights clutter the old Jordaan district that lies just west of the Canal Belt's northern reaches—though 800 of its buildings are protected monuments. But the area does provide an authentic taste of Old Amsterdam. The neighborhood of tightly packed houses and narrow streets and canals was built in the 17th century for craftsmen, tradesmen, and artists. Its name may have come from the French *jardin* (garden), from Protestant French Huguenot refugees who settled here in the late 17th century. Indeed, many streets and canals are named for flowers, trees, and plants. Some of today's streets used to be canals until they were filled in during the 19th century (there's been talk of reversing that and bringing some of the lost canals back).

The neighborhood's modest nature persists even though renewal and gentrification has brought in an influx of offbeat boutiques, quirky stores, cutting-edge art galleries, and trendy restaurants. For a close encounter with the district's unconventional character, see "Walking Tour 3: The Jordaan," p. 191.

THE RED LIGHT DISTRICT

The warren of streets and old canals of the **Rosse Buurt (Red Light District),** around Oudezijds Achterburgwal and Oudezijds Voorburgwal—also known as **De Wallen (the Walls)** or **De Walletjes (the Little Walls)**—is on most people's sightseeing agenda for its open attitude to the world's oldest profession. This is one of the few traditional Amsterdam "industries" still practiced in its original setting, and the first guide to the district's peculiar attractions dates from the 17th century.

However, a visit to this area is not for everyone. If you're liable to be offended by the sex trade exposed in all its garish colors, don't go. If you do choose to go, exercise caution; the area is a center of crime, vice, and drugs. As always in Amsterdam, there's no need to exaggerate the risks. Plenty of tourists visit the Rosse Buurt and suffer nothing more serious than a come-on from one of the prostitutes. Stick to busy streets and be leery of pickpockets at all times. There can be a sinister air to the weird-looking men who gather on the canal bridges; there's a sadder aura around the "heroin whores" who wander the dark streets. Finally, do not take photographs of the women in the windows, many of whom don't want Mom and Dad to know how they earn a living. Large, observant men are on the lookout, and they won't hesitate to throw your camera (and maybe your person) into the canal.

Still, it's extraordinary to view the prostitutes in leather and lace sitting in storefronts listening to their iPods as they knit or adjust their makeup, waiting patiently for customers. The district seems to reflect Dutch pragmatism; if you can't stop prostitution, you can at least confine it to a particular area and impose health, tax, and other regulations on it.

Mirrors on the Walls

The Dutch use the little mirrors you'll see on many house fronts from upper-story windows to see who's knocking at their door.

Whipped into Shape

Back in the 17th century, the City Fathers were disposed to be strict with "fallen women"—when they weren't availing themselves of their services. Some were sent to the **Spinhuis**, a females-only corrections house on Spinhuissteeg, off Oudezijds Achterburgwal, just beyond the Red Light District's southern edge. Here they were returned to the straight and narrow path by a strict regimen of spinning cloth. A relief above the entrance shows women being whipped, accompanied by an inscription in lip-smacking prose: *Schrik niet ik wreek geen quaat maar dwing tot goet. Straf is mijn hand maar lieflyk myn gemoet* (Cry not, I avenge no wrong but compel to the good. Stern is my hand but kind is my aim). The building now houses the University of Amsterdam's Faculty of Politics and Social and Cultural Studies.

The fact is that underneath its tacky glitter, the Red Light District contains some of Amsterdam's prettiest canals and loveliest old architecture, plus some excellent bars and restaurants, secondhand bookstores, and other specialty stores (not all of which aim at erogenous zones). To get there, take tram no. 4, 9, 14, 16, 24, or 25 to the Dam, then pass behind the Grand Hotel Krasnapolsky. See also "Walking Tour 2: The Old Center," p. 186; and "The Red Light District," in chapter 10, which covers the district as an after-dark attraction.

THE JEWISH QUARTER

For more than 350 years, Amsterdam was a center of Jewish life—you might still hear locals calling the city "Mokum," from the Hebrew word *makom,* meaning "sacred place"—and its Jewish community was a major contributor to the city's vitality and prosperity. The Jodenbuurt (Jewish Quarter) was centered on Waterlooplein and neighboring streets such as **Jodenbreestraat (Broad Street of the Jews).** In this area, they built their synagogues and held their market. Of the five synagogues built in the "Jerusalem of the West" during the 17th and 18th centuries, only the **Portuguese Synagogue** (see below) continued to serve as a house of worship after the devastating depletion of the Jewish population during World War II. For more on the district's remaining sights, see "Walking Tour 4: The Jewish Quarter," p. 195.

THE WATERFRONT ★

Visitors suffering from a kind of linguistic seizure could be forgiven for wishing Amsterdam's waterfront had been given a different name. What to make of Het IJ? The first word is the neuter form of the word "the," and pronounced more or less as it looks. But IJ? (Yes, that is two upper-case letters.) *Idge? Eyedge?* Say *Aye,* as in "Aye aye, skipper," and you'll be close enough. The narrow shipping channel takes its name from a river that used to flow into the Zuider Zee hereabout until, centuries ago, its course was washed away by an expanding sea. Then, last century, the Zuider Zee transformed into a freshwater lake called the IJsselmeer (after the IJssel River that still flows into it farther east).

Amsterdam's biggest redevelopment project is underway in the IJ channel's Eastern Harbor, once a major part of Amsterdam Port. City government touts the project as "a new life on the water." Java-Eiland, KNSM-Eiland, and other artificial islands and peninsulas have been cleared of most of their warehouses and other harbor installations. Modern housing and infrastructure take their place. A visit here is a good way to see how Amsterdam sees its future, away from its Golden Age heart.

A fast tram service (line 26) connects Centraal Station with the old Eastern Harbor's redeveloped districts along Het IJ. Among its stops are ones for the Muziekgebouw aan 't IJ and Bimhuis concert halls, the Passenger Terminal Amsterdam cruise-liner dock, and the Eastern Islands' new residential, shopping, and entertainment zones. The service goes out as far as the new IJburg suburb, on an artificial island in the IJsselmeer's southern reaches. See also Science Center NEMO, p. 165.

Some of the focus has switched to the Western Harbor, west of Centraal Station.

6 SIGHTS OF RELIGIOUS SIGNIFICANCE

Religion has always been an important part of Amsterdam's history; hundreds of churches are testimony to the great variety of religious beliefs still alive—if not always thriving—in the city. Most can be visited during regular services; some have open doors during weekdays so that visitors may have a look.

In addition to the churches and a synagogue reviewed below, you can find information about the **Nieuwe Kerk (New Church)** under "The Dam," earlier in this chapter. The **Biblical Museum,** the **Jewish Historical Museum,** and the secret church **Our Lord in the Attic** are covered under "More Museums & Galleries," earlier in this chapter. For another secret church, in a building called **De Rode Hoed,** and for the city's medieval **Begijnhof,** look under "Historical Buildings & Monuments," earlier in this chapter.

Noorderkerk (North Church)   A Greek cross-shaped church, designed by Hendrick de Keyser and dating from 1620, Noorderkerk was built for the Jordaan's poor Calvinist faithful. The four triangular houses tucked into the cross's angles weren't part of de Keyser's original plan; architect Hendrick Staets, unwilling to see so much useful space go to waste, added them after de Keyser died in 1621. This is still a working church with an active congregation. A plaque on the facade recalls the 1941 strike protesting Nazi deportation of the city's Jews. Between May and September, for 14€ ($22), you can take in a classical music recital every Saturday at 2pm. A brief visit (when that's possible) and a turn around the outside should suffice.

Noordermarkt 44–48 (off Prinsengracht). ℭ **020/626-6436.** Free admission. Mon 10:30am–12:30pm; Sat 11am–1pm; Sun (services) 10am and 7pm. Tram: 1, 2, 5, 13, or 17 to Martelaarsgracht; *Stop/Go* minibus.

Oude Kerk (Old Church) ★★   This triple-nave, late-Gothic church—its official name is Sint-Nicolaaskerk (St. Nicholas's Church), but nobody ever calls it that—was begun in 1250 and essentially completed with the extension of the bell tower in 1566. Then, in 1578, Protestant reformers destroyed much of its Catholic ornamentation. On the southern porch, to the right of the sexton's house, is a coat of arms belonging to Maximilian of Austria, who, with his son Philip, contributed to the porch's construction. Rembrandt's wife is entombed in vault 28K, which bears the simple inscription "Saskia Juni 1642." The church contains a magnificent Christian Müller organ (1728) that's regularly used for recitals. An inscription over the entrance to the marriage chapel warns all who enter: *'t is haest getrout dat lange rout (Marry in haste, repent at leisure).* Nowadays, the pretty gabled almshouses around the Oude Kerk feature red-fringed windows through which can be seen the scantily clad ladies of the Red Light District. On a guided tour, climb the 70m (230-ft.) church tower, which holds a carillon of 17th-century Hemony bells, for great views of Old Amsterdam.

Oudekerksplein 23 (at Oudezijds Voorburgwal). 🕓 **020/625-8284** church; 🕓 020/689-2565 tower. www.oudekerk.nl. Church: Admission 5€ ($8) adults, 4€ ($6.40) seniors and students, free for children 11 and under. Mon–Sat 11am–5pm; Sun 1–5:30pm. Tower: Admission 6€ ($9.60); minimum age 12. Sat–Sun 1–5pm; tours every 30 min. Metro: Nieuwmarkt.

Portugese Synagoge (Portuguese Synagogue) Sephardic Jews fleeing Spain and Portugal during the 16th and early 17th centuries established a neighborhood east of the center known as the Jewish Quarter. In 1665, they built an elegant synagogue, modeled on the Temple in Jerusalem, within an existing courtyard facing what's now a busy traffic circle. The total cost of the magnificent building was 186,000 florins, a king's ransom in those days but a small price to pay for the Sephardic Jews, whose community could worship openly for the first time in 200 years. The building was restored in the 1950s, and today it looks essentially as it did 340 years ago, with the women's gallery supported by 12 stone columns to represent the Twelve Tribes of Israel, and the large, low-hanging brass chandeliers that together hold 1,000 candles, all of which are lighted for the private weekly services.

Mr. Visserplein 3 (at Waterlooplein). 🕓 **020/624-5351.** www.esnoga.com. Admission 6.50€ ($10) adults, 5€ ($8) seniors and students, 4€ ($6.40) children 10–17, free for children 9 and under. Apr–Oct Sun–Fri 10am–6pm; Nov–Mar Sun–Thurs 10am–6pm, Fri 10am–2pm. Closed Jewish holidays. Tram: 9 or 14 to Mr. Visserplein.

Sint-Nicolaaskerk (St. Nicholas's Church) Opened in 1887, the city's somewhat gloomy, neo-baroque main Catholic church has twin towers and a high domed cupola. At the heart of what was once the old harbor, it started out as a place of worship for seafarers (of whom St. Nicholas is the patron). Inside, murals illustrate themes from the saint's life; the 1345 Miracle of Amsterdam; and the execution of the Catholic martyrs of Gorcum (Gorinchem).

Prins Hendrikkade 73 (facing Centraal Station). 🕓 **020/330-7812.** www.nicolaas-parochie.nl. Free admission. Mon and Sat noon–3pm; Tues–Fri 11am–4pm. Tram: 1, 2, 4, 5, 9, 13, 16, 17, 24, 25, or 26 to Centraal Station.

Westerkerk (West Church) ★ The Renaissance-style Westerkerk holds the remains of Rembrandt, his mistress Hendrickje Stoffels, and probably his son Titus, all in unmarked graves. It's also where, in 1966, Princess (now Queen) Beatrix and Prince Claus said their marriage vows. The church was begun in 1620 and opened in 1631, with Hendrick de Keyser as the initial designer, whose son Pieter took over after Hendrick's death in 1621. In the church's light and spacious interior is a fine organ.

Get Amsterdam's best views by climbing the 186-step stairway or taking the elevator to the top of the Westertoren, on a guided tour. The 85m (277-ft.) church tower, nick-named "Lange Jan" (Long John), is Amsterdam's tallest, providing a spectacular pan-oramic view of the city—and a 3-centimeter (1-in.) sway on a windy day. On its top is the Holy Roman Empire's blue, red, and gold imperial crown, a symbol bestowed on the then-Catholic city in 1489 by the Habsburg emperor Maximilian. The tower's carillon of 17th-century Hemony brothers bells is among the city's most lyrical.

Westermarkt. 🕓 **020/624-7766** church; 🕓 020/689-2565 tower. www.westerkerk.nl. Church: Free admission. Apr–Sept Mon–Sat 11am–3pm. Tower: Admission 6€ ($9.60); minimum age 6. Apr–Oct Mon–Sat 10am–5:30pm; tours every 30 min. Tram: 13, 14, or 17 to Westermarkt.

Zuiderkerk (South Church)   Three of Rembrandt's children were buried here, in the city's first Protestant church, designed by Hendrick de Keyser and built between 1603 and 1614. In recent years, it's succumbed to a shortage of worshipers and today houses a permanent exhibit on modern urban planning, which shows where Amsterdam's headed and is well worth investing an hour or two in. You can climb the church tower, the Zuidertoren, on a tour; its Hemony carillon still peals out in clear tones every hour, and the city carilloneur plays a 1-hour concert here Thursdays at noon.

Zuiderkerkhof 72 (btw. Nieuwmarkt and Waterlooplein). ℭ **020/552-7987** church; ℭ 020/689-2565 tower. www.zuiderkerk.amsterdam.nl. Church: Free admission. Mon–Fri 9am–4pm; Sat noon–4pm; Tower: 6€ ($9.60) adults, 3€ ($4.80) children 6–12, free for children 5 and under. Apr–Sept Mon–Sat noon–3:30pm (every half-hour). Tram: 9 or 14 to Waterlooplein.

7 MULTIMEDIA ATTRACTIONS

Amsterdam is not only about history and heavy-duty culture. Here's a selection of places with a modern bent.

Heineken Experience   Five minutes into the self-guided multimedia tour at Heineken's old Amsterdam brewery, I was already mentally pinning Frommer's "Overrated" icon to this review. Two things persuaded me not to: First, the further you go, the better it gets; second, the other visitors (mostly young males) were having a whale of a time. But admission is steep—even if you do get two "free" fills of Heineken beer and a keepsake Heineken glass—and it seems like a bunch of Heineken marketing whizzes came up with a brilliant wheeze to repurpose the facility and grow the market. You pay to get hit by a high-energy multimedia assault aimed at fixing the word "Heineken" deep in your psyche, and to receive compelling content like "Water is a vital ingredient in beer-brewing."

The experience, such as it is, unfolds inside former Heineken brewing facilities, which date from 1867. Before the brewery stopped functioning in 1988, it produced more than 100 million liters (26 million gal.) annually. Fermentation tanks, each capable of holding a million glassfuls of Heineken, are still there, along with multistory malt silos and all manner of vintage brewing equipment. You "meet" Dr. Elion, the 19th-century chemist who isolated the renowned Heineken "A" yeast, which gives the beer its taste. In one amusing attraction, you stand on a moving floor, face a large video screen, and get to see and feel what it's like to be a Heineken beer bottle—one of a half-million every hour—careening on a conveyor belt through a modern Heineken bottling plant. Best of all, in another touchy-feely presentation, you "sit" aboard an old brewery dray-wagon, pulled by a pair of big Shire horses on the video screen in front of you, that shakes, rattles, and rolls on a minitour through Amsterdam.

It *is* fun, I have to admit. But serious types can take cold comfort from a multiscreen presentation on the evidently dire state of freshwater resources around the world.

Fun Facts   **Prohibition? No Thanks.**

In April 1933, 100 gallons of beer from the Heineken brewery in Rotterdam arrived in Hoboken, New Jersey. This was the first legal shipment of beer to the U.S. in 13 years.

Artis Zoo **9**
Hermitage Amsterdam **5**
Hollandsche Schouwburg **8**
Hortus Botanicus **6**

Joods Historisch Museum **4**
Museum Het Rembrandthuis **1**
Muziektheater/Stadhuis **2**
Portuguese Synagogue **3**

Tropenmuseum **10**
Verzetsmuseum
(Resistance Museum) **7**

Stadhouderskade 78 (at Ferdinand Bolstraat). ☎ **020/523-9666.** www.heinekenexperience.com. Admission 10€ ($16); children 17 and under admitted only with parental supervision. Tues–Sun 10am–6pm. Closed Jan 1 and Dec 25. Tram: 16, 24, or 25 to Stadhouderskade.

Science Center NEMO ★ **Kids** A paean of praise to science and technology, NEMO is housed in a swooping modern building in the Eastern Dock, designed by Italian architect Renzo Piano. It seems to reproduce the graceful lines of an oceangoing ship. The center is a hands-on experience, through games, experiments, and demonstrations—the motto is: *Forbidden Not to Touch*. Admission, though not exactly cheap, is worth it, and most kids'll likely want to spend hours here.

You'll learn how to steer a supertanker safely into port, boost your earnings on the floor of the New York Stock Exchange, execute a complicated surgical procedure, blow a soap bubble large enough to stand inside, boil potatoes, and play the drums. One exhibit even tries to help you understand the basis of sexual attraction. Questions are asked and answered: Why is water clear but the ocean blue? Why does toothpaste contain sugar? In IStudio Bits & Co, NEMO's digital world, don a virtual-reality helmet and play with images, sounds, and your own imported material. Internet-linked computers on every floor provide additional insights, as do workshops and theater and video productions.

ⓜMoments   Sail Ahoy

Moored alongside NEMO is a full-size replica of the United East India Company (V.O.C.) merchant ship *Amsterdam,* which foundered off Hastings, England, in 1749 on its maiden voyage to Indonesia. The replica moved here from its usual berth across the water at the temporarily closed Scheepvaartmuseum (Maritime Museum). Reenactors create scenes from everyday life on the ship. Sailors fire cannons, sing sea shanties, mop the deck, hoist cargo on board, and attend a solemn "burial at sea." You can watch sailmakers and rope makers at work and see the cook prepare a shipboard meal in the galley.

The ship has the same open hours as NEMO. Admission is 5€ ($8) for ages 4 and up, or 2€ ($3.20) if you already have a ticket for NEMO.

The broad, sloping stairway to NEMO's roof is an attraction unto itself, a place to hang out and (when the sun cooperates) soak up some rays. At the top, you're 30m (98 ft.) above the IJ waterway, with fine views over the city's redeveloped Old Harbor.

Oosterdokskade 2 (off Prins Hendrikkade, over the south entrance to the IJ Tunnel). ℂ 020/531-3233. www.e-nemo.nl. Admission 11.50€ ($18), free for children 3 and under. July–Aug daily 10am–5pm; Sept–June Tues–Sun 10am–5pm (also Mon during school vacations). Closed Jan 1, Apr 30, and Dec 25. Bus: 22 to Kadijksplein.

8   MINOR MUSEUMS

The following is only a sampling of the city's many small museums. See the world through cat eyes in sculptures, paintings, and prints at the **Katten Kabinet (Cat Cabinet),** Herengracht 497 (ℂ 020/626-5378; www.kattenkabinet.nl; tram: 16, 24, or 25). The museum is open Tuesday to Friday from 10am to 4pm, and Saturday and Sunday from noon to 5pm. Admission is 5€ ($8) for adults, 2.50€ ($4) for children ages 4 to 12, and free for children 3 and under.

In Amsterdam, no one ever tosses away an old boat. Many houseboats are moored along the canals, on the river, and in the harbor—2,400 legally occupied houseboats float on the city's waters, costing anything up to 200,000€ ($320,000)—but you won't be able to go aboard most of them unless you know the owner. The *Hendrika Maria,* a former commercial sailing barge built in 1914, is an exception. It's now the **Woonbootmuseum (Houseboat Museum),** facing Prinsengracht 296 (ℂ 020/427-0750; www.houseboat museum.nl; tram: 13, 14, or 17), at Elandsgracht. Visit the original deckhouse where the skipper and his family lived, the cupboard bed in which they slept, and the cargo hold, now equipped as remarkably spacious and comfortable living quarters. How do you get the boat's bottom cleaned? Might you sink? What happens in winter? These and other questions are answered in models, photographs, and books. You can go aboard March to October, Tuesday to Sunday from 11am to 5pm; and November to December and February, Friday to Sunday from 11am to 5pm; it's closed most of January, April 30, and December 25, 26, and 27. Admission is 3.25€ ($5.20) for adults, and 2.50€ ($4) for children under 152-centimeters (59 in.).

Surely the most rollicking museum in town is the **Pianola Museum,** Westerstraat 106 (© 020/627-9624; www.pianola.nl; tram: 3, 10), at Tweede Boomdwarsstraat in the Jordaan. Aficionados congregate in a front-room brown cafe to sip coffee and to listen to, and sing along with, vintage tunes played on some of the three dozen old player-pianos and automated music machines—around half of them still in working order—in this private collection. Among some 14,000 "recordings" on perforated-paper rolls are works by Debussy and Gershwin. The museum is open Sunday from 2 to 5pm, and for groups by appointment. Admission is 5€ ($8) for adults, 4€ ($6.40) for seniors, and 3€ ($4.80) for children; it costs 40€ ($64) minimum for groups.

Geels & Co., a coffee-roasting and tea-importing store in the Red Light District (see "Shopping A to Z," in chapter 9), has been around for more than a century. It has a marvelous collection of antique grinders, roasters, tea canisters, and all sorts of coffee-and-tea–brewing paraphernalia in its small, atmospheric upstairs **Koffie en Thee Museum (Coffee and Tea Museum),** Warmoesstraat 67 (© 020/624-0683; www.geels. nl; tram: 4, 9, 14, 16, 24, or 25), at Oude Brugsteeg. The museum is open Saturday 2 to 4:30pm, and for groups by appointment. Admission for individual visitors is free; for groups, there's a fee.

If pipes are your thing, check out the **Pijpenkabinet (Pipe Cabinet),** Prinsengracht 488 (© 020/421-1779; www.pijpenkabinet.nl; tram: 1, 2, 5, 13, 14, or 17), at Leidsestraat. Housed at Smokiana, a pipe museum-store with a remarkable collection of tribal, antique, and ultramodern puffing equipment (p. 220), Pijpenkabinet is open Wednesday to Saturday from noon to 6pm, and by appointment. Admission is 5€ ($8).

A boutique known for selling modern, fashionable (and occasionally bizarre) eyeglasses is the **Brilmuseum (Eyeglass Museum),** Gasthuismolensteeg 7 (© 020/421-2414; www.brilmuseumamsterdam.nl; tram: 1, 2, 5, 13, 14, or 17), between Singel and Herengracht. It lives up to its billing by displaying a collection of antique eyeglasses and taking you on an eye-opening tour through 700 years of impaired-vision aids. It's quite a spectacle. It's open Wednesday to Friday from noon to 5:30pm, and Saturday from noon to 5pm; admission is free.

A MOVING MUSEUM

The superannuated streetcars of the **Elektrische Museumtramlijn (Electric Tramline Museum),** Amstelveenseweg 264 (© 0900/423-1100; www.museumtram.nl; tram: 16), shake, rattle, and roll back and forth between Amsterdam's old Haarlemmermeer rail station (near the Olympic Stadium), and suburban Amstelveen. Most of the trams are at least 50 years old, and come from Amsterdam, The Hague, Berlin, Vienna, Prague, and other cities. If you feel like a walk in the woods, get out along the way in the Amsterdamse Bos (see "Green Amsterdam," below). Trams run July to October, on Sundays from 11am to 5pm (Aug also Wed 1–5pm). Round-trip tickets are 4€ ($6.40) for adults, 2€ ($3.20) for seniors and children ages 4 to 11, and free for children 3 and under.

9 GREEN AMSTERDAM

Amsterdam is not a notably green city, particularly in the Old Center, where the canal water is the most obvious and visible encroachment of the natural world. Still, the city has around 30 parks.

The famous Vondelpark is named after Amsterdam poet and playwright Joost van den Vondel (1587–1689), who's honored with a sculpture in the park. This mosaic of lakes, meadows, and woodland contains 120 tree varieties that include catalpa, chestnut, cypress, oak, and poplar. Vondelpark (Tram: 1, 2, 3, 5, or 12) lies generally southwest of Leidseplein, and has entrances dotted all around; the busiest is on Stadhouderskade, adjacent to Leidseplein, where a sculpture of the *Maid of Amsterdam,* a symbol of the city, sits over the gate.

Beware the tasty-looking "gâteau" they sell here, or you may find yourself floating above the trees: Drug-laced space-cake is an acquired taste and not everyone is ready to acquire it. Some days, there's so much pot smoke in the air that the trees likely are quite a bit higher than they seem. Otherwise, Vondelpark is a fairly standard park, the site of skateboarding, Frisbee-flipping, in-line skating, model-boat sailing, pickup soccer, softball, and basketball, smooching in the undergrowth, parties, picnics, and arts-and-crafts markets. Topless sunbathing has gone out of fashion, however. Best of all, it's free, or as the Dutch say, *gratis.* Also free are the many concerts, theater and dance performances, and all kinds of other events, including plenty for children, at the **Vondelpark Open-luchttheater (Open-Air Theater).** These run from June to mid-August.

Rent in-line skates from **De Vondeltuin Rent A Skate,** Amstelveenseweg entrance (✆ **020/664-5091**). Including protective gear, it's 5€ ($8) for the first hour and 2.50€ ($4) for each subsequent hour, or 15€ ($24) for a full day (11am–11pm; but it closes earlier if weather's bad), for both adults and children. Bring ID and leave 20€ ($32) as a refundable guarantee.

Should toting along a picnic bag not be your thing, quiet hunger at the casual and superb **Vertigo** (p. 113) on the edge of the park. Or, visit the even more casual **Het Blauwe Theehuis,** Vondelpark 5 (✆ **020/662-0254**), at the park's center. This functionalist-style circular cafe on two levels, with a park-level terrace and an upstairs balcony terrace, is good at any time of day and a fine place for indulging in a continental breakfast of coffee and croissant. At night, there's dancing and live music.

AMSTERDAMSE BOS (AMSTERDAM WOOD) ★

To enjoy fresh air and wide expanses of scenery, head out to this giant park in the southern suburb of Amstelveen. This is nature on the city's doorstep, and covers some 10 sq. km (4 sq. miles). The park was laid out during the Depression years as a public works project. By now, the woodlands, grasslands, moors, and marshes, along with their birds, insects, and small animals (and a herd of Highland cattle to keep the moors in shape), are firmly established. The best way to get to the Amsterdamse Bos from the center city is to take bus no. 170 or 172 from outside Centraal Station. The Amsterdamse Bos is open 24 hours; admission is free.

At the entrance on Amstelveenseweg, stop by the **Bezoekerscentrum (Visitor Center),** Bosbaanweg 5 (✆ **020/545-6100;** www.amsterdamsebos.nl), where you can trace the park's history, learn about its wildlife, and pick up a park map. The center is open daily (except Dec 25–26) from noon to 5pm, and admission is free. Across the way is a bicycle rental shop (✆ **020/644-5473;** www.amsterdamsebosfietsverhuur.nl), open April through October, with fees starting at 9.50€ ($15) per day.

(Moments) Market Makers

Amsterdam has more than 50 outdoor markets every week. Some are permanent or semipermanent, and others just pass through. For details, see "Street Markets," in chapter 9, but three you shouldn't miss are the floating **Bloemenmarkt (Flower Market)** on Singel, the **Waterlooplein Flea Market** on Waterlooplein, and the **Albert Cuypmarkt,** on Albert Cuypstraat.

Then follow the path to a long stretch of water called the **Bosbaan,** a 2km (1¼-mile) competition-rowing course. Overlooking the finishing line, and with a great terrace beside the water, is the fine **Grand-Café De Bosbaan** (② 020/404-4869; www.de bosbaan.nl). Beyond the course's western end is **Boerderij Meerzicht** (② 020/679-2744), a restaurant that sells great Dutch pancakes. It also has peacocks wandering around freely and a playground for kids. South of the course is a big pond, the **Grote Vijver,** where you can rent rowboats and pedal-boats, and the **Openluchttheater (Open-Air Theater),** where performances are presented on many summer evenings. The Japan Women's Club donated the 400 cherry trees of the **Kersenbloesempark (Cherry Blossom Park)** in 2000 to mark 400 years of cultural ties between the Netherlands and Japan.

Horseback riding through the Amsterdamse Bos is available from **De Amsterdamse Manege,** Nieuwe Kalfjeslaan 25 (② 020/643-1342; www.amsterdamse-manege.com).

MORE PARKS

After Vondelpark, the city's other parks are fairly tame, but the following still make pleasant escapes on a warm summer day: **Sarphatipark,** 2 blocks behind the Albert Cuyp Markt in South Amsterdam; **Beatrixpark,** adjacent to the RAI Convention and Exhibition Center; **Rembrandtpark** and **Erasmuspark** in the west city; **Martin Luther Kingpark,** beside the Amstel River; **Oosterpark;** and East Amsterdam's **Flevopark,** which has two swimming pools.

A COLORFUL GARDEN

Hortus Botanicus (Botanical Garden) ★ The Botanical Garden, established here in 1682 (having been founded in 1638 in another location as an apothecaries' garden), is a medley of color and scent, with some 250,000 flowers and 115,000 plants and trees from 8,000 different varieties. It owes its origins to the treasure-trove of tropical plants the Dutch found in their exotic colonies, and its contemporary popularity to the Dutch love affair with flowers. Highlights include the Semicircle, which reconstructs part of the original 1682 design; the Mexico–California Desert House; the Palm House, home to one of the world's oldest palm trees; and the Tri-Climate House, which displays tropical, subtropical, and desert plants.

Plantage Middenlaan 2A (near Artis Zoo). ② 020/625-9021. www.dehortus.nl. Admission 7€ ($11) adults, 3.50€ ($5.60) seniors and children 5–14, free for children 4 and under. Feb–June and Sept–Nov Mon–Fri 9am–5pm, Sat–Sun and holidays 10am–5pm; July–Aug Mon–Fri 9am–9pm, Sat–Sun and holidays 10am–9pm; Dec–Jan Mon–Fri 9am–4pm, Sat–Sun and holidays 10am–4pm. Closed Jan 1 and Dec 25. Tram: 9 or 14 to Plantage Middenlaan.

10 OFFBEAT & ALTERNATIVE AMSTERDAM

Amsterdam's streets constitute an offbeat and alternative spectacle all by themselves. But you can also explore sex in the city, bizarre museums, and creations so ugly they could be modern-art masterpieces.

Erotic Museum As its name suggests, this museum presents an allegedly artistic vision of eroticism; it focuses on prints and drawings, including some by John Lennon. There's a replica of a Red Light District alley, and an extensively equipped S&M playroom, both of which are rather antiseptic and serious. The only humorous note is an X-rated cartoon depicting some of the things Snow White apparently got up to with the Seven Dwarfs that Walt never told us about. Considering all this, it's ironic that the legend on the building's 1685 gable stone reads: *God is myn burgh* (God is my citadel).

Oudezijds Achterburgwal 54 (Red Light District). ✆ **020/624-7303.** www.janot.com. Admission 5€ ($8). Sun–Thurs 11am–1am; Fri–Sat 11am–2am. Tram: 4, 9, 14, 16, 24, 25, or 26 to the Dam.

Hash Marihuana & Hemp Museum ★ Well, it wouldn't really be Amsterdam, would it, without its fascination with intoxicating weeds? This museum will teach you everything you ever wanted to know, and much you didn't, about hash, marijuana, and related products. The museum does not promote drug use but aims to make you better informed before deciding whether to light up and, of course, whether to inhale. One way it does so is by having a cannabis garden in the joint . . . sorry, on the premises. Plants at various stages of development fill the air with an unmistakable, heady, resinous fragrance. And hemp, not plastic, could be the future if the exhibit on the plant's multifarious uses through the ages is anything to go by. Some exhibits shed light on cannabis's medicinal use, while others focus on hemp's use as a natural fiber. Among several notable artworks in the museum's collection is one from which the museum takes a proprietary satisfaction: David Teniers the Younger's painting, *Hemp-Smoking Peasants in a Smoke House* (1660).

Oudezijds Achterburgwal 148 (Red Light District). ✆ **020/623-5961.** www.hashmuseum.com. Admission 5.70€ ($9.10) adults, free for children 12 and under. Daily 10am–10pm. Closed Jan 1, Apr 30, and Dec 25. Tram: 4, 9, 14, 16, 24, or 25 to the Dam.

Sexmuseum Amsterdam Behind its faux-marble facade, this museum isn't as sleazy as you might expect, apart from one room covered with straight-up pornography. Otherwise, presentation tends toward the tongue-in-cheek, and the place seems to be fine with its half-million annual visitors. Exhibits include erotic prints and drawings, and trinkets like tobacco boxes decorated with naughty pictures. Teenage visitors seem to find the whole place vastly amusing, judging by the giggling fits at the showcases. Spare a thought for the models of early erotic photography—slow film speeds in those days made for uncomfortably long posing times!

Damrak 18 (near Centraal Station). ✆ **020/622-8376.** www.sexmuseumamsterdam.com. Admission 3€ ($4.80) from age 16 only. Daily 9:30am–11:30pm. Tram: 1, 2, 4, 5, 9, 13, 16, 17, 24, 25, or 26 to Centraal Station.

Torture Museum You enter through a gloomy tunnel, and emerge with a new appreciation of why the framers of the U.S. Constitution outlawed cruel and unusual punishment. Yet one suspects the motives of the Torture Museum—and its visitors?—are not purely educational. There's a terrible fascination with devices such as the Inquisition chair, the guillotine, and assorted grotesque implements of torture, punishment, and "redemption" favored by civil and ecclesiastic authorities in times not-so-far gone, if gone at all.

11 CONTEMPORARY GALLERIES

The art galleries reviewed below aim to give new talent space to develop and be seen.

De Appel   Named after Amsterdam Cobra artist Karel Appel, this center for contemporary art provides cutting-edge artists, both known and unknown, with space for exhibits, projects, and research. Six yearly presentations of solo or group work are backed up by interaction with the artists through lectures, discussions, and video presentations.

Nieuwe Spiegelstraat 10 (off Keizersgracht). © 020/625-5651. www.deappel.nl. Admission 7€ ($11) adults, free for visitors 18 and under. Tues–Sun 11am–6pm. Closed Jan 1 and Apr 30. Tram: 16, 24, or 25 to Keizersgracht.

Huis Marseille ★   The city's top international photography venue is in a monumental canal-house mansion, the Huis Marseille. Vast display rooms on four floors, renovated and restored to their 17th-century glory, showcase work by international talents. Shows change quarterly, at the beginning of March, June, September, and December. Even if you're not a shutterbug fan, the house alone is worth the visit. French merchant Isaac Focquier built it in 1665 with proceeds from a fortune-making cargo he sailed from Marseilles to Amsterdam. Of note are its period interior, a facade graced by a classical neck gable, and a stone relief of Marseilles with the city's name inscribed in gold letters below.

Keizersgracht 401 (at Leidsegracht). © 020/531-8989. www.huismarseille.nl. Admission 5€ ($8) adults, 3€ ($4.80) students, free for children 17 and under. Tues–Sun 11am–6pm. Closed Jan 1, Apr 30, and Dec 25. Tram: 1, 2, or 5 to Keizersgracht.

SMBA   An initiative by the modern-art Stedelijk Museum, this gallery was described in a Dutch newspaper as a "hatchery for young artistic talent," particularly from Amsterdam. Exhibits change constantly, but the works are always by promising young artists who embrace painting, sculpture, video, installations, or performance art.

Rozenstraat 59 (off Prinsengracht). © 020/422-0471. www.smba.nl. Free admission. Tues–Sun 11am–5pm. Closed Jan 1, Apr 30, and Dec 25. Tram: 13, 14, or 17 to Westermarkt.

12 ESPECIALLY FOR KIDS

Kids may get bored in Amsterdam's art museums, but they're likely to be interested in the **Anne Frankhuis** (see "The Big Three," earlier in this chapter). At **Kindermuseum TM Junior,** Linnaeusstraat 2 (© 020/568-8233; www.tropenmuseumjunior.nl; tram: 9 or 14), a section of the **Tropenmuseum** (p. 150), kids learn about exotic tropical countries and their people through stories, songs, dances, games, and paintings. The **Science Center NEMO** (p. 165) does a good job of appealing to the inner nerd. **Madame Tussauds** (p. 152) is always fun for kids, though if they're too young, they could be frightened by the wax statues.

Older kids might appreciate the sheer white-knuckle excitement of—well, **chess,** actually. It's played with giant plastic pieces on an open-air board on Max Euweplein, named after a Dutch grandmaster, next to the Casino behind Leidseplein. They can even challenge one of the minor masters who hang out around there. If all else fails, take them to

Intersphere Lasergames, Prins Hendrikkade 194 (© **020/622-4809;** www.lasergames. nl; bus: 22, 42, or 43), where in a gloomy, mist-suffused futuristic world they can zap each other until the electric sheep come home.

The street **barrel organ performances** (mixed with the rattle of money as the organ-grinder tries to persuade you to make a donation) are always interesting. There are also the pretty melodies emanating from the bells of five **17th-century carillons:** Westertoren (Tues noon–1pm); Zuidertoren (Thurs noon–1pm); Munttoren (Fri noon–1pm); Oude Kerkstoren (Sat 4–5pm); and Koninklijk Paleis (occasional)—these concert times are in addition to frequent regular chimes. That should hold their attention for around 30 seconds.

Children can be amateur farmers for a while at **Geitenboerderij Ridammerhoeve,** Nieuwe Meerlaan 4 (© **020/645-5034;** www.geitenboerderij.nl; bus: 170 or 172), inside the Amsterdamse Bos (p. 168). They get to feed 150 goats and lambs (along with chickens, a calf or two, and a few potbelly hogs); clean coops and pens; milk a goat; bottle-feed baby animals; and maybe even, between the months of January and April, be lucky enough to see kid goats being born. On Saturdays, they can watch goat's milk being turned into cheese. The farm is open March to October, Wednesday to Monday from 10am to 5pm; and November to February, Wednesday to Sunday from 10am to 5pm. Admission is 1.50€ ($2.40).

Before taking the kids back to the hotel for a nap, take them out to the tiny **Kinderboerderij De Dierencapel,** Bickersgracht 207 (© **020/420-6855;** bus: 18, 21 or 22), an urban petting zoo in the Western Islands neighborhood, west of Centraal Station. Endearing piglets, kids (of the goat species), lambs, chickens, ducks, and rabbits nibble, root, and peck along the banks of the Bickersgracht canal; there's a play area too. It's not a bad place to bring a picnic when the weather's fine. The petting zoo is open Tuesday to Sunday from 9am to 4:30pm; admission is free.

Equally entertaining is **Kinderboerderij De Pijp,** Lizzy Ansinghstraat 82 (© **020/ 664-8303;** www.kinderboerderijdepijp.nl; tram: 12 or 25), a children's farm off Ferdinand Bolstraat in the down-at-the-heels De Pijp (the Pipe) urban district south of the center. Here, in addition to the animals mentioned above, kids can get close to donkeys, ponies, peacocks, and turkeys. The farm is open Monday to Friday from 11am to 5pm, and weekends from 1 to 5pm; admission is free.

A GREAT ZOO

Artis Zoo ★★ **Kids**   If you're at a loss for what to do with the kids, Artis is a safe bet—1.2 million visitors a year agree. Established in 1838, the oldest zoo in the Netherlands houses more than 6,000 animals from 1,400 species. Of course, you'll find the usual tigers, lions, giraffes, wolves, leopards, elephants, camels, monkeys, penguins, and peacocks no self-respecting zoo can do without. The African residents even stroll around on a miniature savanna. Yet there's also much more, for no extra charge. There's the excellent Planetarium (closed Mon mornings), and a Geological and Zoological Museum. The Aquarium, built in 1882 and renovated in the late 1990s, is superbly presented, particularly the sections about the Amazon River, coral reefs, and Amsterdam's own canals. Finally, there's a children's farm, where kids can help tend to the needs of resident Dutch species, including moorland sheep, long-haired Veluwe goats, and tufted ducks. An Insectarium opened in 2005 and a Butterfly Garden in 2006. To rest for a while, dine at Artis Restaurant.

Plantage Kerklaan 38–40 (at Plantage Middenlaan). © **020/523-3400.** www.amsterdamzoo.nl. Admission 18€ ($28) adults, 17€ ($26) seniors, 15€ ($23) children 3–9, free for children 2 and under. May–Oct daily 9am–6pm (Sat to sunset); Nov–Apr daily 9am–5pm. Tram: 9 or 14 to Plantage Kerklaan.

13 ORGANIZED TOURS

A convincing case could be made for the proposition that "disorganized tours"—making it up as you go along—are a better way of getting to the inner core of the Amsterdam experience. But there's no lack of choice or ingenuity among off-the-peg offerings.

CANAL-BOAT CRUISE ★★

Amsterdam's 17th-century Golden Age becomes a vivid reality as you glide through the waterways that were largely responsible for those years of prosperity. You view the canal houses from canal level, just as they were meant to be seen. This is also the best way to see Amsterdam's large and busy harbor. Yes, you have to smile inanely for your boarding picture and sit through a thumbnail-sketch history in several different languages. No matter. The canals are Amsterdam's best starting point. Amsterdammers might scoff as they watch fleets of glass-topped boats prowling around, but secretly, they're proud of everything you will see. "I live here," you can almost hear them thinking. "All this belongs to me."

A typical canal tour-boat itinerary includes Centraal Station, the Haarlemmersluis floodgates (used in the nightly canals flushings), the Cat Boat (a houseboat with a permanent population of some 100 wayward felines), and the city's narrowest building, as well as one of the largest houses still in private hands. You'll also see the official residence of the *burgemeester* (mayor), at Herengracht 502, on the "Golden Bend" (traditionally the best address in the city), many picturesque bridges, including the famous Magere Brug (Skinny Bridge) over the Amstel, and the harbor. While on the canal-boat tour, take note of attractions you'd like to see up close later.

Trips last about an hour and depart at regular intervals from *rondvaart* (excursion) piers in key locations around town. The majority of launches are docked along Damrak and Prins Hendrikkade near Centraal Station, on Rokin near Muntplein, and at Leidseplein. Tours leave every 15 to 30 minutes during summer (9am–9pm), and every 45 to 60 minutes in winter (10am–5pm). Prices vary from company to company, but a basic 1-hour tour is around 8€ ($13) to 12€ ($19) for adults, 4€ ($6.40) to 6€ ($9.60) for children ages 4 to 12, and free for children 3 and under.

The canal tour-boat lines are **Amsterdam Canal Cruises** (✆ 020/626-5636; www.amsterdamcanalcruises.nl); **Canal Company** (✆ 020/626-5574; www.canal.nl); **Holland International** (✆ 020/625-3035; www.hir.nl); **Meyers Rondvaarten** (✆ 020/623-4208; www.meyersrondvaarten.nl); **Rederij Boekel** (✆ 020/612-9905; www.rederijkooij.nl); **Rederij Hof van Holland** (✆ 020/623-7122; www.rederijkooij.nl); **Rederij Lovers** (✆ 020/530-1090; www.lovers.nl); **Reederij P. Kooij** (✆ 020/623-3810; www.rederijkooij.nl); **Rederij Plas** (✆ 020/624-5406; www.rederijplas.nl); and **Blue Boat Company** (✆ 020/679-1370; www.blueboat.nl).

Some lines offer specialized tours and services. These include the **Museum Quarter Line** and the **Canal Bus** (see "Getting Around," in chapter 3), the **Artis Zoo Express** (which plies a regular furrow btw. Centraal Station and the Artis Zoo), cruises amid the Eastern Islands' modern architecture, Red Light District cruises, dinner cruises, jazz cruises, candlelight cruises with wine and cheese, night cruises, and more. See "A Dinner Cruise," in chapter 6 and "More Evening Entertainment," in chapter 10 for information on after-dark tours.

WATER BIKES ★

A water bike is a boat you pedal with your feet. These craft seat two or four people and are rentable from **Canal Bike** (✆ 020/626-5574; www.canal.nl). Amsterdammers look

(Moments) Biking on the Water

A suggested tour by water bike: Start at the Canal Bike mooring on Prinsengracht (at Westermarkt). Pedal south along Prinsengracht, past Lauriergracht, Looiersgracht, and Passeerdersgracht, perhaps diverting into one or more of these quiet side canals if you fancy a closer look at their leafy linings. At Leidsegracht, go straight ahead under the Leidsestraat bridge until you come to Spiegelgracht, where you turn right. Continue to the end, then turn left under the bridge into Lijnbaansgracht.

Turn right at the first corner into a narrow connecting canal that merges with Singelgracht in front of the Rijksmuseum. Go right along this canal, which is bordered by overhanging trees and the back gardens of waterside villas. You pass the Holland Casino Amsterdam, Leidseplein, and the American Hotel.

Keep going, past the Bellevue Theater and the De la Mar Theater, and turn right into Leidsegracht, which brings you back to Prinsengracht and the long home stretch back to Westermarkt.

down their tolerant noses at water bikes. On the other hand, tourists love the things. No prizes for guessing who has more fun. Your water bike, also known as a *pedalo,* comes with a detailed map. It's great fun in sunny weather, and still doable when it rains; boats can be covered with a rain shield. But they don't go very fast and it can get tiring. In summer, rent a water bike for evening rambles, when the canals are illuminated and your bike is kitted out with its own Chinese lantern.

Moorings are on Prinsengracht, beside the Anne Frankhuis (Tram: 13, 14, or 17); on Singelgracht, a few steps from Leidseplein (Tram: 1, 2, 5, 7, or 10) and next to the Rijksmuseum (Tram: 7 or 10); and on Keizersgracht at Leidsestraat (Tram: 1, 2, or 5). You can rent a water bike at one mooring and leave it at another. The canals get busy with tour boats and other small vessels, so proceed carefully, particularly when going under bridges. Rental is available daily from 10am to 10pm in summer, and to 7pm during other seasons. The cost is 8€ ($13) per person hourly for one or two people and 7€ ($11) per person hourly for three or four people. You need to leave a deposit of 50€ ($80). See "Biking on the Water," below, for a suggested tour.

BY VINTAGE BOAT

Using antique IJ passenger ferryboats from 1927, the **Historic Ferry** (© **0900/423-1100;** www.museum-ijveren-amsterdam.nl) takes a 2-hour trip through the eastern harbor and along the IJ channel, with stops at several places where you can disembark (and pick up a later boat if you want). The ferry departs from dock 14 behind Centraal Station. It operates Easter to October, on Sundays and some other days, with departures at 11:30am, and 1:30 and 3:30pm. Tickets are 4.50€ ($7.20) for adults, 3€ ($4.80) for seniors (not all tours) and children ages 4 to 11, and free for children 3 and under. On Saturday, there's a longer cruise (1¹/₂ hr. each way) to Fort Pampus, and one that's 2 hours each way to allow time to tour this old coastal fortification on the IJsselmeer.

BY BICYCLE ★

You'll look pretty conspicuous taking one of the guided tours offered by **Yellow Bike,** Nieuwezijds Kolk 29, off Nieuwezijds Voorburgwal (✆ **020/620-6940;** www.yellow bike.nl; tram: 1, 2, 5, 13, or 17). Why? Because you'll be cycling on a yellow bike along with a dozen other people also on yellow bikes. But you get a close encounter with Amsterdam or its nearby countryside. There are multiple tour options, with the shortest (2 hr.) costing 18€ ($28).

BY TRAM

A vintage **Tourist Tram** (✆ **0900/423-1100**) from the Clanking Twenties shakes, rattles, and rolls between the sights along the tracks on a 1-hour ride through the heart of town. Departures are from Prins Hendrikkade, at Damrak, in front of Centraal Station. The tram runs Sundays and holidays from Easter to September, hourly from 11am to 5pm, and Saturday (July–Aug) from 10am to 5pm. Tickets are valid all day, so you can step on and off at will; they're 8€ ($13) for adults, 5€ ($8) for kids ages 4 to 11, and free for kids 3 and under.

BY BUS

A quick bus tour is a good way to get going on sightseeing in a strange city, and though a boat tour on Amsterdam's canals is a pertinent alternative, you might want to get your bearings on land as well. A basic $2^{1}/_{2}$-hour bus tour is around 20€ ($32); on most tours, children ages 4 to 13 are charged half-fare, and children 3 and under go free. Itineraries vary from line to line, but a typical one might include the Royal Palace, the Mint Tower, the flower market, the old Jewish Quarter, the Waterlooplein flea market, the Museum Quarter, the Jordaan, the Westerkerk, the harbor, the Red Light District, a windmill, a visit to a diamond factory, and shopping and entertainment areas. Good sightseeing lines are the **Best of Holland,** Damrak 34 (✆ **020/420-4000**); **Keytours Holland,** Paulus Potterstraat 8 (✆ **020/305-5333**); and **Lindbergh Tour & Travel,** Damrak 26 (✆ **020/622-2766**).

These and other lines provide a variety of half-day and full-day tours into surrounding areas, particularly between April and October, and special excursions at tulip time and the height of the summer season. Rates vary by company and tour, but typical half-day tours begin around 20€ ($32); full-day tours cost around 44€ ($70); children ages 4 to 13 are generally charged half-fare, and children 3 and under go free.

Typical of the tours on offer is an 8-hour drive that hits the Aalsmeer flower auction, The Hague and its sea-coast resort Scheveningen, Delft, and Rotterdam. A shorter excursion visits just Delft and The Hague. A $4^{1}/_{2}$-hour trip takes you to see the decorated houses and the (occasionally) costumed villagers of Volendam and Marken on the shore of the IJsselmeer, with stops at the windmills of Zaanse Schans and a cheese farm along the way. An additional tour, available during tulip time (late Mar to late May), is a $4^{1}/_{2}$-hour or a 9-hour drive through the flower fields of the Bollenstreek (Bulb District) and to Keukenhof Gardens.

Other tours available include a half-day outing to Haarlem, an 8-hour trip along the IJsselmeer shore and across the Afsluitdijk (Enclosing Dike) to Friesland; a $4^{1}/_{2}$-hour tour via Zaanse Schans to Edam (a cheese town with no market); and a 5-hour trip to visit the Friday Alkmaar cheese market and the 17th-century port of Hoorn.

Though you could see most of Amsterdam's important sights in one long walking tour, it's best to break the city into shorter walks. Luckily, the **VVV Amsterdam** tourist office has done that for you. For 2€ ($3.20), buy a brochure outlining one of four walking tours: *Voyage of Discovery Through Amsterdam, A Walk Through Jewish Amsterdam, A Walk Through the Jordaan,* and *A Walk Through Maritime Amsterdam.*

Amsterdam Walking Tours (✆ **020/640-9072**) leads guided strolls through Old Amsterdam on Saturday and Sunday at 11am.

BY HORSE AND CARRIAGE

These romantic, kid-friendly vehicles run by **Karos** (✆ **020/691-3478;** www.karos.nl) depart from just outside the Royal Palace on the Dam for traipses through the Old City, along the canals, and into the Jordaan. Tours operate April to October, daily from 11am to 6pm (to 7pm in July–Aug), and on a limited schedule in winter. Rides are 35€ ($56) for each 20 minutes.

DIAMOND TOURS

Visitors to Amsterdam during the 1950s and 1960s, when the diamond business was booming, were able to go to Amsterdam's diamond-cutting factories and take tours through their workrooms. Now you'll be lucky to see one lone polisher working at a small wheel set up in the back of a jewelry store or in the lobby of a factory building. Never mind, you still can get an idea of how a diamond is cut and polished. You need no special directions or instructions to find this sightseeing activity; signs all over town direct you to diamond-cutting demonstrations.

Amsterdam's major diamond factories and showrooms are **Amsterdam Diamond Center,** Rokin 1, just off the Dam (✆ **020/624-5787;** tram: 4, 9, 14, 16, 24, or 25); **Coster Diamonds,** Paulus Potterstraat 2–6, near the Rijksmuseum (✆ **020/676-2222;** tram: 2 or 5); **Gassan Diamonds,** Nieuwe Uilenburgerstraat 173–175 (✆ **020/622-5333;** Metro: Waterlooplein); **Holshuijsen Stoeltie,** Wagenstraat 13–17 (✆ **020/623-7601;** tram: 4, 9, or 14); and **Van Moppes Diamonds,** Albert Cuypstraat 2–6 (✆ **020/676-1242;** tram: 16).

---

14 STAYING ACTIVE

Should a steady diet of Indonesian *rijsttafels,* brown-cafe beers and *jenevers,* and exotic smokes in "coffeeshops" begin to take its toll, don't despair. Amsterdam has ways of making you work up some healthy sweat—or at least of watching other people sweat. See also "Green Amsterdam," earlier in this chapter.

SPORTS & OUTDOOR PURSUITS

Bicycling

South of the city is **Amsterdamse Bos,** where you can rent bikes (✆ **020/644-5473;** bus: 170 or 172) for touring the woodland's paths. Of course, you can always do as Amsterdammers do and explore all those city bridges and canals by bicycle (for rental information, see "Bicycles, Mopeds & More" under "Getting Around," in chapter 3).

Bowling

If you find you just have to knock down a few pins, head to **Knijn Bowling,** Scheldeplein 3 (✆ **020/664-2211;** www.knijnbowling.nl; tram: 12 or 25).

Fishing

Anglers should try the **Bosbaan** artificial lake (it's actually an Olympic rowing course) in **Amsterdamse Bos** (see "Green Amsterdam," earlier in this chapter), south of the city. You can get a license from the **Amsterdamse Hengelsportvereniging,** Nicolaas Witsenstraat 10 (© **020/626-4988;** www.ahv.nl; tram: 4 or 25), open Tuesday to Friday.

Fitness Centers

If you don't want to neglect your exercise routine, there are many available centers. Good ones belong to the minichain **Splash** (www.splashhealthclubs.nl), with branches at Looiersgracht 26–30 (© **020/624-8404;** tram: 7, 10, or 17); Lijnbaansgracht 241 (© **020/422-0280;** tram: 7 or 10); and Dokter Meurerlaan 10 (© **020/411-6522;** bus: 19 or 192).

Golf

There are public golf courses in or near Amsterdam at the **Golf Center Amstelborgh,** Borchlandweg 6 (© **020/697-5000;** Metro: Strandvliet); **Golfclub Sloten,** Sloterweg 1045 (© **020/614-2402;** bus: 145); **Waterlandse Golf Club,** Buikslotermeerdijk 141 (© **020/636-1010;** www.waterlandsegolfclub.nl; bus: 100, 104, or 105); and **Openbare Golfbaan Spaarnwoude,** Het Hogeland 2, Spaarnwoude (© **020/538-5599;** www. golfbaanspaarnwoude.nl; bus: 82). Call ahead for greens fees and tee times.

Horseback Riding

Amsterdamse Manege, Nieuwe Kalfjeslaan 25 (© **020/643-1342**; www.amsterdamse-manege.com), offers riding, both indoor and outdoor. Only indoor riding is available at **Nieuw Amstelland Manege,** Jan Tooropplantsoen 17 (© **020/643-2468;** www.nieuw-amstelland.nl). You can rent a horse at **Manege De Ruif,** Sloterweg 675 (© **020/615-6667;** www.manegederuif.nl; bus: 145), then ride it in Amsterdamse Bos.

From the comfort of its upper-floor cafe, watch horses being put through their paces in a sawdust-strewn arena at the regal **Hollandsche Manege,** Vondelstraat 140 (© **020/618-0942;** www.dehollandschemanege.nl; tram: 1). Opened in 1882, this fusion of plaster, marble, and gilded mirrors was designed by Concertgebouw architect Adolf Leonard van Gendt and inspired by Vienna's Spanish Riding School. In addition to being a spectator, you can ride.

Ice-Skating

All those Dutch paintings of people skating and sledding—not to mention the story of Hans Brinker and his silver skates—will surely get you thinking about skating on Amsterdam's ponds and canals (see "Blades on Ice," below). However, doing this won't be easy unless

---

ⒸMoments Blades on Ice

In winter, when the temperature drops low enough for long enough, Amsterdam's canals become sparkling highways through the city. Skating to the strains of classical music is a memorable experience. Little kiosks are set up on the ice to dispense heart-warming liqueurs. Go cautiously when skating under bridges, where the ice is usually thinner, and don't go anywhere the Dutch don't. Few sounds generate more adrenaline than a sudden crackling of ice below, but the Dutch seem to know instinctively if it's just the natural rhythm of things or time to light the afterburners and be gone.

7

(Moments **Get Your Skates On**

Why not strap on in-line skates for the regular **Friday Night Skate?** In summer, this attracts 3,000 skaters. It begins at 8pm from Vondelpark's Filmmuseum and takes a 15km (9-mile) route through the city.

you're willing to shell out for a new pair of skates, since very few places rent them. One that does is **Jaap Eden IJsbanen,** Radioweg 64 (*©* 020/694-9652; www.jaapeden.nl; tram: 9), from November to February, and they even allow you to take skates out of their marvelous outdoor rink, which is popular in wintertime. Unless you're highly competent, watch out for the long lines of speed skaters practicing for the next Eleven Cities Race in Friesland.

In-Line Skating
De Vondeltuin Rent A Skate has a rent shop for in-line skates in Vondelpark, at the Amstelveenseweg entrance (*©* **020/664-5091;** tram: 2).

Jogging
The two main jogging areas are **Vondelpark** in the Center and **Amsterdamse Bos** on the city's southern edge. You can also run along the Amstel River. If you choose to run along the canals, as many do, watch out for uneven cobbles, loose paving stones, and dog poop.

Sailing & Boating
Sailboats, kayaks, and canoes can be rented on the Sloterplas Lake from **Watersportschool De Duikelaar,** Noordzijde 41 (*©* 020/613-8855; www.deduikelaar.nl; tram: 13, 14, or 17). From March 15 to October 15, you can go to the Loosdrecht lakes, southeast of Amsterdam, to rent sailing equipment from **Ottenhome** (*©* 035/582-3331; www.ottenhome.nl; bus: 121 or 122 from Hilversum). Canoes can be rented in **Amsterdamse Bos,** south of the city, for use in the park lakes only.

Snooker & Pool
Locals guzzle beer and get snookered at *carambole,* a devilishly complicated game played on pool tables without pockets. Billiards-type games are an obsession among the brown-cafe contingent; it's as easy to pick up a game as a flea. Try your hand at carambole, and delve deep into billiards, snooker, and pool at the **Pool Centrum Boven 't IJ,** Buikslotermeerplein 145 (*©* 020/634-1792; www.boventij.com; bus: 30, 36, 37, or 46), across the IJ waterway in Amsterdam-Noord (North). Sharps bring their own cues and call ahead to reserve a table. For pickup games, you'd better be good. It's open daily from 10am to 1am (Fri–Sat until 3am).

Squash
Squash courts and far more are at chic **Squash City,** Ketelmakerstraat 6 (west of Centraal Station; *©* 020/626-7883; www.squashcity.nl; bus: 18, 21, or 22).

Swimming
Amsterdam's state-of-the-art swimming facility is centrally located **Het Marnix,** Marnixplein 1 (*©* 020/524-6000; tram: 3 or 10). It opened in 2006 and has two heated pools along with a fitness center and spa, and a cafe-restaurant. The **Zuiderbad** (ca. 1911), Hobbemastraat 26 (*©* 020/679-2217; tram: 2 or 5), a handsome, refurbished place near the Rijksmuseum, sets time aside for those who like to swim in their birthday suits. **De**

Mirandabad, De Mirandalaan 9 (© **020/546-4444;** tram: 25), in Amsterdam-Zuid (South) features an indoor pool with wave machines, slides, and other amusements, and an outdoor pool that's open May to September. Other decent public pools are the **Floraparkbad,** Sneeuwbalweg 5 (© **020/636-8121;** bus: 38), in Amsterdam-Noord, and the **Sloterparkbad,** President Allendelaan 3 (© **020/506-3506;** tram: 7 or 14), in Amsterdam-West.

Table Tennis

Ping-pong to your heart's content at **Tafeltennis Centrum Amsterdam,** Keizersgracht 209 (© **020/624-5780;** tram: 13, 14, or 17), on the Canal Belt, close to Westermarkt.

Tennis

Find indoor courts at **Frans Otten Stadion,** IJsbaanpad 43 (© **020/662-8767;** www. fransottenstadion.nl; tram: 16), close to the Olympic Stadium. For indoor *and* outdoor courts, try **Gold Star,** Gustav Mahlerlaan 20 (© **020/644-5483;** tram: 16 or 24), or **Amstelpark Tennisschool,** Koenenkade 8, Amsterdamse Bos (© **020/301-0700;** www. amstelpark.nl; bus: 166, 170, 171, or 172), which has 36 courts.

WELLNESS ACTIVITIES

The **Body Tuning Clinic,** Jan Luijkenstraat 40 (© **020/662-0909;** www.bodytuningclinic.nl; tram: 2 or 5), will take excellent care of the outer you. At **Sauna Deco,** Herengracht 115 (© **020/627-1773;** www.saunadeco.nl; tram: 1, 2, 5, 13, or 17), in Dutch style, you sweat together in mixed facilities. Soothe away a hard day's stress at **Koan Float,** Herengracht 321 (© **020/555-0333;** www.koan-float.com; tram: 1, 2, or 5), while floating in warm saline water in a soundproof fiberglass capsule with light switches, ambient music, and a two-way intercom; treatments are by appointment only.

SPECTATOR SPORTS
Baseball

Honk if you like baseball (the game is called *honkbal* in Holland). The **Amsterdam Pirates** (www.amsterdampirates.nl) may not be the greatest practitioners of the art, but they have their moments, as you can see at the **Sportpark Ookmeer,** Herman Bonpad 5 (© **020/616-2151;** bus: 19 or 192).

Basketball

MyGuide Amsterdam (www.amsterdambasketball.nl) play their home games at **Sporthallen Zuid,** Burgerweeshuispad 54 (© **020/305-8305;** tram: 16 or 24), close to the Olympic Stadium.

Ice Hockey

The Dutch are known for their skill on ice, as local hotshots the **Amstel Tijgers** (www. amsteltijgerspro.nl) demonstrate at the **Jaap Eden IJsbanen,** Radioweg 64 (© **020/694-9652;** www.jaapeden.nl; tram: 9).

Soccer

Soccer (known as *football* in Europe, and *voetbal* in Dutch) is absolutely the biggest game in Holland. **Ajax Amsterdam** is invariably the best team in the land, and often is among the best in Europe. Ajax plays home matches at a fabulous modern stadium with a retractable roof, the **Amsterdam ArenA,** ArenA Boulevard 1, Amsterdam Zuidoost (© **020/311-1444;** Metro: Strandvliet/ArenA). There's even an on-site Ajax Museum.

8

Strolling & Bicycling in Amsterdam

The best way to discover Amsterdam is on foot. The first tour described here takes you to the essential cultural and architectural sights along the city's 17th-century Golden Age canals. Tours 2, 3, and 4 focus on the Old Center, the Jordaan, and the Jewish Quarter, respectively.

Our fifth tour is no leisurely stroll, but a taste of that quintessential Amsterdam experience: biking. Bicycles are a key part of the mechanism that makes Holland tick, and no trip to Amsterdam is complete without some time in the saddle. This tour pedals you out from the Center, along the Amstel River, to breathe fresh country air at the old riverside village of **Ouderkerk aan de Amstel.**

Part of Amsterdam's enchantment comes from making your own discoveries. On each of my proposed itineraries, you'll come across points of interest I haven't written up for lack of space. It could be an unusually shaped gable, an offbeat boutique, a gaily painted bike, a sunken canal boat, whatever. And here's something to keep your eyes open for: Before house numbers were introduced on canal houses during Napoleon's occupation, engraved gable stones indicating the resident's trade or profession served for identification purposes; you'll still see many of these today.

WALKING TOUR 1   **THE GOLDEN AGE CANALS**

START:	Herenmarkt (off Brouwersgracht).
FINISH:	Amstel River.
TIME:	3 hours to all day, depending on how long you linger along the way.
BEST TIMES:	First thing in the morning from spring through autumn, so you can watch as city life along the canals wakes up and gets going. If you're not an early riser, then any hour (yes, even after dark) is fine.
WORST TIMES:	Mondays, when most museums are closed.

The three 17th-century canals you explore on this tour—**Herengracht (Gentlemen's Canal), Keizersgracht (Emperor's Canal),** and **Prinsengracht (Princes' Canal)**—are the very heart of Golden Age Amsterdam, emblems of the city's wealth and pride in its heyday. Each deserves at least a morning or afternoon to itself. Time being limited, we're going to combine them into one monumental effort. If you're not so pressed, by all means slice the tour up into segments for a more leisurely experience.

You'll stroll along miles of tree-lined canals, crisscrossed by smaller canals, and you'll pass innumerable 17th-century canal houses with gables in various styles (bell, step, neck, and variations), classical facades, warehouses converted to apartments, colorful houseboats moored along the banks, bridges, museums, cafes, restaurants, boutiques, offbeat stores, and battered bikes secured to lampposts. I'm going to mention only the most special sights and point out some insider tips along the way. This should leave you with plenty of space for making your own discoveries.

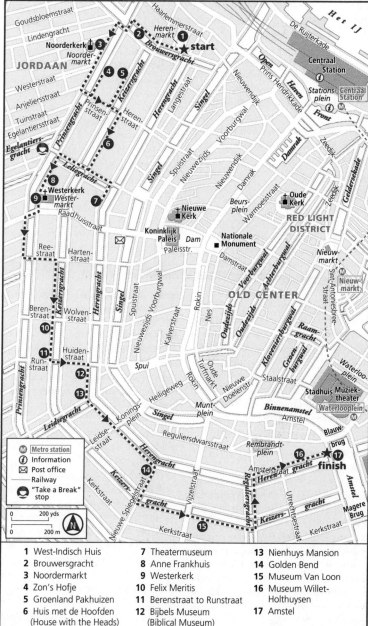

1 West-Indisch Huis	**7** Theatermuseum	**13** Nienhuys Mansion
2 Brouwersgracht	**8** Anne Frankhuis	**14** Golden Bend
3 Noordermarkt	**9** Westerkerk	**15** Museum Van Loon
4 Zon's Hofje	**10** Felix Meritis	**16** Museum Willet-Holthuysen
5 Groenland Pakhuizen	**11** Berenstraat to Runstraat	**17** Amstel
6 Huis met de Hoofden (House with the Heads)	**12** Bijbels Museum (Biblical Museum)	

Take tram 1, 2, 5, 13, or 17 to Martelaarsgracht, or the *Stop/Go* bus (see "Getting Around," in chapter 3) direct to the starting point, on Herenmarkt, just off Brouwersgracht:

❶ West-Indisch Huis

The 17th-century Dutch West India Company's headquarters handled trade—including slave trade—between Holland, the Americas, and Africa. It later became the offices of a social-welfare organization and a Lutheran orphanage, and now houses a U.S.-linked educational institute (see "Historical Buildings & Monuments," in chapter 7).

Walk along tranquil:

❷ Brouwersgracht

Humpback bridges, moored houseboats, and 17th- and 18th-century brewery *pakhuizen* (warehouses) that have been turned into chic, expensive apartments combine to make the Brewers' Canal one of Amsterdam's most photogenic corners. Worth special attention are nos. 204 and 206, **Het Kleine Groene Hert (the Little Green Deer)** and **Het Groote Groene Hert (the Big Green Deer).** Each has a gable crowned with a green-painted deer sculpture. Take note for possible future reference of two fine 17th-century "brown cafes": **Tabac** at Brouwersgracht 101 and **Papeneiland** at Prinsengracht 2–4. In the 17th century, Prinsengracht was home to storekeepers and craftsmen.

Along Prinsengracht, your first stop is:

❸ Noordermarkt

Saturdays from 9am to 5pm, this old market square hosts a farmers' market for "bio" (organic) products. A popular flea market takes over Mondays from 8am to 2pm, at which clothes fashionable a decade or more ago are highly esteemed, and dealers peddle everything from Golden Age antiques to yesterday's junk. Pause for a moment to admire the elaborate gables of the houses at nos. 15–22, each one decorated with an agricultural image—a cow, a sheep, a chicken—from the time when a

livestock market was held here. No. 16 has a Louis XIV neck gable and a gable stone from 1726 depicting Fortuna and advertising the textile store that once occupied the building.

The **Noorderkerk (North Church)**—the last masterpiece by architect Hendrick de Keyser, who was the guiding hand behind many of Amsterdam's historic churches—dominates the square (see "Sights of Religious Significance," in chapter 7). It's something of a rarity in nominally Calvinist Amsterdam, since it has a large and active Calvinist congregation. On the facade, a plaque recalls the February 1941 strike protesting Nazi deportation of the city's Jews. A group of sculptures outside recalls the dead and wounded from the 1934 *Jordaanoproer* street riots protesting poverty; the army suppressed these. If you're lucky, you'll hear the church's carillon playing as you go by.

Continue along Prinsengracht to the bridge at Prinsenstraat, and cross over. A few steps back along the canal on this side is:

❹ Zon's Hofje

At Prinsengracht 159–171, a hidden almshouse surrounds a courtyard garden at the end of a long passageway. People live here, but from 10am to 5pm the outer door is open and you can walk discreetly through the passageway to the courtyard, which belonged to the city's Mennonites. They worshiped at a clandestine church, **De Zon (the Sun),** and held meetings in the courtyard, which they called De Kleine Zon (the Little Sun). In 1720, the church's name was changed to De Arke Noach (Noah's Ark) and in 1755, it was demolished. Above the lintel of nos. 163–165, a carved plaque from the vanished church shows animals piling two by two into Noah's Ark.

Farther back along the canal, at nos. 85–133, is another former almshouse, built for the sick, elderly, and indigent: the carefully restored and immensely restful **Van Brienen's Hofje,** dating from 1804 (and also known as **De Star** after the De

Star Brewery foundation that took over the site in 1841). A wealthy merchant named Jan van Brienen supposedly had it built in gratitude for his escape from a vault in which he'd accidentally been locked. It has a lovely garden with benches, but if you don't want to have to backtrack too far, and aren't much of a *hofje* (almshouse) enthusiast, you can let it alone.

Head down Prinsenstraat to Keizersgracht. A short detour to the left brings you to the:

❺ Groenland Pakhuizen

Built in 1621 to store whale oil, the Greenland Warehouses are now chic apartments (nos. 40–44).

Cross the bridge over Keizersgracht. Note the houseboats moored on the canal. Ahead of you is Herenstraat, and at the far end of this short street, if you want to jog for a look, is Amsterdam's shortest canal, Blauburgwal, all 68m (74 yd.) of it. To stay on route, go right before Herenstraat on Keizersgracht, to the:

❻ Huis met de Hoofden (House with the Heads)

At no. 123, the heads on the 1622 facade by Hendrick de Keyser represent, from left to right, Apollo, Ceres, Mars, Athena, Bacchus, and Diana.

Turn left along Leliegracht, then right on Herengracht, to the:

❼ Theatermuseum

Herengracht was the ultimate address for flourishing 17th-century bankers and merchants. The graceful house at no. 168 was built in 1638 for Michiel Pauw, who established a short-lived trading colony in America at Hoboken, facing Nieuw Amsterdam (New York), and named it Pavonia after his august self. Note the classical neck gable, the city's first of its style. The museum extends into the flamboyant **Bartolotti House** at nos. 170–172, built in 1618 for Guillielmo Bartolotti, who began life as homey old Willem van den Heuvel; he switched to the fancy moniker after making a bundle in brewing and banking (see "More Top Museums & Galleries," in chapter 7).

Backtrack to Leliegracht, and cross over Keizersgracht on the bridge. Note at Keizersgracht 176 a rare Amsterdam Art Nouveau house (1905), designed by architect Gerrit van Arkel, which houses Greenpeace International headquarters. Continue up Leliegracht and take a left on Prinsengracht to the:

❽ Anne Frankhuis

This house at no. 263 is where the young Jewish girl Anne Frank (1929–45) hid from the Nazis and wrote her imperishable diary. The earlier you get here the better, because the line to get in grows as the day progresses (see "The Big Three," in chapter 7).

You might be tempted to stow away on a *pedalo* from the Canal Bikes dock outside the Anne Frankhuis. But if you're more in need of lunch, cross over Prinsengracht by the canal bridge and pop into:

 TAKE A BREAK
Cafe-restaurant **De Prins,** Prinsengracht 124 (☏ **020/624-9382**), which is my Best Value restaurant recommendation, and a great spot for a leisurely meal (see "The Canal Belt," in chapter 6).

Along this bank, at no. 170, Galleria d'Arte Rinascimento sells both old and new hand-painted Delftware from Koninklijke Porceleyne Fles (see "Shopping A to Z," in chapter 9). Continue to Rozengracht and turn left (east) to Westermarkt and its:

❾ Westerkerk

The Dutch Renaissance church, begun by Hendrick de Keyser in 1620, became his son Pieter's project after Hendrick died. The church opened in 1631 (see "Sights of Religious Significance," in chapter 7).

In 1635, French philosopher René Descartes lived in the house at Westermarkt 6; this is where he wrote *Treatise on the Passions of the Soul.* Descartes evidently thought he was in need of some more down-to-earth passion—therefore he was—and had an affair with his maid, which produced a child whose reality could scarcely be doubted. Also on Westermarkt: a somber bronze sculpture of Anne Frank, and the **Homomonument**'s pink marble triangles, dedicated to persecuted gays and lesbians.

Cross over Westermarkt to Rozengracht, which once was a canal. Continue along Prinsengracht to Reestraat, where you turn left. At Keizersgracht go right, across Berenstraat, to Keizersgracht 324:

⑩ Felix Meritis

Jacob Otten Husly built this structure in 1788 as the headquarters of a Calvinist philosophical society. The name (which was the group's motto) means "happiness through merit," and they invited such luminaries as Czar Alexander I and Napoleon to this Palladian setting, with Corinthian columns and triangular pediment, to experience this philosophy's consolations. The building later housed the Dutch Communist Party, and now hosts avant-garde theater, music, and dance performances (see "Other Venues," in chapter 10).

The next stretch of Keizersgracht goes from:

⑪ Berenstraat to Runstraat

On this stretch of Keizersgracht, instead of standing directly in front of buildings of interest, craning your neck skyward, walk along near the canal's bank (on the side with even numbers) and look across the water to the other side, so you can view things in panorama. In summer, though, elm trees screen some facades, and you might prefer to cross over for a closer look.

The third building along from Wolvenstraat (no. 313), an office block from 1914, is almost modern in Keizersgracht-time. Two houses farther down (no. 317) is the stately canalside home that belonged to Christoffel Brants, who counted Peter the Great among his acquaintances. A story goes that Peter sailed into Amsterdam in 1716, planning to stay a night here. The Czar of All the Russias got royally drunk, kept the mayor waiting at a reception in his honor, then retreated to the Russian ambassador's residence (at Herengracht 527) to sleep off his hangover.

Next door (no. 319) is a work by architect Philips Vingboons from 1639, as you can easily tell from the inscribed Latin numerals MDCXXXIX. It's interesting to compare this ornate neoclassical facade with its graceful neck gable to the Theatermuseum building by the same architect, at Herengracht 168 (p. 155).

Note the narrow facade of the seventh building before Huidenstraat (no. 345A), and run your eyes over the trio of graceful neck gables on the last three houses (nos. 353–357).

At Runstraat, cross over to Huidenstraat and go along to Herengracht. Turn right to Herengracht 366–368, for the:

⑫ Bijbels Museum (Biblical Museum)

Comprised of two of a group of four 1660s houses (nos. 364–370) with delicate neck gables, this museum was designed by architect Philips Vingboons for timber merchant Jacob Cromhout. The four structures are known both as the Cromhuithuizen and as the "Father, Mother, and Twins." The museum features Bibles and things biblical, but its canal-house setting and illuminated ceilings by Jacob de Wit are at least as interesting (see "More Top Museums & Galleries," in chapter 7).

Continue a few doors farther along Herengracht, to nos. 380–382, the:

⑬ Nienhuys Mansion

This princely residence was constructed in 1889 for Dutch tobacco tycoon Jacob Nienhuys. Polite society was amused that the coach-house entrance was too narrow for coaches to make the turn in one go. The mansion now houses the **Netherlands Institute for War Documentation** and the **Center for Holocaust and Genocide Studies.** Across the canal, on Herengracht 395's facade (hard to see unless you cross over for a close-up look), a stone cat stalks a carved mouse that's on the facade of the neighboring house, no. 397.

Cross elegant Leidsegracht (dug in 1664 for barge traffic to and from Leiden) to busy Leidsestraat. Go along Leidsestraat to its junction with Keizersgracht, and turn right into:

TAKE A BREAK
Walem, Keizersgracht 449 (☏ **020/625-3544**), a cafe that's just about hung on to its once-undisputed trendy rep, and that (more importantly) still serves great food (see "The Canal Belt," in chapter 6).

Retrace your steps to Herengracht, and turn right to the:

⑭ Golden Bend

You can trace the development of rich folks' wealth and tastes as you progress up the house numbers on this canal section between Leidsestraat and Vijzelstraat, named for its opulent palaces. Built with old money around the 1670s, in the Golden Age's fading afterglow, when French-influenced neoclassicism was all the rage, these mansions are mostly built of sandstone (rather than brick) on double lots with central entrances. Compare these sober baroque facades to the exuberant gabled houses from a half-century earlier, back along the canal. Look across the water to no. 475 for a particularly fine example of the later style. Closer to hand, no. 466 houses Yahoo!'s Dutch headquarters.

Turn right on Nieuwe Spiegelstraat, a street lined with antiques stores, and go along it to Keizersgracht. A short detour to your right brings you to No. 529, which in 1781–82 was the residence of John Adams, the then U.S. ambassador to the Netherlands, and later the second U.S. president. The canalside house was in effect the first-ever embassy of the United States, and a plaque placed there in 2005 by Amsterdam's John Adams Institute records the fact. Turn around and cross over on the bridge at Nieuwe Spiegelstraat to the far bank of Keizersgracht, for the:

⑮ Museum Van Loon

This museum (at no. 672) gives a rare glimpse beyond a patrician post–Golden Age house's gables (see "More Top Museums & Galleries," in chapter 7).

Cross Reguliersgracht and return to Herengracht—from the bridge over Reguliersgracht at Herengracht, you can see no fewer than 15 bridges (including the one you're standing on). Skim the edge of neat little Thorbeckeplein, and go right along the canal across Utrechtsestraat, a cornucopia of good restaurants and variegated stores, to the:

⑯ Museum Willet-Holthuysen

At Herengracht 605, this patrician canal house dating from 1687 is richly decorated in Louis XIV style. A table, under a big chandelier in the dining salon, is set for a meal being served more than 300 years late (see "More Top Museums & Galleries," in chapter 7).

Stroll to the end of Herengracht and finish at the:

⑰ Amstel River

At this point, the river should be thick with houseboats and canal barges. To your left is the refurbished **Blauwbrug (Blue Bridge),** built in 1884 (p. 158); to your right is the famous **Magere Brug (Skinny Bridge),** a double drawbridge (p. 158). Step out onto either of these for great views of the comings and goings on the water.

Walking the short distance along the river to Waterlooplein, or backtracking to Utrechtsestraat, puts you on the tram net. If you're footsore and hungry, hobble the short distance to:

WINDING DOWN
Café Schiller, Rembrandtplein 36 (☏ **020/624-9864**), where you can take the weight off your feet amid Art Deco surroundings, or on the glassed-in terrace next to the square (see "The Bar Scene," in chapter 10).

START:	The Dam.
FINISH:	Prins Hendrikkade, close to Centraal Station.
TIME:	2½ to 4 hours or more, depending on how long you spend in museums, attractions, cafes, and stores (and perusing the windows in the Red Light District).
BEST TIMES:	If you want to visit one or more of the museums or other attractions, most of them open at 10am (some are closed Mon). Morning is a good time to do the Red Light District, because by then most of its bizarre night owls—and raptors—have crashed for the day.
WORST TIMES:	Daylight hours are bad for perusing the Red Light District if you want to be there when business is humming. Then again, after-dark hours are bad for perusing the Red Light District if you *don't* want to be there when business is humming. It's a free country; the choice is yours.

This tour takes you past some of the main city-center points of interest in the **Nieuwe Zijde (New Side)**. It then goes into the **Oude Zijde (Old Side)**, the oldest part of town, the first part of which is a place of tranquil canals; then it weaves through the bawdy **Red Light District,** a sex-for-sale zone which actually occupies a handsome area of 16th-century canals and gabled houses. "Ordinary" people still live in this area and go on with their daily lives, as you'll observe if you take your eyes for a moment off the barely clad women behind red-lit windows. I don't recommend you do the Red Light section after dark; the district is seedier and more sinister then, and while it's fascinating, it no longer falls under the category of a casual stroll through town.

The starting point, reached by tram 1, 2, 4, 5, 9, 13, 14, 16, 17, 24, or 25, is the:

❶ Dam

It can be one hot Dam at times, especially in summer, when the city's main monumental square becomes a hangout for young and old, visitors and natives (see "The Dam," in chapter 7). Don't waste your time looking for a dam on the Dam, though; there hasn't been one here for centuries. Let's make a clockwise circuit of the square.

Dominating the western side is the neoclassical:

❷ Koninklijk Paleis (Royal Palace)

Constructed between 1648 and 1655 as the Stadhuis (Town Hall), this was later chosen to be the royal family's official residence (see "The Dam," in chapter 7).

Cross over Mozes en Aäronstraat to the:

❸ Nieuwe Kerk

Since 1814, all the kings and queens of the Netherlands have been inaugurated at the New Church (Dutch monarchs are not uppity enough to actually be crowned). Built between the late 15th and mid–17th centuries in elaborate late-Gothic style, the Nieuwe Kerk often hosts temporary exhibits expensive enough to maybe make you think twice (see "The Dam," in chapter 7).

Outside the church, take narrow Eggertstraat at the side of the Nieuwe Kerk's cafe, 't Nieuwe Kafé. On adjoining Gravenstraat, at no. 18, is:

❹ De Drie Fleschjes

A character-rich *proeflokaal* (tasting house) dating from 1650, where merchants sampled liqueurs and spirits, it now specializes in *jenever* (Dutch gin). Among a warren of tiny alleyways around here, Blaeustraat, behind a locked gate next to De Drie Fleschjes, recalls the store at nearby Damrak 46 where the 17th-century mapmaker Johannes Blaeu sold his superb world atlases.

Return to the north side of the Dam and glance upward at the painted 15th-century wall sculpture of Sinter Claes (St. Nicholas), the city's patron saint, and

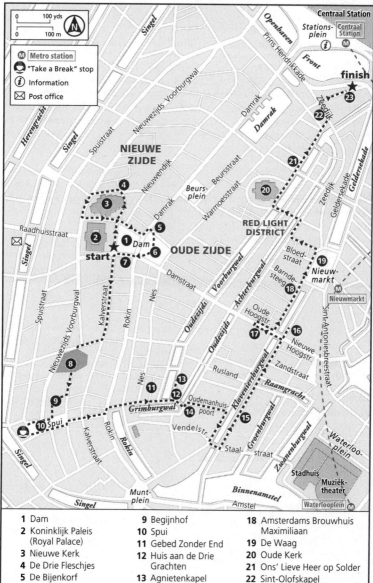

1 Dam
2 Koninklijk Paleis (Royal Palace)
3 Nieuwe Kerk
4 De Drie Fleschjes
5 De Bijenkorf
6 Nationaal Monument
7 Madame Tussauds
8 Amsterdams Historisch Museum
9 Begijnhof
10 Spui
11 Gebed Zonder End
12 Huis aan de Drie Grachten
13 Agnietenkapel
14 Oudemanhuispoort
15 Poppenhuis
16 Trippenhuis
17 Oost-Indisch Huis
18 Amsterdams Brouwhuis Maximiliaan
19 De Waag
20 Oude Kerk
21 Ons' Lieve Heer op Solder
22 Sint-Olofskapel
23 Sint-Nicolaaskerk

Santa Claus's forerunner, on the building just before the corner at Damrak.

Cross over busy Damrak to Amsterdam's answer to Bloomingdale's:

❺ De Bijenkorf

"The Beehive" department store dates from 1915 (see "Shopping A to Z," in chapter 9). In front is the **NH Grand Hotel Krasnapolsky** (p. 83). A short stroll along Damstraat at the side of the hotel would bring you right into the Red Light District, but we're not going there—not yet!

Cross over to the:

❻ Nationaal Monument

Holland's obelisk-shaped World War II memorial was erected in 1956 (see "The Dam," in chapter 7).

From here, cross over to the Amsterdam Diamond Center on the corner of Rokin, then cross over busy Rokin to:

❼ Madame Tussauds

Amsterdam's Madame Tussauds contains characters with a peculiarly Dutch waxen stare (see "The Dam," in chapter 7).

Continue to Kalverstraat, and go left on this bustling, pedestrians-only shopping street lined with department stores and cheap, cheerful boutiques. Turn right on Sint-Luciënsteeg to the:

❽ Amsterdams Historisch Museum

A porch from 1592 that used to be the city orphanage's entrance is now the museum entrance. The outer courtyard was for boys (to the left are cupboards where they stored their tools), and the inner courtyard was for girls (see "More Top Museums & Galleries," in chapter 7). Exit the museum through the **Schuttersgalerij,** a covered arcade lined with group portraits of 16th- and 17th-century militia companies (p. 144).

On the right side of narrow Gedempte Begijnensloot is the entrance to the:

❾ Begijnhof

Devout women lived in this cloister from the 14th century onward. The house at no. 34, Amsterdam's oldest, was built in 1425 and is one of only two timber houses remaining in the city (see p. 154 in chapter 7).

Pass between nos. 37 and 38, to:

❿ Spui

An elegant and animated square, Spui has at its west end a statue of a small boy, *Het Lieverdje* **(the Little Darling),** meant to represent a typical Amsterdam kid. Across the street, at no. 21, is the **Maagdenhuis,** the University of Amsterdam's main downtown building.

Go up on Spuistraat, to:

 TAKE A BREAK
Café Luxembourg, Spuistraat 24 (☎ **020/620-6264**), which the *New York Times* considers "one of the world's great cafes," for drinks, snacks, or one of their renowned sandwiches (see "The Old Center," in chapter 6).

Walk to the end of Spui and cross over Rokin, past a statue of Queen Wilhelmina, a canal tour-boat dock, and the Allard-Pierson Museum (see "More Top Museums & Galleries," in chapter 7). Go straight ahead on Lange Brugsteeg to Grimburgwal, in the district known as De Wallen (the Walls). The first street on the left, Nes, is lined with alternative theaters. Keep straight ahead, though, to:

⓫ Gebed Zonder End

This alleyway's odd name, which means "Prayer Without End," comes from the convents that used to be here. It's said that the murmur of prayers from behind the walls could always be heard.

Stay on Grimburgwal across Oudezijds Voorburgwal and Oudezijds Achterburgwal. Between these two canals and the adjacent Grimburgwal canal is the:

⓬ Huis aan de Drie Grachten

At Oudezijds Voorburgwal 249, the House on the Three Canals (1609) is a handsome redbrick, step-gabled, Dutch Renaissance house.

Go a short way along Oudezijds Voorburgwal to the:

⑬ Agnietenkapel

You'll easily recognize the building at no. 231 by its elaborate ornamental gateway from 1571. This was St. Agnes Convent's chapel until the Protestants took Amsterdam over. The Agnietenkapel later formed part of the **Athenaeum Illustre,** the city's first university, and now houses the university museum (which isn't very interesting unless there's a special exhibit).

Return to the House on the Three Canals and cross the bridge to Oudezijds Achterburgwal's far side, where you pass the **Gasthuis,** once a hospital and now part of the University of Amsterdam.

Turn right into the:

⑭ Oudemanhuispoort

A secondhand book market (Mon–Sat from 10:30am–6pm) popular with students occupies this dimly lit arcade. Midway along, on the left, a doorway leads to a courtyard garden with a statue of Minerva. At the far end of the arcade, above the exterior doorway, is *The Liberality,* a sculpture of a seated female figure with three objects: a cornucopia symbolizing abundance, a book symbolizing wisdom, and an oil lamp symbolizing enlightenment. An old man and woman represent old age and poverty. City sculptor Antonie Ziesenis created these statues in 1785.

Turn right on Kloveniersburgwal, cross over the canal at the next bridge, and go left on the far bank of the canal to Kloveniersburgwal 95, the:

⑮ Poppenhuis

Architect Philips Vingboons designed this classical mansion in 1642 for Joan Poppen, a dissolute grandson of a rich German merchant and heir to his fortune. The youth hostel next door at no. 97 was originally a home for retired sea captains.

Continue on Kloveniersburgwal—behind the buildings to your right front as you cross Raamstraat, you'll see the tip of the Zuiderkerk (South Church) spire—to Kloveniersburgwal 29, the:

⑯ Trippenhuis

The Trip brothers commissioned Philips Vingboons to create their ideal mansion (1664). They were arms dealers, which accounts for the martial images and emblems about the house. Originally, there were two houses behind a single classical facade, but the two have since been joined. It now houses the **Royal Netherlands Academy of Science.**

Backtrack to the canal bridge and cross over to Oude Hoogstraat and the:

⑰ Oost-Indisch Huis

Enter the East India House (1606) via a courtyard on the left side of the street, at no. 24. Once the headquarters of the V.O.C., the Vereenigde Oostindische Compagnie (United East India Company), it now belongs to the University of Amsterdam (see "Historical Buildings & Monuments," in chapter 7). Next door, at Oude Hoogstraat 22, is Amsterdam's narrowest house, just 2.02m (6⅔ ft.) wide.

Back on Kloveniersburgwal, go left. At no. 26 is the Klein Trippenhuis, the narrow house of the Trip brothers' coachman (see "The Smallest Houses," in chapter 7), which now houses a fetishist fashion store called Webers. Note a few doors along, at nos. 10–12, the drugstore Jacob Hooy & Co., which has dispensed medicinal relief since 1743. A little farther along, at nos. 6–8, is the:

⑱ Amsterdams Brouwhuis Maximiliaan

The city's smallest brewery, in a surviving portion of the 16th-century **Bethaniënklooster (Bethanien Convent),** produces 10 different beers and serves them from copper vats. The nuns who once brewed beer here have long since departed, but this brewery maintains their beer-making tradition. It's got a rustic-chic, wood-floored bar and a restaurant attached. A part of the old convent, which belonged to the Sisters of St. Mary Magdalen of Bethanien, has been restored and is now used as a concert hall for chamber music recitals.

In the center of Nieuwmarkt, the large, open square dead ahead, is:

⑲ De Waag

This massive edifice was once one of the city's medieval gates, and later the Weigh House and guild offices (see "Historical Buildings & Monuments," in chapter 7). It now houses a specialized educational and cultural institute (rarely open to the public), and a fashionable cafe-restaurant, **In de Waag** (see "The Old Center," in chapter 6).

Take a turn around bustling **Nieuwmarkt,** the center of Amsterdam's diminutive **Chinatown** and site of a summertime Sunday antiques market, from May through October.

Now we're going to head into the **Red Light District.** If you don't want to come along, go instead along Zeedijk at the northwest corner of Nieuwmarkt and I'll pick you up again farther along that street (skip to no. 22 on this tour). In compensation, you'll surely notice—you can't easily miss it—the Buddhist **Fo Guang Shan He Hua Temple** at Zeedijk 106–116, on the left, about midway along the street. It's open Monday to Saturday from noon to 5pm, and Sunday from 10am to 5pm. Admission's free, but donations are welcomed.

If, on the other hand, you have no objection to viewing the Red Light District in all its scuzzy glory, take Monnickenstraat to Oudezijds Achterburgwal and turn right, past windows that frame prostitutes waiting for customers or that have closed curtains to signify that a deal has been done, to the next bridge. Then go through Oude Kennissteeg (or take a neighboring street if this narrow alleyway is closed) directly ahead to Oudezijds Voorburgwal. Should you require proof that you can do more here than ogle the "views" through the multitudes of red-lit windows, turn right to no. 57, a 1615 baroque Renaissance canal house by architect Hendrick de Keyser, dubbed **De Gecroonde Raep (the Crowned Turnip)**

for its facade's motif. Take in its graceful accolade arches, double pilasters, and window cartouches.

Cross over the canal by the nearest bridge, to the:

⑳ Oude Kerk

Rembrandt's wife Saskia is interred within the Old Church, the city's first great Gothic church (see "Sights of Religious Significance," in chapter 7). Nowadays, the pretty little gabled almshouses around the church have red-fringed windows in which you can see scantily clad hookers.

Go north on Oudezijds Voorburgwal to no. 40:

㉑ Ons' Lieve Heer op Solder

Visit Our Lord in the Attic, a hidden Catholic church in a superb example of a 17th-century patrician canal house (see "Sights of Religious Significance," in chapter 7).

A couple of blocks north, at no. 14, on the corner of Oudezijds Armsteeg, you'll notice a step-gabled, redbrick building that leans crazily out over the sidewalk—careful not to trip over its projecting basement. It's called **Het Wapen van Riga (the Arms of Riga),** and it was built in 1605 in Dutch Renaissance style by a merchant from the Baltic city of Riga. It now houses a Leger des Heils (Salvation Army) hostel.

At the end of Oudezijds Voorburgwal, turn right on Sint-Olofssteeg to Zeedijk, one of the city's oldest streets—it was a center for prostitution and drugs until it was cleaned up in the 1990s. (Welcome back to anyone who forewent the Red Light District.) Go left now, to:

㉒ Sint-Olofskapel

The fishermen's dog that, according to some city legends, marked the spot where Amsterdam began by throwing up, is said to have done the deed on the site of St. Olaf's Chapel, at Zeedijk 2A. Supposedly, fishermen founded the chapel in gratitude for their escape from the sea. But discrepancies exist: The chapel was built around 1425 and Amsterdam dates from the end of the 12th century. Sometimes you can enter the church, which was over-restored in the 1990s and reopened as a congress center, via a tunnel under Zeedijk from the NH Barbizon Palace (see below); you'll see its spacious columned interior.

From here, continue past two great Amsterdam taverns: **Het Elfde Gebod** at Zeedijk 5, which stocks 50 different kinds of beer, and the traditional bar **In 't Aepjen** at Zeedijk 1, in one of Amsterdam's two surviving timber houses (the other is in the Begijnhof, see above), which dates from 1550.

Emerge on Prins Hendrikkade and go right to:

❷ Sint-Nicolaaskerk

The city's main Catholic church (since Protestants took over most of the others

during the Reformation), St. Nicholas's dates from 1887 and was originally the harbor church—primarily, but not exclusively, for seamen (see "Sights of Religious Significance," in chapter 7).

From here, you can get to Centraal Station by just crossing over busy Prins Hendrikkade. But before doing so, take a break next door at:

WINDING DOWN
Hudson's, in the NH Barbizon Palace (see "The Waterfront," in chapter 5), Prins Hendrikkade 59–72 (📞 **020/556-4564**), a tony place that serves light food and drinks.

WALKING TOUR 3   **THE JORDAAN**

START:	Brouwersgracht.
FINISH:	Noordermarkt.
TIME:	Allow between 2 and 2½ hours.
BEST TIMES:	Anytime, but if you want to visit one of the Jordaan's lively markets, go on Monday morning or on Saturday. On Monday there's a flea market on Noordermarkt, and a textiles market on Westerstraat where you find, among other items, fabrics and secondhand clothing. On Saturday, Noordermarkt hosts a bird market and a farmers' market with organic produce, and Lindengracht has a general street market.
WORST TIMES:	If you hate street markets, you won't want to go plowing through them on the days mentioned above. Don't visit the *hofjes* (almshouses) on the route too early or too late.

It's easy to get lost in the character-rich maze of the Jordaan—not that getting lost is a bad thing. It affords you an opportunity to make your own discoveries, which is the key to appreciating the Jordaan. Among the district's sights are several of the delightful, centuries-old almshouses known as *hofjes*. Students, seniors, and people requiring supervised accommodations live in these small houses. If you enter their courtyards, be sure to tread softly.

To avoid an overly long walk, I've restricted this tour to the northern—and more interesting—half of the Jordaan, from Brouwersgracht down to about Rozengracht. That leaves the southern half, from Rozengracht to Leidsegracht, for your own perusal.

Take tram 1, 2, 5, 13, or 17 to Martelaarsgracht, or the *Stop/Go* bus (see "Getting Around," in chapter 3) direct to the starting point, on:

❶ Brouwersgracht

A walk northwest along this venerable houseboat-lined canal (see stop 2 in Walking Tour 1), takes you across Lindengracht, past a 1979 bronze sculpture of

writer Theo Thijssen (1879–1943) with one of his popular fictional characters, the Jordaan schoolchild Kees de Jongen. Farther along, across Willemstraat, look across the water to the modern De Blauwe Burgt apartment block for an idea of how the new complements (or degrades) the old.

Go left on tree-shaded:

❷ Palmgracht

This street was once a canal. The house at nos. 28–38 hides a small cobblestone courtyard garden behind an orange door that's the entrance to the **Raepenhofje,** an almshouse dating from 1648. The turnip on the gable stone is a pun on the original owner's name, Pieter Adriaenszoon Raep (*raep* means "turnip" in Dutch). Across the courtyard, at nos. 20–26, is the **Bossche-hofje,** which Arent Dirkszoon Bossch built in 1648.

Go left on Palmdwarsstraat and cross over Willem-straat (which used to be a canal called Gouds-bloemgracht), onto Tweede Goudsbloemdwarsstraat. Cross over Goudsbloemdwarsstraat to:

❸ Lindengracht

Like Palmgracht, Lindengracht was once a canal, and is now the scene of a lively Saturday street market. Continue along to the **Suyckerhoff Hofje,** at nos. 149–163. The 15 small houses (originally there were 19) of this pretty *hofje* were built in 1670 by order of Pieter Janszoon Suyckerhoff's 1667 testament, which aimed to provide refuge for Protestant widows and women of good moral standing and "tranquil character," who'd been abandoned by their husbands. The door may appear to be locked, but you can usually open it during daylight hours and walk along the narrow entrance corridor to a flower-filled courtyard garden.

Farther up, at Lindengracht 171, you pass the Old Jordaan–style coffeehouse **Oor**—this isn't a dope-dealing "coffeeshop" but the genuine article—in a building from 1884.

Take the first street on the left, Tweede Lindendwarsstraat, to:

❹ Karthuizersplantsoen

Nothing's left of the Carthusian monastery built in 1394. It stretched from here to Lijnbaansgracht before being demolished in the 1570s during Amsterdam's transition from Catholicism to Protestantism. A children's playground is now where the monastery's cemetery once was. There are still sights to see here, however: At Karthuizersstraat 11–19 is a row of neck-gabled houses from 1737, named after the four seasons (Lente, Zomer, Herfst, and Winter). Next-door (forgive the unusual numbering) at nos. 69–191, is the 1650 **Huyszitten-Weduwenhof,** a large interior courtyard surrounded by houses that were once poor widows' homes—they now board students.

Go left on Tichelstraat, cross Westerstraat, once a broad canal, and continue along a string of *dwarsstraten* (side streets)—Tweede Anjeliersdwarsstraat, Tweede Tuindwarsstraat, and Tweede Egelantiersdwarsstraat—it may take you longer to pronounce the names of these lively little cafe-lined streets than to walk through them—to:

❺ Egelantiersgracht

On the way you'll notice the Westerkerk's tall spire, called the Westertoren, which has a carillon that breaks into song at every opportunity (see "Sights of Religious Significance," in chapter 7). Genuine Jordaaners, it is said, are born within earshot of the bells.

Named for the eglantine rose, or sweetbriar, Egelantiersgracht is one of the city's most elegant and tranquil small canals. Its many interesting 17th- and 18th-century houses afford a tantalizing insight into the kinds of modestly elegant living quarters successful Amsterdam artisans could aspire to.

On the gable stone of a trio of simple bell gables at nos. 61–65 is a carved falcon.

If the door's open, peek into the **Andrieshofje** at nos. 107–145. Cattle farmer Ivo Gerrittszoon provided funds in his will to build these 36 almshouses; they were completed in 1617 and remodeled in 1884. A corridor decorated with Delft blue tiles leads up to a small courtyard with a leafy garden. An old water pump stands here, as does a stone bearing the inscription: *Vrede Sy Met U* (Peace be with you).

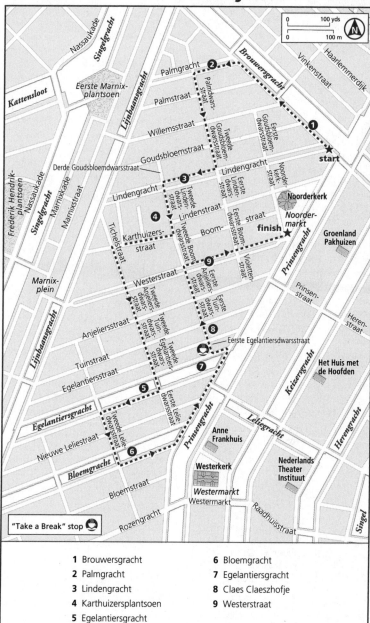

"Take a Break" stop 🍲

1 Brouwersgracht
2 Palmgracht
3 Lindengracht
4 Karthuizersplantsoen
5 Egelantiersgracht

6 Bloemgracht
7 Egelantiersgracht
8 Claes Claeszhofje
9 Westerstraat

Retrace your steps to turn right on Tweede Leliedwarsstraat (from 1637 to 1696, the famous Blaeu family of cartographers lived at no. 76) and continue to:

6 Bloemgracht

The grandest of the Jordaan canals was originally home to workers who produced dyes and paints. Architect Hendrick de Keyser built the three step-gabled houses at nos. 87–91 in 1642—they're gems, and now house a foundation established to preserve the architect's works. Their carved gable stones represent a townsman, a countryman, and a seaman.

Nos. 77 and 81 are former sugar refineries from 1752 and 1763, respectively. Their gable stones, De Saayer (the Sower) and De Jonge Saayer (the Young Sower), are of recent origin.

Walk east toward Prinsengracht, where you can see the Westertoren again. Go left on Prinsengracht to:

7 Egelantiersgracht

You visited this canal earlier at a point farther west. A hardware store at nos. 2–6, at the corner of Prinsengracht, is a fine example of Amsterdam School architecture from 1917, with its intricate brickwork and cast-iron, Art Nouveau–influenced ornaments. To the store's left, at no. 8, a 1649 step-gabled house is decorated with sandstone ornaments and gable stones that depict St. Willibrord and a brewer.

On Egelantiersgracht is a particularly good place to:

> ☕ **TAKE A BREAK**
> Though there are plenty of cafes in the Jordaan at which you can rest your legs and quench your walker's thirst, the best terrace is along the waterside at **'t Smalle,** Egelantiersgracht 12 (📞 **020/623-9617**). This cafe serves snacks like *bitterballen* and homemade soups (see "The Bar Scene," in chapter 10).

When you've finished your break, turn right off Egelantiersgracht to another sequence of side streets— Eerste Egelantiersdwarsstraat, Eerste Tuindwarsstraat, and Eerste Anjeliersdwarsstraat. On the way, at Eerste Egelantiersdwarsstraat 1–3, is a passage leading to the:

8 Claes Claeszhofje

Claes Claesz Anslo, a cloth merchant, founded this (now handsomely restored) almshouse in 1616. It's also known as the **Anslohofje**—a plaque on the neighboring entrance bears Anslo's coat of arms. Also note the "writing hand" gable stone at no. 52. Tiny apartments surround two equally minuscule courtyards.

Continue through those three side streets to:

9 Westerstraat

This broad street, formerly a canal known as Anjeliersgracht, hosts a Monday street market. At Westerstraat 109, at the corner of Eerste Anjeliersdwarsstraat, you pass a characteristic Jordaan bar, **Café Nol.** Across the street is the **Pianola Museum,** Westerstraat 106 (see "Minor Museums," in chapter 7).

Continue east on Westerstraat to Noordermarkt (see stop 3 in Walking Tour 1).

> ☕ **WINDING DOWN**
> A cafe that's a contender for serving the best *appelgebak met slagroom* (apple pie with cream) in town, **Winkel,** Noordermarkt 43 (📞 **020/623-0223**), also does a fair breakfast and snacks. It's a little gloomy (okay, *atmospheric*) inside, but has a great sidewalk terrace on Westerstraat and a sliver of patio on Noordermarkt.

START:	Waterlooplein.
FINISH:	*The Dockworker* statue, on Jonas Daniël Meijerplein.
TIME:	Allow between 1½ and 3 hours, not including museum and rest stops.
BEST TIMES:	Monday to Saturday from 10am to 5pm, when the Waterlooplein flea market is open.
WORST TIMES:	During a street battle on Waterlooplein between the Dutch riot police and demonstrators protesting the construction of the Town Hall and Opera House—but hey, the Battle of Waterlooplein was decades ago and the tear gas has long since dissipated.

I need to advise you right from the get-go that the **Jodenbuurt (Jewish Quarter)** has changed almost beyond recognition since World War II. The Holocaust decimated most of the area's Jewish population, and wartime damage followed by postwar redevelopment eliminated much of its physical character. Some of the places you'll encounter on this tour actually no longer exist or are in ruins, others have been put to quite different purposes, and a few may seem like a minor reward for the effort you'll expend in getting to them. But Amsterdam was once renowned as the "Jerusalem of the West," and there remain mementos and memorials of what was a thriving Jewish community.

You can edit the tour to just its highlights by deleting waypoints 7 to 13—but if you do this, consider excepting waypoint 10 from that equation, and take the tram from Waterlooplein to visit the Hollandsche Schouwburg.

You can go by tram 9 or 14, or by Metro train, to Waterlooplein, where from Monday to Saturday you'll be able to take in the:

❶ Waterlooplein Flea Market

If you like flea-market shopping, beware: You may need to continue this tour tomorrow. In the middle of the square are the city's modern opera and ballet house, the **Muziektheater** (p. 228), and the **Stadhuis (Town Hall).**

Assess the likelihood of getting your feet wet at the **Normaal Amsterdams Peil (Normal Amsterdam Level),** a fixed point against which experts measure sea level—NAP is Europe's standard for altitude measurements. Beside a bronze plaque in the passageway between the Muziektheater and the Town Hall are three acrylic columns filled with water. The first two show the current sea level at Vlissingen in the province of Zeeland and IJmuiden on the North Sea coast west of Amsterdam; the third, 4.6m (15 ft.) above your head, shows the high-water mark during the disastrous Zeeland floods of 1953.

Also on Waterlooplein is the:

❷ Mozes en Aäronkerk

This started as a secret church for Catholics who were forbidden to worship in public when the Calvinists rose to power in the 16th century.

From Waterlooplein, go right on the little street with the big name of Houtkopersdwarsstraat, then left on Jodenbreestraat to the:

❸ Museum Het Rembrandthuis

"Jewish Broad Street" was for centuries the center of Amsterdam's Jewish life. Now, its north side consists of mostly modern buildings with little in the way of distinctive character. On the south side, though, at nos. 4–6, is the stellar Rembrandt House Museum. Rembrandt wasn't Jewish, but while living in this house (see "More Top Museums & Galleries," in chapter 7) in what was then a primarily Jewish neighborhood, he often painted or sketched portraits of his Jewish friends and neighbors.

Cross over the Sint-Antoniesluis bridge, pausing to enjoy the handsome views up and down the canal. On the south bank of Oude Schans lies an island that from the 17th century until World War II was home to many Jewish diamond workshops and other small crafts houses. Walk a little way along Sint-Antoniesbreestraat, to no. 69, to view the magnificent:

➍ Huis De Pinto

The mansion dates from the early years of the 17th century. In 1651, it came into the possession of the Jewish businessman and scholar Isaäc de Pinto, and later in the century was remodeled in the ornate Italian Renaissance style. It now houses a branch of the Amsterdam Public Library.

Return to Waterlooplein. Keeping the Zwanenburgwal canal to your right, walk down to the bridge that leads to Staalstraat, and cross over to:

> **TAKE A BREAK**
> **Puccini,** Staalstraat 17 (✆ 020/
> 427-8341), a delightful place to
> stop for coffee and homemade desserts
> (fruit pies, cakes, and luscious pastries),
> which you can watch prepared before
> your very eyes.

Go back over the bridge and turn right, to the:

➎ Jewish Resistance Fighters Memorial

This is the black marble monument to Jews who tried to resist Nazi oppression and to the people who helped them.

Turn left at the monument and walk toward the Blauwbrug (Blue Bridge), dead ahead. Just before the bridge, look for the outline of:

➏ Megadlei Yethomin

This orphanage, established in 1836, was for German and East European Jewish boys. During World War II, the boys were deported to Sobibor concentration camp. After the war, the orphanage reopened, this time as a home for boys who wanted to get to Israel; it successfully placed many orphans in Israel before closing in 1955. Only the building's outline remains today, as a memorial to the orphans and their

caretaker who died in Sobibor. The rest was demolished in 1977 to make way for the Metro, and later, for the new Town Hall and the Muziektheater.

Continue to the Blauwbrug. Don't cross over, but continue straight ahead, keeping the Amstel River to your right. Go left on Nieuwe Herengracht just before the handsome drawbridge ahead of you, and walk to:

➐ Nieuwe Herengracht 33

There was space for just 10 people in this home for Portuguese Jewish seniors, yet they had their own synagogue inside.

Walk to the end of Nieuwe Herengracht and turn right across Vaz Diasbrug. Look back down the canal as you cross the bridge for a picture-perfect view of canal houses and houseboats. Continue along this street, which is now Weesperstraat, until you reach a:

➑ Small garden

This resting spot contains a monument to the Dutch people who protected their Jewish compatriots during World War II. The memorial, from 1950, is a white limestone altar, and has five reliefs of mourning men, women, and children.

Continue along Weesperstraat to Nieuwe Kerkstraat. Go left to:

➒ Nieuwe Kerkstraat 127

Formerly the Metaarhuis, this is where the bodies of people who died at the Nieuwe Keizersgracht hospital were cleansed in accordance with Jewish ritual.

Walk farther along and cross the bridge at the end of Nieuwe Kerkstraat; veer to the left a bit and you'll be on Plantage Kerklaan. Walk down Plantage Kerklaan to the traffic lights and take a left on Plantage Middenlaan. To your left, at Plantage Middenlaan 24, is the:

➓ Hollandsche Schouwburg

Only the shell remains of this old theater (see "Historical Buildings & Monuments," in chapter 7). Here, Nazis processed many of Amsterdam's Jewish victims before they deported them to concentration camps. Some deportees' children were able to sneak across the street to a kindergarten— these lucky ones were saved by residents in the attached houses. A plaque on the

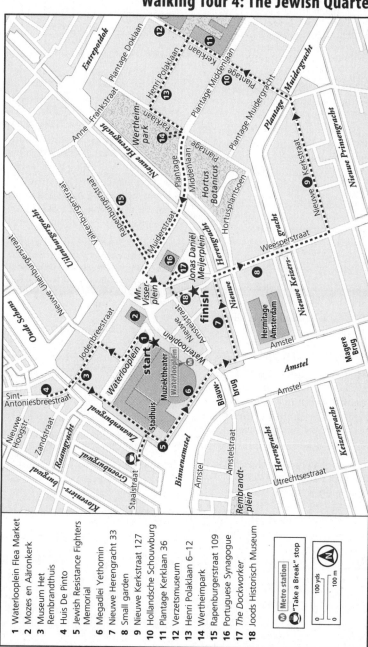

1 Waterlooplein Flea Market
2 Mozes en Aäronkerk
3 Museum Het Rembrandthuis
4 Huis De Pinto
5 Jewish Resistance Fighters Memorial
6 Megadlei Yethomin
7 Nieuwe Herengracht 33
8 Small garden
9 Nieuwe Kerkstraat 127
10 Hollandsche Schouwburg
11 Plantage Kerklaan 36
12 Verzetsmuseum
13 Henri Polaklaan 6–12
14 Wertheimpark
15 Rapenburgerstraat 109
16 Portuguese Synagogue
17 The Dockworker
18 Joods Historisch Museum

Ⓜ Metro station
☕ "Take a Break" stop

0   100 yds
0   100 m

school building celebrates the children's escape. Opposite the theater, notice the bright primary colors of architect Aldo van Eyck's **Moederhuis** (1978), a residence for single mothers.

Go back to the traffic lights, turn left, and continue along Plantage Kerklaan. On the right side of the street, you'll soon come to:

⓫ Plantage Kerklaan 36

A plaque at this address commemorates Jewish resistance fighters who attempted to destroy the city registers to prevent the Nazis from discovering how many Jews were in Amsterdam and where they lived. This brave effort could have kept thousands of Amsterdam Jews from dying in concentration camps. But tragically, the attempt failed and 12 resistance fighters were executed.

The building now houses offices for **Artis Zoo** (see "Especially for Kids," in chapter 7).

Stay on Plantage Kerklaan, but cross over to the other side of the street, to the:

⓬ Verzetsmuseum

The Resistance Museum at no. 61A (see "More Top Museums & Galleries," in chapter 7) is quite small; it eerily evokes the dark years of Amsterdam's Nazi occupation and the slow but sure implementation of Hitler's "Final Solution" to rid the world of Jews.

Backtrack to Henri Polaklaan and turn right, to:

⓭ Henri Polaklaan 6–12

Built in 1916, this is the former Portuguese Jewish Hospital. The pelican on the facade is a symbol of the Portuguese Jewish community.

Go left at the end of Henri Polaklaan, to Plantage Parklaan, and, on the corner of Plantage Middenlaan, go right, into:

⓮ Wertheimpark

Though really more like a large garden with benches, this small park is a good place for a rest. At its heart is a memorial (1993) to Auschwitz victims by Dutch

sculptor Jan Wolkers (who died in 2007). Six large broken-seeming mirrors laid flat on the ground reflect a shattered sky and cover a buried urn containing ashes of those who died in the concentration camp. NOOIT MEER AUSCHWITZ (Never Again Auschwitz), reads the dedication. An information board lists in impersonal round numbers some of the Holocaust's gruesome statistics: Of Holland's 140,000 Jews, 107,000 were deported to concentration camps. Just 5,200 returned. Of the 95,000 sent to Auschwitz and Sobibor, fewer than 500 survived. One of those who perished (at Bergen-Belsen) was Anne Frank. At the park's far end, there's a street named after her.

Exit the park through the gate you came in and go right on Plantage Middenlaan. On the other side of the street is Hortus Botanicus, the city's botanical garden (see "Green Amsterdam," in chapter 7). Keep going, across the bridge over Nieuwe Herengracht. At Mr. Visserplein, turn right and walk on until you come to:

⓯ Rapenburgerstraat 109

Bet Hamidrash Ets Haim (Study House of the Tree of Life) was once a center of Jewish learning where people studied Jewish law and devotionals. The building dates from 1883.

Return to Mr. Visserplein and head to the:

⓰ Portuguese Synagogue

This large and distinguished-looking building will be to your left (see "Sights of Religious Significance," in chapter 7).

Make a left on Jonas Daniël Meijerplein. On the square, pause to view:

⓱ The Dockworker

Nazis forced many Jews to wait in this area for deportation to concentration camps. This bronze statue by Mari Andriessen was erected in 1952; it commemorates the 1941 February Strike by Amsterdam workers protesting the Nazis' persecution of Amsterdam's Jews. The strike, one of the biggest collective anti-Nazi actions in all of occupied Europe, was ruthlessly suppressed.

Turn onto Nieuwe Amstelstraat, for the entrance (at no. 1) to the:

⑱ Joods Historisch Museum

The building that now houses the Jewish Historical Museum once comprised four separate synagogues built by Jewish refugees from Germany and Poland in the 17th and 18th centuries (see "More Top Museums & Galleries," in chapter 7). Across the street from the museum is the **Arsenal,** which served as a munitions

storage space in the 19th century. It's now part of the museum.

> **WINDING DOWN**
> **Grand Café Dantzig aan de Amstel,** Zwanenburgwal 15 (☏ **020/620-9039**), is a large, modern, trendy place built into a corner of the Stadhuis (City Hall) complex. An alfresco terrace beside the Amstel River soaks up sunrays.

BIKE TOUR · ALONG THE AMSTEL RIVER

START:	Waterlooplein.
FINISH:	Amstel Station.
TIME:	Allow between 3 and 4 hours, not including rest stops.
BEST TIMES:	May to September, outside of rush hour (rush hour is around 8–10am and 5–7pm).
WORST TIMES:	A cold winter's day won't suit sensible folks—but the Dutch don't mind.

This biking route begins in the city center and follows a scenic, relatively quiet way through the city, emerging into the countryside alongside the Amstel River for a short but glorious hop out to the pretty village of **Ouderkerk aan de Amstel.** Also see "Bicycling in Amsterdam," in chapter 3.

The starting point is Waterlooplein and the:

❶ Amstel River

The Amstel is likely to be fairly busy with waterborne traffic, and has houseboats moored along both banks.

Continue to the:

❷ Magere Brug

Known as the Amstel's "Skinny Bridge," the Magere Brug is actually an 18th-century replacement for the original 17th-century bridge. Cross over to the west (left) bank and cycle south along the Amstel. On the river's other side, you can see the **Koninklijk Theater Carré** see "The Performing Arts," in chapter 10). Continue over Sarphatistraat, which you'll easily recognize by its tram lines.

Detour around a break in the road, cross busy Stadhouderskade, and get back to the river at:

❸ Amsteldijk

Keep pedaling south on this road, enjoying the riverside views, until you reach the

Berlagebrug (Berlage Bridge), where you need to be careful, as the traffic gets noticeably busier at this point.

Stay on Amsteldijk until you arrive at:

❹ Martin Luther Kingpark

Most of the road traffic swings away to the right on President Kennedylaan at this park, but stay on Amsteldijk, which gradually becomes almost rural, though with houseboats alongside the road in place of country cottages. Up ahead, you'll hear a noise like a substantial storm; it means you're just getting closer to the highway bridge that carries the city's A10 ring road (beltway) across the river. Go under the bridge and finally you're out in the country, passing:

❺ Amstelpark

The riverside stays tranquil and scenic from now on. Continue past the statue of Rembrandt and a windmill at the park's end. Around this characteristic old Dutch

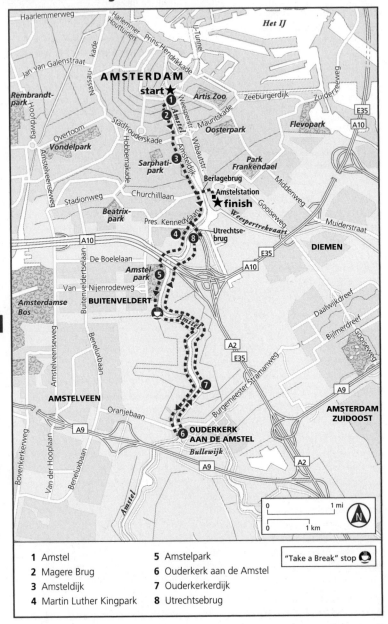

1 Amstel
2 Magere Brug
3 Amsteldijk
4 Martin Luther Kingpark

5 Amstelpark
6 Ouderkerk aan de Amstel
7 Ouderkerkerdijk
8 Utrechtsebrug

"Take a Break" stop

scene, there'll likely be busloads of tourists photographing Rembrandt, the windmill, themselves, and everything in sight, probably including you as you glide past. Beyond this is:

TAKE A BREAK
Klein Kalfje, Amsteldijk 355 (✆ **020/644-5338**), a small atmospheric Dutch cafe with a riverside terrace and canal barges moored alongside. A road separates the terrace from the cafe. There used to be an unofficial traffic sign here that indicated CAUTION: WAITER CROSSING.

You pass cottages and villas all the way to:
❻ Ouderkerk aan de Amstel
The village has an abundance of cafes and restaurants with riverside or sidewalk terraces. If you've still got energy, explore the village before settling down at one of the terraces for something restorative.

To return, switch to the right bank of the river, on:
❼ Ouderkerkerdijk
Narrower than Amsteldijk, this road has almost no traffic. Along the way, you'll pass a windmill and several tiny hamlets.

Recross the Amstel at the:
❽ Utrechtsebrug
Now you return to Amsteldijk and busy city streets. At Berlagebrug, recross the river and pedal the short distance to Amstel Station, where you, your bike, and your weary legs can board a Metro train back to Waterlooplein. Or you can bike back along either bank.

Shopping in Amsterdam

From its earliest days Amsterdam has been a trading city. First, trade centered on the fish that the original dammers of the Amstel caught in the river and on the Zuider Zee; later, during the 17th century, Dutch East and West India companies' ships carried back spices, furs, flower bulbs, and artifacts, all of which would be bought and sold in Amsterdam.

The fish were sold where a major department store—**De Bijenkorf**—now stands, and early townspeople brought calves to market on **Kalverstraat**, still a popular shopping street. The luxury items available today are the same sort of goods Dutch merchants sold in the 17th-century Golden Age, and the junk you buy in Waterlooplein's flea market is much the same as it has been for hundreds of years.

Adding a modern dimension to this tradition-laden scene are the funky boutiques scattered around Amsterdam, and adding sparkle are the diamond cutters. Amsterdam has a full range of shopping options, from small and highly individualistic—perhaps eccentric—boutiques showcasing small-name designers to chains, department stores, and malls.

---

1 THE SHOPPING SCENE

Shopping can be an interesting extension to your Amsterdam experience, because the center city is small enough that stores and attractions are often right beside each other. Rather than going on dedicated shopping expeditions, it may make more sense to simply drop into close-by stores while you're touring.

OPEN HOURS Regular store hours in Amsterdam are Monday, Tuesday, Wednesday, and Friday from 9 or 10am to 6pm (some stores don't open until as late as 1pm on Mon), Thursday from 9 or 10am to 9pm, and Saturday from 9 or 10am to 5pm. Many stores open on Sunday too, usually from noon to 5pm.

PRICES All applicable taxes are included in amounts shown on tags and display cards. End-of-season and other special sales occur occasionally throughout the year.

DUTY-FREE ITEMS If you are traveling from one E.U. country to another, you can't buy duty-free goods at airports, on ferries, or at border crossings; you can make duty-free purchases only when traveling to or from the E.U. from a nonmember country. Some duty-free shopping centers, like the one at Amsterdam's Schiphol Airport, offer reduced prices (close to duty-free prices) for intra-E.U. travelers.

BEST BUYS

Should an item in an Amsterdam store window take your fancy or fill a specific need, buy it. But often, prices and selections in Holland are too close to—or more expensive than—what you'd find at home to justify the extra weight in your suitcase or the expense

(Tips) Tax Return

If you live outside the European Union (E.U.), you're entitled to a refund of the value-added tax (BTW) paid on purchases totaling 50€ ($80) or more in a day, at a store that subscribes to the refund system, identified by a TAX-FREE SHOPPING sticker. On high-ticket items, the 13.5% savings can be significant. You must export the purchases within 3 months.

To obtain your refund, ask the store for a **global refund check.** When you leave the E.U., present this check along with your purchases and receipts to Customs. They'll stamp the check, and then you can get the refund in cash or paid to your credit card at any **International Cash Refund Point.** At Schiphol Airport, this is the **Global Refund Cash Refund Office;** refunds are also available from the airport branch of **ABN-AMRO bank.**

For a list of International Cash Refund Points, and for more information, contact **Europe Tax-Free Shopping,** Leidsevaartweg 99, 2106 AS Heemstede, the Netherlands (© **023/524-1909;** www.globalrefund.com).

of shipping. Exceptions are the special items that the Dutch produce to perfection—Delftware, pewter, crystal, and old-fashioned clocks—or commodities in which they've significantly cornered a market, like diamonds.

None of the aforementioned items are inexpensive, unfortunately, and you'll want to do some homework to be able to make canny shopping decisions. But you can find excellent values and take home treasures from Holland that will please you more and longer than the usual souvenirs. If money's a consideration, focus on less costly Dutch specialties: cheese, flower bulbs, and chocolate.

ANTIQUES All those tankards, pipes, cabinets, clocks, kettles, vases, and other bric-a-brac you see in old Dutch paintings still show up among stores' treasures on **Nieuwe Spiegelstraat.** It's the 21st century's good fortune that since the 17th century, the Dutch have saved everything, from Chinese urns to silver boxes, cookie molds to towering armoires. With around 160 antiques stores, there's no lack of choice in Amsterdam.

ART Galleries abound in Amsterdam, particularly in the canal area near the Rijksmuseum, and their exhibitions prove that Dutch painters are as prolific in the 21st century as they were in the Golden Age. The VVV Tourist Information Office publication *Amsterdam Day by Day* is your best guide to who's showing what, and where.

CHEESE Holland is known for its cheese *(kaas)*. Gouda *(khow-duh)* and Edam *(ay-dam)* are the two most familiar Dutch cheeses. You have the choice between factory cheese, made from pasteurized milk, or *boerenkaas,* farm cheese produced the old way with fresh, unpasteurized milk straight from the cow. *Boerenkaas* is more expensive, but has more taste. Another choice is between *jonge* (young) and old *(oude)* cheese. Young cheese is sweeter, moister, and has that melt-in-your-mouth quality, while old cheese has a sharper, drier taste, and a crumbly texture.

CHOCOLATE Droste, Verkade, and van Houten are three of the best names to look for. Or seek out the small specialty stores that still hand-fill bonbon boxes.

204 **CIGARS** Holland is one of the world's predominant cigar-producing centers. Serious smokers know that Dutch cigars are different, and drier, than Cuban or American smokes. It's partly because of the Indonesian tobacco and partly because of how the cigar's made. Whatever the reason, Dutch cigars can be a pleasant change for American tobacco enthusiasts.

CRYSTAL & PEWTER If you recall classic Dutch still-life paintings portraying happy scenes of 17th-century family life, you'll know that crystal and pewter objects are part of Holland's heritage. Crystal has long been associated with the towns of Leerdam and Maastricht (to spot the genuine article, look for the four triangles of the **Royal Leerdam** label), and pewter of Tiel.

Note: The Dutch government bans the use of lead as a hardening agent, but this assurance only protects you from toxicity in new pewter, so don't buy any antiques for use with food or drink.

DELFTWARE & MAKKUMWARE Three main types of delftware are available in Amsterdam: Delftware, Makkumware, and junk. None of it is cheap. With a lowercase *d,* delftware is an umbrella name for all Dutch hand-painted earthenware pottery resembling ancient Chinese porcelain, whether it is blue and white, red and white, or polychrome, and regardless of the Dutch city in which it was produced. Delftware, or Delft Blue (with a capital *D*), refers to the predominantly, but not exclusively, blue-and-white products of the Delft-based firms **De Koninklijke Porceleyne Fles** and **De Delftse Pauw.** Similarly, *makkumware* is synonymous with polychrome pottery, whereas Makkumware is the hand-painted polychrome earthenware produced only in Makkum, a town in Friesland province, by the family-owned firm **Koninklijke Tichelaars,** which was founded in 1594.

Genuine Delftware and Makkumware are for sale in specialized stores all over the country (De Delftse Pauw sells its pottery only from its factory and by mail order), but it is far more interesting to go to the workshops in the towns and see how they are made. Little has changed over the centuries, and all the decorating is still done by hand. This makes it quite pricey, but each piece is a unique product, made by craftsmen. Some of the numerous copies of De Porceleyne Fles and Tichelaars products are nearly equal in quality, while others miss by miles the delicacy of the brush stroke, the richness of color, or the sheen of the secret glazes that make the items produced by these firms so highly prized.

SHOPPING IN AMSTERDAM

9

THE SHOPPING SCENE

Blue Days

Only a few remain of the more than 30 potteries in Delft that in the 17th century worked overtime to meet the newly affluent Dutch's clamoring demand for Chinese-style vases, urns, wall tiles, and knickknacks. Originally, pottery made in Delft was white, to imitate tin-glazed products from Italy and Spain. During the 16th century, superior-quality Chinese porcelain, decorated in blue, was imported to Holland. Delftware factories refined their products accordingly, using a white tin glaze to cover the red clay, then decorating it in blue. This Delft Blue became famous the world over; it was less expensive than Chinese porcelain, and skillfully made. Polychrome decorations were also used, on both white and black backgrounds.

To be sure that you're looking at a *real* Delft vase, look on the bottom for the distinc- tive three-part De Porceleyne Fles hallmark: an outline of a small pot, above an initial *J* crossed with a short stroke, above the scripted word *Delft*. To distinguish Tichelaars products, look for two scripted *T*s overlapped like crossed swords.

DIAMONDS   Since the 15th century, Amsterdam has been a major diamond-cutting center and is one of the world's best places to shop for diamond jewelry and unmounted stones in all gradations of color and quality. Most Dutch jewelers issue certificates for sold diamonds that spell out carat weight, cut, color, and other pertinent identifying details, including imperfections.

FLOWER BULBS   Nothing is more Dutch than a tulip—even though the flower's natural home is on the high plains of Turkey and Iran—and no gift to yourself will bring more pleasure than bulbs to remind you of Holland when they pop up at home every spring. You may have a problem making your choices, however, since there's an incredible array of colors and shapes among the more than 800 varieties of tulip bulbs available, not to mention more than 500 kinds of daffodils and narcissi, and 60 varieties of hyacinth and crocus. Many growers and distributors put together combination packages with various amounts of bulbs that are coordinated according to the colors of the flowers they will produce, but it's fun—since so many bulbs are named for famous people—to put together your own garden party with Sophia Loren, President Kennedy, Queen Juliana, even Cyrano de Bergerac!

In Amsterdam, you can't do better than to buy them from Singel's **Flower Market** (see later in this chapter). And don't worry about failure rates or bug-ridden bulbs—the Dutch have been perfecting their growing methods and strengthening their stock for more than 400 years. Not all bulbs are certified for entry into other countries, so look for the num- bered phyto-sanitary certificate attached to the label—these allow you to import bulbs.

Say It with Flowers

Holland has long had a close relationship with flowers, and it's not merely that the tulip fields south of Haarlem are a springtime blaze of color that attracts worldwide admirers. Flowers have deeper roots in this land of flat, green polders. Amsterdam's flower market is only the best-known example of a sales network that makes a flower store a vital service in Dutch towns and villages.

Maybe because so many people live side by side in such a small, well- ordered country, flowers provide a breath of fresh air, a touch of the natural world when much of the environment is artificial. A Dutch house without flow- ers would be like Edam without the cheese. Gardens, balconies, rooftop ter- races, window boxes, and vases, are all pressed into service. Additionally, no visit to a dinner party would be complete without an accompanying bunch of flowers for the host. And Dutch men don't share the macho hang-up that some nationalities have at being seen carrying flowers in public.

TRADITIONAL CLOCKS Two types of handcrafted clocks have retained popularity through the centuries. One is the Zaandam clock, or *Zaanseklok,* identified by its ornately carved oak or walnut case, brass panels, tiny windows on the dial face, and the motto *Nu Eick Syn Sin* ("To each his own"). The other is the Frisian clock, or *Friese Stoelklok,* which is even more heavily decorated, customarily with hand-painted scenes of the Dutch countryside, a smiling moon face, or ships at sea that may bob back and forth in time with the ticks.

GREAT SHOPPING AREAS

A few shopping streets are pedestrians-only, some are busy thoroughfares, and others are peaceful canalside esplanades or fashionable promenades. Yet others are in suburban malls, or opening up in new waterfront development zones. Each segment in this ever-growing network has developed its own identity or predominant selection of goods as a specialty. To get you on your way, here are three suggested shopping itineraries:

- If you're looking for jewelry, trendy clothing, or athletic gear, begin at the Dam's department stores. Follow Kalverstraat to turn right at Heiligeweg; and continue shopping until you reach Leidseplein. Heiligeweg becomes Leidsestraat after it crosses Koningsplein, but it's really one long street, so you can't get lost.
- If you're feeling rich or simply want to feast your eyes on lovely things (fashion, antiques, and art), begin at the Concertgebouw and walk along Van Baerlestraat toward Vondelpark. Turn right onto elegant Pieter Cornelisz Hooftstraat. At the end of the street, by the canal, turn right again and walk to the Rijksmuseum, then turn left across the canal. Straight ahead is Spiegelgracht, a small and quiet bit of canal that's the gateway to the best antiques-shop street in Amsterdam, Nieuwe Spiegelstraat.
- Finally, if your idea of a good shopping day includes fashion boutiques, funky specialty stores, and a browse through a flea market or secondhand store, cut a west-to-east path through the old city by beginning at Westermarkt and crisscrossing the canals. Reestraat, Hartenstraat, Wolvenstraat, and Runstraat—these are among the *Negen Straatjes* (Nine Little Streets) that connect the big canals in this part of town— are particularly good choices with lots of fun shops. At the Dam, take Damstraat and its continuations (Oude Doelenstraat, Hoogstraat, and Nieuwe Hoogstraat) to Sint-Antoniesbreestraat, and its continuation, Jodenbreestraat, to Nieuwe Uilenburger-straat, to Waterlooplein and the flea market. Alternatively, at the Dam, follow Rokin to Muntplein and walk from there to Waterlooplein.

To plan your own shopping route through Amsterdam, here are brief descriptions of the major shopping streets and what you can expect to find along each of them:

KALVERSTRAAT At one end of this long, pedestrians-only shopping street is the Dam; at the other is the Muntplein traffic hub. In between is a hodgepodge of shopping possibilities—punky boutiques, athletic-shoe emporiums, stores selling dowdy raincoats and conservative business suits, bookstores, fur salons, maternity and baby stores, record stores, and more. Interspersed is everything in the way of fast food, from *frites* to *poffertjes.* The mid-brow **Vroom & Dreesman** department store has its main entrance on Kalverstraat, as does the elegant **Maison de Bonneterie,** and the **Kalvertoren Shopping Center,** a mall with 45 stores, plus cafes and restaurants, hosts the cheap 'n' cheerful department store **Hema.**

ROKIN Parallel to Kalverstraat and also running from the Dam to Muntplein is Rokin. Along here, you'll find art galleries, antiques stores, and elegant fashion boutiques.

HEILIGEWEG & LEIDSESTRAAT The shopping parade that begins on Kalverstraat continues around the corner on Heiligeweg, across Koningsplein and along Leidsestraat, all the way to Leidseplein.

PIETER CORNELISZ HOOFTSTRAAT & VAN BAERLESTRAAT Known locally as "P.C. Hooftstraat," or just "the P.C. Hooft" (pronounced pay-say-*hoaft*), this is where well-dressed, well-coiffed Amsterdammers buy everything from lingerie to light bulbs. Along its 3 short blocks, stores sell furniture, antiques, toys, shoes, chocolates, Persian rugs, designer clothes, fresh-baked bread, fresh-caught fish, china, books, furs, perfume, leather goods, office supplies, flowers, and jewelry. Around the corner on Van Baerlestraat are more boutiques, shoe stores, and enough branches of major banks to guarantee that you can continue to buy as long as your plastic holds out.

NIEUWE SPIEGELSTRAAT & SPIEGELGRACHT This is Amsterdam's antiques esplanade, and though it covers only a short 4-block stretch, it's one of Europe's finest antiques-hunting grounds. At one end is the Rijksmuseum; at the other is Herengracht's Golden Bend, where Amsterdam's wealthiest burghers once lived. Now that these gabled homes have been turned over to banks and embassies, it seems that all the treasures they once contained have found their way around the corner to the antiques stores. Among the items you might see are dolls with china heads, rare editions of early children's books, Indonesian puppets, Persian tapestries, landscape paintings, art prints and reproductions, brass Bible stands, candlesticks, copper kettles, music boxes, and old Dutch clocks.

AMSTELVEEN This new town built around an old village south of Amsterdam offers up clean, efficient living in a garden city. The shopping center has many of the non-specialist types of outlets—department stores, boutiques, toy stores, and the like—that you'll find throughout Amsterdam. Here, however, they're in an enclosed mall and you can visit them all a lot quicker. So if you don't like shopping but can just about tolerate it if you get through it quickly, this may be the place for you. Take the no. 5 tram from Centraal Station to the terminus, which is right beside the Amstelveen mall; the ride takes about 25 minutes.

Other Shopping Areas

For more antiques stores, look along Prinsengracht between Leidsestraat and Westermarkt. For Amsterdam's up-and-coming funky boutiques, look along the canals east and west of the Dam, or in the nest of streets beyond Westermarkt known as the Jordaan.

---

2 SHOPPING A TO Z

Here is a selection of interesting Amsterdam stores, some of which you might not otherwise have found. Use this list to save you time and trouble with your shopping list, or simply to locate interesting stores.

ANTIQUES

Mathieu Hart ★ This discreet store has been in business as a fine antiquarian since 1878. If you're interested in an artistic view of Amsterdam or the Dutch countryside, Mathieu Hart stocks color etchings of Dutch cities alongside rare old prints, 18th-century Delftware, and grandfather clocks. Rokin 122 (at Spui). ✆ **020/623-1658.** www.hartantiques.com. Tram: 4, 9, 14, 16, 24, or 25 to Spui.

SHOPPING IN AMSTERDAM

9

SHOPPING A TO Z

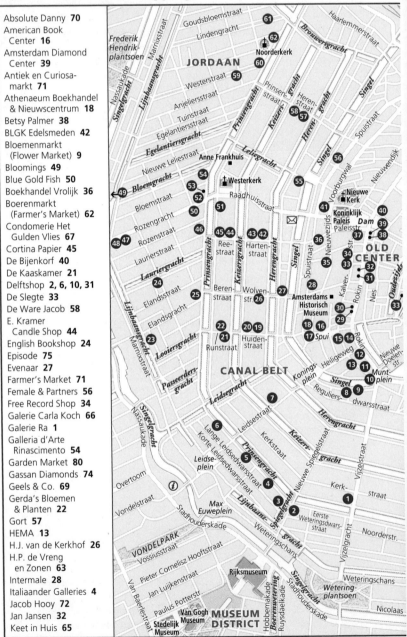

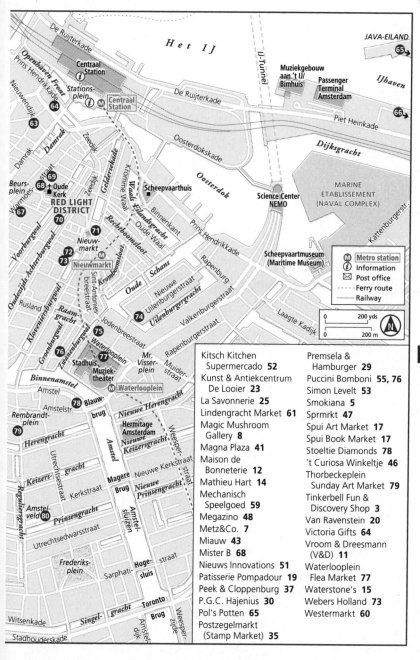

Kitsch Kitchen
  Supermercado **52**
Kunst & Antiekcentrum
  De Looier **23**
La Savonnerie **25**
Lindengracht Market **61**
Magic Mushroom
  Gallery **8**
Magna Plaza **41**
Maison de
  Bonneterie **12**
Mathieu Hart **14**
Mechanisch
  Speelgoed **59**
Megazino **48**
Metz&Co. **7**
Miauw **43**
Mister B **68**
Nieuws Innovations **51**
Patisserie Pompadour **19**
Peek & Cloppenburg **37**
P.G.C. Hajenius **30**
Pol's Potten **65**
Postzegelmarkt
  (Stamp Market) **35**

Premsela &
  Hamburger **29**
Puccini Bomboni **55, 76**
Simon Levelt **53**
Smokiana **5**
Sprmrkt **47**
Spui Art Market **17**
Spui Book Market **17**
Stoeltie Diamonds **78**
't Curiosa Winkeltje **46**
Thorbeckeplein
  Sunday Art Market **79**
Tinkerbell Fun &
  Discovery Shop **3**
Van Ravenstein **20**
Victoria Gifts **64**
Vroom & Dreesmann
  (V&D) **11**
Waterlooplein
  Flea Market **77**
Waterstone's **15**
Webers Holland **73**
Westermarkt **60**

Premsela & Hamburger ★ Opposite the Allard-Pierson Museum (p. 143), this jewelry and antique silver establishment—purveyors to the Dutch court—opened in 1823. Inside their brocaded display cases and richly carved cabinets is a variety of exquisite, distinctive items. You can find decorative Old Dutch silver objects fashioned by 17th-century crafters. Feast your eyes on an 18th-century perpetual calendar, a silver plaque depicting the entrance to an Amsterdam hospital, and a variety of sterling silverware. A workshop on the premises designs, makes, and repairs jewelry. Open Monday to Friday from 9:30am to 5:30pm. Rokin 98 (at Spui). ✆ **020/627-5454.** www.premsela.com. Tram: 4, 9, 14, 16, 24, or 25 to Spui.

ART

Posters and reproductions of famous artworks are an excellent item to buy in Amsterdam. The Dutch are known for their high-quality printing and color-reproduction work, and one of their favorite subjects is Holland's rich artistic treasure-trove. Choose any of the three major art museums listed below as a starting point.

For van Gogh prints, the **Van Gogh Museum,** Paulus Potterstraat 13 (✆ **020/570-5200;** tram: 2, 3, 5, or 12), is an excellent good source for reproductions. At **Museum Het Rembrandthuis,** Jodenbreestraat 4 (✆ **020/624-9486;** tram: 9 or 14), you can buy a mounted Rembrandt etching for 15€ to 20€ ($24–$32); it's not an original, of course, but it is an individually produced high-quality modern printing done by hand in the traditional manner. For something simpler (and cheaper) to remind you of the great master, Het Rembrandthuis also sells mass-printed reproductions of the etchings and small packets of postcard-size reproductions in sepia or black and white on a thick, fine-quality paper stock.

Here are just a few of Amsterdam's 140 or so galleries that display and sell photography, sculpture, and contemporary, modern, and ethnic art.

Galerie Carla Koch For ceramics and glassware, this waterfront gallery employs some of the raciest design talent in Holland; their products are always different and interesting, if inevitably not to everyone's taste. Open Thursday to Saturday from noon to 6pm, and the first Sunday of the month from 2 to 6pm. Detroit Building (6th Floor), Veemkade 500 (at Piet Heinkade). ✆ **020/673-7310.** www.carlakoch.nl. Tram: 26 to Kattenburgerstraat.

Italiaander Galleries This gallery displays a permanent exhibition of art from around the world (particularly Africa and Asia), and all sorts of ethnic jewelry. Open Wednesday to Saturday from noon to 5:30pm. Prinsengracht 526 (at Spiegelgracht). ✆ **020/625-0942.** Tram: 1, 2, or 5 to Prinsengracht.

BOOKS

American Book Center ★ Laying claim to be the biggest U.S.-style bookstore in Europe, the ABC stocks magazines and hardcover books, hot off the presses. Prices are higher than back in the States, but the selection beats any airport or hotel gift store, with a range of categories including ancient civilizations, astrology, baby care, science, science fiction, and war. Students and teachers get 10% off simply by showing a school ID. Spui 12. ✆ **020/625-5537.** www.abc.nl. Tram: 1, 2, or 5 to Spui.

Athenaeum Boekhandel & Nieuwscentrum You can't miss this place. It's always crowded with book lovers, students, and scholars. The Art Nouveau Athenaeum is best known for its nonfiction collection and has books in a number of languages. Magazine stands are on the sidewalk. Spui 14–16. ✆ **020/514-1460.** www.athenaeum.nl. Tram: 1, 2, or 5 to Spui.

Albert Cuypmarkt **4**	De Waterwinkel **1**
Carla V **2**	Oilily **5**
Coster Diamonds **6**	Van Moppes Diamonds **3**

De Slegte You won't find too many English-language books here—most are in Dutch or other languages—but there are a few, and if you collect books as a hobby, you might come across a real gem. It's probably one of Amsterdam's biggest, most-visited bookstores. Kalverstraat 48–52 (at Gapersteeg). ☏ 020/622-5933. www.deslegte.com. Tram: 4, 9, 14, 16, 24, or 25 to the Dam.

English Bookshop On the edge of the Jordaan, this small bookstore has a wonderful selection of books in English, mainly fiction and biography, and a small selection of British magazines. Occasionally, you can find a great book at a discount. It's open Tuesday to Friday from 1 to 6pm and Saturday from 11am to 5pm. Lauriergracht 71 (at Hazenstraat). ☏ 020/626-4230. www.englishbookshop.nl. Tram: 7, 10, or 17 to Elandsgracht.

Evenaar Since you're traveling, you may be in the mood for travel literature. Evenaar, which is close to Spui, sells not only travel guides but also a wide range of travel literature and large-format photo books about travel and anthropology. It's also got secondhand and antique travel books. It's open Monday to Friday from noon to 6pm, Saturday from 11am to 5pm. Singel 348 (at Oude Spiegelstraat). ✆ 020/624-6289. www.evenaar.net. Tram: 1, 2, or 5 to Spui.

Waterstone's This branch of a British chain has a large stock of fiction and nonfiction titles. You'll probably be able to find almost anything you're looking for on one of the three floors here. Kalverstraat 152 (at Spui). ✆ 020/638-3821. www.waterstones.com. Tram: 1, 2, 4, 5, 14, 16, 24, or 25 to Spui.

CRAFTS & CURIOS

Blue Gold Fish (Finds) "Dive into the pool of fantasy," say the owners of this colorful store and gallery. There's no real rhyme or reason to the items for sale. Still, there's unity in diversity in the more-or-less fantastic design sensibility that goes into each piece. It's open Monday to Saturday from 11:30am to 6:30pm. Rozengracht 17 (at Westermarkt). ✆ 020/623-3134. Tram: 13, 14, or 17 to Westermarkt.

Cortina Papier If you'd like the kind of personal journal that would have looked good in *The English Patient* or *Dances with Wolves,* this is your place. Cortina showcases fancy notebooks, agenda and address books, writing paper, envelopes, and other fine stationery. Reestraat 22 (btw. Prinsengracht and Keizersgracht). ✆ 020/623-6676. www.cortina papier.nl. Tram: 13, 14, or 17 to Westermarkt.

E. Kramer Candle Shop Illuminate everything from a romantic candlelit dinner to a wake. Some of the candles are little melting works of art while others are outrageously kitschy. The store also sells scented oils and incense. Reestraat 20 (btw. Prinsengracht and Keizersgracht). ✆ 020/626-5274. Tram: 13, 14, or 17 to Westermarkt.

La Savonnerie This is the kind of clean-living store that a raffish place like Amsterdam can't use enough of. You can buy artisanal soap in all shapes and sizes. How about a soap chess set, soap alphabet blocks, or soap animals? You can also buy personalized soap and even make your own. Prinsengracht 294 (at Elandsgracht). ✆ 020/428-1139. www.savonnerie.nl. Tram: 7, 10, or 17 to Elandsgracht.

Nieuws Innovations This is a source for all kinds of offbeat souvenirs, such as pens in the shape of fish, lipstick, and (perhaps too near the bone for Amsterdam) syringes; washcloths in the form of hand-glove puppets; spherical dice; and many other hard-to-define but colorful little bits and pieces. Prinsengracht 297 (at Westermarkt). ✆ 020/627-9540. Tram: 13, 14, or 17 to Westermarkt.

't Curiosa Winkeltje This place sells knickknacks such as colored bottles and glasses, modern versions of old tin cars and other children's toys from the 1950s and earlier, big plastic butterflies, banana-shaped lamps, and many other such useful things. Prinsengracht 228 (at Leliegracht). ✆ 020/625-1352. Tram: 13, 14, or 17 to Westermarkt.

DELFTWARE

Delftshop ★ Delft's four upscale souvenir stores offer a good selection of quality porcelain from De Porcelyne Fles (Delft), Tichelaars (Makkum), and Heinen. The Muntplein store has the additional attraction of being inside the medieval Munttoren (Mint Tower). Spiegelgracht 13 (at Prinsengracht). ✆ 020/421-8360. www.jorritheinen.com. Tram: 7 or

Prinsengracht. Rokin 44 (south of the Dam). ℂ 020/620-1000. Tram: 4, 9, 14, 16, 24, or 25 to the Dam. Muntplein 12 (at Singel). ℂ 020/623-2271. Tram: 4, 9, 14, 16, 24, or 25 to Muntplein.

Galleria d'Arte Rinascimento   This well-stocked emporium sells hand-painted Delftware of every conceivable type from De Porcelyne Fles (see "Delftware & Makkumware," earlier in this chapter). You can buy the junk and the real thing, too. Both the knockoffs and the genuine articles come in elegant as well as sublimely ridiculous shapes: ceramic clogs, Christmas ornaments, contorted vases, and the like. Don't miss the cabinet of superb, multicolored (and pricey) Makkumware porcelain from Koninklijke Tichelaars. Prinsengracht 170 (facing the Anne Frank House). ℂ 020/622-7509. www.delft-art-gallery.com. Tram: 13, 14, or 17 to Westermarkt.

DEPARTMENT STORES

De Bijenkorf ★★   Amsterdam's best-known department store is the one with the best variety of goods. The ground floor has the usual ranks of cosmetic counters, plus a men's department and odds and ends such as socks and stockings, handbags and belts, costume jewelry, and stationery. And umbrellas—plenty of umbrellas! On upper floors, there's everything from ladies' fashions to down comforters, plus a bookstore, several eating spots, and a luggage section at which you can pick up an extra suitcase or bag to tote home your purchases. Records, color TVs, books, shoes, clothing, personal effects, appliances—it's all here. Several worthwhile eateries include **La Ruche** ★, a classy Rietveld-style cafeteria on the second floor (its big windows afford a fine view of the Dam), and the more intimate fourth-floor **Literair Café,** where you can have sushi, sandwiches, and light snacks. Dam 1. ℂ 0900/0919. www.bijenkorf.nl. Tram: 4, 9, 14, 16, 24, or 25 to the Dam.

HEMA   This cheap 'n' cheerful chain department store is the Woolworth's of Holland, selling things like socks, toothbrushes, chocolate, cookies, and cheese. If you can't figure out where to find something, your best bet is to look here. Kalvertoren Shopping Center, Kalverstraat 212 (close to Muntplein). ℂ 020/422-8988. www.hema.nl. Tram: 4, 9, 14, 16, 24, or 25 to Muntplein.

Maison de Bonneterie   This elegant store carries exclusive women's fashions, Gucci bags, Fieldcrest towels, and a star-studded cast of brand-name household goods and personal items. Rokin 140–142 (close to Muntplein). ℂ 020/531-3400. www.debonneterie.nl. Tram: 4, 9, 14, 16, 24, or 25 to Muntplein.

Metz&Co. ★★   This dramatic store, built in 1891 for a company founded in 1740, is the store of choice for Amsterdam's power shoppers. It sells modern furniture, fabrics, kitchenware, and other home-based items. The in-store rooftop cafe **Metz,** designed by De Stijl architect Gerrit Rietveld in 1933, has a section in the cupola for special events and affords a spectacular panoramic view across Amsterdam's rooftops. Leidsestraat 34–36 (at Keizersgracht). ℂ 020/520-7020. www.metzandco.com. Tram: 1, 2, or 5 to Keizersgracht.

Peek & Cloppenburg   Occupying an unbeatable central location just off the Dam, this is a moderately upmarket department store with a difference, one that focuses on each of its floors on clothes and fashion, for both men and women. The wide-ranging stock goes all the way from street wear to black-tie and evening-gown wear, and takes in a sporty, outdoors look along the way. Dam 20. ℂ 020/623-2837. www.peekandcloppenburg. nl. Tram: 4, 9, 14, 16, 24, or 25 to the Dam.

Sprmrkt ★ An Aladdin's cave filled with wonderful things, this rambling but stylish lifestyle store with no vowels in its name stocks everything from vintage furniture to books, CDs, and the latest designer fashions and accessories. Rozengracht 191–193 (at Lijnbaansgracht). ℂ 020/330-5601. www.sprmrkt.nl. Tram: 13, 14, or 17 to Rozengracht/Marnixstraat.

Vroom & Dreesmann (V&D) Less polished and pretentious than Metz&Co. (see above), and highly successful as a result, this is the Amsterdam branch of a department-store chain that pops up in key shopping locations all over Holland. V&D is a no-nonsense sort of store with a wide range of middle-of-the-road goods—and prices and service to match. Its vast multilevel **La Place** food depot has something for everyone. Kalverstraat 203 (at Muntplein; there's also an entrance on Rokin). ℂ 0900/235-8363. www.vroomendreesmann.nl. Tram: 4, 9, 14, 16, 24, or 25 to Muntplein.

DIAMONDS

These reputable stores offer guided diamond-cutting and polishing tours for free, and sales of the finished product: **Amsterdam Diamond Center,** Rokin 1–5 (ℂ 020/624-5787; www.amsterdamdiamoncenter.com; tram: 4, 9, 14, 16, 24, or 25), at the Dam; **Coster Diamonds,** Paulus Potterstraat 2–8 (ℂ 020/305-5555; www.costerdiamonds.com; tram: 2 or 5), at the Rijksmuseum; **Gassan Diamonds,** Nieuwe Uilenburgerstraat 173–175 (ℂ 020/622-5333; www.gassandiamonds.com; Metro: Waterlooplein), at Oudeschans; **Stoeltie Diamonds,** Wagenstraat 13–17 (ℂ 020/623-7601; www.stoeltiediamonds.com; tram: 4, 9, or 14), at Rembrandtplein; and **Van Moppes Diamonds,** Albert Cuypstraat 2–6 (ℂ 020/676-1242; www.moppesdiamonds.com; tram: 16, 24, or 25), at Ruysdaelkade.

FASHIONS

Paris may set the styles, but young Dutch women—and some of their mothers—often know better than the French how to make them work. Whatever the current European fashion rage is, you can expect to see it in store windows all over Amsterdam, and in all price ranges. It's fun to ferret out the new, young crop of Dutch designers who regularly open stores in unpredictable locations all over town.

Carla V ★ Irrepressible Dutch designer Carla van der Vorst owns this posh Museum District boutique specializing in custom ladies' leather clothing. Look for coats, skirts, bags, belts, and more. Skinflints should abstain. Cornelis Schuytstraat 45 (at Johannes Verhulststraat). ℂ 020/672-0404. www.carlav.nl. Tram: 2 to Cornelis Schuytstraat.

Megazino Large for Amsterdam, this designer outlet store in the Jordaan sells everything from Armani, Gucci, and Prada to Calvin Klein and Dolce & Gabbana—all at 30% to 50% off the original price. It's a great place to burn some plastic without breaking the bank. Rozengracht 207–213 (at Lijnbaansgracht). ℂ 020/330-1031. www.megazino.nl. Tram: 13, 14, or 17 to Westermarkt.

Miauw ★ This two-room store is owned by one of Amsterdam's renowned designers, Analik. One room is filled with small pieces of clothing for young and skinny women, the other with funky handbags and other accessories designed by local Dutch artists. Hartenstraat 36 (at Keizersgracht). ℂ 020/422-0561. www.analik.com. Tram: 13, 14, or 17 to Westermarkt.

Van Ravenstein ★★ You're likely to bump into media stars, gallery owners, and the moneyed creative crowd of both sexes at this small boutique, buying the latest creations by Dutch and Belgian designers; Victor and Rolf, Martin Margiela, Dirk Bikkembergs, Dries van Noten, and Bernhard Willhelm are stock in trade. In the basement, a collection

of last season's discards is on sale. Keizersgracht 359 (at Huidenstraat). ℂ 020/639-0067. Tram:
1, 2, or 5 to Keizersgracht.

Webers Holland ★   The venerable 17th-century **Klein Trippenhuis** (p. 158), a
protected historical monument, is the counterintuitive setting for this avant-garde, sexy,
humorous—and, to a degree, in-your-face—store for women. The designer fashions here
are mainly by co-proprietor Désirée Webers, but other Dutch and international designers
are represented. It's open Sunday and Monday from 1 to 7pm, and Tuesday to Saturday
from 11am to 7pm. Kloveniersburgwal 26 (at Nieuwmarkt). ℂ 020/638-1777. www.webers
holland.nl. Metro: Nieuwmarkt.

FLOWERS

Bloomings   This friendly florist in the Bos en Lommer neighborhood sells expertly
arranged flowers and exquisite vases of all shapes and sizes. Lucellestraat 20 (at Bos en Lom-
merweg). ℂ 06/2421-3723. www.bloomings-amsterdam.nl. Tram: 14 to Egidiusstraat.

Gerda's Bloemen & Planten ★   One of the most elegant florists in the city boasts a
fantastic selection of exotic flowers and unusual plants artfully arranged and presented at its
Canal Belt store. Runstraat 16 (at Keizersgracht). ℂ 020/624-2912. Tram: 1, 2, or 5 to Spui.

FOOD & DRINK

De Kaaskamer ★   Possibly Amsterdam's best cheese store, with deli delights to boot.
You may have a hard time choosing from the 300 different cheeses for sale, including
rows and rows of authentic wheels of aged Gouda stamped with their farm of origin, and
cumin-flavored *komijnenkaas.* They will vacuum-pack and courier cheese anywhere for
travelers. Runstraat 7 (at Keizersgracht). ℂ 020/623-3483. Tram: 1, 2, or 5 to Spui.

De Ware Jacob   Since 1970 this small but charming Canal Belt wine shop has carried
the finest wines from boutique wineries around the world. Herenstraat 41 (at Keizersgracht). ℂ 020/623-9877. Tram: 13, 14, or 17 to Westermarkt.

De Waterwinkel   Quality and purity are the watchwords at the tastefully designed
Water Shop. More than 100 varieties of mineral water from around the planet, ranging
from ordinary to designer, are for sale here. Some bottles are miniature works of art.
Roelof Hartstraat 10 (at Roelof Hartplein). ℂ 020/675-5932. www.dewaterwinkel.nl. Tram: 3, 5,
12, or 24 to Roelof Hartplein.

Geels & Co. ★   Devotees of the legal drug from Colombia and other coffee-producing
nations will be tempted by the smell of fresh-roasted coffee beans at this coffee-roasting
and tea-importing establishment in a 17th-century building. Geels & Co. has been going
strong since 1864, and goes a long way toward raising the tone of shabby Warmoesstraat
on the Red Light District's edge. Offerings (besides coffee, of course) include beverage
accessories, tastings by appointment, old-fashioned fudges and toffees, and a coffee-and-
tea museum on the second floor (p. 167). Warmoesstraat 67 (at Oude Brugsteeg). ℂ 020/
624-0683. www.geels.nl. Tram: 4, 9, 14, 16, 24, or 25 to the Dam.

H.P. de Vreng en Zonen ⓜoments   This traditional distillery, founded in 1710, creates Dutch liqueurs and gins according to old-fashioned methods, *sans* additives. Try the
Old Amsterdam *jenever* or some of the more flamboyantly colored liquids, like the
bright-green plum liqueur *Pruimpje prik in;* some supposedly have aphrodisiac power. A
chance to see the collection of 15,000 miniature bottles alone makes a visit worthwhile.
Nieuwendijk 75 (at Martelaarsgracht). ℂ 020/624-4581. www.oudamsterdam.nl. Tram: 1, 2, 5, 13,
or 17 to Martelaarsgracht.

(Tips) **Night Owls**

A local *avondwinkel* **(evening store)** is a resource not to be ignored for keeping you stocked with after-hours munchies. Suppose you feel like an evening in your hotel, and you either don't fancy the room-service menu or your hotel doesn't provide one. Not to worry: There's bound to be an evening store close to the hotel (ask the front desk). Many can prepare takeout meals to about the same standard as you would find in a typical Dutch *eetcafé*, for 10% to 20% less than restaurant prices. Hours are usually from 5 to 11pm or midnight.

Jacob Hooy (Finds) You'll feel like you've stepped back into history when you visit this store, which opened in 1743. For the past 130 years, the Oldenboom family has operated this wonderland of fragrant smells from more than 600 different herbs and spices, and 30 different teas, all sold loose by weight. Wooden drawers and barrels hand-scripted in gold lettering store everything. Across the counter are fishbowl jars in racks containing some 30 types of licorice and other *dropjes* (drops or lozenges) that range in taste from sweet to sour to salty. Health foods, homeopathic products, and natural cosmetics are also available here. Kloveniersburgwal 12 (at Nieuwmarkt). (C) 020/624-3041. www.jacobhooy. nl. Metro: Nieuwmarkt.

Patisserie Pompadour The counter display here is amazing. It groans under the weight of some 50 kinds of luscious pastries and tarts, complemented by endless dollops of whipped cream. Enjoy these genuine Dutch treats in the exquisite Louis XVI tearoom or wrapped to go. A second branch is across town on Kerkstraat. It's open Tuesday to Friday from 9am to 6pm, and Saturday from 9am to 5pm. Huidenstraat 12 (at Herengracht). (C) 020/623-9554. www.patisseriepompadour.com. Tram: 1, 2, or 5 to Spui. Kerkstraat 148 (at Nieuwe Spiegelstraat). (C) 020/330-0981. Tram: 1, 2, or 5 to Keizersgracht.

Puccini Bomboni A long, open table supports fresh, handmade pralines in a plethora of shapes and styles—pure, milk, white—at each of Puccini Bomboni's two branches. Peruse the multifarious merchandise and breathe in its sultry scents to the strains of soft classical music. There are at least six liqueur-filled varieties and more than 20 with non-alcoholic, often exotic, fillings—you can try these little chocolate heavens with flavors like Drambuie, Calvados, cognac, rum, marzipan, ginger, nutmeg, cinnamon, fig, lemon grass, thyme, and many more. Singel 184 (at Oude Leliestraat). (C) 020/427-8341. www.puccini bomboni.com. Tram: 1, 2, 5, 13, or 17 to the Dam. Staalstraat 17 (at Waterlooplein). (C) 020/626-5474. Tram: 9 or 14 to Waterlooplein.

Simon Levelt Founded in 1839 as H. Keijzer, this tea-and-coffee store now belongs to a chain that was founded in 1817. Consider taking home several 100-gram tea packets from different parts of the globe: Ceylon Melange (or Delmar Melange), an English-style blend from Sri Lanka; Darjeeling First Flush, from India; Yunnan, from China; and Java O. P. (Orange Pekoe), from Indonesia—all these teas are popular with the Dutch. To come away with a delightful gift, select from an assortment of tea boxes. Prinsengracht 180 (at Westermarkt). (C) 020/624-0823. www.simonlevelt.nl. Tram: 13, 14, or 17 to Westermarkt.

Episode Jackets, dresses, scarves, belts, funky brooches, boots—you'll find all these and more at this unisex vintage shop. Specialties include flamboyant evening gowns and leather jackets, all in pretty good shape and reasonably priced. Waterlooplein 1. ✆ 020/320-3000. www.episode.eu. Tram: 9 or 14 to Waterlooplein.

Magic Mushroom Gallery How to define this place that treads a thin line? It sells "natural drugs" and "psychoactive mushrooms" that are much better for you, so they say, than illegal narcotics. Improve your sex life with Yohimbe Rush and Horn E, boost your energy with Space Liquid and Herbal Booster, grow your own Mexican mushrooms, then unwind with After Glow and Rapture. Singel 524 (at the Flower Market). ✆ 020/422-7845. www.magicmushroom.com. Tram: 4, 9, 14, 16, 24, or 25 to Muntplein.

GAY & LESBIAN

Boekhandel Vrolijk ★ The city's main bookstore for gays and lesbians stocks a wide range of books, many of them in English. It's invariably cheaper to buy here than at the gay sections of general bookstores, but is still likely to be more expensive than at home. Paleisstraat 135 (at the Dam). ✆ 020/623-5142. www.vrolijk.nu. Tram: 1, 2, 4, 5, 9, 13, 14, 16, 17, 24, or 25 to Centraal Station.

Intermale In addition to books, magazines, and greeting cards in English, this large bookstore stocks Dutch and German periodicals. It claims to have the largest collection of books of interest to gay men in Europe. Spuistraat 251–253 (at Spui). ✆ 020/625-0009. www.intermale.nl. Tram: 1, 2, or 5 to Spui.

Mister B This airy store is world-famous for its high-quality leather goods, from basic trousers and chaps to more revealing fetish wear. The store's window often displays erotic art, S&M accessories, and a selection of piercing jewelry—it ensures many a gaping tourist. Visiting tattoo and piercing artists from around the world make guest appearances. Racy postcards are available. Warmoesstraat 89 (edge of the Red Light District). ✆ 020/788-3060. www.misterb.com. Tram: 1, 2, 4, 5, 9, 13, 14, 16, 17, 24, or 25 to Centraal Station.

GIFTS

Victoria Gifts Dutch clockmakers turn out timepieces with soft-toned chimes in Old Dutch–style handcrafted cases covered with tiny figures and mottoes, hand-painted Dutch scenes, and decorated porcelain insets. This small store has some of these treasures along with Delftware, embroidered flags, chocolates, and other gifts at reasonable prices. Prins Hendrikkade 47 (opposite Centraal Station). ✆ 020/427-2051. www.victoriagifts.nl. Tram: 1, 2, 4, 5, 9, 13, 16, 17, 24, or 25 to Centraal Station.

HABERDASHERY

H.J. van de Kerkhof This store's walls are lined with spools of ribbon and cord, and its notebooks filled with examples of patches and appliqués. Key tassels and tiebacks come in all sizes, including very large. Wolvenstraat 9–11 (at Herengracht). Closed Fri–Sun. ✆ 020/623-4666. Tram: 1, 2, or 5 to Spui.

HOUSEHOLD

Kitsch Kitchen Supermercado ★ The name just about says it all. You'll want to put on your shades before entering this world of glaringly bright colors. Kitsch Kitchen's

From Ships to Shops

KNSM-Eiland (KNSM Island), in the redeveloping Eastern Harbor area, has a streetload of interior design stores. The island is named after the Dutch initials of the old Royal Dutch Steamship Line that was based there—the Koninklijke Nederlandse Stoomboot Maatschappij. Shops here include **Pol's Potten,** KNSM-laan 39 ((*C* 020/419-3541; www.polspotten.nl), for furnishings, accessories, kitchen stuff, and knicknacks by hip young designers; and **Keet in Huis,** KNSM-laan 297 ((*C* 020/419-5958; www.keetinhuis.nl), for children's lifestyles. Tram: 10.

utensils and household fittings—not just for kitchens—come in plastic, enamel, and papier-mâché. A separate department caters to culinary-oriented kids. Rozengracht 8–12 (at Westermarkt). (*C* 020/622-8261. www.kitschkitchen.nl. Tram: 13, 14, or 17 to Westermarkt.

JEWELRY

BLGK Edelsmeden   This store is run by a group of jewelry designers who produce and sell affordable jewelry with character. Each designer has a unique slant: Some pieces represent a new and fresh spin on classic forms, while others are more innovative and imaginative. It's open Tuesday to Friday from 11am to 6pm, and Saturday from 11am to 5pm. Hartenstraat 28 (at Herengracht). (*C* 020/624-8154. www.blgk.nl. Tram: 13, 14, or 17 to Westermarkt.

Galerie Ra   Marvelous contemporary designs and materials turn jewelry into an art form here. Owner Paul Derrez specializes in stunning modern jewelry in gold and silver, and goes a bit further, turning feathers, rubber, foam, and other materials into pieces he describes as "playful." It's open Tuesday to Friday from 10am to 6pm, and Saturday from 10am to 5pm. Vijzelstraat 90 (at Keizersgracht). (*C* 020/626-5100. www.galerie-ra.nl. Tram: 16, 24, or 25 to Keizersgracht.

Gort ★   This beautiful little shop specializes in unique and innovative jewelry design. If you like modern, minimalist designs, then this could be the place for you. Herenstraat 11 (at Herengracht). (*C* 020/620-6240. www.juweliergort.nl. Tram: 13, 14, or 17 to Westermarkt.

KIDS

Some museum gift stores are good sources for toys and other children's knickknacks. Try the stores at the **Theatermuseum,** Herengracht 168 ((*C* 020/551-3300; tram: 13, 14, or 17), for masks, costumes, and minitheaters; Science Center **NEMO,** Oosterdokskade 2 ((*C* 0900/919-1100; bus: 22), for scientific and educational toys and gadgets; and both the **Tropenmuseum,** Linnaeusstraat 2 ((*C* 020/568-8215; tram: 7, 9, 10, or 14), and **Artis Zoo,** Plantage Kerklaan 38–40 ((*C* 020/523-3400; tram: 9 or 14), for model animals and eco-stuff.

Mechanisch Speelgoed ★ (Kids) (Finds)   Your grandparents, when they were children, surely would have appreciated this old-fashioned toy store in the Jordaan. And plenty of today's kids seem equally attracted by this tiny shop's trove of traditional games, wooden houses, and other delights like tin drums, rag dolls, teddy bears, masks, and costumes. Tin toys are upstairs and other toys are downstairs. It's open Monday, Tuesday, and Thursday to Saturday from 10am to 6pm. Westerstraat 67 (at Violettenstraat). (*C* 020/638-1680. Tram: 3 or 10 to Marnixplein.

Oilily (Kids)   Amsterdam's most upscale children's clothing store has been on the fashion scene since 1963 (they now sell some women's clothing, too). They are known for extremely colorful designs of very high quality. Pieter Cornelisz Hooftstraat 131–133 (at Van Baerlestraat). ✆ 020/672-3361. www.oilily-world.com. Tram: 2, 3, 5, or 12 to Van Baerlestraat.

Tinkerbell Fun & Discovery Shop (Kids)   This is the place to find treasures for kids. The toys here don't blink, bleep, or run out of batteries—many are actually made from wood. But none of this is old-fashioned—this is real up-to-the-minute gear. Spiegelgracht 10–12 (at Prinsengracht). ✆ 020/625-8830. www.tinkerbelltoys.nl. Tram: 7 or 10 to Spiegelgracht.

MALLS

Magna Plaza ★   Magna Plaza isn't actually a department store, but a mall, located amid the extravagant neo-Gothic architecture of the former central Post Office, which dates from 1908. The Plaza's four elegant, column-lined floors are decked with around 50 specialist stores of all kinds. Yet it's small enough to function almost like a department store does. Nieuwezijds Voorburgwal 182 (behind the Royal Palace). www.magnaplaza.nl. Tram: 1, 2, 5, 13, 14, or 17 to the Dam.

MUSIC

Free Record Shop   No, the records here aren't free, sadly, but this store's large ground floor and basement hold an incredible number of cassettes, CDs, and videos at competitive prices. Kalverstraat 32 (at the Dam). ✆ 020/626-5808. www.freerecordshop.nl. Tram: 4, 9, 14, 16, 24, or 25 to the Dam.

SEX

Amsterdam's free and easy—you could even say laid-back—attitude to the mysteries of the flesh has spawned a vast range of stores devoted to satisfying customers' needs, whether real or pure fantasy. Many of these stores are down-and-dirty, sleazeball kinds of places, but not all. Here are some with a sense of style.

Absolute Danny   Owner Danny Linden, a graduate of Amsterdam's Fashion Academy and the Academy of Fine Arts, brings her artistic sensibilities to bear on the erotic lifestyle her store supports. You'll find everything from sexy tableware (if you can imagine such a thing) to S&M clothing and accessories in leather and latex to sexy lingerie. It's open Monday to Saturday from 11am to 9pm, and Sunday from noon to 9pm. Oudezijds Achterburgwal 78 (close to Nieuwmarkt). ✆ 020/421-0915. www.absolutedanny.com. Metro: Nieuwmarkt.

Condomerie Het Gulden Vlies ★ (Finds)   This store on the edge of the Red Light District claims to be the world's first specialized condom store—the start of a whole new protection racket. It stocks a vast range of these singular items, in all shapes, sizes, and flavors, from common brands to flashy designer fittings, all but guaranteeing your apparel of choice. It's open Monday to Wednesday, Friday, and Saturday from noon to 6pm, and Thursday from noon to 8pm. Warmoesstraat 141 (behind De Bijenkorf). ✆ 020/627-4174. www.condomerie.com. Tram: 4, 9, 14, 16, 24, or 25 to the Dam.

Female & Partners   Here, you'll find all sorts of lingerie and female-oriented sex articles, like dildos and other imaginative toys. This chic store caters to women who like women, women who like men, and those who like both, and is close to the Royal Palace (p. 152). Not that the queen has anything to do with it, so far as I know. If the vibrator display makes you hesitant to enter, you can order the goods by phone, mail, or Internet.

It's open Tuesday to Saturday 11am to 6pm, and Sunday and Monday 1 to 6pm. Spuist-raat 100 (at Nieuwe Sparpotsteeg). ℂ **020/620-9152**. www.femaleandpartners.nl. Tram: 1, 2, 5, 13, 14, or 17 to the Dam.

SMOKING ARTICLES

P.G.C. Hajenius ★   This store has been Amsterdam's leading purveyor of cigars and smoking articles since 1826, first with a store on the Dam and then (since 1915) in its present elegant Art Deco headquarters. Cigars are the house specialty; there's a room full of Havanas, and Hajenius also sells cigars from Sumatra, Brazil, and more. One good gift idea is the long, handmade clay pipes you see in old paintings—they're uniquely Dutch. Other good gifts include the ceramic pipes, some painted in the blue-and-white Chinese-inspired patterns of Delftware. You can also find lighters, cigarette holders, clippers, and flasks. Rokin 92–96 (at Spui). ℂ **020/623-7494**. www.hajenius.com. Tram: 4, 9, 14, 16, 24, or 25 to Spui.

Smokiana   This is where to buy that unique pipe into which tobacco can be tamped with an air of deliberate insouciance, and the resulting fug flaunted in the faces of non-smokers everywhere. Smokiana stocks a vast range of pipes from the antique to the exotic to the downright weird. While you're here, be sure to step into the **Pijpenkabinet (Pipe Cabinet),** an in-store museum (p. 167). It's open Wednesday to Saturday from 11am to 6pm. Prinsengracht 488 (at Leidsestraat). ℂ **020/421-1779**. www.pipeshop.nl. Tram: 1, 2, or 5 to Prinsengracht.

SHOES

Betsy Palmer ★   Imelda Marcos would not approve. There are no classic shoes here, but there's an incredible collection of trendy women's footwear, with obscure but fun brands like Sexy Chic, Sunloving Babe, and Serious Partying. Rokin 9–15 (at the Dam). ℂ **020/422-1040**. www.betsypalmer.com. Tram: 4, 9, 14, 16, 24, or 25 to the Dam.

Jan Jansen ★★   Award-winning Dutch shoe designer Jan Jansen sells his men's and women's footwear in this chic store. Well-heeled customers can choose each piece of leather to make up exclusive shoes. You can special-order colors and sizes if you can't find yours—it takes about 3 weeks and they will mail your shoes to you. Rokin 42 (btw. the Dam and Spui). ℂ **020/625-1350**. www.janjansenshoes.com. Tram: 4, 9, 14, 16, 24, or 25 to the Dam or Spui.

3 STREET MARKETS

Amsterdammers are traders to the tips of their fingers, as you'll quickly find if you visit a street market, but they won't bargain with you—they have much less interest in hag-gling, or margin in their prices, than their counterparts in countries farther south. They're simply too practical to quote a ridiculous price in the expectation that it'll be cut in half or that you'll be fool enough to pay it. No, Dutch street merchants exhibit their enthusiasm for trade in a more stolid way—simply by being permanent. Many of Amsterdam's open-air salesmen are at the stalls, vans, tents, and barges of the city's mar-kets 6 days a week, 52 weeks a year. In all, Amsterdam and its outlying neighborhoods have more than 50 outdoor markets every week, on any given day, except Sunday, when you have a choice of several.

Finding a bargain-basement souvenir is easy at the **Waterlooplein Flea Market** ★, on Waterlooplein (Tram: 9 or 14). All kinds of stuff is here, not all of it junk, and a constant press of people with good buys on their minds. This is Amsterdam's classic market: It's often said that in its glory days before World War II, when it was a fixture of the city's Jewish community, you could find amazing antiques amid the lesser goods—possibly even a dusty old Rembrandt. Today, however, your luck is more apt to run in the opposite direction. Most merchants work out of tents, and some sell *patates frites met mayonnaise* (french fries eaten Dutch style, with mayonnaise) from vans that are a long way from the pushcarts of yesteryear; but among old CDs and leather jackets, you'll still find cooking pots, mariners' telescopes, coal scuttles, bargain watches, nuts and bolts, and decent prints of Dutch cities. The market is open Monday to Saturday from 10am to 5pm.

At the **Bloemenmarkt (Flower Market)** ★, Singel (Tram: 4, 9, 14, 16, 24, or 25), at Muntplein, awnings stretch to cover some 15 stalls of brightly colored blossoms, bulbs, and potted plants. This row of permanently moored barges is one of Amsterdam's stellar spots, though you might find it overrated, especially since it doesn't look like it's actually floating—and indeed, most of it isn't. Still, this is probably the most atmospheric place to buy fresh-cut flowers, bright and healthy plants, ready-to-travel packets of tulip bulbs, and any necessary home-gardening accessory. A stroll down that fragrant line is surely one of Amsterdam's most heart-lifting experiences. An added plus is that tulips here cost a few cents less than at the flower stands around town. The market is open daily from 8am to 8pm.

At the colorful, kilometer-long **Albert Cuypmarkt** (www.albertcuypmarkt.com), Albert Cuypstraat (Tram: 16, 24, or 25), you find just about anything your imagination can conjure: 350 stalls sell different types of foods, clothing, flowers, plants, and textiles. Cheesemongers slice wedges from Frisbee-shaped disks of Edam. The market is open Monday to Saturday from 9am to 6pm.

The Friday **book market** at Spui (Tram: 1, 2, or 5) has around 25 booths with secondhand books. You can often find some great deals (even for books in English), and perhaps even a rare book or two. Just about any subject is available, both fiction and nonfiction. The market is open Friday from 10am to 6pm.

Local artists mount outdoor exhibits at the **Spui Art Market,** April to November, Sunday from 10am to 6pm.

Kunst & Antiekcentrum De Looier ★, Elandsgracht 109 (© **020/624-9038;** www.looier.nl; tram: 7, 10, or 17), is a big indoor antiques market spread through several old warehouses in the Jordaan. Individual dealers rent small stalls and corners to showcase their best wares. The old armoires and other heavy pieces of traditional Dutch furniture are likely too large to consider buying, but many dealers offer antique jewelry, prints and engravings, old porcelain table settings, bathroom fixtures, 19th-century tin toys, Delft tiles, furniture, Dutch knickknacks, and much more. De Looier is open Saturday to Thursday from 11am to 5pm.

(Fun Facts   **Borrowed Blooms**

Berliner Klaus-Günter Neumann wrote the classic "Dutch" song *Tulips from Amsterdam*—in German.

Local artists come to show off their wares at the **Thorbeckeplein Sunday Art Market,** Thorbeckeplein (© **075/670-3030;** tram: 4, 9, or 14). Picking your way through the tables, you'll find sculptures, ceramics, paintings, jewelry, and mixed-media pieces. The market runs from April to October, Sunday from 11am to 6pm.

The **Boerenmarkt (Farmers' Market;** www.boerenmarktamsterdam.nl) at Noordermarkt (Tram: 3 or 10), also known as the **Bio Market,** caters to Amsterdam's infatuation with health foods and natural products, sold by green-living enthusiasts who know and love what they do. Popular items include fruit and vegetables, homemade bread, colorful Dutch cheeses, and natural soap. It takes place on Saturday from 9am to 5pm. A similar **Farmers' Market** at Nieuwmarkt (Metro: Nieuwmarkt) operates on the same day and hours. Bargains may be thin on the ground but quality is pretty much assured. The crowd browsing here is invariably large.

Other enjoyable street markets include the **Westermarkt,** which sells textiles and clothes on Westerstraat, at Noordermarkt, Monday from 9am to 1pm; the **Lindengracht** general market, on the long Jordaan street of the same name, Saturday from 9am to 5pm; the **garden market,** at Amstelveld, on Prinsengracht near Vijzelstraat, Easter to Christmas, Monday from 3 to 6pm; the **Postzegelmarkt (Stamp Market),** around Nieuwezijds Voorburgwal 276, on Wednesday and Saturday from 1 to 4pm; and the **Antiek en Curiosamarkt,** Nieuwmarkt (Metro: Nieuwmarkt), for antiques and curios, May to October, Sunday from 9am to 6pm.

Amsterdam After Dark

Nightlife in Amsterdam, like an Indonesian *rijsttafel*, is a bit of this and a bit of that. The cultural calendar is full, but not jammed. There's a strong jazz scene, good music clubs, and enjoyable English-language shows at the little cabarets and theaters along the canals. The club and bar scene can be entertaining if not outrageous; the dance clubs may indeed seem quiet and small to anyone used to the flash of clubs in New York City, Los Angeles, or London. However, the brown cafes—the typical Amsterdam pubs—have never been better. And there are always the movies: You can watch first-run U.S. blockbuster hits with their English soundtracks intact.

Hot and cool at the same time, **Leidseplein** is the center of Amsterdam's nightlife, with some of the city's most popular restaurants, bars, and nightspots all within dancing distance of each other around the square. Leidseplein never really closes, so you can greet the dawn and start again. **Rembrandtplein** is a brash and brassy square that really comes alive at night, when it's awash with neon. Although it has a more downscale reputation than Leidseplein, this area often seems even more intent on having fun, and there are enough hip, sophisticated places to go around. These two areas are connected by **Reguliersdwarsstraat,** which has some good cafes, including a few gay ones, and also several fine clubs and restaurants. The **Rosse Buurt (Red Light District)** serves up its own unique brand of nightlife, and adjoining this is **Nieuwmarkt,** which has become a popular alternative hangout.

INFORMATION

Your best source of information for nightlife and cultural events is *Amsterdam Day by Day,* the VVV Tourist Office's monthly program guide in English, which costs 1.95€ ($3.10). It provides a complete cultural guide to Amsterdam, with listings for concerts and recitals, theater, cabaret, opera, dance performances, rock concerts, art films, film festivals, special museum and art gallery exhibitions, and lots more. Many hotels have copies available for guests, in some cases for free, or you can get one at the VVV offices (p. 26 for addresses and hours). There's also the free monthly listings magazine *De Uitkrant* from the Amsterdams Uitburo (see below), which you can pick up at many performance venues; it's in Dutch, but it isn't difficult to understand the listings information.

TICKETS

If you want to attend any of Amsterdam's theatrical or musical events (including rock concerts), make it your first task on arrival to get tickets. The **Amsterdams Uitburo**

Impressions

It often seems to me that the night is much more alive and richly colored than the day.

—Vincent van Gogh, September 8, 1888

> **(Tips)** **That's the Ticket for Youth**
>
> If you're interested in cultural events and are under age 26, go by the **Amsterdams Uitburo** (see above) to pick up a 15€ ($24) **CJP (Cultural Youth Pass).** This pass grants free or reduced admission to most museums and discounts on many cultural events. For more information, go to www.cjp.nl.

(AUB) Ticketshop, Leidseplein 26 (© **0900/0191** or 31-20/621-1288 from outside the Netherlands; www.uitburo.nl; tram: 1, 2, 5, 7, or 10), can reserve tickets for almost every venue in town, for a reservations charge of 2€ ($3.20) per ticket when you buy at its office, 2.50€ ($4) when you buy online, and 3€ ($4.80) when you buy by phone. Discounted last-minute tickets may be available. Using this service instead of chasing down tickets on your own can save you precious hours. The office is open Monday to Saturday from 10am to 7:30pm, and Sunday from noon to 7:30pm. You can purchase tickets with a credit card by phone daily from 9am to 8pm, and online at any time.

The **VVV Amsterdam** tourist information office (p. 26 for addresses and hours) can also reserve performance tickets, and charges 2.50€ ($4) for the service. Most upmarket and many mid-level hotels will reserve tickets as well; ask at the concierge desk.

1 THE PERFORMING ARTS

CLASSICAL MUSIC

Amsterdam's top orchestra is the famed **Koninklijk Concertgebouworkest (Royal Concertgebouw Orchestra)** (© 02/305-1010; www.concertgebouworkest.nl), which performs mainly in the **Concertgebouw,** and gives occasional open-air concerts in the **Vondelpark.** The Concertgebouw Orchestra, under Latvian lead conductor Mariss Jansons, can produce any of the great classical works at the tap of a baton, yet is also willing to go out on a limb from time to time with modern and experimental pieces.

The city's other full orchestra, the **Nederlands Philharmonisch Orkest (Netherlands Philharmonic Orchestra)** (© 02/521-7500; www.orkest.nl), fondly known as the NedPhO, isn't far behind its illustrious cousin, if behind at all. The NedPhO has found its niche in an adventurous repertoire, which includes opera collaborations. Its main Amsterdam concert venue is also the Concertgebouw, though it is based at the **Beurs van Berlage,** and it shows up regularly for opera in the **Muziektheater.**

Holland's other top orchestras, such as The Hague's **Residentie Orchestra** and the **Rotterdam Philharmonic,** as well as visiting orchestras from abroad, also appear regularly at Amsterdam venues.

When it comes to chamber music, the **Nederlands Kamerorkest (Netherlands Chamber Orchestra)** (© 02/521-7500; www.orkest.nl), the **Amsterdam Baroque Orchestra** (www.tonkoopman.nl), and the **Orkest van de Achttiende Eeuw (Orchestra of the Eighteenth Century)** (www.orchestra18c.com) provide plenty of possibilities, often playing with authentic period instruments and ably supported by the **Nederlands Kamerkoor (Netherlands Chamber Choir)** (© 020/578-7978; www.nederlandskamerkoor.nl). You often hear these outfits in the Concertgebouw's Recital Hall, at the

of these venues, see "Major Concert Halls & Theaters," below.

OPERA

Productions by **De Nederlandse Opera (Netherlands Opera)** (℃ **020/551-8922;** www.dno.nl), under Pierre Audi's artistic direction, dominate the **Muziektheater**'s schedule, and attract a devoted following.

DANCE

The Dutch take pride in the growing international popularity and prestige of their major dance companies. **Het Nationale Ballet (National Ballet)** (℃ **020/551-8225;** www. het-nationale-ballet.nl), based at the **Muziektheater,** has a repertoire of both classical and modern works, many by choreographers George Balanchine and Hans van Manen. The **Nederlands Dans Theater (Netherlands Dance Theater)** (℃ **070/880-0100;** www. ndt.nl), choreographed by Czech artistic director Jiri Kylián, is based in The Hague but frequently comes to the Muziektheater. Both companies are usually accompanied by the specialized **Netherlands Ballet Orchestra.**

THEATER

Amsterdammers speak English so well that Broadway and London roadshows and English-language touring companies sometimes make Amsterdam a stop on their European itineraries. However, many of Amsterdam's theatergoing opportunities are more experimental and avant-garde, and most of them are in Dutch.

MAJOR CONCERT HALLS & THEATERS

Some tickets for the **Muziektheater** and the **Concertgebouw** are eminently affordable, even for visitors whose financial assets are severely limited. Seeing the resident Netherlands Opera, National Ballet, or Royal Concertgebouw Orchestra is well worth a bit of financial trimming in other departments.

Beurs van Berlage ★ The former home of the Amsterdam Stock Exchange now houses the **Netherlands Philharmonic Orchestra** and the **Netherlands Chamber Orchestra.** What was once the exchange's trading floor, built in 1903 by Amsterdam School architect Hendrik Petrus Berlage, has since 1988 been a concert venue with two halls: the 665-seat Yakult Zaal and the 200-seat AGA Zaal. Holland's **Concertzender** classical radio station is also based here. Damrak 213 (at Beursplein). ℃ **020/521-7520.** www. berlage.com. Tickets 15€–75€ ($24–$120). Box office Tues–Fri 12:30–6pm, Sat 12:30–5pm, and 1¹/₄ hr. before performances begin. Tram: 4, 9, 14, 16, 24, or 25 to the Dam.

Concertgebouw ★★★ The Concertgebouw (Concert Building), home base of the **Royal Concertgebouw Orchestra,** opened its doors in 1888 and is said to be one of the world's most acoustically perfect concert halls. Musical performances have a distinctive richness of tone that is as much a pleasure for the performer as for the audience. During the musical season (Sept–Mar) and the annual **Holland Festival** (p. 33), the world's greatest orchestras, ensembles, conductors, and soloists perform here. Concerts and recitals happen every day and often there's a choice of two programs at the same time on the same evening: one in the Grote Zaal (Great Hall), the other in the smaller Kleine Zaal (Little Hall). Don't worry about your location—every seat in the Grote Zaal has a clear view. It's even possible to sit onstage behind the performers; tonal quality is altered there, however, so those seats are actually cheaper.

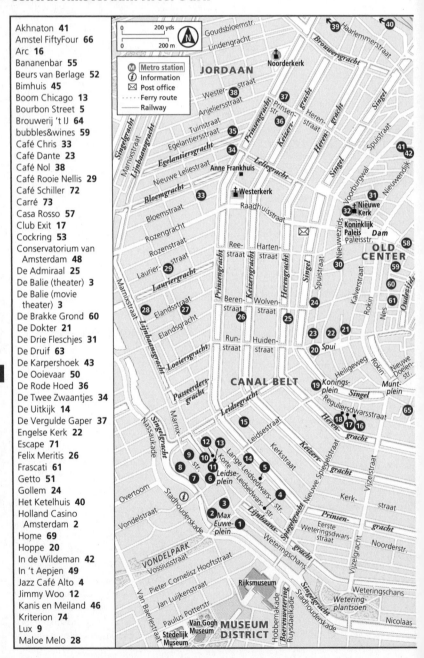

Akhnaton **41**
Amstel FiftyFour **66**
Arc **16**
Bananenbar **55**
Beurs van Berlage **52**
Bimhuis **45**
Boom Chicago **13**
Bourbon Street **5**
Brouwerij 't IJ **64**
bubbles&wines **59**
Café Chris **33**
Café Dante **23**
Café Nol **38**
Café Rooie Nellis **29**
Café Schiller **72**
Carré **73**
Casa Rosso **57**
Club Exit **17**
Cockring **53**
Conservatorium van
  Amsterdam **48**
De Admiraal **25**
De Balie (theater) **3**
De Balie (movie
  theater) **3**
De Brakke Grond **60**
De Dokter **21**
De Drie Fleschjes **31**
De Druif **63**
De Karpershoek **43**
De Ooievaar **50**
De Rode Hoed **36**
De Twee Zwaantjes **34**
De Uitkijk **14**
De Vergulde Gaper **37**
Engelse Kerk **22**
Escape **71**
Felix Meritis **26**
Frascati **61**
Getto **51**
Gollem **24**
Het Ketelhuis **40**
Holland Casino
  Amsterdam **2**
Home **69**
Hoppe **20**
In de Wildeman **42**
In 't Aepjen **49**
Jazz Café Alto **4**
Jimmy Woo **12**
Kanis en Meiland **46**
Kriterion **74**
Lux **9**
Maloe Melo **28**

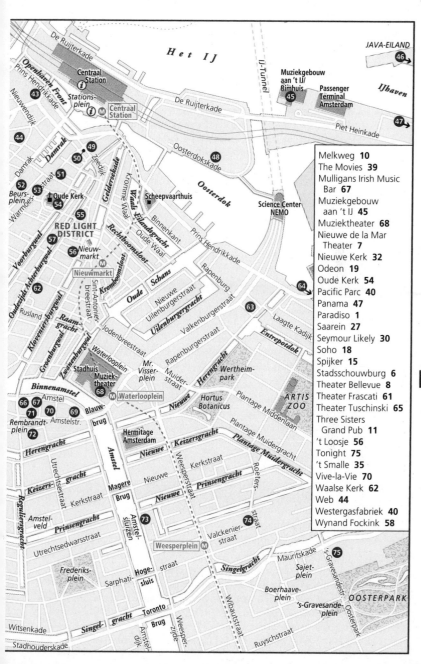

Melkweg **10**
The Movies **39**
Mulligans Irish Music
 Bar **67**
Muziekgebouw
 aan 't IJ **45**
Muziektheater **68**
Nieuwe de la Mar
 Theater **7**
Nieuwe Kerk **32**
Odeon **19**
Oude Kerk **54**
Pacific Parc **40**
Panama **47**
Paradiso **1**
Saarein **27**
Seymour Likely **30**
Soho **18**
Spijker **15**
Stadsschouwburg **6**
Theater Bellevue **8**
Theater Frascati **61**
Theater Tuschinski **65**
Three Sisters
 Grand Pub **11**
't Loosje **56**
Tonight **75**
't Smalle **35**
Vive-la-Vie **70**
Waalse Kerk **62**
Web **44**
Westergasfabriek **40**
Wynand Fockink **58**

(Moments) Vondelpark Open-Air Theater

From June to mid-August, the stage at the **Vondelpark Openluchttheater**
(© **020/673-1499**) is set for theater, all kinds of music (including concerts by
the Royal Concertgebouw Orchestra), dance, operetta, and more.

There are **free lunchtime rehearsal concerts** at 12:30pm on Wednesdays during
the October to June concert season. These may feature chamber music, symphonic performances, or abbreviated previews of a full concert to be played that same evening.
Concertgebouwplein 2–6. © **020/671-8345** (daily 10am–5pm; 24-hr. information line
© 020/675-4411). www.concertgebouw.nl. Tickets 15€–100€ ($24–$160); summer
concerts (Aug) 30€ ($48). Box office daily 9:30am–7pm, until 8pm for same-day
tickets; phone orders 10am–3pm. Tram: 3, 5, or 12 to Museumplein; 16 to
Concertgebouwplein.

Koninklijk Theater Carré   This big, plush Royal Carré Theater on the banks of the
Amstel River, built in the 19th century, used to be a full-time circus arena. These days,
clowns and animals are infrequent visitors, though spectacles such as the Flying Karama-
zov Brothers fill the gap. In addition to opera, modern dance, and ballet, look for lavish
Dutch-language productions of top Broadway and London musicals—*Les Misérables,
The Phantom of the Opera, Miss Saigon, Evita, Cats,* and *42nd Street* have all been on the
bill. On occasion, a visiting show is in English. Top rockers and pop stars have performed
here, but the biggest names now strut their stuff at Amsterdam ArenA (see below). Get
tickets as far in advance as possible—the hottest shows always sell out quickly. Amstel
115–125. © **0900/252-5255.** www.theatercarre.nl. Tickets 15€–125€ ($24–$200). Box office Mon–
Sat 10am–7pm, Sun 1–7pm. Tram: 7 or 10 to Weesperplein.

Muziekgebouw aan 't IJ ★   Opened in 2005 in a spectacular piece of modern
architecture on the IJ waterfront, this is the home of the former **Muziekcentrum De
IJsbreker,** the once-grungy foundation for avant-garde and experimental music. This
ocean of glass is very far from being grungy. The main hall seats around 750 and a smaller
foyer hall has space for 125. Performances here feature modern, old, jazz, electronic, and
non-Western music, along with small-scale musical theater, opera, and dance. Visit the
concert hall's in-house cafe-restaurant, the **Star Ferry;** it became one of Amsterdam's hit
eateries the moment it opened. In fine weather, you can dine outside on its waterfront
terrace. From the Center, it's just a short walk or tram ride here. Piet Heinkade 1 (IJ waterfront, just east of Centraal Station). © **020/788-2000.** www.muziekgebouw.nl. Tickets 10€–60€
($16–$96). Box office Mon–Sat from noon to 7pm. Tram: 25 or 26 to Muziekgebouw.

Muziektheater ★★   In the 1980s, construction of this superbly equipped 1,600-
seat auditorium sparked street riots that sent tear gas drifting across what is now the stage.
Today, it's the performances that cause a stir. The Muziektheater is one of the city's stellar
performance venues and home base of the highly regarded **Netherlands Opera** and
National Ballet. Like at the Concertgebouw, there are free "musical lunches" from October to June—these half-hour concerts are on Tuesdays at 12:30pm (doors open at
12:15pm). Waterlooplein 22 (at the Amstel River). © **020/625-5455.** www.hetmuziektheater.nl.
Tickets 20€–90€ ($32–$144). Box office Mon–Sat 10am–6pm, Sun 11:30am–6pm. Tram: 9 or 14
to Waterlooplein.

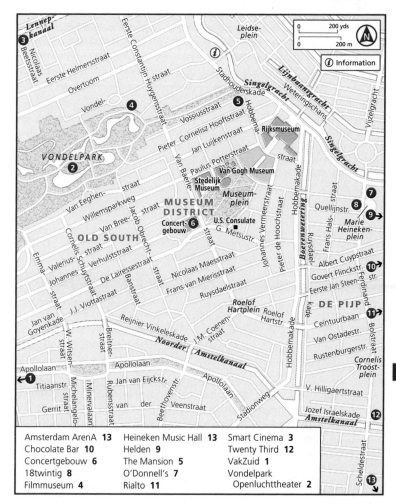

Amsterdam ArenA **13**	Heineken Music Hall **13**	Smart Cinema **3**
Chocolate Bar **10**	Helden **9**	Twenty Third **12**
Concertgebouw **6**	The Mansion **5**	VakZuid **1**
18twintig **8**	O'Donnell's **7**	Vondelpark
Filmmuseum **4**	Rialto **11**	Openluchttheater **2**

Stadsschouwburg   The plushly upholstered, 950-seat Municipal Theater is Amsterdam's principal venue for mainstream Dutch theater. Dutch (and occasionally, English) productions of international plays, both classic and modern, are presented here, as are opera and ballet performances. The 1894 baroque theater stands on the site of earlier theaters that were destroyed by fire. Performances usually start at 8pm. Leidseplein 26. ☎ **020/624-2311.** www. stadsschouwburgamsterdam.nl. Tickets 10€–50€ ($16–$80). Tram: 1, 2, 5, 7, or 10 to Leidseplein.

Other Venues

In addition to the major ones, there are plenty of other venues in Amsterdam. No fewer than 42 of the city's churches are equipped with organs, some of them historic works of

AMSTERDAM AFTER DARK

10

THE PERFORMING ARTS

(Tips) **What to Wear**

If you intend to go to the opera, a classical music concert, or the theater, don't worry about what to wear, since Amsterdam has a very informal dress code—no code at all, really. Of course, you might want to dress up, and in fact many people do, but you'll never be turned away for being improperly dressed.

art in their own right. Four churches in particular—the **Engelse Kerk,** Begijnhof 48 ((*C*) **020/624-9665;** tram: 1, 2, 4, 5, 9, 14, 16, 24, or 25); **Nieuwe Kerk,** the Dam ((*C*) **020/626-8168;** www.nieuwekerk.nl; tram: 1, 2, 4, 5, 9, 13, 14, 16, 17, 24, or 25); **Oude Kerk,** Oudekerksplein 23 ((*C*) **020/625-8284;** www.oudekerk.nl; Metro: Nieuwmarkt); and **Waalse Kerk,** Walenpleintje 157 ((*C*) **020/623-2074;** www.waalsekerk-amsterdam.nl; tram: 4, 9, 14, 16, 24, or 25)—are regularly in use for baroque chamber music and organ recitals.

Holland's oldest and largest clandestine church (for more than 2 centuries after Amsterdam's 1578 Protestant revolution other Christian denominations were forbidden to worship openly), is the Remonstrant Church, in a one-time hat store called **De Rode Hoed (the Red Hat),** Keizersgracht 102 ((*C*) **020/638-5606;** tram: 13, 14, 17)—look for a red hat on the fine canalside building's gable stone. The chapel in back, with an upper-floor balcony and an impressive organ, dates from 1630 and is now a venue for classical music concerts and debates.

A place worth checking out for potential new talent is the city's music school, the **Conservatorium van Amsterdam,** Oosterdokskade 151 ((*C*) **020/527-7550;** www. conservatoriumvanamsterdam.nl; Metro: Centraal Station), which moved to a shiny new home on redeveloped Oosterdokseiland, just east of Centraal Station, in 2008.

Theaters, some of which occasionally feature performances in English, include **De Balie,** Kleine Gartmanplantsoen 10 ((*C*) **020/623-2904;** www.debalie.nl; tram: 1, 2, 5, 7, or 10); **Theater Bellevue,** Leidsekade 90 ((*C*) **020/530-5301;** www.theaterbellevue.nl; tram: 1, 2, 5, 7, or 10), which also hosts modern dance; **De Brakke Grond,** at the Vlaams Cultureel Centrum, Nes 43 ((*C*) **020/626-0044;** www.brakkegrond.nl; tram: 4, 9, 14, 16, 24, or 25), which has mostly Flemish theater; **Felix Meritis,** Keizersgracht 324 ((*C*) **020/626-2321;** www.felixmeritis.nl; tram: 1, 2, or 5); **Theater Frascati,** Nes 63 ((*C*) **020/626-6866;** www.theaterfrascati.nl; tram: 4, 9, 14, 16, 24, or 25), which focuses on modern theater; **Nieuwe de la Mar Theater,** Marnixstraat 404 ((*C*) **020/623-3462;** www.nieuwedelamartheater.nl; tram: 1, 2, 5, 7, or 10); and the **Westergasfabriek,** Haarlemmerweg 8–10 ((*C*) **020/488-7778;** www.westergasfabriek.com; bus: 22), a multipurpose arts complex in an old gas works building. For open-air theater in summer, there's the **Vondelpark Openluchttheater,** Vondelpark ((*C*) **020/673-1499;** www.openlucht theater.nl; tram: 1, 2, or 5).

2 THE CLUB & MUSIC SCENE

Visiting a jazz club or music bar is always a good way to round off your day.

JAZZ & BLUES

Jazz, Dixieland, and blues may be American musical forms, but Europeans—and certainly the Dutch—have adopted them with gusto. July is the best month for jazz lovers in Europe: Three major festivals are scheduled almost back-to-back in France, Switzerland, and Holland, including the 3-day **North Sea Jazz Festival** (www.northseajazz. com), held at Rotterdam's **Ahoy** (ⓒ **010/293-3300;** www.ahoy.nl). The festival convenes the international jazz world's biggest names with more than 100 concerts involving more than 600 artists.

Described below are a few of the jazz hangouts that dot Amsterdam's cityscape.

Bimhuis ★   Since 2005, a shiny metal box with windows has been home to the city's premier jazz, blues, and improvisational club. It's an extension of the new **Muziekgebouw aan 't IJ.** This venue represents a big change from its previous tatty premises amid the old warehouses of the Oude Schans canal, but the "Bim," as locals affectionately call it, has handled the move well—and in truth, the new purpose-built venue is a big improvement acoustically and in other respects, even if it's lost some street cred along the way. Top local and international musicians regularly perform here. Piet Heinkade 3 (IJ waterfront, just east of Centraal Station). ⓒ **020/788-2188.** www.bimhuis.nl. 10€–30€ ($16–$48). Tram: 25 or 26 to Muziekgebouw.

Bourbon Street ★★   This intimate little cafe hosts local blues, jazz, soul, and funk talent from the States and elsewhere. There's a cover charge for well-known groups or musicians, but the music plays well into the night. Leidsekruisstraat 6–8 (off Leidseplein). ⓒ **020/623-3440.** www.bourbonstreet.nl. No cover, except for special acts. Tram: 1, 2, 5, 7, or 10 to Leidseplein.

Jazz Café Alto   A regular quartet plays jazz nightly to a diverse crowd in this small, comfortable cafe. There are also guest combos and occasional blues as well—the music is always top-notch. On Wednesday evening, noted saxophonist Hans Dulfer plays, sometimes accompanied by his equally noted daughter, Candy. Korte Leidsedwarsstraat 115 (off Leidseplein). ⓒ **020/626-3249.** www.jazz-cafe-alto.nl. No cover. Tram: 1, 2, 5, 7, or 10 to Leidseplein.

Maloe Melo ★   This small club isn't the Mississippi Delta, but Amsterdam's "home of the blues" features live blues most nights, though some evenings feature jazz and country. Tuesday and Thursday nights are for jams, which pack the place. Music quality varies from sounds lovingly created by capable amateurs to, occasionally, those cooked up by a big name. A pleasantly intimate setting and eager audiences always make for a good time. Lijnbaansgracht 163. ⓒ **020/420-4592.** www.maloemelo.nl. Cover 5€ ($8). Tram: 7, 10, or 17 to Elandsgracht.

ROCK & POP

Nothing changes faster in Holland—or exhibits more variety—than the pop music scene, whether the latest craze is rock, reggae, new wave, or whatever. Performers en route to world-class stardom always seem to turn up in Amsterdam, and few of their shows have difficulty selling out. Big stars and large-scale productions are occasionally featured at **Koninklijk Theater Carré** (see "Major Concert Halls & Theaters," above). Rock stars strut their stuff at the giant **Amsterdam ArenA,** ArenA Boulevard, Amsterdam Zuidoost (ⓒ **020/311-1313;** www.amsterdamarena.nl; Metro: Bijlmer/ArenA), the Ajax soccer club's stadium in the southeastern suburbs, which has a sliding roof to keep out the ubiquitous Dutch rain.

AMSTERDAM AFTER DARK

10

THE CLUB & MUSIC SCENE

Near Amsterdam ArenA, the smaller **Heineken Music Hall** ★, Arena Blvd. 590 (⌀ **0900/6874-24255;** www.heineken-music-hall.nl; Metro: Bijlmer/ArenA), hosts more intimate concerts. Performers have included Avril Lavigne, Alanis Morissette, Duran Duran, the Black Eyed Peas, Michael Bolton, Marilyn Manson, and Meat Loaf, among others.

For ticket info, go to **Mojo Concerts** (⌀ **0900/300-1250;** www.mojo.nl).

DANCE CLUBS

For local residents, the Amsterdam club scene is generally a members-only situation. But as a tourist, you can simply show up and, so long as your attire and behavior suit management's sensibilities, you shouldn't have problems getting past the bouncer. Drinks can be expensive—a beer or Coke averages 5€ ($8), and a whiskey or cocktail, 8€ ($13)—but you can nurse just one drink while you dance the night away, or down a quick beer and move on if the crowd or the music mix isn't your style. The places listed below are some of the most popular at press time, and in Amsterdam, the nightclub hierarchy doesn't change very quickly. But don't hesitate to ask around for new places once you get here.

Akhnaton   Jazz, African, and salsa music are regular features at this spot that caters to a youthful, multiethnic, hash-smoking crowd of joyful dancers. Nieuwezijds Kolk 25 (near Centraal Station). ⌀ 020/624-3396. www.akhnaton.nl. Cover 3€–6€ ($4.80–$9.60). Tram: 1, 2, 5, 13, or 17 to Martelaarsgracht.

Escape ★★   Three dance floors, a great sound system, and a healthy mix of local and international DJs make this one of the prime choices for the young and trendy. Rembrandtplein 11. ⌀ 020/622-1111. www.escape.nl. Cover 8€–15€ ($13–$24). Tram: 4, 9, or 14 to Rembrandtplein.

Home   This ultratrendy place tends to attract Dutch celebs (and wannabes) and offers a variety of music on its three floors, depending on the night—but the main deal here is house. Wagenstraat 3–7 (off Rembrandtplein). ⌀ 020/620-1375. www.clubhome.nl. Cover 10€–12€ ($16–$19). Tram: 4, 9, or 14 to Rembrandtplein.

Jimmy Woo ★   A Hong Kong–style club, Jimmy Woo attracts a slow-burning crowd, but the slow-starting music gets spikier and the vibes begin to smolder the later it gets. Guest-list entry only on some nights makes this luxe spot occasionally hard to get into. Korte Leidsedwarsstraat 18 (off Leidseplein). ⌀ 020/626-3150. www.jimmywoo.com. Cover 15€–20€ ($24–$36). Tram: 1, 2, 5, 7, or 10 to Leidseplein.

The Mansion ★   Hotshot DJs jet in from around Europe for this swank venue's Friday and Saturday club nights. At other times, the former royal mansion on the edge of Vondelpark, which dates from 1905, gets by on its suite of über-plush restaurants and cocktail bars. Hobbemastraat 2 (off Leidseplein). ⌀ 020/616-6664. www.the-mansion.nl. Cover 15€–25€ ($24–$40). Tram: 2 or 5 to Hobbemastraat.

Pacific Parc   Step on the gas for hip-hop and Latin dance at this cavernous place, in the unlikely setting of the Westergasfabriek, a disused gas plant in the Westerpark district west of Centraal Station. It's now a cultural center, restaurant, and bar (open longer hours than the dance club) with an outdoor terrace. This club was born hip and has stayed that way, so it's often crowded and hard to get in. Haarlemmerweg 6–10 (west of Centraal Station). ⌀ 020/488-7778. www.pacificparc.nl. No cover. Tram: 10 to Van Halstraat.

Panama ★★   A waterfront building from 1899 that used to be a power station houses this hip club. The attractive bar/restaurant in the lobby opens up into the cavernous club, which hosts big-name DJs and special events, depending on the day and seasons. This is a see-and-be seen place for 30- to 40-something professionals. So dress to impress and bring some attitude. Oostelijke Handelskade 4. ✆ **020/311-8686.** www.panama.nl. Cover 10€–25€ ($16–$40). Tram: 10 or 26 to Rietlandpark.

Paradiso ★ This old church has been transformed into a space that presents an eclectic variety of music, both live and canned. A dark and somewhat forbidding exterior belies the bright inside. The majestic interior has lofty ceilings and a high balcony encircling the room, which affords great views of the central dance floor. The club revels in name DJs and has popular theme nights, ranging from jazz to disco to raves. The Friday-night VIP Club is stylish. Weteringschans 6–8 (near Leidseplein). ✆ **020/626-4521.** www.paradiso.nl. Cover 8€–18€ ($13–$29). Tram: 1, 2, 5, 7, or 10 to Leidseplein.

Tonight ★★ A former 17th-century orphanage chapel with frescoed walls is the atmospheric, if unlikely, setting for one of Amsterdam's hottest clubs. DJs rustle up music from the '60s to the '90s, drawing a surprisingly youthful crowd to the Timezone club nights, where funk, soul, and New York disco reign. 's Gravesandestraat 51 (near the Tropenmuseum). ✆ **020/850-2400.** www.hotelarena.nl. Cover 6€–10€ ($9.60–$16). Tram: 7 or 10 to Korte 's Gravesandestraat.

MULTIDIMENSIONAL VENUES

Melkweg ★★ **Finds** A one-time hippie haven in an old dairy factory, the Melkweg (Milky Way) constantly reinvents its multimedia persona. It houses a reasonably priced international restaurant (**Eat@Jo's**), coffeeshop, bar, art center, dance floor, cinema, theater, concert hall, photo gallery, and exhibition space. You need to get a temporary membership before they let you in, but it's worth it. International big-name groups perform here, and DJs spin a musical mix ranging from ska to house. Friday night is called **Electric Circus,** and it's a multimedia music extravaganza. Melkweg's organizers have always embraced liberalism and experimentalism, and its theater showcases new groups, both international and local, and performances ranging from comedy to multicultural and gay- and lesbian-oriented. The entire setup is a throwback to Amsterdam's glory days in the '60s, but is big enough, and wise enough, to accommodate the latest trends as well. Lijnbaansgracht 234A (near Leidseplein). ✆ **020/531-8181.** www.melkweg.nl. Cover 5€–10€ ($8–$16) plus 3€ ($4.80) monthly club membership. Box office Mon–Fri 1–5pm, Sat–Sun 4–6pm. Tram: 1, 2, 5, 7, or 10 to Leidseplein.

Odeon ★ Your feet might not know what to do at first amid the graceful surroundings of this reconverted old canalside building (1663). The period ceiling paintings and stucco decor seem more suited to minuets than disco moves. A mix of '50s–'80s music is played. In addition to dance at the Odeon Club, there's a chic restaurant, the Cocktailbrasserie; a laid-back cellar cafe/brasserie, the Café Odeon; the funky Odeon Bar; and a performance hall that's used for music concerts, from classical to jazz and rock, as well as theater, lectures, and other events (until it gets made over to dance-club mode in the late evening). Singel 460 (near Muntplein). 𝄯 020/521-8555. www.odeonamsterdam.nl. Cover 5€–15€ ($8–$24). Odeon Club: Fri–Sat 11pm–5am. Tram: 1, 2, or 5 to Koningsplein.

COMEDY THEATER

Boom Chicago ★ (Finds)   Since 1993, Boom Chicago has been successfully importing American and British brands of comedy to Amsterdam. *Time* magazine compared them to Chicago's famous Second City comedy troupe, and the *Chicago Tribune's* critic reported back to the Windy City that "big talents turn in a very funny show." The partly scripted, partly improvised humor takes aim at life in Amsterdam, the Dutch, tourists, and any other convenient target. Dutch audiences don't have much problem with the English sketches, and often seem to get the joke ahead of the native English speakers in attendance. Spectators sit around candlelit tables for eight and can dine on what the *Wall Street Journal* called "surprisingly good food" and a drink while enjoying the show. The restaurant opens at 7pm (it closes when the theater closes), and meals cost 16€ to 20€ ($26–$32) per person. Leidseplein Theater, Leidseplein 12. 𝄯 020/423-0101. www.boomchicago. nl. Cover 15€–35€ ($24–$56) (not including dinner). Box office daily noon–8:30pm. Tram: 1, 2, 5, 7, or 10 to Leidseplein.

3 THE BAR SCENE

Amsterdam's more than 1,400 cafes and bars are a hard act to follow. A lot of Amsterdammers still start their day at their favorite cafe (usually a so-called brown cafe), have lunch there, return for drinks before dinner, and then go back for a bit of socializing, a game of snooker, and some live (or canned) music and a singalong. Since everyone goes to cafes, they are the ultimate democratic institutions. You, the street sweeper, drink with the CEOs and politicos and speak your mind about everything from croquettes to geopolitics. The average price for a beer in Amsterdam is 1.50€ to 3€ ($2.40–$4.80)—clubs and hotel bars will charge more.

BROWN CAFES

You haven't really tasted Dutch beer until you've tasted it in Holland, served Dutch-style in a real *bruine kroeg* (brown cafe). These traditional Dutch bars are unpretentious, unpolished institutions filled with camaraderie, like a British pub or an American neighborhood bar. In a brown cafe, pouring another beer is much more important than dusting off the back bottles on the bar; the ritual is to draw a beer to get as much foam as possible, then to use a wet knife to shave off the head between a series of final fill-ups.

Even if you're not a beer lover, venturing into a brown cafe in Amsterdam will give you a peek into the city's everyday life. In old neighborhoods, brown cafes are on almost every corner—you can't miss them. Most have lacy curtains on the bottom half of the window, and perhaps a cat sleeping on the ledge. In winter (and sometimes into spring), their front doors are hung with a thick drape to keep out drafts. Once inside, you'll find the smoky, mustard brownness that's unique to an Amsterdam brown cafe, the result of years—no, centuries—of thick smoke and warm conversation.

There may be booths or little tables sprinkled around, but the only spots of color and light will be the shining metal of the beer tap and, perhaps, a touch of red still showing in the Persian rugs thrown across the tables (a practice that's typically Dutch, if you recall the old paintings). You'll feel the eons of conviviality the minute you walk into a really

⸜**Fun** Facts **A Lost Art?**

Today's Amsterdammers are no more than a pale shadow of their esteemed ancestors when it comes to quaffing beer. In 1613, Amsterdam's 518 taverns assured one for every 200 inhabitants. Today, the ratio has slipped to one per 725. The 17th century, clearly, was a Golden Age in more senses than one.

old, really *brown* brown cafe. Some have been on their corners since Rembrandt's time, haunted by the ghosts of drinkers past. The best of them are on the Prinsengracht, below Westermarkt, at the Dam, at Leidseplein, on Spui, or with a bit of searching, on tiny streets between canals.

Café Chris ★　Amsterdam's oldest remaining drinking den opened in 1624 and has been going strong ever since. It's said to be where the builders of Westerkerk (p. 163) were paid every week or two. There are a lot of curious old features at this bar that keep drawing people year after year, including the quirky toilet in the bathroom, which, oddly, flushes from outside the door and inside the bar! On Sunday nights, loud opera music engulfs the bar, attracting a cultured bohemian crowd. Bloemstraat 42 (near Westermarkt). ✆ **020/624-5942.** www.cafechris.nl. Tram: 13, 14, or 17 to Westermarkt.

De Druif　This is one of those places that not many visitors know about, though it's the third-oldest tavern in town. "The Grape" is on the waterfront and mainly frequented by a friendly local crowd. The bar's mythology has it that the Dutch naval hero, Piet Heyn, was a frequent patron (he lived nearby). However, as happens often when good beer is at hand, this is a tall tale told from wishful thinking—the bar opened in 1631 and Heyn died in 1629. Rapenburgerplein 83 (behind the Eastern Dock). ✆ **020/624-4530.** Bus: 22 to Kadijksplein.

De Karpershoek　Opened in 1629, this bar—the city's second oldest—was once a favorite hangout of sailors and seamen. Nowadays, given its prime location across the street from Centraal Station, the clientele is a mix of Dutch regulars, commuters popping in for a quick drink, and tourists, some of whom seem to settle in nicely while others look out of place, as if they've wandered in by mistake. The floor is covered with sand, just like it was in the 17th century. Martelaarsgracht 2 (facing Centraal Station). ✆ **020/624-7886.** Tram: 1, 2, 5, 13, or 17 to Martelaarsgracht.

De Vergulde Gaper　This place is a double delight: In bad weather, you can retreat into the warm, cozy interior, decorated with vintage posters and old medicine bottles (it used to be a pharmacy). In good weather, you can sit on a terrace beside the Prinsengracht—if you can get a seat. There's an unseemly dash whenever a table is vacated. Prinsenstraat 30 (at Prinsengracht). ✆ **020/624-8975.** Tram: 1, 2, 5, 13, or 17 to Martelaarsgracht.

Gollem　More than 200 kinds of beer are for sale in this ever-popular brown cafe near Spui. Many of them are imported, many of them favorites from Belgium, but do look for some weird-and-wonderful brews from other parts of the world. Raamsteeg 4 (off Spui). ✆ **020/626-6645.** www.cafegollem.nl. Tram: 1, 2, or 5 to Spui.

Hoppe ★　Standing room only is often the space situation here, and the crowds sometimes overflow onto the sidewalk. It seems that, quite by accident, Hoppe has become a tourist attraction. Locals love this spot, which dates from 1670. Trendy young

AMSTERDAM AFTER DARK

10

THE BAR SCENE

Message in the Bottle

You can smooth the process of conversing with locals in a bar if you can bandy about some Dutch drinking terminology. The most common word for a glass of *jenever* (Dutch gin) is a *borrel* (*bo*-rel) or the diminutive *borreltje* (*bo*-rel-che), though you'll also hear it called a *vaderlandje* (*fader*-lant-che), meaning "little fatherland," and other terms such as *hassebassie* (*hass*-uh-bassie), *keiltje* (*kyle*-che), *piketanussie* (*pik*-et-an-oossee), *recht op neer* (*rekht op near*), and *slokkie* (*slok*-ee). Avant-garde imbibers may ask for an "uppercut" to prove their international credentials. A glass of *jenever* filled to the brim, as tradition mandates that it must be, is called a *kamelenrug* (cam-*ay*-len-rookh), meaning "camel's back," or an *over Het IJ-kijkertje* (*over het eye kyk*-erche), meaning "view over the IJ" (an Amsterdam water channel). *Jenever* is often ordered with a beer chaser. The barkeep will place the *kopstoot* (*cop*-stoat), meaning "knock on the head," of a *stelletje* (*stel*-etche), meaning "couple," on the bar. Beer or *pils* (*pilss*) in a small glass is called a *colaatje pils* (*co*-la-che *pilss*); a *kabouter pils* (ka-*bou*-ter *pilss*), meaning "dwarf beer"; or a *lampie licht* (*lam*-pee *likht*), meaning "little lamp." Ale in a large glass is known as a *bakkie* (*bak*-ee) or a *vaas*, which means jar or vase. If it's served in a half-liter (1-pint) glass, it's known locally as an *amsterdammertje* (little Amsterdammer).

So if you breeze into a brown cafe, park yourself at the bar, and call the bartender over for a *"Recht op neer borrel,"* then ask him to "make sure it's a proper *over Het IJ-kijkertje,* put a *kopstoot* with it, a *colaatje* if you please, and set up a *bakkie* for later," you should get on swimmingly (of course, they might also send for the men in white coats).

professionals often pass through for a drink on their way home, mingling with hardened drinkers who pass through at any time and rarely leave. A convivial, smoky atmosphere and authentic decor make it a great place to while away an afternoon. It's worth stopping by just to see. Spui 18–20. © 020/420-4420. Tram: 1, 2, or 5 to Spui.

In de Wildeman Tucked away in a medieval alley, this wood-paneled *bier-proeflokaal* (beer-tasting house) dates from 1690. The tiled floor and rows of bottles and jars behind the counters are remnants of earlier days, when it functioned as a distillery. Today, it serves 17 draft and 200 bottled beers from around the world. It's a laid-back atmosphere, with mostly hard-drinking but very friendly locals ranging from 30- to 50-something. There's a separate room for nonsmokers. Kolksteeg 3 (off Nieuwezijds Voorburgwal). © 020/638-2348. www.indewildeman.nl. Tram: 1, 2, 5, 13, or 17 to Nieuwezijds Kolk.

't Loosje This is a friendly place in the up-and-coming Nieuwmarkt area, popular with students, artists—and guidebook writers. It was built around 1900 and was originally used as a waiting room for the horse-drawn tram. The walls are still ornamented with tiles from that period and a painting of the South Holland Beer Brewery. There are lots of beers on tap. Nieuwmarkt 32–34. © 020/627-2635. Metro: Nieuwmarkt.

't Smalle ★ For an authentic brown cafe experience—though it opened only in 1978—stop by this place, which in 1786, Pieter Hoppe used as a warehouse and distillery for his Hoppe *jenever* and as a *proeflokaal* (tasting house). The air is invariably thick with cigar smoke, *jenever* vapor, and animated conversation. You're unlikely to find a free seat, but you can escape the crush out on the canalside terrace, a perfect place to watch bikes and boats going by. Egelantiersgracht 12 (at Prinsengracht). ℂ 020/623-9617. Tram: 13, 14, or 17 to Westermarkt.

TASTING HOUSES

There are only three differences between a brown cafe and a *proeflokaal,* or tasting house: what you drink, how you drink it, and who owns the place. A *proeflokaal'*s decor will still be basically brown and typically Old Dutch—and its age may be even more impressive than that of its beer-swilling neighbors—but in a tasting house, you traditionally order *jenever* (Dutch gin, taken "neat," without ice) or another product of the distillery that owns the place. Then, to drink your libation, custom decrees that you lean over the bar with your hands behind your back to take the first sip from your full-to-the-brim *borreltje* (small drinking glass).

Brouwerij 't IJ ★★   In addition to the usual features, this slightly down-at-the-heels *proeflokaal* has a small brewery and a fascinating location—it's in the De Gooyer windmill in the city's old harbor area. You can take guided tours of the beer-making facilities (Fri at 4pm), then taste the brewery's Pilzen or Mug Bitter brews, or the slightly stronger Pasij or Zatte brews. Columbus, a hearty wheat beer that's reddish, flavorful, and fierce (almost 10% alcohol by volume), is the new brew of choice among many Amsterdam barflies. Funenkade 7 (at Sarphatistraat). ℂ 020/320-1768. www.brouwerijhetij.nl. Tram: 10 to Hoogte Kadijk.

De Admiraal   This tasting house has a small and pleasant outdoor cafe patio. Inside, sofas and big cozy armchairs make things comfortable, as do 15 different *jenevers* and 55 liqueurs, plus a fair Dutch dinner-and-snacks menu. Herengracht 319 (along the canal near Oude Spiegelstraat). ℂ 020/625-4334. Tram: 1, 2, or 5 to Spui.

De Dokter   This antiques-filled tasting house is near Spui, the Student Quarter's main square. Ask to sample the homemade *boeren jongens* and *boeren meisjes,* the brandied fruits—raisins and apricots—that serve as the traditional introduction to "spirits" for Dutch *jongen* and *meisjes*—boys and girls. Rozenboomsteeg 4 (off Spui). ℂ 020/626-4427. www.cafe-de-dokter.nl. Tram: 1, 2, 4, 5, 9, 14, 16, 24, or 25 to Spui.

De Drie Fleschjes   Not much has changed in this tidy tasting house ("The Three Little Bottles") since its 1650 opening, except that in 1816, Heindrik Bootz liqueurs took over. Fifty-two wooden casks along the wall face the bar. It's open Monday to Saturday from noon to 8:30pm, Sunday from 3 to 8pm. Gravenstraat 18 (off the Dam, behind the Nieuwe Kerk). ℂ 020/624-8443. Tram: 1, 2, 4, 9, 14, 16, 24, or 25 to the Dam.

De Ooievaar   This tiny place, Holland's smallest *proeflokaal,* dispenses *jenevers* and Oudhollandse liqueurs. It's a pleasant place, with a bright bar area to offset the brown walls and wooden casks. Sint Olofspoort 1 (at Zeedijk). ℂ 020/625-7360. Tram: 1, 2, 4, 5, 9, 13, 16, 17, 24, 25, or 26 to Centraal Station.

In 't Aepjen   An old sailor's tavern near the waterfront, this small traditional Dutch bar is housed in one of Amsterdam's two surviving timber buildings, which dates from 1550. The "ape" of the name refers to images of monkeys in the tap room. Zeedijk 1 (at Prins Hendrikkade). ℂ 020/626-8401. Tram: 1, 2, 4, 5, 9, 13, 16, 17, 24, 25, or 26 to Centraal Station.

Great Dutch Drinks

The Dutch are famous for their gin, or *jenever,* and their beer. The former is a fiery, colorless liquid served ice-cold and drunk "neat"—it's not a mixer. You can get flavored *jenever*—from berry to lemon—and just as with Dutch cheese, you can get **oude** or **jonge** (old or young) *jenever*—every bar has a wide selection on its shelves. But while cheese gets harder and sharper with age, *jenever* grows smooth and soft; *jonge* is less sweet and creamy than *oude*. All are known for their delayed-action effectiveness, so beware if you don't feel it right away.

As for **beer,** you can get regular **Heineken, Grolsch,** or **Amstel**—called *pils* in Amsterdam, or you can try something different as you make the rounds. I happen to like the *witte* (white) beer, which is sweeter than *pils:* Belgian **Hoegaarden** is a good example. On the opposite end of the spectrum are the Belgian dark beers, like **De Koninck** or **Duvel.** Belgian beers are quite popular in Holland and are, in general, better made and more artisanal than the native brews.

Wynand Fockink ★ (Finds) Don't waste your breath—regulars here know all about the English pronunciation bomb hidden in the Dutch name. This popular old-world *proeflokaal,* tucked away in a quiet alleyway off brash Damstraat, dates from 1679. Aficionados of the 50 varieties of Dutch *jenever* and 70 traditional liqueurs on hand often have to maneuver for elbowroom to raise their glasses. One of the wow-worthy attractions here is the collection of liqueur bottles on which are painted portraits of every Amsterdam mayor since 1591. It's open daily from 3 to 9pm. The attached *lunchlokaal* is, as its name implies, open for lunch. Pijlsteeg 31 (off the Dam). © 020/639-2695. www.wynand-fockink.nl. Tram: 4, 9, 14, 16, 24, or 25 to the Dam.

MODERN CAFES

Amsterdam has many contemporary cafes that are neither brown cafes nor friendly watering holes (though many examples in both categories are acceptably trendy). You may hear some contemporary cafes described as "white cafes," as distinct from brown cafes. You may also hear talk of the "coke-trail circuit," though that's a bit passé nowadays. Besides the trendy cafes listed below, you might want to check out some of Amsterdam's "Grand Cafes" reviewed in chapter 6: **De Jaren, Café Luxembourg, De Balie,** and **Grand Café l'Opera.**

bubbles&wines This fancy champagne and wine bar (think subdued lighting, dark wood surfaces, and red tones) serves an extensive roster of champagne and wine labels, along with light snacks. It's just a few minutes' walk from the Dam. Nes 37 (at Pieter Jacobszstraat). © 020/422-3318. www.bubblesandwines.com. Tram: 4, 9, 14, 16, 24, or 25 to the Dam.

Café Dante This is art-gallery chic. The owners cover the walls with a different modern art exhibit every month. Feel free to wander in and around. Spuistraat 320 (at Spui). © 020/638-8839. Tram: 1, 2, or 5 to Spui.

Smoking Coffeeshops

Amsterdam's reputation as a wild party town is in part a result of its tolerance toward cannabis. Yet the practice is technically illegal and only just tolerated. Local producers are allowed to operate so long as they don't go in for large-scale production. Individuals are allowed to be in possession of up to 30 grams (about 1 oz.) for personal use, but can only purchase 5 grams (about $1/6$ oz.) at a time. "Coffeeshops" in Amsterdam are places where a customer can purchase marijuana or hashish. They are licensed and controlled and provide a place where patrons can sit and smoke all day if they so choose; they are not allowed to sell alcohol, and only some serve food (usually light snacks)—but the coffee is not bad. Warmoesstraat, on the edge of the Red Light District, is lined with coffeeshops, making it a prime spot for coffeeshop crawls by bands of young tourists (they're usually dazed by the end of the evening, as you can imagine, so things are quite mellow).

Some notable coffeeshops: the **Rookies**, Korte Leidsedwarsstraat 145–147 (© **020/694-2353;** www.rookies.nl); friendly **Sheeba**, Warmoesstraat 73 (© **020/512-3127**); **Borderline**, Amstelstraat 37 (© **020/622-0540**); and the brash **Bulldog Palace**, Leidseplein 15 (© **020/627-1908;** www.bulldog.nl). Like the John Travolta character Vincent Vega in *Pulp Fiction*, you'll find it's mostly fellow tourists you'll be gazing at through the fug of bitter-smelling smoke in these places.

Toker's tip: Don't buy on the street. You stand a fair chance of being ripped off, the quality will be questionable, and there may be unpleasant additives.

Café Schiller ★   A bright glassed-in terrace on the square and a finely carved Art Deco interior make a nice backdrop for the friendly, laid-back atmosphere, good food, and lively crowd of artistic and literary types on offer here. Rembrandtplein 36. © 020/624-9864. Tram: 4, 9, or 14 to Rembrandtplein.

Chocolate Bar ★   The hippest bar in the Pijp also serves up delicious light meals. DJs spin great music on the weekends, and there's a terrace for when the weather's fine. Eerste Van der Helststraat 62A (at Govert Flinckstraat). © 020/675-7672. www.chocolate-bar.nl. Tram: 16 or 24 to Albert Cuypstraat.

18twintig ★★   Soft chairs, long banquettes, and chandeliers draw a hip, youthful crowd to "18twenty," in the Pijp district, to sip mojitos and other cocktails, graze on plates of tempura, and dance to DJs on Friday and Saturday nights. Ferdinand Bolstraat 18–20 (at Marie Heinekenplein). © 020/470-0651. www.18twintig.nl. Tram: 16, 24, or 25 to Stadhouderskade.

Frascati   Frascati belongs to a category similar to Schiller's (see above), except that in this case, the café's good looks have a theatrical bent. The surrounding neighborhood is rife with alternative theater, and Frascati is a major player in this scene. Nes 59 (behind Rokin). © 020/624-1324. www.theaterfrascati.nl. Tram: 4, 9, 14, 16, 24, or 25 to Spui.

Impressions

I just wanna get, like, stoned out of my head all day.
—Young American, overheard entering a coffeeshop

Helden ★   A young well-heeled crowd sinks into the sofas and sips martinis and mojitos over soft music at this trendy place in the Pijp district. The food's good, too, and there's a pleasant summer terrace where you can lounge alfresco. Eerste Van der Helststraat 42 (at Quellijnstraat). © 020/673-3332. www.helden.nu. Tram: 16 or 24 to Stadhouderskade.

Kanis en Meiland   On a redeveloped island named KNSM Eiland in the old Eastern Docks Area, this cafe takes its moniker from a clever play on the islet's name. Equally inventive is a time-warp design that has you stepping from 1990s functional urban architecture on the outside into a traditional brown cafe interior. The illusion is genuine enough that K&M has become a near-classic on the city's cafe roster and a legend in its own lunchtime for freshly made snacks. Levantkade 127. © 020/418-2439. www.kanisen meiland.nl. Bus: 32 to Levantkade.

Lux   Although the Leidseplein area is quite touristy, laid-back Lux draws in a healthy dose of locals with its chic attitude. Sit on the upper level to enjoy a sweeping view of the place. Marnixstraat 403 (at Leidseplein). © 020/422-1412. Tram: 1, 2, 5, 7, or 10 to Leidseplein.

Seymour Likely   Woe unto you if you enter here wearing out-of-date duds. And it's no use wailing that they were the latest and hippest thing only yesterday—that's the whole point. The lips of all those beautiful young things inside that aren't on a glass, or each other, will curl into a sneer. Nieuwezijds Voorburgwal 250 (near Amsterdam Historical Museum). © 020/627-1427. Tram: 1, 2, 5, 13, or 17 to Nieuwezijds Voorburgwal.

VakZuid ★   Located inside the Olympic Stadium used for the 1928 Games, this chic cocktail bar/lounge/restaurant/club evokes the interior design of that period in an updated form, and has a large canalside terrace. Olympisch Stadion 35 (at Stadionplein in Amsterdam-Zuid). © 020/570-8400. www.vakzuid.nl. Tram: 16 or 24 to Stadionplein.

ENGLISH & IRISH PUBS

Mulligans Irish Music Bar   Both the Irish music and *craic* (pronounced "crack," and meaning fast wit and good conversation, not that other stuff) at Mulligans have been lively since its 1988 opening. Bring an instrument and you may be allowed to play. Amstel 100 (off Rembrandtplein). © 020/622-1330. www.mulligans.nl. Tram: 4, 9, or 14 to Rembrandtplein.

O'Donnell's   A happy, boisterous place where the Guinness is good and the bartenders are Irish and friendly, this neighborhood Irish pub pulls in many of the young, up-and-coming professionals who live in the Pijp, not least for its down-to-earth food—Guinness stew, fish and chips, grilled lamb chops—and busy sidewalk terrace. Ferdinand Bolstraat 5 (at Marie Heinekenplein). © 020/676-7786. Tram: 16 or 24 to Stadhouderskade.

Three Sisters Grand Pub   There's an English-style pub on the first floor, with lots of snug corners for conversation about Shakespeare or Manchester United over pints of warm ale (they have cold beers too), and a New York steakhouse upstairs. Leidseplein 2. © 020/428-0428. Tram: 1, 2, 5, 7, or 10 to Leidseplein.

The Jordaan is Amsterdam's iconoclastic working-class district. It has suffered from the depredations of gentrifiers, demolition experts, and cleaner-uppers, but still retains its distinctive style and preoccupation with itself. Cafes here are old-style, colorful, and working class (a bit like London's Cockney pubs). You might even take in a singsong of incredibly schmaltzy old Dutch songs about stolen kisses behind the windmill.

Café Nol   A bit younger and cooler than your average Jordaan cafe, but not by much, this place is decked out with crystal chandeliers, mirrors, a red carpet, and hanging potted plants. It caters to a mix of young, cool Jordaaners and old-timers who have lived in the neighborhood for ages. Young folks love to sing here. Westerstraat 109 (near Noordermarkt). ✆ 020/624-5380. www.cafenolamsterdam.nl. Tram: 3 or 10 to Marnixplein.

Café Rooie Nellis   The kitschy decor here has to be seen to be believed—and even then you might not. The same family has owned this place for generations; it's real down-home Jordaan. Laurierstraat 101 (off Prinsengracht). ✆ 020/624-4167. Tram: 13, 14, or 17 to Westermarkt.

De Twee Zwaantjes   The two swans of the cafe's name would find it hard to spread their wings here. But the little place's intimacy means you're brought face-to-face with the Jordaanese in all their glory. On some evenings, they'll break into traditional Dutch song. Prinsengracht 114 (at Egelantiersgracht). ✆ 020/625-2729. www.detweezwaantjes.nl. Tram: 13, 14, or 17 to Westermarkt.

COCKTAILS WITH A VIEW

Twenty Third   Even a low-rise city like Amsterdam has a high-rise hotel with a roof-top cocktail lounge. This one is located on the 23rd floor. The drink prices are a little higher than what you'd find at ground level, but the view is worth the cost. From a comfortable vantage point in Amsterdam South, the big picture windows provide a sweeping panorama of the city. In the Hotel Okura Amsterdam, Ferdinand Bolstraat 175. ✆ 020/678-7111. www.okura.nl. Tram: 25 to Ferdinand Bolstraat.

THE GAY & LESBIAN SCENE

Amsterdam's gay scene is strong, and there is no lack of gay bars and nightspots. Below are listings of some of the most popular spots for gay men. For lesbians, the scene is a little more difficult to uncover. Places that are hot now might not be later, so contact **COC,** Rozenstraat 14 (✆ 020/626-3087; www.cocamsterdam.nl; tram: 13, 14, or 17), the Organization of Homosexuals in the Netherlands. The office and telephone lines operate daily from 10am to 5pm. More information is available from the **Gay and Lesbian Switchboard** (✆ 020/623-6565). *Gay News Amsterdam,* a monthly newspaper in English, is available for free in gay establishments throughout Amsterdam.

Most of the city's gay bars and other venues are in well-defined areas. For frivolous, old-style camp, look along the Amstel near **Muntplein** and on **Halvemaansteeg.** The trendier places are along **Reguliersdwarsstraat.** Casual locals head for **Kerkstraat,** on both sides of Leidsestraat. Lesbian bars are more thinly spread. There are few of them, but there are no neighborhoods or streets that specialize in lesbian bars. Amstel and Amstelstraat at Rembrandtplein, the Jordaan, and to a limited extent the edge of the Red Light District are the likeliest zones to check out.

Amstel FiftyFour   One of Amsterdam's most venerable gay bars, on gay-friendly Amstel, has had a makeover, changing it from a cozily old-fashioned place to one which, if not exactly hip, has a definite sense of style. It remains engagingly convivial, and the regulars will occasionally break into song. Amstel 54 (behind Rembrandtplein). ℂ 020/623-4254. www.amstelfiftyfour.nl. Tram: 4, 9, or 14 to Rembrandtplein.

Arc ★★   Arc, one of the most attractive and trendy bars in the city, pulls in both gays and straights. The friendly, 20- and 30-something mixed crowd is very hip. Many opt to lounge the night away here and indulge in the delicious appetizer platters. Reguliersdwarsstraat 44 (a block behind the Flower Market). ℂ 020/689-7070. www.bararc.com. Tram: 1, 2, or 5 to Koningsplein.

Soho   Open until 4am on weekends (3am weekdays), this place doesn't get going until late (after 11pm) and is the city's quintessential gay pub. Reguliersdwarsstraat 36 (behind the Flower Market). ℂ 020/422-3312. www.pubsoho.eu. Tram: 1, 2, or 5 to Koningsplein.

Getto   This bar and restaurant attracts an equal mix of boys and girls with its hip interior and such events as "Club Fu" karaoke (first Mon of each month) and bingo (every Thurs). An eclectic dinner menu offers food from around the world, whether vegetarian or Cajun crocodile steak, and the kitchen stays open until 11pm. Open Wednesday, Thursday, and Sunday from 5pm to 1am, Friday and Saturday from 5pm to 2am. Warmoesstraat 51 (Red Light District). ℂ 020/421-5151. www.getto.nl. Tram: 1, 2, 4, 5, 9, 13, 14, 16, 17, 24, or 25 to Centraal Station.

Saarein   Once a female-only enclave with a feisty atmosphere, this bar is now open to both genders and has livened up a bit. Attractions include pool, darts, and pinball. The change in atmosphere has included the addition of food, with a well-priced Continental dinner menu served from 6 to 9:30pm. Open Sunday to Thursday from 5pm to 1am, Friday and Saturday from 5pm to 2am. Elandstraat 119 (Jordaan). ℂ 020/623-4901. www.saarein.nl. Tram: 7, 10, or 17 to Marnixstraat.

Spijker   This long-standing neighborhood bar attracts a casual crowd that extends a friendly welcome to visitors. The pinball machine and pool table are social focal points, and side-by-side video screens broadcast an amusing juxtaposition of cartoons and erotica. Lively staffers keep the atmosphere relaxed with a varied selection of music and stiff drinks. Happy "hour" draws crowds in daily from 5 to 7pm. Open Sunday to Thursday from 1pm to 1am, Friday and Saturday from 1pm to 3am. Kerkstraat 4 (corner with Leidsegracht). ℂ 020/620-5919. www.spijkerbar.nl. Tram: 1, 2, or 5 to Prinsengracht.

Vive-la-Vie   This lesbian bar celebrated its 20th anniversary in 2000. It attracts a young, lively crowd before club-hopping time, and lipstick isn't forbidden. The sidewalk terrace offers great summertime relaxation and a fine view of the flocks of tourists in

---

For Women Only

Amsterdam is very much a center of women's activism, and there are many women's centers around the city. **Vrouwenhuis (Women's House)**, at Nieuwe Herengracht 95 (ℂ 020/625-2066), has a cafe that opens on Wednesday from noon to 5pm and Thursday from noon to 9pm.

neighboring Rembrandtplein. Open Sunday to Thursday from 2:30pm to 1am, Friday and Saturday from 3pm to 3am. Amstelstraat 7 (off Rembrandtplein). ✆ 020/624-0114. www. vivelavie.net. Tram: 4, 9, or 14 to Rembrandtplein.

Web Behind its corrugated metal facade, this popular after-work drinks venue has a raunchy atmosphere and plenty of space to walk. Tuesday is "beer bust" (an intense beer-drinking session) and Wednesday is prize-draw night. On Sunday evening at 7pm, line up for the food buffet. Open Sunday to Thursday from 2pm to 1am, Friday and Saturday from 2pm to 2am. St. Jakobsstraat 6 (at Nieuwendijk). ✆ 020/623-6758. Tram: 1, 2, 5, 13, or 17 to Nieuwezijds Kolk.

Clubs
Club Exit ★ On a street that has no shortage of gay venues, Exit stands out for having some of the best DJs in town, who spin up a pounding mix of techno, progressive house, and hip-hop for a hot-to-trot 20s and up crowd that runs from regular guys to fashion queens. There's a large dark room and live strip shows, to go along with happy house and other music. Reguliersdwarsstraat 42 (behind the Flower Market). ✆ 020/638-5700. www. clubexit.eu. Cover 10€–15€ ($16–$24). Tram: 1, 2, or 5 to Koningsplein.

Cockring This none-too-subtly named gay disco is the most popular in town. On the dance floor, DJs lay down no-nonsense, hard-core, high-decibel dance and techno music. More relaxed beats in the sociable upstairs bar make for a welcome break. Live shows with male strippers keep things hot. Warmoesstraat 96 (Red Light District). ✆ 020/623-9604. www.clubcockring.com. Cover 6€–12€ ($9.60–$19). Tram: 4, 9, 14, 16, 24, or 25 to the Dam.

4 THE RED LIGHT DISTRICT

Prostitution is legal in the Netherlands, and in Amsterdam, most of it is concentrated in the Red Light District. Even if you don't want to play, this is a place you may want to see at night, when the red lights reflect from the canals' inky surfaces. Lots of visitors come here out of curiosity or just for fun. There's no problem with wandering around, and you don't need to worry much about crime as long as you stick to busier streets—and keep an eye out for pickpockets. Visiting women going around in groups of two or more won't be noticed any more than anyone else, but a single female might be subject to misrepresentation. See also "Offbeat & Alternative Amsterdam," in chapter 7, and "Walking Tour 2: The Old Center," in chapter 8, both of which have sections that cover the Red Light District as a daytime attraction.

The Red Light District, known in Dutch as *Rosse Buurt,* isn't very big. The easiest way in is on **Damstraat,** beside the Krasnapolsky Hotel on the Dam. Then stick to the main

Impressions

A night on the town in the world's tawdriest city . . . smoking coffeehouses, peep shows, and live sex shows in Amsterdam (if your sensibilities can handle it).
—Online promo for *Secrets of the Untourist*, 2007

drag on **Oudezijds Voorburgwal,** as far north as the **Oude Kerk,** the venerable Old Church, which stands watch over this passable representation of Sodom and Gomorrah. If you don't mind the weird-looking, sad-sack males and the heroin whores hanging around on the bridges, you can go farther in to the parallel canal, **Oudezijds Achterburgwal,** and to **Nieuwmarkt**'s cluster of good bars and Chinese restaurants.

In recent years, as part of a continuing effort to clean up the "unsavory" side of Amsterdam, the mayor forced the closure of a third of the red-light windows and bought up properties to be rented as fashion boutiques and other upscale small businesses. Some of the more raucous sex clubs may also be shuttered.

Despite this effort, "ladies of ill repute" still populate the many red-fringed window parlors; they're minimally dressed, and tap (or pound) on the windows as potential customers go by. Then there are peep-show joints with private cabins, dark and noisy bars, theaters offering a popular form of performance art, bookstores filled with the illustrated works of specialists in a wide range of interpersonal relationships, video libraries, and dedicated apparel and appliance stores.

For safety's sake, stick to the main streets and the crowds. It's asking for trouble to go off on your own at night down some of those narrow, dark side streets and connecting lanes between the canals—some are so narrow you literally have to squeeze past other people, and on slow days, hookers come out from behind their windows to turn some of that squeezing into a marketing move. The main streets are usually busy and brightly lit (what with all those red lights and neon signs) and most clubs have security, since they have a vested interest in not having their customers bothered. Remember, though, that the industries active here attract less savory types, including muggers, pickpockets, drug dealers, junkies, street prostitutes, pimps, and weird folks in general. But there are also plenty of tour groups who seem to be having a great time, judging by all the laughing they do as they go around.

Without going into detail about the services on offer in the Red Light District, here are a couple of places that have shown an enduring popularity with visitors.

Bananenbar Bananas are an essential prop in the nightly drama here, and audience participation is encouraged. Needless to say, the show is mainly of interest to red-blooded males on temporary vegetarian diets. Let your sense of taste be your guide. Oudezijds Achterburgwal 37. ✆ **020/622-4670.** www.janot.com. Tram: 1, 2, 4, 5, 9, 13, 16, 17, 24, or 25 to Centraal Station.

Casa Rosso In its own words, Casa Rosso puts on "one of the most superior erotic shows in the world, with a tremendous choreography and a high-level cast." Not everyone would describe it in those exact words, perhaps, but this is the local market leader in live shows. Oudezijds Achterburgwal 106–108. ✆ **020/627-8943.** www.janot.com. Tram: 4, 9, 14, 16, 24, or 25 to the Dam.

5 MORE EVENING ENTERTAINMENT

EVENING CANAL-BOAT TOURS

Even if you took a daytime canal-boat tour, come back for cocktails. Special candlelit wine-and-cheese cruises operate nightly year-round, except for December 31. Libations and nibbles are served as you glide through the canal district, which is quiet and calm at night. It's a leisurely, convivial, and romantic way to spend an Amsterdam evening. Among the recommended operators is **Rederij Lovers** (✆ **020/530-1090;** www.lovers. nl). Boats depart from the tour-boat piers on Prins Hendrikkade, opposite Centraal Station. The 2-hour cruises cost about 22€ ($35). Reservations are required.

Then there's the Saturday evening Jazz Cruise, by **Canal Bus** (✆ **020/623-9886;** www.canal.nl). As you cruise through the romantically lit canals, a live band entertains you with $1^1/_2$ hours of jazz. While you stomp, you can slurp and chomp on unlimited amounts of wine, beer, soft drinks, Dutch cheese, and nuts. The Jazz Cruise departs from the Canal Bus dock on Singelgracht, at Stadhouderskade (Tram: 7 or 10), opposite the Rijksmuseum, April to November, Saturday at 8 and 10pm. Reservations are required, and tickets are 28€ ($45).

MOVIES

In Amsterdam, you'll find a dozen or more first-run features, most of them Hollywood's finest, in English with Dutch subtitles. You can find showtimes in various publications available free from movie theaters—in Dutch, a movie theater is called a *bioscoop*—as well as hotels and cafes. Most of the information is in Dutch, but the movie titles and screening times are hard to get wrong. Admission prices are around 8€ ($13), depending on the day, time, and movie, and you can reserve advance tickets for a small charge. A string of commercials and trailers always precedes the main feature (except at art-house cinemas).

Note: If all of a sudden there's a break in the film, which happens at some movie theaters, don't fret; this is a *pauze* and it lasts about 15 minutes. It can be incredibly annoying, especially as it seems always to come during an arresting on-screen moment, but at least it gives you time to visit the toilet, buy an ice cream, or grab a smoke.

Multiplexes are to be found around Leidseplein, on Kleine-Gartmanplantsoen, Marnixstraat, and Lijnbaansgracht; around Rembrandtplein, on Vijzelstraat and Reguliersbreestraat; and in Amsterdam-Zuidoost on ArenA Boulevard.

Movie Theaters of Note

De Balie   This all-purpose cultural center has an eclectic calendar of workshops, lectures, and film festivals. You can view controversial and award-winning features and documentaries and lots of interesting movies from around the world that don't make it to mainstream theaters. Kleine-Gartmanplantsoen 10 (at Leidseplein). ✆ **020/553-5151.** www. debalie.nl. Tram: 1, 2, 5, 7, or 10 to Leidseplein.

Filmmuseum ★   Much more than just a museum, this striking venue inside the Vondelpark has two theaters (one of them with an Art Deco interior) that schedule interesting retrospectives and film festivals. *Note:* In 2010, the Filmmuseum is due to move to a brand-new facility in Amsterdam-Noord, on the north shore of the IJ waterway. Vondelpark 3 (at Vondelstraat). ✆ **020/589-1400.** www.filmmuseum.nl. Tram: 1 to Eerste Constantijn Huygensstraat; 3 or 12 to Overtoom.

Through a Glass, Clearly

One of the city's simplest, and cheapest, evening activities is walking along the canals and looking into the houses as you pass. You may think I'm making the shocking suggestion that you window-peep, but in Amsterdam, it's not peeping. The Dutch take great pride in their homes and keep their curtains open in the evening because they want you to see how tidy and *gezellig* (cozy, homey, warm, and inviting) their living quarters are. This doesn't mean you should linger on the sidewalk gawking, but a leisurely peek inside at the decor is okay.

Theater Tuschinski ★★   This theater is well worth a visit for its extravagant, Art Deco style from 1921. On its upper balconies, you'll sit on plush chairs and can sip champagne during the flick. Reguliersbreestraat 26–34. (© **0900/1458.** www.tuschinski.nl. Tram: 4, 9, or 14 to Rembrandtplein.

Small Art-House & Alternative Theaters

Lesser-known films are often screened at **De Uitkijk,** Prinsengracht 452 (© **020/623-7460;** www.uitkijk.nl; tram: 1, 2, or 5); **Het Ketelhuis,** Westergasfabriek, Harlemmerweg 8–10 (© **020/488-7788;** www.ketelhuis.nl; bus: 18 or 22); **Kriterion,** Roetersstraat 170 (© **020/623-1708;** www.kriterion.nl; tram: 7 or 10); **Melkweg Cinema,** Lijnbaansgracht 234A (© **020/531-8181;** www.melkweg.nl; tram: 1, 2, 5, 7, or 10); **Rialto,** Ceintuurbaan 338 (© **020/676-8700;** www.rialtofilm.nl; tram: 3); **Smart Cinema,** Eerste Constantijn Huygensstraat 20 (© **020/427-5951;** www.smartprojectspace.net; tram: 3 or 12); and the **Movies,** Haarlemmerdijk 161 (© **020/638-6016;** www.themovies. nl; tram: 3).

AMSTERDAM'S CASINO

Holland Casino Amsterdam, in the Lido, Max Euweplein 62 (© **020/521-1111;** www. hollandcasino.com; tram: 1, 2, 5, 7, or 10), at Leidseplein, is the only legal casino in town. This place deals in European gambling, with an emphasis on roulette, baccarat, punto banco, blackjack, and others, though there are also abundant one-armed bandits, which the Dutch call "fruit machines." You need correct attire to get in (jacket and tie or turtleneck for men), and you also need to bring your passport to register at the door. The minimum age is 18. The casino is open daily (except May 4 and Dec 31) from 12:30pm to 3am. Admission is 5€ ($8). Wednesday is "ladies day," and admission is free for all female visitors.

Side Trips from Amsterdam

Amsterdam is the brightest star in a galaxy of cities and towns that together form what the Dutch call the **Randstad (Rim City),** a budding megalopolis that stretches from Amsterdam to Rotterdam and contains two-thirds of the country's 16 million inhabitants.

Both **Noord-Holland (North Holland)** province, to which Amsterdam belongs, and neighboring **Zuid-Holland (South Holland)** province afford a variety of options for a day outside the city. It won't be a day in the outback, exactly, but you don't have to go far from Amsterdam to see the flat in the *polder* (the Dutch word for land reclaimed from water) landscape, with its tulips, windmills, rivers, and dikes, where Rembrandt strolled sketchbook in hand. You can climb tall towers, visit cheese markets and multifarious museums, ride a steam train, tour the world's largest harbor, and see giant locks and tiny canals.

On your first day of touring, I suggest you travel from Amsterdam to **Haarlem,** and maybe squeeze into the same day a visit to the North Sea coast at nearby **Zandvoort,** which has a fine beach and a casino. On your second day of touring, head to **Hoorn** on the IJsselmeer. If you're driving, take in **Volendam** and **Marken** along the way. From Hoorn, continue along the lakeshore to **Enkhuizen** and the **Afsluitdijk (Enclosing Dike).**

With more time, you can alternate days spent in Amsterdam with visits to, for instance, the **Bulb Fields** and **Keukenhof Gardens** when it's tulip time; **Zaanse Schans** for its windmills; **Leiden** for the Pilgrim Fathers; **Delft** for Holland's historical royal city; **The Hague** for the government seat and home-base for the royal family; and **Rotterdam** for Europe's largest and the world's second-busiest port (after Shanghai).

---

1 HAARLEM ★★

18km (11 miles) W of Amsterdam

If you have only a day to travel beyond Amsterdam, spend it in the small city of Haarlem (pop. 150,000)—it's traditionally considered the capital's little sister city, though since it was likely founded in the 10th century, it's actually older than Amsterdam. Granted municipal status by Count Willem II of Holland in 1245, it's where Frans Hals, Jacob van Ruisdael, and Pieter Saenredam lived and painted their famous portraits, landscapes, and church interiors during the same years that Rembrandt lived and worked in Amsterdam.

Some visitors even prefer to "commute" to Amsterdam from here, since Haarlem has a similar 17th-century look, but by being thoroughly provincial, prosperous, and conservative (meaning there's only a tiny red-light district here), it gets along nicely without the many hassles that accompany the capital's eccentric lifestyle. You can easily get around this quaint, quiet city of music and art on foot, and Haarlem is home to the **Frans Hals**

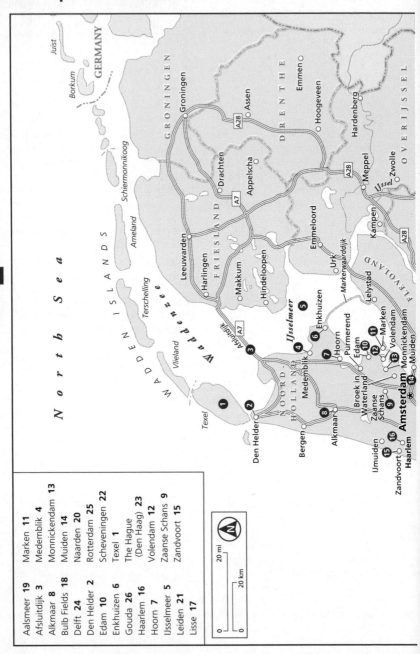

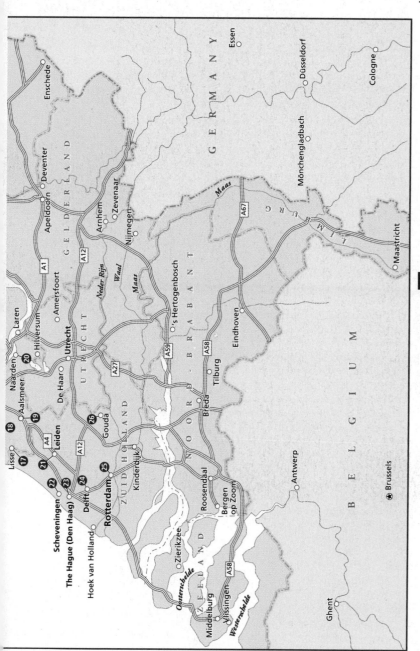

Museum (see below), one of Holland's premier art museums. In addition, it's close to the North Sea beaches and to the bulb fields, in the heart of an area dotted with elegant manors and picturesque villages.

ESSENTIALS

GETTING THERE Trains depart at least every half-hour from Amsterdam Centraal Station for Haarlem; the trip takes 15 minutes. A round-trip ticket is 6.40€ ($10). Buses depart every 15 minutes or so from outside Centraal Station, but they take longer than the train. By car from Amsterdam, take N5 and A5.

VISITOR INFORMATION VVV Haarlem, Stationsplein 1, 2011 LR Haarlem (© 0900/616-1600; fax 023/534-0537; www.vvvzk.nl) is just outside the rail station. The office is open April to September, Monday to Friday from 9am to 5:30pm and Saturday from 10am to 4pm; October to March, Monday to Friday from 9:30am to 5pm and Saturday from 10am to 3pm.

WHAT TO SEE & DO

The historic center is a 5- to 10-minute walk from the graceful 1908 Art Nouveau rail station (with decorative painted tiles and a fine restaurant), most of it on pedestrian-only shopping streets. First-time visitors generally head straight to the **Grote Markt ★★**, the central market square. Most points of interest in Haarlem are within easy walking distance of the Grote Markt. The monumental buildings, dating from the 15th to the 19th centuries, around the tree-lined square are a visual minicourse in the development of Dutch architecture. Here stands Haarlem's 14th-century **Stadhuis (Town Hall),** a former hunting lodge which Holland's counts rebuilt in the 17th century. It contains a magnificent 1629 tapestry, *Crusades,* by Josef Thienpont of Oudenaarde.

Adjacent to the Grote Markt, the splendid **Sint-Bavokerk (St. Bavo's Church) ★**, Oude Groenmarkt 23 (© 023/553-2040; www.bavo.nl), also known as the Grote Kerk (Great Church), soars skyward. Finished in 1520 after a relatively short building period, it has a rare unity of structure and proportion. The interior is light and airy, with whitewashed walls and sandstone pillars. Look for painter **Frans Hals**'s **tombstone** and for a **cannonball** that's been embedded in the wall ever since it came flying through a window during the Spanish siege in 1572 to 1573. The elegant wooden tower is covered with lead sheets and adorned with gilt spheres.

Mozart (at just 10 years old), Handel, Mendelssohn, Schubert, and Liszt all visited Haarlem to play the church's magnificent, soaring **Christian Müller Organ** (1738). It has 5,068 pipes and is nearly 30m (98 ft.) tall, and when it's going, it can blow your socks off. Jan van Logteren crafted its woodwork. Enjoy the organ in a free recital Tuesday at 8:15pm from May to October; in July and August there's an additional free recital on Thursday at 3pm. From May to October, church services using the organ take place Sunday at 10am; June to October there's an additional 7pm Vespers and Cantata service. St. Bavo's is open Monday to Saturday from 10am to 4pm. Admission is 2€ ($3.20) for adults, and 1.25€ ($2) for children ages 12 to 16, and free for children 11 and under.

Haarlem's finest attraction is the **Frans Hals Museum ★★**, Groot Heiligland 62 (© 023/511-5775; www.franshalsmuseum.com), housed in galleries that were the rooms of handsome gabled cottages of the Oudemannenhuis (1608), an almshouse for retired gentlemen, arranged around a courtyard garden. The famous paintings by Antwerp-born Frans Hals (ca. 1580–1686) and other Haarlem School masters hang in settings that look like the 17th-century houses they were intended to adorn. Hals,

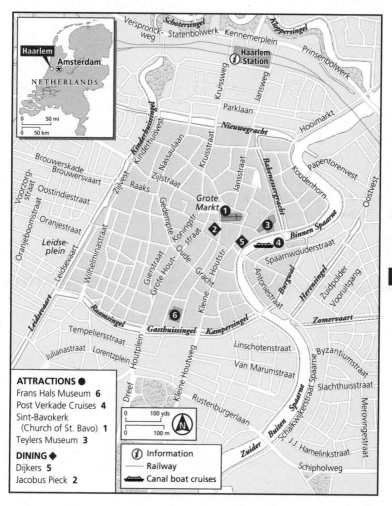

Haarlem

Amsterdam

NETHERLANDS

0   50 mi
0   50 km

Verspronck-weg Schotersingel Statenbolwerk Kennemerplein Koppersingel

Haarlem Station Prinsenbolwerk

Kruisweg Jansweg

Parklaan

Nieuwegracht Hooimarkt

Kinderhuissingel Kinderhuisvest Nassaulaan Kruisstraat Jansstraat Bakenessergracht Papentorenvest Koudenhorn Oostvest

Brouwerskade Brouwersvaart Zijlvest Raaks Zijlstraat

Voorzorg-straat Oostindiestraat Oranjeboomstraat Oranjestraat

Leidse-plein Wilhelminastraat Gedempte Oude Gracht Koningstr.

Grote Markt ❶ ❷ ❸ Binnen Spaarne

❺ ❹ Spaarnwouderstraat

Leidsevaart Leidsevaart Raamsingel Gierstraat Grote Hout-straat Kleine Houtstr. Antoniestraat Burgwal Herensingel Zuidpolder Vooruitgang

Tempeliersstraat Gasthuissingel Kampersingel Zomervaart

Julianastraat Lorentzplein Houtplein Linschotenstraat Byzantiumstraat Slachthuisstraat Merovingenstraat

Van Marumstraat

Dreef Kleine Houtweg Rustenburgerlaan Spaarne Schalkwijkerstraat Spaarne Buiten Spaarne Slachthuisstraat

0   100 yds
0   100 m
N

Zuider J.J. Hamelinkstraat Schipholweg

ATTRACTIONS ●
Frans Hals Museum **6**
Post Verkade Cruises **4**
Sint-Bavokerk
(Church of St. Bavo) **1**
Teylers Museum **3**

DINING ◆
Dijkers **5**
Jacobus Pieck **2**

ⓘ Information
— Railway
🚢 Canal boat cruises

who died here, earned his bread and butter by painting members of the local Schutters (Musketeers) Guild. Typified by his *Officers of the Militia Company of St. George* (ca. 1627), five other such works hang in the museum, along with six more Hals paintings. Other exhibits include fine collections of antique silver, porcelain, clocks, and a superb dollhouse-like piece from around 1750 that's actually an exquisitely detailed miniature replica of an Amsterdam merchant's canal house. The museum is open Tuesday to Saturday from 11am to 5pm, and Sunday and holidays from noon to 5pm; it's closed January 1 and December 25. Admission is 7.50€ ($12) for adults, 3.75€ ($6) for visitors ages 19 to 24, and free for visitors 18 and under.

From St. Bavo's, it's a short walk to Holland's oldest and perhaps most unusual museum, the **Teylers Museum,** Spaarne 16 (© **023/531-9010;** www.teylersmuseum. nl). Its diverse collection encompasses drawings by Michelangelo, Raphael, and Rembrandt; fossils, minerals, and skeletons; physics instruments; and an odd assortment of inventions, including the world's largest electrostatic generator (1784) and a 19th-century radarscope. The museum is open Tuesday to Saturday from 10am to 5pm, and Sunday and holidays from noon to 5pm; it's closed January 1 and December 25. Admission is 7€ ($11) for adults, 2€ ($3.20) for children ages 6 to 18, and free for children 5 and under.

Organized Tours

An ideal way to view Haarlem is by canal tour-boat. Tours are operated by **Post Verkade Cruises** (© **023/535-7723;** www.postverkadecruises.nl), from the Spaarne River dock next to the Gravenstenenbrug, a handsome lift bridge. April to October, Tuesday to Sunday, boats depart hourly from noon to 4pm on a 45-minute cruise. Tickets are 9.50€ ($15) for adults, 4.50€ ($7.20) for children ages 3 to 12, and free for children 2 and under. In addition, there are longer cruises that go outside of town, candlelight cruises, and more.

WHERE TO DINE

Dijkers INTERNATIONAL   Near the start of a short but chic shopping street a block south of the Grote Markt, this tiny restaurant, popular with locals, serves an unlikely mix of Italian and Asian dishes, from Thai green curry to lighter fare such as club and toasted sandwiches—the mozzarella and prosciutto club sandwich is an excellent choice for a quick bite at lunch. A bright, orange-toned designer-ish setting with transparent plastic chairs meshes nicely with the breezy service. On warm sunny days, a few tables are set out on the sidewalk.

Warmoesstraat 5–7 (off Oude Groenmarkt). © 023/551-1564. www.restaurantdijkers.nl. Main courses 13€–23€ ($21–$37); *dagschotel* 12€ ($19). AE, MC, V. Mon 11am–4pm; Tues–Sat 11am–4pm and 5:30–10pm.

Jacobus Pieck ★ DUTCH/INTERNATIONAL   This popular cafe-restaurant has a lovely shaded terrace in the garden for fine-weather days; inside, it's bustling and stylish. Outside or in, you get excellent food for reasonable prices and friendly, efficient service. Lunchtime features generous sandwiches and burgers, and salads that are particularly good. Main dinner courses range from pastas and Middle Eastern or Asian dishes to wholesome Dutch standards.

Warmoesstraat 18 (off Oude Groenmarkt). © 023/532-6144. www.jacobuspieck.nl. Main courses 16€–18€ ($26–$29); *dagschotel* 12€ ($19). AE, MC, V. Mon 11am–4pm; Tues–Sat 11am–4pm and 5:30–10pm.

2 ZANDVOORT

24km (15 miles) W of Amsterdam; 7km (4¹/₂ miles) W of Haarlem

If you feel like drawing a breath of fresh sea air and you don't have much time for it, do what most Amsterdammers do: Head for Zandvoort. On the North Sea coast just west of Haarlem and on the same rail line from Amsterdam, the resort is brash in summer, though it often looks forlorn in the off season.

GETTING THERE   Trains depart hourly from Amsterdam Centraal Station for Zandvoort. Transfer at Haarlem (where the Zandvoort train usually waits on the adjacent platform). During summer months, extra trains go direct from Centraal Station. In either case, the trip time is around 30 minutes, and a round-trip ticket is 8.70€ ($14). Buses depart every 30 minutes from outside Centraal Station, but they take longer than the train. By car, go via Haarlem, on N5, A5, and N200, but be ready for long traffic lines in summer.

VISITOR INFORMATION   VVV **Zandvoort,** Bakkerstraat 2B (at Kerkstraat), 2042 HK Zandvoort (© **023/571-7947;** fax 023/571-7003; www.vvvzk.nl) is opposite the bus station in the center of town. The office is open Monday to Friday from 9:30am to 12:30pm and 1:30 to 4:30pm, Saturday from 10am to 4:30pm, and Sunday from 11am to 4:30pm.

WHAT TO SEE & DO

There isn't much more to Zandvoort than its **beach,** but what a beach! In summer, this seemingly endless stretch of smooth sand is lined with dozens of temporary beach cafe-restaurants. Besides the mainstream sections, there are gay and naturist zones where the shocking sight of a clothed individual can generate considerable moral outrage. **Windsurfing** is pretty good, and Zandvoort hosts international competitions in this sport, and in **catamaran racing.** The sea—a soup of suspended sand, jellyfish, and seaweed—doesn't look inviting, but the Dutch swim in it anyway (in summer).

The Dutch Formula One Grand Prix motor race used to happen at **Circuit Park Zandvoort,** Burg van Alphenstraat 63 (© **023/574-0740**), in the north of the town. Now, the circuit hosts only smaller events. If you come on a summer weekend, you might find a Formula Three training session or a Porsche meeting underway.

Equally racy, and far less noisy, is **Holland Casino Zandvoort,** Badhuisplein 7 (© **023/574-0574;** www.hollandcasino.com), behind the seafront promenade. You'll find roulette, blackjack, punto banco, slot machines, and more. The dress code is "correct" (collar and tie for men), and minimum age is 18. You need your passport to get in. The casino is open daily (except May 4 and Dec 31) from 12:30pm to 3am. Admission is 5€ ($8); Wednesday is "ladies day," with no cover charge for females.

(Tips   **Hot Jets**

How about a jetfoil ride to the seacoast? **Connexxion Fast Flying Ferries** (© **020/ 639-2247;** www.connexxion.nl), runs a scheduled service on the Noordzeekanaal between Amsterdam and Velsen-Zuid. At the nearby seaport of IJmuiden (connected with the jetfoil dock by frequent bus service), you can view the three great locks of the **North Sea Canal,** and visit the **fish auctions** at Halkade 4, held Monday to Friday from 7 to 11am. Jetfoils depart from a dock behind Amsterdam Centraal Station, Monday to Saturday every half-hour from 7am to 9pm, and Sunday from 8:45am to 10:30pm; the trip takes 30 minutes. Round-trip tickets are 8.30€ ($13) at peak times and 7€ ($11) at off-peak times for adults, 4.85€ ($7.75) for children ages 4 to 11, and free for children 3 and under.

Find solitude amid nature by walking some of the 2,500 hectares (6,200 acres) of sand dunes, deciduous and pine forest, grassland, and small lakes in the **Nationaal Park Zuid-Kennemerland** (www.npzk.nl), north of town. Reinforced by native vegetation, these dunes play an important part in the defenses against the sea and are designated nature reserves. Stroll along pathways once used by fishermen's wives bringing their husbands' catch from the coast to market, through the woods on the landward side and westward across the dunes toward the sea. A variety of plants, some of them rare, occupy this relatively small area, and you can spot up to 230 species of birds, including rare crossbills and sea eagles. The beach is never far away.

Even in winter, it's an Amsterdam tradition to take the train to Zandvoort, stroll up and down the shore for an hour or so, then repair to one of the town's cafes, such as **Het Wapen van Zandvoort,** Gasthuisplein 10 (© 023/571-4638), and **Café Alex,** Gasthuisplein 9A (© 023/571-9205), a few blocks back from the seafront, in the heart of town.

11

3 THE IJSSELMEER ★★

Some of Holland's most popular places—**Hoorn, Edam,** and **Marken** among them—lie along this great lake's western shore. Painterly light washes through clouds, and luminous mists seem to merge water and sky. Cyclists test both speed and endurance, zipping round the 400km (250-mile) circumference in bright Lycra blurs, or plodding along on the lonesome dike-top. The IJsselmeer (pronounced *Eye*-sselmeer) hosts fleets of traditional Dutch *boter* and *skûtsje* sailing ships, fishing smacks, modern sailboats, powerboats, and canoes. Its waters are an important feeding ground for migrating and resident birds.

VOLENDAM, MARKEN ★ & MONNICKENDAM
18km (11 miles), 16km (10 miles), and 14km (9 miles) NE of Amsterdam

Volendam and Marken are combined on bus-tour itineraries from Amsterdam as a kind of packaged-Holland-to-go. Nonetheless, it's possible to have a delightful full day in the bracing air of these two lakeside communities, where a few residents (fewer all the time) may be seen going about their daily business in traditional dress. Monnickendam lies between them.

Essentials
GETTING THERE **Arriva** buses depart every 15 to 30 minutes from outside Amsterdam Centraal Station. Nos. 110, 112, 116, and 118 go to Volendam; nos. 111 and 115 go to Monnickendam; and no. 111 goes on to Marken. Trip time to Volendam is 35 minutes; to Monnickendam, 30 minutes; and to Marken, 45 minutes. The round-trip fare is around 5€ ($8).

Driving to Marken, which was once an island, you cross over a 3km-long (2-mile) causeway from Monnickendam. You then need to leave your car in a parking lot outside the village before walking through the narrow streets to the harbor.

VISITOR INFORMATION **VVV Volendam,** Zeestraat 37, 1131 ZD Volendam (© 0299/363-747; fax 0299/368-484; www.vvv-volendam.nl) is just off Julianaweg in the heart of town. The office is open mid-March to the end of October Monday to Saturday from 10am to 5pm; and November to mid-March Monday to Saturday from 10am to 3pm.

By the Side of the Zuider Zee

Only in Holland could you say, "This used to be a sea." The IJsselmeer actually was once a sea, until the Dutch decided they didn't want it to be one anymore—it was always threatening to flood Amsterdam and other towns and villages along its low-lying coastline.

For centuries, the Dutch have been protecting themselves from encroaching seas and snatching more land to accommodate their expanding population. One of their most formidable opponents was the Zuider Zee (Southern Sea), an incursion of the North Sea that washed over Frisian dunes to flood vast inland areas between A.D. 200 and 300. Over the centuries, the Zuider Zee continued to expand, and in the 1200s, a series of storms drove its waters far inland.

Despite the sea's reputation as a graveyard of ships, the sleepy, picturesque villages that today line the IJsselmeer's shores presented quite a different picture when their harbors were alive with great ships that sailed for the Dutch West and East India Companies. North Sea fishermen added to the maritime traffic as they returned to Zuider Zee home ports, and Amsterdam flourished as ships from around the world sailed to its front door.

Still, as early as the 1600s, there was talk of driving back the sea and reclaiming the land it covered. Parliament got around to authorizing the project in 1918, and in the 1920s, work was begun. In 1932, in an unparalleled engineering feat, the North Sea was sealed off, from Noord-Holland to Friesland, by the 30km (19-mile) Afsluitdijk (Enclosing Dike), and the saltwater Zuider Zee became the freshwater IJsselmeer lake.

What to See & Do

A small Catholic town on the mainland, **Volendam** lost most of its fishing industry to the enclosure of the Zuider Zee. It's geared now for tourism in a big way and has souvenir shops, boutiques, cafes, and restaurants. Lots of people come to town to pig out on the town's near-legendary *gerookte paling* (smoked eel), and to visit such attractions as the **fish auction,** the **diamond cutter,** the **clog maker,** and the **old house** with a room entirely wallpapered in cigar bands. Still, Volendam's boat-filled harbor, tiny streets, and traditional houses maintain an undeniable enchantment. If you must have a snapshot of yourself in traditional Dutch costume—local women wear white caps with wings—this is a good place to do it.

Volendam's historic rival, **Marken,** is Protestant and was an island until a narrow causeway connected it to the mainland. It remains insular. Smaller and less rambunctious than Volendam, it is rural, with clusters of farmhouses dotted around on the polders. A white-painted **lighthouse** stands on the IJsselmeer shore. One half of Marken village, **Havenbuurt,** consists of stilted green-and-white–painted houses grouped around a tiny harbor. A **clog maker** works in summer in the village car park. Four old smokehouses in the other half of the village, **Kerkbuurt,** serve as the **Museum Marken,** Kerkbuurt 44–47 (© 0299/601-904; www.markermuseum.nl), which covers traditional furnishings, costumes, and more. The museum is open Easter Friday to September, Monday to

---

Moments **Perchance to Dream**

To overnight in traditional style in Volendam and Monnickendam, ask at their VVV offices about sleeping aboard one of the old wooden IJsselmeer *boters* and *skûtsjes* (sailing ships) moored in the harbor (this option isn't available in Marken). It's a romantic, if somewhat cramped, way to spend the night.

Saturday from 10am to 5pm, and Sunday from noon to 4pm; and October Monday to Saturday from 11am to 4pm, and Sunday from noon to 4pm. Admission is 2.50€ ($4) for adults, 1.25€ ($2) for children ages 5 to 12, and free for children 4 and under.

Marken doesn't go all gushy for tourists—though a tax levied on every tour goes directly into village coffers. The village merely feeds and waters its visitors, and allows them to wander around its pretty streets gawking at locals going about their daily routines of hanging out laundry, washing windows, and shopping for groceries. Some residents occasionally wear traditional dress—for women, caps with ribbons and black aprons over striped petticoats—but as much to preserve the custom as for tourists.

By way of contrast to its two neighbors, **Monnickendam** doesn't pay much attention to tourists at all, but gets on with its own life as a boating and fishing center, as you can see in its busy **harbor.** Take a walk through streets lined with gabled houses and stop to admire the 15th-century late Gothic **Sint-Nicolaaskerk (St. Nicholas's Church),** at Zarken 2. Be sure to visit the **Stadhuis (Town Hall),** at Noordeinde 5, which began life as a private residence in 1746 and has an elaborately decorated ceiling. Across the street, a 15th-century tower, the **Speeltoren,** has a carillon that chimes every hour, accompanied by a parade of mechanical knights. Inside is the town museum, **Museum de Speeltoren,** Noordeinde 4 (© **0299/652-203;** www.despeeltoren.nl), open early April to May and mid-September to mid-October, Saturday and Sunday from 10am to 4pm; and June to mid-September, Tuesday to Sunday from 10am to 4pm. Admission is 1.50€ ($2.40) for adults, and .50€ (80¢) for children.

Where to Stay

Hotel Spaander ★   This old-fashioned hotel has real harbor flavor to go with its lakeside setting. The public spaces have an Old Dutch interior look, appropriate to a lodging that started out in 1881, and the entire space is a kind of art gallery, speckled with a thousand 19th-century paintings. Its guest rooms, however, are modern, brightly furnished, comfortable, and attractive. The hotel's two dining rooms, an old-style inn and an elegant sun lounge, serve local IJsselmeer and other Dutch specialties, like smoked eel. The outside terrace cafe is great when the weather is fine.

Haven 15–19 (north end of the harbor), 1131 EP Volendam. © **0299/363-595.** Fax 0299/369-615. www. spaander.nl. 79 units. 95€–169€ ($152–$270) double; 169€ ($270) suite. Rates include continental breakfast. AE, DC, MC, V. Parking 5€ ($8). **Amenities:** 2 restaurants; 2 bars; small heated indoor pool; exercise room; sauna; smoke-free rooms. *In room:* TV, minifridge (some rooms), high-speed Internet, hair dryer.

Where to Dine

De Taanderij ★ DUTCH/FRENCH   Lunch at this little *eethuis* at the harbor's end (yes, seafood is served). For dessert, try the traditional Dutch treat of *koffie en appelgebak met slagroom* (coffee with apple pie and cream) or *poffertjes* (small fried pancake puffs coated with confectioners' sugar and filled with syrup or liqueur). The interior is an elegant and cozy interpretation of old Marken style. When the weather's good, a terrace spreads onto the harborside, where you can absorb the sunshine, the tranquil view over the IJsselmeer, and of course, the menu's luscious goodies.

Havenbuurt 1, Marken. © **0299/602-206.** Main courses 15€–19€ ($24–$30); snacks 4€–13€ ($6.40–$21). AE, MC, V. Apr–Sept Tues–Sun 11am–10pm; Oct–Mar Tues–Sun 11am–7pm.

EDAM ★
18km (11 miles) NE of Amsterdam; 2km (1 mile) N of Volendam

A little way inland from the IJsselmeer, Edam (pronounced *ay*-dam) gives its name to one of Holland's most famous cheeses. Don't expect to find it in the familiar red skin, though—that's for export. In Holland, the skin is yellow. This pretty little town (pop. 7,000), a whaling port during Holland's 17th-century Golden Age, is centered around canals you cross by way of drawbridges that offer views of canal houses, gardens, and teahouses.

Essentials
GETTING THERE There is frequent service by **Arriva** bus nos. 110, 112, 113, 114, 116, 117, and 118 from outside Amsterdam Centraal Station, a 35-minute ride. By car from Amsterdam, drive via Monnickendam and Volendam (see "The IJsselmeer," p. 254).

VISITOR INFORMATION **VVV Edam,** Stadhuis (Town Hall), Damplein 1, 1135 BK Edam (© **0299/315-125;** fax 0299/374-236; www.vvv-edam.nl) is in the town center. The office is open May to October, Monday to Saturday from 10am to 5pm; November to April, Monday to Saturday from 10am to 3pm.

What to See & Do
This was once a port of some prominence, and a visit to the modest **Edams Museum,** Damplein 8 (© **0299/372-644;** www.edamsmuseum.nl), opposite the former Town Hall, gives you a peek not only at its history but also at some of its most illustrious citizens over the centuries. Look for the portrait of Pieter Dirckz, a one-time mayor and proud possessor of what is probably the longest beard on record anywhere: It was 2.5m (8 ft.) long! An intriguing feature of this merchant's house (ca. 1530) is the cellar, which is actually a box floating on water, constructed that way so changing water levels wouldn't upset the house's foundations. The museum is open late March to late October, Tuesday to Saturday from 10am to 4:30pm, and Sunday from 1 to 4:30pm. Admission is 3€ ($4.80) for adults, 1.50€ ($2.40) for seniors, 1€ ($1.60) for children ages 6 to 17, and free for children 5 and under.

Take a look at the lovely wedding room in the **Stadhuis (Town Hall),** and if you visit during summer months, don't miss the cheese-making display at the **Kaaswaag (Weigh House).** The **Speeltoren (Carillon Tower)** from 1561 tilts a bit and was very nearly lost when the church to which it belonged was destroyed.

HOORN ★★
32km (20 miles) NE of Amsterdam; 17km (11 miles) N of Edam

Historically, Hoorn (pronounced *Hoarn*) is one of the great names in Dutch seafaring. Even now, with the open sea no longer on its doorstep, it remains water-oriented and is a busy IJsselmeer sailing center. On a tour of the graceful Golden Age town, be sure to visit the old harbor, the **Binnenhaven.** Hoorn (pop. 69,000) is the hometown of Willem Cornelisz Schouten, who in 1616 rounded South America's southernmost tip, which he dubbed Kap Hoorn (Cape Horn) in his town's honor.

GETTING THERE   Trains depart at least every hour from Amsterdam Centraal Station to Hoorn; trip time is 40 minutes, and a round-trip ticket is 13€ ($21). Buses depart every hour or so from outside Centraal Station, but they take longer than the train. By car from Amsterdam, take A7/E22 north.

VISITOR INFORMATION   VVV Hoorn, Veemarkt 4, 1621 JC Hoorn (© **072/511-4284;** fax 0229/215-023; www.vvvhoorn.nl) is between the rail station and the center. The office is open May to August Monday from 1 to 6pm, Tuesday, Wednesday, and Friday from 9:30am to 6pm, Thursday from 9:30am to 9pm, and Saturday from 9:30am to 5pm; September to April, Monday from 1 to 5pm, and Tuesday to Saturday from 9:30am to 5pm.

What to See & Do

Visit the **Westfries Museum,** Rode Steen 1 (© **0229/280-022;** www.wfm.nl), in a 1632 building containing a wide-ranging historical collection that includes armor, weapons, paper cuttings, costumes, toys, naive paintings (which embody a deliberately childlike style), coins, medals, jewels, civic guards' paintings, and porcelain. A second-floor exhibit details the town's maritime history, with an emphasis on ships and voyages of the United East India Company (V.O.C.). There are fine tapestries and 17th- and 18th-century period rooms. A basement exhibit showcases a collection of Bronze Age relics. The museum is open Monday to Friday from 11am to 5pm, Saturday and Sunday from 1 to 5pm; it's closed January 1, April 30, 3rd Monday in August, and December 25. Admission is 5€ ($8) for adults, and 3.50€ ($5.60) for seniors and children ages 5 to 16.

During summer, an antique steam tram, the **Museumstoomtram Hoorn-Medemblik** (© **0229/214-862;** www.museumstoomtram.nl) transports tourists from Hoorn to nearby **Medemblik** (see below). Round-trip tickets are 19€ ($30) for adults, 14€ ($22) for children ages 4 to 12, and free for children 3 and under.

Where to Dine

De Hoofdtoren ★ DUTCH   Boat lovers will want to linger on this cafe-restaurant's terrace in the midst of the busy harbor, surrounded by traditional IJsselmeer sailing ships and pleasure boats large and small. The restaurant is housed in an old defense tower that dates from 1532—its one-time purpose was to protect the harbor entrance; its interior retains many antique features. Traditional Dutch fare and grilled meat and fish specialties are served at dinner. During the day, there's a lunch-and-snacks menu.

Hoofd 2. © **0229/215-487.** www.hoofdtoren.nl. Main courses 17€–20€ ($27–$32). AE, DC, MC, V. Daily 10am–10pm.

De Waag FRENCH   This grand cafe in the monumental Weigh House from 1609 is open all day, for breakfast, lunch, and dinner. It stands on one of the country's squares, surrounded by 17th-century buildings from the town's heyday. You can still see antique weighing scales in the wood-beamed interior.

Rode Steen 8. © **0229/215-195.** www.dewaaghoorn.nl. Main courses 13€–23€ ($21–$37). MC, V. Daily 10am–1am.

A 400-boat herring fleet once sailed out of Enkhuizen. Then in 1932 came the Enclosing Dike (see below), closing off the North Sea. Today, the town looks to pleasure boating, tourism, and bulb-growing for its livelihood, and boasts one of the country's most fascinating open-air museums (see below).

Essentials

GETTING THERE Trains depart at least every hour from Amsterdam Centraal Station, going via Hoorn; trip time is 1 hour, and a round-trip ticket is 18€ ($29). Buses depart every half-hour or so from outside Hoorn rail station. By car from Amsterdam, drive to Hoorn, then, take N302 northeast.

VISITOR INFORMATION VVV Enkhuizen, Tussen Twee Havens 1, 1601 EM Enkhuizen (② 0228/313-164; fax 0228/315-531; www.vvvenkhuizen.nl) is at the harbor. The office is open April to October, daily from 9am to 5pm.

What to See & Do

From a dock in Veerhaven next to Enkhuizen rail station, or from another next to the dike road from Enkhuizen to Lelystad, take a boat over to one of Holland's finest museums, the **Zuiderzeemuseum ★★**, Wierdijk 12–22 (② 0228/351-111; www.zuiderzee museum.nl), dedicated to re-creating the historic way of life on the shores of the old Zuider Zee. Its two sections, **Indoor** and **Outdoor,** feature many exhibits, of which the most dramatic are 130 complete old buildings. Farmhouses, public buildings, stores, and a church have been moved here from lakeside villages, and from elsewhere in Holland, brought together to form a cobblestone-street village. There are, too, examples of the fishing boats that provided the incomes on which villagers depended. The museum is open daily from 10am to 5pm. The Indoor section is open daily from 10am to 5pm; closed January 1 and December 25. Admission is 13€ ($20) for adults, 12€ ($19) for seniors, 7.50€ ($12) for children ages 4 to 12, and free for children 3 and under.

MEDEMBLIK
46km (29 miles) NE of Amsterdam; 14km (9 miles) NW of Enkhuizen

Medemblik is a small IJsselmeer town with busy twin harbors. Founded in the 7th century, it later joined the powerful Hanseatic League trading federation.

There are two great ways to get to Medemblik in the summer. One is onboard the 1956 passenger (and bike) ferry *Friesland* from Enkhuizen (see above). Another is from Hoorn (see above) by **antique steam train,** which arrives at an old station. Tourist information is available from VVV Medemblik, Kaasmarkt 1, 1671 BH Medemblik (② 072/511-4284; fax 072/511-7513; www.vvvmedemblik.nl).

Adjacent to Medemblik's **Oosterhaven (East Harbor)**—its twin is called the **Westerhaven (West Harbor)**—is the moated **Kasteel Radboud,** Oudevaartsgat 8 (② 0227/541-960; www.kasteelradboud.nl), an 8th-century castle refortified by the count of Holland in 1289 against a possible rebellion by the troublesome Frisians. The remaining section has been restored to its 13th-century state and is well worth a visit. The castle is open May to mid-September, Monday to Saturday from 11am to 5pm, and Sunday from 2 to 5pm; and mid-September to April, Sunday from 2 to 5pm (and during school vacations 11am–5pm). Admission is 5€ ($8) for adults, 3€ ($4.80) for seniors and children ages 5 to 13, and free for children 4 and under.

(Moments) **By Bicycle to Hoorn**

For a great day trip from Amsterdam, go by bike along the IJsselmeer shore to Hoorn, and return by train (with your bike). (Do this on a halfway decent bike, not a decrepit old Amsterdam bike.) Riding along between the polders and the lake is a perfect Dutch experience—but you need to be ready for some vigorous pedaling. You can't get lost if you stay on the road that runs along the IJsselmeer and keep the lake to your immediate right.

Board the IJ ferry at the pier behind Centraal Station and cross to Amsterdam North. Take Durgerdammerdijk, a road leading east alongside the IJsselmeer shore to Durgerdam, a lakeside village huddled below water level behind a protective dike, with its roofs sticking up over the top. Ride either next to the houses and the polders or up on the dike-top path, immersed in wind, rain, and shine—and with fine lake views.

Beyond Uitdam, either go left on the lakeside road through Monnickendam to Volendam, or right on the causeway to Marken. The first option cuts overall distance because Marken is a dead end and you need to come back across the causeway again. But in summer, you can take the *Marken Express* passenger boat (and take your bike on as well), which sails hourly from Marken to Volendam. One way or the other, you'll arrive in Volendam.

Go inland a short way along a canal that runs from the lakeside dike to Edam, famed for its cheese. Cross over the canal on the bridge at Damplein in Edam's center, and go back along the far bank to regain the IJsselmeer shore. Up ahead is a straight run north to Hoorn through the pastoral villages of Warder, Etersheim, Schardam, and Scharwoude.

After exploring Hoorn—or flopping down exhausted in a cafe—follow the green-painted signs pointing the way to the station for the train ride back to Amsterdam.

AFSLUITDIJK (ENCLOSING DIKE) ★
62km (38 miles) N of Amsterdam; 30km (19 miles) NW of Enkhuizen

It's hard to grasp what a monumental work the great barrier that separates the salty Waddenzee from the freshwater IJsselmeer is until you drive its 30km (19-mile) length. The Afsluitdijk connects the provinces of **Noord-Holland** and **Friesland.** Dr. Cornelis Lely came up with the plans in 1891, but construction was delayed for 25 years while he tried to convince the government to allocate funding.

Massive effort went into building the dike, which is 100m (330 ft.) wide and 7m (23 ft.) above mean water level. Many communities around the shores of what used to be the saltwater Zuider Zee lost their livelihood when access to the open sea was shut off. Some of the fishing boats that now sail the IJsselmeer hoist dark-brown sails as a sign of mourning for their lost sea fishing industry.

Midway along the dike's length, at the point where it was completed in 1932, stands a **monument** to the men who put their backs to the task, and a memorial to Dr. Lely. Stop for a snack at **Afsluitdijk Café** in the monument's base and pick up an illustrated booklet that explains the dike's construction. For those crossing over by bike or on foot, **261**

there's a bike path as well as a pedestrian path.

4 ZAANSE SCHANS ★★

16km (10 miles) NW of Amsterdam

Nestled like a pearl at the heart of the Zaanstreek district is **Zaanse Schans** (© **075/616-2862;** www.zaanseschans.nl), a replica village of houses, workshops, and windmills moved to this site when industrialization leveled their original locations. Though most of the distinctive green-painted timber houses are inhabited by those who can afford and appreciate their historic timbers (and have the patience for the pedestrian traffic from the tour buses), a few can be visited as museums.

Trains depart every 20 minutes from Amsterdam Centraal Station via Zaandam to Koog-Zaandijk station, from where it's a 1km (²/₃-mile) walk to Zaanse Schans. Or, take **Connexxion** bus no. 91 from outside Amsterdam Centraal Station for the 40-minute ride direct. By car from Amsterdam, take A8 north, then switch to A7/E22 north to exit 2, from where you can follow the signs to Zaanse Schans.

Adding to the pleasure of just walking through the Zaanse Schans, you can visit three of the five working industrial **windmills** on the site: a sawmill (the wind-powered sawmill was invented in the Zaan district in 1592), and mills that specialized in producing paint, vegetable oil (two mills), and the renowned Zaanse mustard; three smaller mills are speckled around. At one time the Zaanstreek had more than 1,000 windmills. Only 13 have survived, including these 8. Reconstruction of a second sawmill that was demolished in 1942 is underway. A short tour shows you just how these wind machines worked. Stop, too, at an 18th-century **grocery store,** an old-style **bakery,** and a **clog workshop** to see how the wooden shoes called *klompen* are made.

Most of these and other attractions are open March to October, daily from 10am to 5 or 6pm, and November to February, Saturday and Sunday from around 11am to 4pm; open hours for some sites are more restricted. Admission varies from free to 1€ to 2.50€ ($1.60–$4) for adults, .50€ to 1€ (80¢–$1.60) for children ages 5 to 12, and free for children 4 and under.

Tour the **Zaans Museum,** Schansend 7 (© **075/616-2862;** www.zaansmuseum.nl), at the site, where this fascinating district's history is told. The architecturally novel museum is open daily from 9am to 5pm. Admission is 4.50€ ($7.20) for adults, 2.70€ ($4.30) for seniors, and free for children 17 and under.

For a view from a different perspective, take a 45-minute **cruise** on the **Zaan River** aboard a **Rederij De Schans** tour boat (© **075/614-6762;** www.rederijdeschans.nl).

ⓘTips Get Your Clogs On

Wood clogs are still a fixture in many farming areas, where they're much more effective against wet and cold than leather shoes or boots. If you plan to buy a pair, Zaanse Schans is a good place to do it. Traditionally, clogs with pointed toes are for women and rounded toes are for men. They must be worn with heavy socks, so when buying, add the width of one finger when measuring for size.

Boats depart from a river dock next to the **De Huisman windmill,** April to September, hourly from 10am to 4pm. Cruises are 6€ ($9.60) for adults, 3€ ($4.80) for children ages 3 to 12, and free for children 2 and under.

WHERE TO DINE

De Hoop Op d'Swarte Walvis ★ CONTINENTAL   A stellar restaurant with a mouthful of a name borrowed from a 19th-century local whaling ship, the "Hope for the Black Whale" occupies a refined brick building that now stands amid Zaanse Schans's green-painted houses, having been originally constructed as an orphanage in nearby Westzaan. Its glass pavilion and memorable outdoor terrace overlook the Zaan River and the waterside villas on the far bank. Gastronomes can expect an unforgettable treat from the hands of master chef Jan Willem Teunis, with subtle mixtures of superior produce prepared to perfection.

Kalverringdijk 15, Zaanse Schans. © **075/616-5629.** www.dewalvis.nl. Main courses 17€–30€ ($27–$48); 4-course menu 48€ ($77). AE, DC, MC, V. Sun–Fri noon–10pm; Sat 6–10pm.

---

5 TULIPS & CHEESE

The place to see flowers in their full glory is **Keukenhof,** where vast numbers of tulips and other flowers create dazzling mosaics of color. Combine your visit with a trip through the **bulb fields.** And if all of the above isn't Dutch enough for you, there's always the incomparable **Alkmaar cheese market.**

KEUKENHOF ★★

26km (16 miles) SW of Amsterdam

In **Keukenhof,** Stationsweg 166A, Lisse (© **0252/465-555;** www.keukenhof.nl), gardens and flowers at their peak have short seasons, but if you're here in the spring, you'll never forget a visit. This park's meandering 32 hectares (79 acres) of wooded green are in the heart of the bulb-producing region, planted each fall by the major Dutch growers (each plants his own plot or establishes his own greenhouse display). Come spring, the bulbs burst forth and produce not hundreds, or even thousands, but *millions* (more than 7 million at last count) of tulips of hundreds of varieties, narcissi, daffodils, hyacinths, bluebells, crocuses, lilies, amaryllis, and many others. The color blaze is everywhere in the park; it's also in the greenhouses, next to the brooks and shady ponds, along the paths and in the neighboring fields, in neat little plots and helter-skelter on the lawns, and alongside the inevitable windmill. Keukenhof claims to be the world's greatest flower show, and nearly a million visitors come each year to evaluate this claim. Count on spending an entire morning or afternoon here, and grab a quick bite at one of several on-site cafes so that you don't have to go looking for a place to eat when you'd rather be enjoying the flowers. The park is open from around March 20 to around May 20, daily from 8am to 7:30pm. Admission is 14€ ($22) for adults, 13€ ($21) for seniors, 6.50€ ($10) for children ages 4 to 11, and free for children 3 and under. Special train/bus connections run via Haarlem and nearby Leiden.

THE BULB FIELDS ★

The largest bulb growers are in the southern part of Noord-Holland province and the northern corner of Zuid-Holland, with the heaviest concentration lying between Haarlem and Leiden. Each year from mid-March until late April, the bulb fields cover a

Impressions

Aalsmeer is an auction house in the sense that Shanghai is a city or Everest a mountain.

—*National Geographic* (Apr 2001)

strip of land 16km (10 miles) long and 6km (4 miles) wide with tulips, crocuses, daffodils, narcissi, hyacinths, lilies, and more. A signposted **Bollenstreek (Bulb District)** route that covers about 60km (38 miles) makes viewing the flowers easy (VVV tourist information offices provide a detailed "Bulb Route" brochure). Roadside stalls sell flower garlands—do as the natives do and buy one for yourself and another for the car.

To get to the bulb fields from Amsterdam, either drive first to Haarlem, then south on N206 through De Zilk and Noordwijkerhout, or on N208, through Hillegom, Lisse, and Sassenheim. Alternatively, go south from Amsterdam on A4/E19, past Schiphol Airport, to exit 4 (Nieuw-Vennep), and then northwest on N207 for 8km (5 miles) until you hit N208.

AALSMEER

18km (11 miles) SW of Amsterdam

Selling flowers and plants nets 1.5€ billion ($2.4 billion) a year at the **Bloemenveiling (Flower Auction)** ★, Legmeerdijk 313 (② **0297/393-939;** www.flora.nl), in the lakeside community of Aalsmeer close to Schiphol Airport. Every day, the auction vends 19 million cut flowers and 2 million plants, in 12,000 varieties, from 7,000 nurseries, representing 30% of the worldwide trade. So vast is the auction house that 120 soccer fields would fit inside.

Get here early to see the biggest array of flowers in the distribution rooms, and to have as much time as possible to watch the computerized auction. Buyers sit in rows in five auditorium-style auction halls; they have microphones to ask questions and buttons to electronically register their bids. As the bunches of tulips or daffodils go by the stand on carts, they're auctioned in a matter of seconds. A mammoth timer, which starts at 100 and counts clockwise to 1, determines the bidding: The winning, and only, bid is placed by the person who stops the clock. It's like a gigantic game of chicken. Press too early and you pay more than necessary; wait too long and someone else already has the lot.

The auction is held Monday to Friday from 7 to 11am (there's little point in arriving after 9:30am). Admission is 5€ ($8) for adults, 3€ ($4.80) for children 6 to 11, and free for children 5 and under. Connexxion bus no. 172 goes there from outside Amsterdam Centraal Station. By car, take A4/E19 south to the Hoofddorp junction, then go southeast on N201.

ALKMAAR

30km (19 miles) N of Amsterdam

Every Friday morning during the long Dutch summer season, a steady parade of tourists arrives to visit the famous cheese market in this handsome, canal-lined town (pop. 94,000), founded in the 10th century. It's quite a show they're on their way to see. For other towns with a cheesy disposition, see also the sections on Edam in "The IJsselmeer," earlier in this chapter, and on Gouda in "Delft, Leiden & Gouda," later in this chapter.

GETTING THERE   Trains depart at least every hour from Amsterdam Centraal Station to Alkmaar; the trip takes around 35 minutes by fast train. A round-trip ticket is 12€ ($19). By car from Amsterdam, take A8, N246, N203, and A9 north.

VISITOR INFORMATION   **VVV Alkmaar,** Waagplein 2, 1811 JP Alkmaar (© **072/511-4284;** fax 072/511-7513; www.vvvalkmaar.nl) is in the center. The office is open Monday to Friday from 10am to 5:30pm (Apr–Sept Fri from 9am), and Saturday from 9:30am to 5pm.

What to See & Do

At the Friday morning **Kaasmarkt (Cheese Market)** ★ in Waagplein, yellow-skinned Edam, Gouda, and Leidse (Leiden) cheeses are piled high on the cobblestone square. The carillon in the 16th-century **Waaggebouw (Weigh House)** tower hourly showers the streets with tinkling Dutch folk music, accompanying a jousting performance of mechanical knights. The square is filled with sightseers, barrel organs, souvenir stalls, and tangible excitement. White-clad *kaasdragers* (cheese porters) dart around wearing colored lacquered-straw hats in red, blue, yellow, or green as a sign of which more-than-400-year-old guild they belong to. Porters, who aren't permitted to smoke, drink, or curse while on duty, are so proud of their standards that every week they post on a "shame board" the name of any carrier who indulged in profanity or showed up late at the auction.

Bidding is carried on in the traditional Dutch manner of hand clapping to bid the price up or down; a good, solid hand clap seals the deal. Once a buyer has accumulated his lot of cheeses, teams of porters move in with shiny, shallow barrows, and, using slings that hang from their shoulders, carry the golden wheels and balls of cheese to the scales in the Weigh House for the final tally. The market is held from the first Friday of April to the first Friday of September, from 10am to 12:30pm.

6 DEN HELDER & TEXEL

The harbor town and navy base of Den Helder, at the tip of Noord-Holland province, is the gateway to the island of Texel.

DEN HELDER

67km (42 miles) N of Amsterdam; 31km (19 miles) NW of Medemblik

Den Helder has Holland's most important navy base and hosts the annual Navy Days, a national fleet festival, in July.

Essentials

GETTING THERE   Trains depart at least every hour from Amsterdam Centraal Station for Den Helder; the trip takes around 75 minutes. A round-trip ticket is 23€ ($37). By car from Amsterdam, take A8, A9, and N9 north.

VISITOR INFORMATION   **VVV Den Helder,** Bernhardplein 18, 1781 HH Den Helder (© **0223/625-544;** fax 0223/614-888; www.vvvkopvannoordholland.nl) is next to the rail station. The office is open Monday from 10:30am to 5:30pm, Tuesday to Friday from 9:30am to 5:30pm, and Saturday from 9:30am to 5pm.

What to See & Do

For an insight into the Royal Netherlands Navy's illustrious past, by way of models, marine paintings, weapons and equipment, and some real warships, visit the

Marinemuseum (Navy Museum), Hoofdgracht 3 (© **0223/657-534;** www.marine museum.nl), just 200m (660 ft.) west of the Texel ferry dock. Several retired combatants on display include the steam-and-sail ram *De Schorpioen,* built in 1868. Now tied to a dock, the *Scorpion* was once a vessel with a sting in its bow, from which a below-the-water ram could deal fatal blows to enemy ships—not that it ever did. The steam engine still works, and you can visit the captain's cabin and crew's quarters. Equally fascinating is the dry-landed submarine *Tonijn (Tunny),* which has a torpedo emerging from its front tube—go aboard to experience a submariner's claustrophobic quarters. The museum is open May to October, Monday to Friday from 10am to 5pm, and Saturday, Sunday, and holidays from noon to 5pm; November to April, Tuesday to Friday from 10am to 5pm, and Saturday, Sunday, and holidays from noon to 5pm; it's closed January 1 and December 25. Admission is 6€ ($9.60) for adults, 3€ ($4.80) for children ages 5 to 15, and free for children 4 and under.

While you're in naval mode, visit the **Nationaal Reddingmuseum Dorus Rijkers (Dorus Rijkers National Lifeboat Museum),** Oude Rijkswerf, Willemsoord 60G (© **0223/618-320;** www.reddingmuseum.nl), which chronicles the Lifeboat Service's history. The museum is open April to October and Christmas school vacation, Monday to Friday from 10am to 5pm, and Saturday and Sunday from noon to 5pm; November to mid-December, Sunday from noon to 5pm; closed January 1 and December 25. Admission is 5.50€ ($8.80) for adults, 5€ ($8) for seniors, 4.50€ ($7.20) for children ages 5 to 15, and free for children 4 and under.

The Bulb District between Leiden and Haarlem (see above) may be better known, but around Den Helder is Holland's largest area of **bulb fields;** the serried ranks of spring tulips look every bit as colorful here as there.

TEXEL ★

69km (43 miles) N of Amsterdam

A short ferry trip from Den Helder, family-orientated Texel (pronounced *Tess*-uhl) is the largest and most populated of the Wadden Islands archipelago. With just 14,000 permanent inhabitants, that's not saying much. Texel, 24km (15 miles) long and 9km (6 miles) wide, has a varied landscape of tidal gullies, sand dunes, and rolling meadows. Its entire North Sea shoreline is just one long beach. It has the serenity intrinsic to islands, even with the many visitors who pour in during summer months.

Essentials

GETTING THERE   The **TESO** line (© **0222/369-600;** www.teso.nl) operates car-ferry service from Den Helder, across the Marsdiep strait, to 't Horntje on Texel—a 20-minute trip. A connecting bus shuttles hourly between Den Helder rail station and the Den Helder ferry dock. Ferries depart hourly at peak times and reservations are not accepted. Return fares for cars, including two passengers, are Friday to Monday 18€ ($29), and Tuesday to Thursday 12€ ($19); for passengers alone, return fares are 3€ ($4.80) for adults, 1.50€ ($2.40) for children ages 4 to 11, and free for children 3 and under. Bicycles and mopeds cost 2.50€ ($4).

VISITOR INFORMATION   **VVV Texel,** Emmalaan 66, 1791 AV Den Burg (© **0222/ 314-741;** fax 0222/310-054; www.texel.net), is just off the main road into town from the ferry harbor. The office is open Monday to Friday from 9am to 5:30pm, and Saturday from 9am to 5pm.

Cars are permitted on Texel and buses connect the villages and the main beaches, but the best way to get around and to respect the island's environment is to go by bike. Bring yours over for free on the ferry, or rent one from dozens of outlets around the island.

Exploring Texel

Beaches, sailing, biking, hiking, and bird-watching are Texel's big attractions, but eating, drinking, and partying certainly have a place too. The main village, **Den Burg,** is a bustling settlement near the center of the island. For a glimpse of historical island life, visit its moderately interesting, centrally located **De Oudheidkamer,** Koogerstraat 1 (© **0222/313-135**), in the island's oldest house, which was built in 1599 and furnished in a style from around 1900. The museum is open April to October, daily from 10am to 12:30pm and 1:30 to 3:30pm. Admission is 1.60€ ($2.55) for adults, 1.40€ ($2.25) for seniors, .90€ ($1.45) for children ages 4 to 13, and free for children 3 and under.

You're allowed to freely visit the dune and forest area belonging to the **Staatsbosbeheer (State Forest Authority),** so long as you stick to the marked trails. Wildlife biologists from **EcoMare,** Ruijslaan 92 (© **0222/317-741;** www.ecomare.nl), a Wadden Islands research center, conduct guided tours of some of these areas. EcoMare's visitor center, amid the sand dunes just south of a coastal village called **De Koog,** houses a small natural history museum featuring Texel's geology, plants, and its wildlife of land, sea, and air. The Wadden Sea is rich in seals, and EcoMare has a seal rehabilitation facility that cares for weak and injured seals until they are strong enough to be returned to the sea. Another of their rehabilitation projects cares for birds affected by pollution and other hazards. The center is open daily from 9am to 5pm. Admission is 8.50€ ($14) for adults, 5.50€ ($8.80) for children ages 4 to 13, and free for children 3 and under.

Some 300 bird species frequent Texel, of which around 100 breed on the island. Among the avian stars: oyster-catchers, Bewicks swans, spoonbills, eider ducks, Brent geese, avocets, marsh harriers, snow buntings, ringed plovers, kestrels, short-eared owls, and bar-tailed godwits. Observe these and more in the **De Schorren, De Bol,** and **Dijkmanshuizen**—three protected nature reserves that you can only enter if you're on an EcoMare-conducted tour.

7 CASTLE COUNTRY

In earlier times, the territory southeast of Amsterdam was a place of strategic importance, as evidenced by the grand military constructions still standing today, such as the 13th-century Muiderslot moated castle in Muiden and the star-shaped fortifications of Naarden.

MUIDEN

13km (8 miles) SE of Amsterdam

A 14th-century, fairy-tale–princess castle, with a moat, turrets, and stout crenelated walls, **Muiderslot** ★, Herengracht 1 (© **0294/261-325;** www.muiderslot.nl), perches on the bank of the Vecht River just outside the small IJsselmeer harbor town of Muiden, a handsome place with gabled waterfront houses. Count Floris V of Holland, who in 1275 granted toll privileges to the vibrant new Aemstelledamme (Amsterdam) settlement,

built the castle around 1280, and was murdered here by rival nobles in 1296 (see
"Amsterdam's Origins," in chapter 2).

Muiderslot is where poet Pieter Cornelisz Hooft found both a home and employment when he served as castle steward and local bailiff for 40 years in the early 17th century. The castle is furnished essentially as Hooft and his artistic circle of friends—known in Dutch literary history as the *Muiderkring* (Muiden Circle)—knew it. You'll find distinctly Dutch carved cupboard beds, heavy chests, fireside benches, and mantelpieces. The castle is open April to October, Monday to Friday from 10am to 5pm, Saturday, Sunday, and holidays from noon to 6pm; November to March, Saturday and Sunday from noon to 6pm. Admission is 8.75€ ($14) for adults, 6.25€ ($10) for children ages 4 to 12, and free for children 3 and under. By car from Amsterdam, take A1/E231 east.

NAARDEN
19km (12 miles) E of Amsterdam

This small town doesn't have too much to recommend in it, but it does have one of Holland's best-preserved rings of old military fortifications.

Essentials
GETTING THERE   Trains depart every hour or so from Amsterdam Centraal Station for Naarden-Bussum station; the trip takes around 25 minutes. A round-trip ticket is 7.60€ ($12). By car from Amsterdam, take A1/E231 east.

VISITOR INFORMATION   VVV Naarden, Adriaan Dortsmanplein 1B, 1411 RC Naarden (© 035/694-2836; fax 035/694-3424; www.vvvhollandsmidden.nl) is located inside the old town's walls. The office is open May to mid-September, Tuesday to Friday from 10am to 3pm, and Saturday from 10am to 2pm; mid-September to April, Saturday from 10am to 2pm.

What to See & Do
Much in the spirit of locking the barn door after the horse was gone, Naarden erected its star-shaped double fortifications after the Don Fadrique Álvarez de Toledo and his Spanish troops brutally sacked the town in 1572. The fortifications were begun in 1580 and completed in 1730, and since the inner ring wasn't completed until 1685, the French were able to storm the works in 1673.

Beneath the **Turfpoort,** one of six bastions, visit the casemates (artillery vaults) which house the **Nederlands Vestingmuseum (Dutch Fortification Museum),** Westwalstraat 6 (© 035/694-5459; www.vestingmuseum.nl), filled with cannon, muskets, accoutrements, and documentation. The museum is open mid-March to October, Tuesday to Friday from 10:30am to 5pm, and Saturday, Sunday, and holidays from noon to 5pm; November to mid-March, Sunday, and Saturday before Christmas to Sunday after New Year, Tuesday to Friday from 10:30am to 5pm, and Sunday from noon to 5pm; it's closed January 1, December 25 and 31. Admission is 5.50€ ($8.80) for adults, 4.50€ ($7.20) for seniors, 3€ ($4.80) for children 5 to 12, and free for children 4 and under.

Also take in the town's 15th-century late-Gothic **Grote Kerk (Great Church),** Markstraat (© 035/694-9873), noted for its 45m (148-ft.) tower, fine acoustics, and annual pre-Easter performances of Bach's *St. Matthew Passion.* The church is open June to September daily from 1 to 4pm. Admission is free.

8 THE HAGUE ★★★

50km (31 miles) SW of Amsterdam

Amsterdam may be the capital of the Netherlands, but The Hague ('s-Gravenhage, or more commonly Den Haag, in Dutch) has always been the seat of government and Dutch monarchs' official residence. This tradition began in 1248, when Count Willem II of Holland was crowned king of the Romans in the German city of Aachen, but chose to live at the Binnenhof palace in what's now The Hague. Sophisticated, full of parks and elegant homes, the city has an 18th-century French look that suits its role as the Dutch nation's diplomatic center. Nowadays, as the seat of the International Court of Justice, the city's name is associated with international law.

ESSENTIALS

GETTING THERE The Hague is an easy day trip from Amsterdam, with frequent train service from Amsterdam Centraal Station. The trip takes around 50 minutes. A round-trip ticket is 18€ ($29). Note that The Hague has two main rail stations, Centraal (CS) and Hollands Spoor (HS); most city sights are closer to Centraal Station, but some trains stop only at Hollands Spoor. By car from Amsterdam, take A4/E19.

VISITOR INFORMATION VVV Den Haag, Hofweg 1 (mailing address: Postbus 85456, 2500 CD Den Haag; © 0900/340-3505; fax 0900/352-0426; www.denhaag. com; tram: 1 or 16), is outside the Binnenhof (Parliament). The office is open Monday to Friday from 10am to 6pm, Saturday from 10am to 5pm, and Sunday from noon to 5pm.

WHAT TO SEE & DO

The Hague's most notable attraction is the impressive **Binnenhof (Inner Court),** Binnenhof 8A (© 070/364-6144; www.binnenhofbezoek.nl; tram: 10, 16, or 17), complex of Parliament buildings, in the center. Join a tour to visit the lofty, medieval **Ridderzaal (Hall of the Knights);** this is where the queen delivers a speech from the throne each third Tuesday in September. If you're lucky enough to be here on that day, be sure to be here to see her arrive and depart in her golden coach—like Cinderella—drawn by high-stepping royal horses. Government business permitting, you can tour the two chambers of the **Staaten-Generaal (States General),** the Dutch Parliament. Guided tours (the only way guests are permitted to visit) take place Monday to Saturday hourly from 10am to 4pm (closed holidays and during special events), and cost 6€ ($9.60) or 8€ ($13) for adults, and 5€ ($8) or 7€ ($11) for seniors, students, and children 12 and under, depending on the tour. Reserve ahead of time by phone, and confirm that tours are happening on the day you intend to visit. Admission to the Parliament exhibit in the Hall of Knights reception room is free.

ⓕ Fun Facts   Hard-Handed Boosters

In an ironic counterpoint to The Hague's genteel image, fans of the city's soccer club, ADO Den Haag, have about the worst reputation in the land for hooliganism.

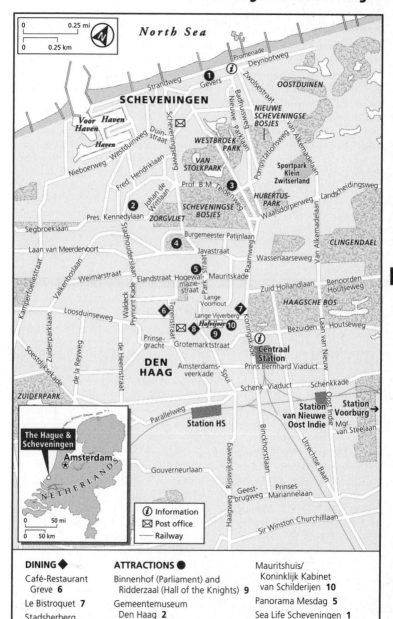

DINING ◆

Café-Restaurant
  Greve **6**

Le Bistroquet **7**

Stadsherberg
  't Goude Hooft **8**

ATTRACTIONS ●

Binnenhof (Parliament) and
  Ridderzaal (Hall of the Knights) **9**

Gemeentemuseum
  Den Haag **2**

Madurodam **3**

Mauritshuis/
  Koninklijk Kabinet
  van Schilderijen **10**

Panorama Mesdag **5**

Sea Life Scheveningen **1**

Vredespaleis (Peace Palace) **4**

Adjacent to the Binnenhof is the neoclassical **Mauritshuis** ★★, Korte Vijverberg 8 (© **070/302-3456;** www.mauritshuis.nl; tram: 10, 16, or 17), built in 1637 as the residence of Count Johan Maurits van Nassau-Siegen, court dandy and cousin of the ruling Oranje-Nassaus (House of Orange). Today, it houses the **Koninklijk Kabinet van Schilderijen (Royal Cabinet of Paintings),** an impressive art collection which King Willem I gave to the nation in 1816. Highlights include 13 Rembrandts, three Frans Hals, and three Vermeers (including his famous *View of Delft* and *Girl With a Pearl Earring*), plus hundreds of other paintings by the likes of Bruegel, Rubens, Steen, and Holbein. The gallery is open April to September, Monday to Saturday from 10am to 5pm, and Sunday and holidays from 11am to 5pm; and October to March, Tuesday to Saturday from 10am to 5pm, and Sunday and holidays from 11am to 5pm; it's closed January 1 and December 25. Admission is 9.50€ ($15) for adults, and free for visitors 18 and under.

Venture beyond the center to visit the **Gemeentemuseum Den Haag (the Hague Municipal Museum)** ★, Stadhouderslaan 41 (© **070/338-1111;** www.gemeentemuseum. nl; tram: 10 or 17), from 1935. Designed by Hendrik Petrus Berlage, the museum possesses a world-famous collection of works by De Stijl artist Piet Mondrian (1872–1944), including his last work, *Victory Boogie Woogie* (1944). There's more art (from the 19th c. onward), decorative arts, musical instruments, and fashion. The museum is open Tuesday to Sunday and holidays from 11am to 5pm; it's closed January 1 and December 25. Admission is 9€ ($14) for adults, 7€ ($11) for seniors, 5.50€ ($8.80) for students, and free for visitors 18 and under.

Andrew Carnegie donated the famous **Vredespaleis (Peace Palace),** Carnegieplein 2 (© **070/302-4242;** www.vredespaleis.nl; tram: 1 or 10), as a home for the **International Court of Justice** and the **Permanent Court of Arbitration.** The palace is open for guided tours only, Monday to Friday at 10 and 11am, and 2, 3 and 4pm (there isn't always a 4pm tour); these should be reserved at least 1 or 2 days ahead of time (© **070/302-4137;** fax 070/302-4234; guidedtours@planet.nl), though booking a week ahead would better guarantee securing a spot. Guides usually speak English, but it can't hurt to confirm this for your chosen time. Also note that you can only visit the Peace Palace's museum on the 11am and 3pm tours. Tours last 50 minutes without the museum visit and 1¹/₂ hours with. They're 5€ ($8) for adults, 3€ ($4.80) for children ages 5 to 12, and free for children 4 and under; add 3€ ($4.80) per person for the museum visit.

Not far away, in the **Scheveningse Bosjes (Scheveningen Woods),** is the enchanting **Madurodam** ★, George Maduroplein 1 (© **070/416-2400;** www.madurodam.nl; tram: 9), a miniature village in 1:25 scale. It presents many of the country's most historic buildings in miniature, with lights that work, bells that ring, and trains that run. It's open April to June, daily from 9am to 8pm; July to August, daily from 9am to 11pm; and September to March, daily from 9am to 6pm. Admission is 14€ ($22) for adults, 13€ ($20) for seniors, 9.75€ ($16) for children ages 3 to 11, and free for children 2 and under.

If you don't have time to visit Scheveningen (see below), you can still see the resort town, kind of, at **Panorama Mesdag,** Zeestraat 65 (© **070/364-4544;** www.panorama-mesdag.com; tram: 1 or 10), a superb panoramic painting of the resort town as it was in 1880, done in the style of The Hague school—its perimeter is 119m (395 ft.)! View it Monday to Saturday from 10am to 5pm, Sunday and holidays from noon to 5pm; it's closed January 1 and December 25. Admission is 6€ ($9.60) for adults, 5€ ($8) for

---

(Moments) Rising Roses

In Westbroekpark's **Rosarium,** more than 20,000 roses of 300 varieties bloom each year between July and September. Its grounds are open daily from 9am to 1 hour before sunset.

---

seniors and students, 2.50€ ($4) for children ages 3 to 13, and free for children 2 and under.

Scheveningen ★
5km (3 miles) NW of The Hague center

A chic beach resort with a notoriously hard-to-pronounce name, Scheveningen (try *Skhe*-ven-ing-en) is virtually a part of The Hague. It sports a cast of upscale restaurants with international cuisine, accommodations in all price ranges, international-name boutiques, and abundant nighttime entertainment. Until the early 19th century, this was a sleepy fishing village. You might still sight costumed fishermen's wives near the harbor—they dress up in traditional Dutch garb only for special events, like *Vlaggetjesdag* (Flag Day) around the first week of June (see "When to Go," in chapter 3) when the first of the new season's herring are landed.

To get there from The Hague, take tram nos. 1 or 9 to the beach at Gevers Deynootplein in front of the Kurhaus Hotel; 11 to the beach between the Kurhaus and the fishing harbor; and 10 or 17 to the harbor area. Tourist information is available from **VVV Scheveningen,** Gevers Deynootweg 1134 (mailing address: Postbus 85456, 2500 CD Den Haag; © **0900/340-3505;** fax 070/352-0426; www.denhaag.com; tram: 1 or 9), at the Palace Promenade mall. The office is open Monday to Friday from 9:30am to 5:30pm, Saturday from 10am to 5pm, and Sunday from 10am to 3pm.

In Scheveningen, you can stroll on dunes, go deep-sea fishing in the North Sea, and splash in the waves. The beach zone is called Scheveningen Bad—but it looks pretty good. A 3km (2-mile) promenade borders the wide sand beach and has as its highlight the **Scheveningen Pier ★** (© **070/306-5500;** www.pier.nl; tram: 1 or 9), jutting out onto the North Sea. There's plenty to do here, from a casino, cafe-restaurant, and 60m-high (200-ft.) observation tower, to a "play island" for kids.

At **Sea Life Scheveningen,** Strandweg (aka the Boulevard) 13 (© **070/354-2100;** www.sealife.nl; tram: 1), an aquarium, you can observe denizens of the deep, including sharks, swimming above your head in a walk-through underwater tunnel. The aquarium is open August, daily from 10am to 7pm; and September to July, daily from 10am to 6pm; it's closed December 25. Admission is 12€ ($19) for adults, 11€ ($18) for seniors and visitors with disabilities, 8.50€ ($14) for children ages 3 to 11, and free for children 2 and under.

Tuxedoed croupiers serve up blackjack and roulette at **Holland Casino Scheveningen,** Kurhausweg 1 (© **070/306-7777;** www.hollandcasino.com; tram: 1 or 9), across from the restored 19th-century Kurhaus Hotel. There's roulette, blackjack, punto banco, slot machines, and more. The dress code is "correct" (collar and tie for men), and the minimum age is 18. You need your passport to get in. The casino is open daily (except

> **(Tips** **Riding the Rails**
>
> **Netherlands Railways** (📞 **0900/9292;** www.ns.nl) trains run frequently
> throughout the day from Amsterdam Centraal Station to all of the cities and
> many of the towns described in this chapter. Trip times are short: Rotterdam, the
> most distant destination in this chapter, is just an hour away.

May 4 and Dec 31) from 12:30pm to 3am. Admission is 5€ ($8); Wednesday is "ladies
day," and admission is free for all visitors.

WHERE TO DINE

Café-Restaurant Greve ★ MEDITERRANEAN   What was once a car showroom
is now a popular cafe-restaurant. Its large windows look out on lively Torenstraat, and
the restaurant is intimate with its low ceiling, candlelight, and wooden tables. There's a
small a la carte menu, but together with the list of daily specials it's difficult to make a
choice. An ideal solution for small appetites is to choose a dish either as a starter or as a
main course. Fish and lamb dishes, like bouillabaisse or lamb cutlets with feta cheese and
ouzo sauce, are popular.

Torenstraat 138 (at Veenkade). 📞 **070/360-3919.** www.greve.nl. Main courses 12€–20€ ($19–$32). AE,
DC, MC, V. Cafe daily 10am–1am. Restaurant Mon–Sat 6–11pm; Sun 6–10pm. Tram: 17 to Noordwal.

Le Bistroquet ★ CONTINENTAL   This small, popular restaurant in the city center
is one of The Hague's finest. Its quietly elegant dining room features lovely table settings.
The menu, though short, is to the point, and covers lamb, fish, and poultry dishes. A fine
choice is the three variations of Texel lamb with roasted garlic and a basil sauce. Seafood
checks in with an excellent lemon-crusted halibut served with asparagus, scallop-stuffed
cannelloni, and a parsley sauce.

Lange Voorhout 98. 📞 **070/360-1170.** www.bistroquet.nl. Reservations recommended on weekends.
Main courses 23€–39€ ($37–$62). AE, DC, MC, V. Mon–Fri noon–2pm and 6–10pm; Sat 6–10pm. Tram: 10,
16, or 17 to Kneuterdijk.

Stadsherberg 't Goude Hooft ★★ DUTCH/CONTINENTAL   There's an old
Dutch flavor to this wonderful cafe-restaurant overlooking the city's market square. Its
1600s exterior cloaks a 1939 interior installed after a fire. In fact, the establishment dates
back to 1423, and was originally a tavern before being transformed in 1660 into a coffeehouse, and finally a cafe-restaurant in 1939. Wood beams, brass chandeliers, and
rustic furnishings harmonize with stained-glass windows, medieval banners, and murals.
An extensive menu covers everything from snacks to light lunches to full dinners. Look
for dishes like Guinea fowl with thyme sauce, or red perch with saffron sauce. This also
is a good place to drop by for a cocktail and snack, or just for a beer or coffee. There's a
sidewalk terrace on Dagelijkse Groenmarkt.

Dagelijkse Groenmarkt 13 (at the Grote Kerk). 📞 **070/346-9713.** www.tgoudehooft.nl. Main courses
12€–27€ ($19–$43). AE, DC, MC, V. Mon noon–6pm; Tues–Wed and Fri–Sat 10am–7pm; Thurs 10am–
9:30pm; Sun 11am–6pm. Tram: 17 to Gravenstraat.

9 ROTTERDAM

58km (36 miles) SW of Amsterdam

For a change from the thick blanket of history in and around Amsterdam, consider a visit to this cutting-edge Dutch city. Here, instead of the usual Dutch web of little streets and alleyways, there's a spacious and elegant shopping mall; instead of Amsterdam's miles of winding canals, there's the world's busiest ocean harbor: Europoort.

Rotterdam is fascinating to see and experience, particularly considering that this city was a living monument to Holland's 17th-century Golden Age until it was bombed to rubble during World War II. At the war's end, rather than try to re-create the old, Rotterdammers looked on their misfortune as an opportunity and approached their city as a clean slate. They relished the chance to create an efficient, elegant, and workable modern city. The result won't be to everybody's taste, but does attest to their ability to find impressive solutions.

ESSENTIALS

GETTING THERE At least two trains run each hour from Amsterdam Centraal Station to Rotterdam Centraal Station; the trip takes around 1 hour. A round-trip ticket is 24€ ($38). By car from Amsterdam, take A4/E19 to The Hague, then A13/E19 to Rotterdam.

VISITOR INFORMATION VVV Rotterdam's mailing address is Postbus 30235, 3001 DE Rotterdam (© 0900/403-4065; fax 010/413-3124; www.vvvrotterdam.nl). The **VVV Rotterdam Store,** Coolsingel 5 (at Hofplein), is open for visits Monday to Thursday from 9am to 6pm, Friday from 9am to 9pm, Saturday from 9am to 5:30pm, and Sunday from 10am to 5pm. The **VVV Rotterdam Info Cafe** in the Grand Café-Restaurant Engels, Stationsplein 45 (Weena entrance), is open Monday to Saturday from 9am to 5:30pm, and Sunday from 10am to 5pm.

SPECIAL EVENTS Each year, for 3 days every July, jazz greats from around the world gather in Holland for the **North Sea Jazz Festival** (© 015/214-8393; www.northsea jazz.nl). This nonstop extravaganza features star performances by internationally acclaimed musicians, in some 200 concerts of jazz, blues, bebop, and world music, at the giant **Ahoy** venue.

WHAT TO SEE & DO

Another of Holland's fine-art treasure-troves is the **Museum Boijmans van Beuningen** ★, Museumpark 18–20 (© 010/441-9400; www.boijmans.rotterdam.nl; tram: 4 or 5). Dutch painters share wall space with an international contingent that includes Salvador Dalí and Man Ray, Titian and Tintoretto, Degas and Daumier. Fine collections of porcelain, silver, glass, and Delftware are also on display. The museum is open Tuesday to Sunday from 11am to 5pm; it's closed January 1, April 30, and December 25. Admission is 9€ ($14) for adults, 4.50€ ($7.20) for students, free for visitors 17 and under, and free for all visitors on Wednesday.

Not all of Rotterdam is spanking new. A neighborhood the German bombers missed is the tiny harbor area known as **Delfshaven (Delft Harbor),** where the Puritans known as Pilgrims embarked on the first leg of their trip to Massachusetts. This is a pleasant place to spend an afternoon. Wander into the church in which the Pilgrims prayed before

> ## Fun Facts Working People
>
> So hard-working are Rotterdam's citizens that they are said to be "born with their sleeves already rolled up."

departure, peek into antiques shops and galleries, and check on the progress of this historic area's housing renovations.

Two interesting places to visit in Delfshaven are the **Zakkendragershuisje (Sack Carriers' Guild House),** Voorstraat 13–15, where artisans demonstrate the art of pewter casting, and the adjoining warehouses that together make up the **Museum De Dubbelde Palmboom (Double Palm Tree Museum),** Voorhaven 12 (✆ **010/476-1533;** www. hmr.rotterdam.nl; Metro: Delfshaven), which displays objects unearthed during the excavations of Rotterdam. Both are open Tuesday to Sunday from 11am to 5pm (closed Jan 1, Apr 30, Dec 25). Admission is 3€ ($4.80) for adults, and free for children 17 and under.

Harbor Tours

An essential part of the Rotterdam experience is taking a **Spido Harbor Tour** (✆ **010/ 275-9988;** www.spido.nl; Metro: Leuvehaven). It's an unforgettable experience to board a boat that seems large in comparison to the canal launches of Amsterdam—two tiers of indoor seating and open decks—and then to feel dwarfed by the hulking oil tankers and container ships that glide like giant whales into their berths along the miles of docks. April to September, departures from a dock below the Erasmus Bridge are every 30 to 45 minutes from 9:30am to 5pm; and October to March, two to four times a day. The basic tour, offered year-round, is a 75-minute sail along the city's waterfront; between April and September, it's possible to take an extended ($2^{1}/_{4}$-hr.) trip daily at 10am and 12:30pm; and on a limited schedule in July and August, you can make all-day excursions along Europoort's full length and to the Delta Works sluices. Tours are 9.80€ ($16) for adults, 5.80€ ($9.30) for children ages 4 to 11, and free for children 3 and under.

WHERE TO DINE

Brasserie Henkes ★ CONTINENTAL   Henkes' Brasserie is an ideal place to appreciate the special atmosphere of old **Delfshaven (Delft Harbor).** The waterside terrace invites you to while away a sunny afternoon, interrupted only by a leisurely stroll down the harbor, then to return for dinner. Inside, the old Henkes' *jenever* (Dutch gin) distillery has been completely transformed; the interior now features the furnishings of a 19th-century Belgian insurance bank. Warm woodwork and brass chandeliers create a dining room on a grand scale. Enjoy seafood and meat dishes or seasonal specialties like venison with chocolate-port sauce.

Voorhaven 17 (at Delfshaven). ✆ **010/425-5596.** www.henkes.nl. Main courses 15€–20€ ($24–$32); fixed-price menu 28€ ($45). AE, DC, MC, V. Daily 11:30am–midnight; kitchen closes at 10pm. Metro: Delfshaven.

Grand Café-Restaurant Engels INTERNATIONAL   This marvelous eatery is actually a complex of four restaurants, each dedicated to a different international cuisine: Don Quijote (Spanish), Tokaj (Hungarian), the Beefeater (British), and Brasserie Engels (Dutch/Continental). Tokaj and Don Quijote offer live music. Each restaurant offers an

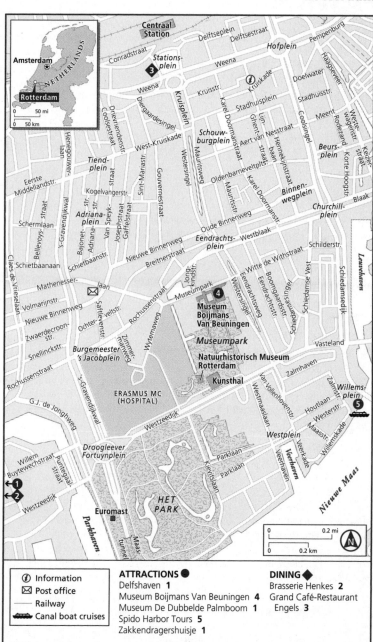

Amsterdam

NETHERLANDS

Rotterdam

0   50 mi
0   50 km

Centraal Station

Delftseplein

Delftsestraat

Hofplein

Pempenburg

Conradstraat

Stations-plein

Weena

Haagseveer

Weena

Kruisstr.

Kruiskade

Doelwater

Schouwburgplein

Stadhuisplein

Stadhuisstr.

Meent

Weste-wagenstr.

Rodezand

Beurs-plein

Keizer-straat

Korte Hoogstr.

Binnen-wegplein

Churchill-plein

Blaak

Oude Binnenweg

Westblaak

Schilderstr.

Eendrachts-plein

Nieuwe Binnenweg

Breitnerstraat

Witte de Withstraat

Leuvehaven

Schiedamsedijk

Museumpark

4

Museum Boijmans Van Beuningen

Museumpark

Natuurhistorisch Museum Rotterdam

Kunsthal

Schiedamse Vest

Vasteland

ERASMUS MC (HOSPITAL)

Westzeedijk

Van Vollenhovenstr.

Zalmhaven

Willems-plein

5

Droogleever Fortuynplein

Westplein

Maasstr.

Willemskade

1

2

Euromast

HET PARK

Nieuwe Maas

Parkhaven

Maas-tunnel

0   0.2 mi
0   0.2 km

(i) Information
✉ Post office
— Railway
⛴ Canal boat cruises

ATTRACTIONS ●
Delfshaven **1**
Museum Boijmans Van Beuningen **4**
Museum De Dubbelde Palmboom **1**
Spido Harbor Tours **5**
Zakkendragershuisje **1**

DINING ◆
Brasserie Henkes **2**
Grand Café-Restaurant Engels **3**

Grand Harbor

A dredged deepwater channel connects Rotterdam with the North Sea and forms a 32km-long (20-mile) harbor known as **Europoort** (*"poort"* is pronounced like "port" in English). This handles more ships and more cargo every year than any other port in the world—20,000 ships and more than 300 million metric tons of cargo. You may think visiting a harbor is boring business on a vacation, but Rotterdam's is one of the most memorable sights in Holland.

a la carte menu (listing full dinners, light meals, sandwiches, omelets, and snacks) and vegetarian options.

Stationsplein 45 (next to Centraal Station, in the Groothandelsgebouw). ☏ **010/411-9550.** www.engels. nl. Main courses 16€–20€ ($26–$32); fixed-price menus and buffet 19€–24€ ($30–$38). AE, DC, MC, V. Daily 8am–1am. Metro: Centraal Station.

10 DELFT, LEIDEN & GOUDA

These three historic towns in Zuid-Holland province are generally similar in character. It won't likely be possible to do all three on a time-limited side tour from Amsterdam, but a visit to any one of them will add a whole new dimension to your trip.

DELFT ★★

54km (33 miles) SW of Amsterdam

Yes, this is the home of the famous blue-and-white porcelain, and you can visit the factory where it's produced. But don't let Delftware be your only reason to visit. The small, handsome city was the cradle of the Dutch Republic, is the burial place of the royal family, and was the birthplace and inspiration of artist Jan Vermeer, the 17th-century master of light and subtle emotion. Quiet and intimate, Delft has flowers in its flower boxes and linden trees bending over gracious canals.

Essentials
GETTING THERE   There's hourly train service from Amsterdam. The ride there takes around 1 hour and a round-trip ticket costs 21€ ($34). From The Hague, go by tram, for about 1.35€ ($2.15) one-way. By car, the town is just off A13/E19, the Hague-Rotterdam expressway.

VISITOR INFORMATION   **Tourist Information Delft,** Hippolytusbuurt 4, 2611 HN Delft (☏ **0900/515-1555** from inside Holland, 31-15/215-4051 from abroad, fax 015/215-4051; www.delft.nl) is in the center of town. The office is open April to September, Sunday and Monday from 10am to 6pm, Tuesday to Friday from 9am to 6pm, and Saturday from 10am to 5pm; October to March, Sunday from 11am to 3pm, Monday from 11am to 4pm, and Tuesday to Saturday from 10am to 4pm.

What to See & Do
Vermeer's house is long gone, as are his paintings. But you can visit the **Oude Kerk (Old Church),** Heilige Geestkerkhof (☏ **015/212-3015;** www.oudekerk-delft.nl), where he's

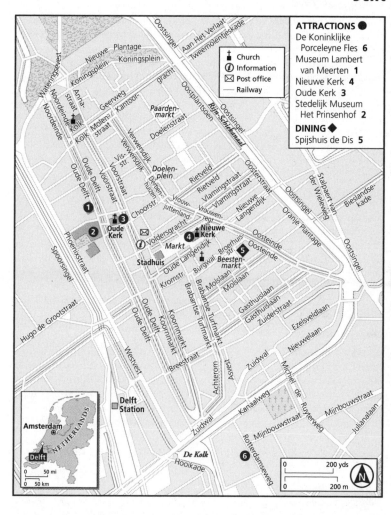

ATTRACTIONS ●
De Koninklijke
   Porceleyne Fles **6**
Museum Lambert
   van Meerten **1**
Nieuwe Kerk **4**
Oude Kerk **3**
Stedelijk Museum
   Het Prinsenhof **2**
DINING ◆
Spijshuis de Dis **5**

Church
Information
Post office
Railway

buried; it's noted for its 27 stained-glass windows by Joep Nicolas. You should also visit the **Nieuwe Kerk (New Church)** ★, Markt (© **015/212-3025;** www.nieuwekerk-delft. nl), where Prince William of Orange and other members of the House of Oranje-Nassau are buried. Climb its tower, which is 109m (357 ft.) high. Both churches are open April to October, Monday to Saturday from 9am to 6pm; November to March, Monday to Friday from 11am to 4pm, and Saturday from 11am to 5pm. Combined admission is 3.20€ ($5.10) for adults, 2.70€ ($4.30) for seniors, 1.60€ ($2.55) for children ages 5 to 14, and free for children 4 and under; admission to the Nieuwe Kerk tower is 2.70€ ($4.30) for adults, 2.20€ ($3.50) for seniors, 1.10€ ($1.75) for children ages 5 to 14, and free for children 4 and under.

The **Stedelijk Museum Het Prinsenhof,** Sint-Agathaplein 1 (📞 **015/260-2358;** www.prinsenhof-delft.nl), on the nearby Oude Delft canal, is where William I of Orange (William the Silent) lived and had his headquarters over the years during which he helped found the Dutch Republic. He was assassinated here in 1584 by Balthasar Gérard, a French Catholic, and you can see the bullet holes from the fusillade that felled him in the stairwell. Today, the Prinsenhof is a museum of paintings, tapestries, silverware, and pottery, and is the site of the annual **Delft Art and Antiques Fair,** held in late October or early November. The museum is open Tuesday to Saturday from 10am to 5pm, and Sunday and holidays from 1 to 5pm; it's closed January 1 and December 25. Admission is 6€ ($9.60) for adults, 5€ ($8) for seniors and children ages 12 to 16, and free for children 11 and under.

In the same neighborhood, view a fine collection of old Delft tiles displayed in the wood-paneled setting of a 19th-century mansion-museum called **Lambert van Meerten,** Oude Delft 199 (📞 **015/260-2358;** www.lambertvanmeerten-delft.nl). The museum is open Tuesday to Saturday from 10am to 5pm, and Sunday and holidays from 1 to 5pm; it's closed January 1 and December 25. Admission is 6€ ($9.60) for adults, 5€ ($8) for seniors and children ages 12 to 16, and free for children 11 and under.

To witness a demonstration of the traditional art of making and hand-painting Delft-ware, visit the factory and showroom at **De Koninklijke Porceleyne Fles,** Rotterdamseweg 196 (📞 **015/251-2030;** www.royaldelft.com; bus: 63, 121, or 129 to Jaffalaan), founded in 1653. It's open from the third week in March to October, daily from 9am to 5pm; November to the third week in March, Monday to Saturday from 9am to 5pm; it's closed December 25 to January 1. Admission is 4€ ($6.40) for adults, and free for children 12 and under (for group visits, it's 2.50€/$4).

Where to Dine

Spijshuis de Dis ★ DUTCH   Some of Holland's best Dutch cooking is at this atmospheric restaurant east of the market. Traditional plates presented in modern variations include *Bakke pot*—a served-in-the-pan stew made from three kinds of meat (beef, chicken, and rabbit) in beer sauce and VOC mussels (named after the Dutch initials for the United East India Company), with garlic, ginger, and curry. Steaks and lamb filet are other specialties. If you're feeling decadent, go for the luscious dessert of vanilla ice cream with hot cherries, whipped cream, and cherry brandy.

Beestenmarkt 36 (2 blocks from the Markt). 📞 **015/213-1782.** www.spijshuisdedis.com. Main courses 14€–22€ ($22–$35); fixed-price menu 30€ ($48). AE, DC, MC, V. Thurs–Tues 5–9:30pm.

LEIDEN ★

36km (22 miles) SW of Amsterdam

Stately yet bustling, the old heart of Leiden is classic Dutch, and filled with handsome, gabled brick houses along canals spanned by graceful bridges. The Pilgrims lived here for 11 years before sailing to North America on the *Mayflower.* Leiden's proudest homegrown moment came in 1574, when it became the only Dutch town to withstand a Spanish siege. This is also the birthplace of the Dutch tulip trade—and of Rembrandt. The home of the oldest university in the Netherlands is here too, founded in 1575. With 14 museums, covering subjects ranging from antiquities, natural history, and anatomy to clay pipes and coins, Leiden seems perfectly justified in calling itself Holland's *Museumstad* (Museum City).

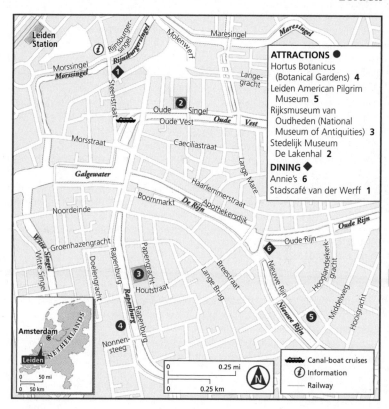

Essentials

GETTING THERE   Trains run frequently (four to six trains per hour) from Amsterdam Centraal Station. The ride takes around 35 minutes and is 14€ ($22) round-trip. Leiden Centraal Station is about a 10-minute walk northwest of the center. By car, take A4/ E19.

VISITOR INFORMATION   VVV Leiden, Stationsweg 2D, 2312 AV Leiden (✆ 0900/ 222-2333; fax 071/516-1227; www.leiden.nl), is just outside the rail station. The office is open Monday from 11am to 5:30pm, Tuesday to Friday from 9:30am to 5:30pm, Saturday from 10am to 4:30pm, and (Apr–Aug) Sunday from 11am to 3pm.

What to See & Do

Among the spectacular antiquities at the **Rijksmuseum van Oudheden (National Museum of Antiquities)** ★★, Rapenburg 28 (✆ 071/516-3163; www.rmo.nl), is the 4.5m-high (15-ft.), 1st-century-A.D. Temple of Taffeh, which the Egyptian government gave to the Dutch nation for its assistance with saving monuments before the construction of the Aswan High Dam. The museum is open Tuesday to Friday from 10am to

> **Fun Facts** **Intelligence Test**
>
> As a reward for their heroic resistance during the 1574 Spanish siege, Prince William of Orange offered the people of Leiden a choice—a tax break or a university. They chose the university.

5pm, and Saturday, Sunday, and holidays from noon to 5pm (closed Jan 1, Oct 3, Dec 25). Admission is 8.50€ ($14) for adults, 7.50€ ($12) for seniors, 5.50€ ($8.80) for children ages 4 to 17, and free for children 3 and under.

The university's **Hortus Botanicus (Botanical Gardens,** ca. 1587), Rapenburg 73 (© **071/527-7249;** www.hortus.leidenuniv.nl), are also noteworthy. In 1592, botanist Carolus Clusius (see the "Roots of a Love Affair" box, below) brought the first tulip bulbs to Holland and planted them here—but he never got to see them flower because rivals stole them. The gardens are open April to October, daily from 10am to 6pm; November to February, Sunday to Friday from 10am to 4pm; and March daily 10am to 4pm. They're closed January 1, the last week in December, and October 3. Admission is 5€ ($8) for adults, 3€ ($4.80) for seniors, 2.50€ ($4) for children ages 4 to 12, and free for children 3 and under.

Visit the **Stedelijk Museum De Lakenhal,** Oude Singel 28–32 (© **071/516-5360;** www.lakenhal.nl), to view works by native sons Rembrandt and Jan Steen, plus period rooms from the 17th to 19th centuries, and temporary modern-art exhibits. Also on display is Leiden's pride and joy: a copper stewpot said to have been retrieved by a small boy who crawled through a chink in the city wall just minutes after the lifting of the Spanish siege. In the enemy's camp, he found this very pot full of boiling stew and brought it back to feed Leiden's starving inhabitants. Ever since, stew has been a national dish and is still traditionally prepared for the Leiden city holiday, October 3, the anniversary of its liberation. Every year on this day, *haring en witte brood* (herring and white bread) are distributed, just as they were in 1574. The museum is open Tuesday to Friday from 10am to 5pm, and Saturday, Sunday, and holidays from noon to 5pm; October 3 10am to noon; it's closed January 1 and December 25. Admission is 4€ ($6.40) for adults, 2.50€ ($4) for seniors, and free for children 17 and under.

Leiden & the Pilgrims

To touch base with the Pilgrims, who lived in Leiden between 1609 and 1620, pick up the VVV brochure *A Pilgrimage Through Leiden: A Walk in the Footsteps of the Pilgrim Fathers.* The walk starts at the **Lodewijkskerk (Louis Church),** which was used as a meeting place by the town's cloth guild. William Bradford, who later became the governor of New Plymouth (Plymouth, Massachusetts), was a member of this guild. The walk takes you past the **Groenehuis (Green House)** on William Brewstersteeg, where in an attached printing shop, William Brewster's and Thomas Brewer's *Pilgrim Press,* published the religious views that so angered King James and the Church of England. Plaques at the brick **Sint-Pieterskerk (St. Peter's Church),** in a small square off Kloksteeg, memorialize the Pilgrims, who worshiped here and lived in its shadow.

An almshouse, the **Jean Pesijnhofje,** now occupies the restored **Groene Port (Green Door)** house on Kloksteeg in which Rev. John Robinson and 21 Pilgrim families lived.

Robinson was forced to stay behind because of illness and is buried in the church. The almshouse is named for Jean Pesijn, a Belgian Protestant who joined the Leiden community along with his wife, Marie de la Noye, and whose son Philip sailed for North America in 1621, where his surname would change to Delano. On July 21, 1620, the 66 departing Pilgrims boarded barges at Rapenburg Quay for the trip by canal from Leiden to the harbor of Delft, now Delfshaven in Rotterdam. From there, they sailed on the *Speedwell* for England, where the *Mayflower* awaited them.

At the **Leiden American Pilgrim Museum**, Beschuitsteeg 9 (© **071/512-2413;** www.rootsweb.ancestry.com), you'll hear a recorded commentary about the Pilgrims and see photocopies of documents relating to their 11-year residence in Leiden. The museum is open Wednesday to Saturday from 1 to 5pm. Admission is 3€ ($4.80), and free for children 5 and under.

Leiden & Rembrandt

In 1606, the great artist Rembrandt van Rijn was born in Leiden. He later moved to Amsterdam, where he won fame and fortune—and later suffered bankruptcy and obscurity. In his hometown, a **Rembrandt Walk** includes the site of the birthplace (since demolished), the Latin School he attended as a boy, and his first studio.

Where to Dine

Annie's DUTCH/CONTINENTAL   This lively restaurant at water level has vaulted cellars that are a favorite eating spot for students and locals, who spill out onto the waterfront terrace in fine weather. When the canals are frozen, the view of skaters practicing their turns is enchanting. The dinner menu is simple but wholesome and, during the day, you can enjoy sandwiches or tapas.

Hoogstraat 1A (at Oude Rijn). © **071/512-5737.** www.anniesverjaardag.nl. Main courses 8.75€–16€ ($14–$26). No credit cards. Sun–Thurs 10am–1am; Fri–Sat 10am–2am.

Stadscafé van der Werff ★ CONTINENTAL   This relaxed cafe-restaurant in a grand 1930s villa on the old town's edge is popular with the town's students and citizens. Even if you're not having dinner, enjoying dishes like an Indonesian satay, or the surf-and-turf *kalfsbiefstukje met gebakken gambas en een kreeftensaus* (beefsteak with fried prawns in lobster sauce), you can still while away your evening just having a drink and reading a paper. The cafe is open until 1am.

Steenstraat 2 (off Beestenmarkt). © **071/513-0335.** www.stadscafevanderwerff.nl. Main courses 13€–20€ ($21–$32). AE, DC, MC, V. Daily 9am–1am.

Roots of a Love Affair

In the spring of 1594, a respected yet perennially grouchy botanist, Carolus Clusius, strode into the Hortus Botanicus, the University of Leiden's research garden. He stopped beside an experiment begun the previous year, and cast a critical eye over some colorful tulips waving in the breeze. Clusius was no admirer of humanity, but flowers were something else, so we may suppose that his dyspeptic disposition softened for a moment as he admired the first tulips ever grown in Holland. A nation's love affair with a flower had begun.

40km (25 miles) S of Amsterdam

In addition to its famous cheese, Gouda (pronounced *Khow*-dah) is noted for its candles: Each year, in the middle of December, the market and the Town Hall are ravishingly candlelit (see "When to Go," in chapter 3).

Essentials

GETTING THERE   Trains depart every hour from Amsterdam Centraal Station, via Leiden or Rotterdam, for Gouda; on the fastest trains, the trip takes 50 minutes. A round-trip ticket is 18€ ($29). By car from Amsterdam, take A4/E19 and N207 south.

VISITOR INFORMATION   VVV Gouda, Markt 27, 2801 JJ Gouda (© **0900/4683-2888;** fax 0182/583-210; www.vvvgouda.nl), is open Monday from 1 to 5:30pm, Tuesday to Friday from 9:30am to 5:30pm, Saturday from 10am to 4pm, and Sunday (July–Aug) noon to 4pm.

What to See & Do

Come here on a Thursday between 10am and 12:30pm from about the third week in June to the first week in September, when the lively **Goudse kaasmarkt (Gouda cheese market)** ★ brings in farmers driving brightly painted wagons piled high with round cheeses in orange skins. Walk to the back of the **Stadhuis (Town Hall)** to sample Gouda cheese. This stone building, with stepped gables and red shutters, is reputed to be Holland's oldest town hall, and parts of its Gothic facade date from 1449.

The monumental **Waag (Weighing House)** ★, Markt 35–36 (© **0182/529-996;** www.goudakaas.nl), dating from 1669, is Gouda's pride. An exhibit inside uses interactive audiovisual media to tell the story of cheese—visitors learn all about the manufacturing process, from grass to cow to milk to cheese, and taste the finished product. The exhibit also explains Gouda's importance as a center of Dutch dairy production. The museum is open from the first week in April to October, Tuesday to Wednesday and Friday to Sunday from 1 to 5pm, and Thursday from 10am to 5pm. Admission is 3.50€ ($5.60) for adults, 2€ ($3.20) for children ages 5 to 12, and free for children 4 and under.

Holland's longest church—and one of its most majestic—**Sint-Janskerk (Church of St. John),** Achter de Kerk 16 (© **0182/512-684;** www.st-janskerkgouda.nl), south of the Markt, has 64 stained-glass windows, made collectively of 2,412 panels. Some date back as far as the mid-1500s. To see the contrast between that stained-glass art of long ago and the work being carried out today, take a look at the most recent window, no. 28A, commemorating World War II in Holland. The church is open March to October,

---

ⒻFun Facts   Smoke It and See

Gouda has been the center of a thriving clay-pipe industry since the 17th century. One local style of pipe has a pattern on the bowl that's invisible when the pipe is new and only appears as the pipe is smoked and darkens. It's called a "mystery pipe," because the designs vary and buyers never quite know what they're getting.

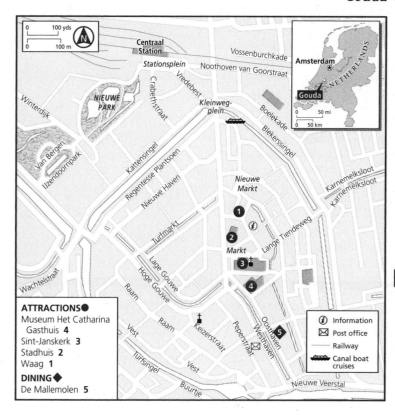

ATTRACTIONS ●
Museum Het Catharina
  Gasthuis **4**
Sint-Janskerk **3**
Stadhuis **2**
Waag **1**

DINING ◆
De Mallemolen **5**

ℹ Information
✉ Post office
···· Railway
⛴ Canal boat cruises

Monday to Saturday from 9am to 5pm; and November to February, Monday to Saturday from 10am to 4pm. Admission is 2.50€ ($4) for adults, 2.25€ ($3.60) for seniors and students, 2€ ($3.20) for school students, 1.75€ ($2.80) for children ages 5 to 12, and free for children 4 and under.

A 1665 mansion houses the **Museum Het Catharina Gasthuis,** Achter de Kerk 14 (© **0182/331-000**), close to Sint-Janskerk. The jewel of its collections, a gold chalice Countess Jacqueline of Bavaria presented to Gouda's Society of Archers in 1465, disappeared for more than a century before turning up in the Town Hall attic. There are colorful guild relics, antique furniture and pipes, *plateel* (a colorful pottery that is Gouda's answer to Delftware), and a terra-cotta plaque with a Latin inscription proclaiming that the humanist Erasmus may have been born in Rotterdam but he was conceived in Gouda. The museum is open Monday to Saturday from 10am to 5pm, and Sunday from noon to 5pm (closed Jan 1 and Dec 25). Admission is 4€ ($6.40) for adults, and free for those 18 and under.

De Mallemolen CLASSIC FRENCH   This excellent traditional restaurant is on what's known as "Rembrandt's corner." The restaurant has an Old Dutch look, though its cuisine is chiefly French. Dishes include tournedos with gooseliver in red-wine sauce. There's an antique windmill on the same street.

Oosthaven 72. ☏ **0182/515-430.** www.mallemolen.com. Reservations recommended on weekends. Main courses 18€–25€ ($29–$40); fixed-price menus 30€–53€ ($48–$85). AE, DC, MC, V. Wed–Sun 5pm–midnight.

Appendix A: Fast Facts, Toll-Free Numbers & Websites

1 FAST FACTS: AMSTERDAM

AREA CODES See "Staying Connected" in chapter 3 for info..

ATM NETWORKS & CASHPOINTS You will find automated teller machines (ATMs) at Schiphol Airport, Centraal Station, other main rail stations, and throughout the city. Among the centrally located ATMs accessible by cards linked to the Cirrus and PLUS networks and the major credit and charge cards are those at **ABN AMRO Bank,** Dam 2 (tram: 4, 9, 14, 16, 24, or 25) and Leidsestraat 1 (tram: 1, 2, or 5), at Leidseplein; **Rabobank,** Dam 16 (tram: 4, 9, 14, 16, 24, or 25); and **Fortis Bank,** Singel 548 (tram: 4, 9, 14, 16, 24, or 25), at the Flower Market.

BABYSITTERS Many hotels can arrange babysitters. A reliable local organization is the **Stichting Oppascentrale Kriterion** (℅ 020/624-5848; www.kriterionoppas. org), which has vetted babysitters who are students over 18. Rates are 6€ ($9.60) an hour, with extra charges for Friday- and Saturday-evening reservations, and for sending sitters to hotels.

BUSINESS HOURS **Banks** are open Monday to Friday from 9am to 4 or 5pm (on Thurs, some stay open until 7pm). **Offices** are generally open Monday to Friday from 9 or 10am to 4 or 5pm. Regular **shopping** hours are Monday from 10 or 11am to 6pm; Tuesday, Wednesday, and Friday from 9am to 6pm; Thursday from 9am to 9pm (Thurs is *koopavond/* late shopping evening); and Saturday from 9am to 5pm. Some stores are open Sunday from noon to 5pm.

CAR RENTALS See "Toll-Free Numbers & Websites," p. 291.

CURRENCY EXCHANGE In addition to the banks and VVV Amsterdam tourist offices, **GWK Travelex** exchanges give a fair deal; they're located at Schiphol Airport (℅ 020/653-5121); Centraal Station (℅ 020/627-2731; tram: 1, 2, 4, 5, 9, 13, 16, 17, 20, 24, 25, or 26); Damrak 125 (℅ 020/620-3236; tram: 4, 9, 14, 16, 24, or 25); Dam 23–25 (℅ 020/625-0922; tram: 4, 9, 14, 16, 24, or 25); Leidseplein 31A (℅ 020/626-7000; tram: 1, 2, 5, 7, or 10), and at some international border crossings and main rail stations. GWK provides cash advances to holders of American Express, Diners Club, Master-Card, and Visa cards, and can arrange transfers through **Western Union.**

Hotels and currency-exchange offices, which are open regular hours plus evenings and weekends, often charge a low commission (or none at all) but may give a low exchange rate.

Should you need emergency cash during the weekend when all banks are closed, have money wired to you via **Western Union** (© 800/023-5172; www.western union.com); see information for GWK, above.

DRINKING & DRUG LAWS There is no minimum legal drinking age in the Netherlands—but other laws may be used against a parent, guardian, or other third party who permits or causes a minor to abuse alcohol. For purchasing drinks that have less than 15% alcohol by volume, the minimum legal age is 16; for drinks with more than 15% alcohol by volume, the minimum legal age is 18. In both cases ID must be produced.

Using narcotic drugs is officially illegal in the Netherlands. Peddling drugs is a serious offense, and buying on the street is illegal. But in licensed premises, Amsterdam allows the sale of up to 5 grams ($^1/_5$ oz.), and possession of 30 grams ($^1/_5$ oz.) of hashish or marijuana for personal use (since you are allowed to buy only 5 grams at a time, you might conceivably face questions if you actually have 30 grams on you). Not every municipality in the Netherlands is as liberal-minded as Amsterdam when it comes to smoking pot—and even Amsterdam isn't so tolerant that you should just light up on the street, in cafes, or on trams and trains (though enough dopey people do). Possessing and using hard drugs like heroin, cocaine, and ecstasy is an offense, and the police have swept most of the downtown heroin-shooters away from the tourist centers. However, drug abusers are considered a medical and social problem here rather than merely a law-enforcement issue.

DRIVING RULES See "Getting There & Getting Around," p. 35.

ELECTRICITY Like in most of Europe, Australia, and New Zealand, the Netherlands uses 220–240 volts AC (50 cycles), compared to 110–120 volts AC (60 cycles) in Canada and the United States. Upward converters that change 110–120 volts to 220–240 volts are difficult to find in Holland, so bring one with you.

Bring a **connection kit** of the right power and phone adapters, a spare phone cord, and a spare Ethernet network cable— or find out whether your hotel supplies them to guests.

EMBASSIES & CONSULATES Both the U.S. and the U.K. have consulates in Amsterdam and embassies in The Hague (Den Haag). Other English-speaking countries have embassies only in The Hague.

The consulate of the **United Kingdom** is at Koningslaan 44, 1070 AL Amsterdam (© 020/676-4343; www.britain.nl; tram: 2). The embassy of the **United Kingdom** is at Lange Voorhout 10, 2514 ED Den Haag (© 070/427-0427; www.britain.nl).

The consulate of the **United States** is at Museumplein 19, 1071 DJ Amsterdam (© 020/575-5309; http://netherlands. usembassy.gov; tram: 3, 5, 12, or 16). The embassy of the **United States** is at Lange Voorhout 102, 2514 EJ Den Haag (© 070/ 310-2209; http://netherlands.usembassy. gov).

The embassy of **Australia** is at Carnegielaan 4, 2517 KH Den Haag (©070/ 310-8200; www.australian-embassy.nl).

The embassy of **Canada** is at Sophialaan 7, 2514 JP Den Haag (© 070/311-1600; www.canada.nl).

The embassy of **Ireland** is at Dr. Kuijperstraat 9, 2514 BA Den Haag (© 070/ 363-0993; www.irishembassy.nl).

The embassy of **New Zealand** is at Carnegielaan 10, 2517 KH Den Haag (© 070/346-9324; www.nzembassy.com).

EMERGENCIES For police assistance, an emergency doctor or an ambulance with paramedics, and for the fire department, call © 112.

GASOLINE (PETROL) A gas (petrol) station is a *benzinestation,* a *pompstation,* or a *tankstation* in Dutch. Gasoline is lead-free and sold in two varieties: euro 95 or euro 98 (for its octane number). Diesel is sold in all stations; *autogas,* also known as LPG (liquid petroleum gas), is sold in many. The Netherlands "boasts" some of the highest gasoline prices in the world, around $2^1/_2$ times the price in the U.S., but only about a tenth more than in the U.K. Taxes are already included in the printed price. One U.S. gallon equals 3.8 liters, and 1 imperial gallon equals 4.4 liters.

HOLIDAYS See "Amsterdam Calendar of Events," in chapter 3.

HOSPITALS Two hospitals with an emergency service are the **Onze-Lieve-Vrouwe Gasthuis,** Oosterpark 9 (ⓒ 020/599-9111; www.olvg.nl; tram: 3, 7, or 10), Amsterdam-Oost; and the **Academisch Medisch Centrum (AMC),** Meibergdreef 9 (ⓒ 020/566-9111; www.amc.uva.nl; Metro: Holendrecht), Amsterdam-Zuidoost.

HOT LINES For rape and sexual abuse, dial **De Eerste Lijn** (ⓒ 020/612-7576).

INSURANCE **Medical Insurance** For travel overseas, most U.S. health plans (including Medicare and Medicaid) do not provide coverage, and the ones that do often require you to pay for services upfront and reimburse you only after you return home.

As a safety net, you may want to buy travel medical insurance, particularly if you're traveling to a remote or high-risk area where emergency evacuation might be necessary. If you require additional medical insurance, try **MEDEX Assistance** (ⓒ 410/453-6300; www.medexassist.com) or **Travel Assistance International** (ⓒ 800/821-2828; www.travelassistance.com; for general information on services, call the company's **Worldwide Assistance Services, Inc.,** at ⓒ 800/777-8710).

Canadians should check with their provincial health plan offices or call **Health Canada** (ⓒ 866/225-0709; www.hc-sc.gc.ca) to find out the extent of their coverage and what documentation and receipts they must take home in case they are treated overseas.

Travelers from the U.K. should carry their European Health Insurance Card (EHIC), which replaced the E111 form as proof of entitlement to free/reduced cost medical treatment abroad (ⓒ 0845/606-2030; www.ehic.org.uk). Note, however, that the EHIC covers only "necessary medical treatment," and for repatriation costs, lost money, baggage, or cancellation, travel insurance from a reputable company should always be sought (www.travelinsuranceweb.com).

Travel Insurance The cost of travel insurance varies widely, depending on the destination, the cost and length of your trip, your age and health, and the type of trip you're taking, but expect to pay between 5% and 8% of the vacation itself. You can get estimates from various providers through **InsureMyTrip.com.** Enter your trip cost and dates, your age, and other information, for prices from more than a dozen companies.

U.K. citizens and their families who make more than one trip abroad per year may find an annual travel insurance policy works out cheaper. Check **www.moneysupermarket.com,** which compares prices across a wide range of providers for single- and multi-trip policies.

Most big travel agents offer their own insurance and will probably try to sell you their package when you book a holiday. Think before you sign. **Britain's Consumers' Association** recommends that you insist on seeing the policy and reading the fine print before buying travel insurance. The **Association of British Insurers** (ⓒ 020/7600-3333; www.abi.org.uk) gives advice by phone and publishes *Holiday Insurance,* a free guide to policy provisions and prices. You might also shop around for better deals: Try **Columbus Direct** (☎ 0870/033-9988; www.columbusdirect.net).

Trip-Cancellation Insurance Trip-cancellation insurance will help retrieve your money if you have to back out of a trip or depart early, or if your travel supplier goes bankrupt. Trip cancellation traditionally covers such events as sickness, natural disasters, and State Department advisories. The latest news in trip-cancellation insurance is the availability of **expanded hurricane coverage** and the **"any-reason"** cancellation coverage—which costs more but covers cancellations made for any reason. You won't get back 100% of your prepaid trip cost, but you'll be refunded a substantial portion. **TravelSafe** (☎ 888/885-7233; www.travelsafe.com) offers both types of coverage. Expedia also offers any-reason cancellation coverage for its air-hotel packages. For details, contact one of the following recommended insurers: **Access America** (☎ 866/807-3982; www.accessamerica.com); **Travel Guard International** (☎ 800/826-4919; www.travelguard.com); **Travel Insured International** (☎ 800/243-3174; www.travelinsured.com); and **Travelex Insurance Services** (☎ 888/457-4602; www.travelex-insurance.com).

INTERNET ACCESS Many hotels, coffeehouses (note that this generally doesn't mean pot-selling "coffeeshops"), and other businesses offer Internet access. The number of dedicated Internet cafes is in rapid decline. The **Mad Processor,** Kinkerstraat 11–13 (☎ 020/612-1818; www.madprocessor.com; tram: 7, 10, or 17), is open daily from noon until 1 or 2am; access is 2€ ($3.20) per hour.

LANGUAGE Dutch people speak Dutch, of course, but English is the second language of the Netherlands and is taught in school from the early grades.

The result is that nearly everyone speaks English fluently—so you may speak English in Amsterdam almost as freely as you do at home, particularly to anyone providing tourist services, whether a hotel receptionist, waitperson, or store clerk (cabdrivers might be another story).

LAUNDROMATS A laundromat is called a *wassalon* or *wasserette* in the Netherlands. These are generally open daily from 7 or 8am to 9 or 10pm. Some central locations: Oudebrugsgracht 22 (tram: 4, 9, 14, 16, 24, or 25), between Damrak and Nieuwendijk; Ferdinand Bolstraat 9 (tram: 16, 24, or 25), near the Heineken Experience; and Rozengracht 59 (tram: 13, 14, or 17), or on the edge of the Jordaan. For dry cleaning, go to **Palthé,** Vijzelstraat 59 (☎ 020/623-0337; tram: 16, 24, or 25), just south of Muntplein.

LOST & FOUND Don't be optimistic about your chances. There are plenty of honest Amsterdammers, but they're generally out of town when you lose something. For items lost on the city's trams, buses, and Metro trains, call ☎ 0900/8011; for railway trains and stations, call ☎ 0900/321-2100; and for Schiphol Airport, call ☎ 0900/0141.

Be sure to tell all of your credit card companies the minute you discover your wallet has been lost or stolen and file a report at the nearest police precinct. Your credit card company or insurer may require a police report number or record of the loss. Most credit card companies have an emergency toll-free number to call if your card is lost or stolen; they may be able to wire you a cash advance immediately or deliver an emergency credit card in a day or two. Local emergency numbers to call are **American Express** (☎ 020/504-8666); **Diners Club** (☎ 0800/555-1212); **MasterCard** (☎ 1-800/307-7309 or 1-636/722-7111 in the U.S.); **Visa** (☎ 0800/022-3110).

If you need emergency cash over the weekend when all banks in Amsterdam are closed, you can have money wired to you via **Western Union** (© 1-800/325-6000 in the U.S.; www.westernunion.com).

MAIL Most offices of **TNT Post** are open Monday to Friday from 9am to 5pm. The office at Singel 250, at the corner of Raadhuisstraat (tram: 13, 14, or 17), is open Monday to Friday from 7:30am to 6pm, and Saturday from 9am to noon. Standard postage for a postcard or letter to the U.S., Canada, Australia, or New Zealand is .92€ ($1.45); to the U.K. and Ireland, it's .80€ ($1.30). To appear really conversant, address your letters home in Dutch: Verenigde Staten van Amerika, Kanada, Groot-Britannië, Ierland, Australië, Nieuw-Zeeland.

MAPS See "Visitor Information," in chapter 3.

MEASUREMENTS See the chart on the inside front cover of this book for details on converting metric measurements to nonmetric equivalents.

NEWSPAPERS & MAGAZINES The main British and Irish daily newspapers, and the *International Herald Tribune, Wall Street Journal Europe, USA Today, Time, Newsweek, U.S. News & World Report, Business Week, Fortune, The Economist,* and more are available at the **American Book Center,** Spui 12 (© 020/625-5537; tram: 1, 2, or 5), and **Waterstone's,** Kalverstraat 152 (© 020/638-3821; tram: 4, 9, 14, 16, 24, or 25). Newsstands at Schiphol Airport and Centraal Station also stock a wide range of international publications.

PASSPORTS The websites listed provide downloadable passport applications as well as the current fees for processing applications. For an up-to-date, country-by-country listing of passport requirements around the world, go to the "International Travel" tab of the U.S. State Department at **http://travel.state.gov.**

For Residents of Australia You can pick up an application from your local post office or any branch of Passports Australia, but you must schedule an interview at the passport office to present your application materials. Call the **Australian Passport Information Service** at © 131-232, or visit the government website at www.passports.gov.au.

For Residents of Canada Passport applications are available at travel agencies throughout Canada or from the central **Passport Office,** Department of Foreign Affairs and International Trade, Ottawa, ON K1A 0G3 (© 800/567-6868; www.ppt.gc.ca). *Note:* Canadian children who travel must have their own passports. However, if you hold a valid Canadian passport issued before December 11, 2001, that bears the name of your child, the passport remains valid for you and your child until it expires.

For Residents of Ireland You can apply for a 10-year passport at the **Passport Office,** Setanta Centre, Molesworth Street, Dublin 2 (© 01/671-1633; www.irlgov.ie/iveagh). Those 17 and under age and 66 and over must apply for a 3-year passport. You can also apply at 1A South Mall, Cork (© 21/494-4700) or at most main post offices.

For Residents of New Zealand You can pick up a passport application at any New Zealand Passports Office or download it from the website. Contact the **Passports Office** at © 0800/225-050 in New Zealand or 04/474-8100, or log on to www.passports.govt.nz.

For Residents of the United Kingdom To pick up an application for a standard 10-year passport (5-year passport for children 15 and under), visit your nearest passport office, major post office, or travel agency or contact the **United Kingdom Passport Service** at © 0870/521-0410 or search its website at www.ukpa.gov.uk.

For Residents of the United States: Whether you're applying in person or by mail, you can download passport applications from the U.S. State Department website at **http://travel.state.gov**. To find your regional passport office, check the U.S. State Department website or call the **National Passport Information Center** toll-free number (© **877/487-2778**) for automated information.

PHARMACIES In the Netherlands a pharmacy is called an *apotheek,* and it dispenses both prescription and non-prescription medicines. Regular hours are Monday to Saturday from 9am to 5:30pm. A centrally located pharmacy is **Dam Apotheek,** Damstraat 2 (© **020/624-4331;** tram: 4, 9, 14, 16, 24, or 25), close to the National Monument on the Dam. Pharmacies post details of nearby all-night and Sunday pharmacies on their doors.

POLICE Holland's emergency phone number for the police *(politie)*—along with the fire department and the ambulance service—is © **112.** For routine matters, visit a district police office. A centrally located one is at Lijnbaansgracht 219 (© **0900/8844;** tram: 1, 2, 5, 7, or 10), off Leidseplein; calling its number can also provide details about other district police offices.

SMOKING In a city where smoking hashish is an acceptable use of the public air, it used to be that there was no mercy shown to anyone who squirmed at the thought of mere tobacco. Since July 1, 2008, all that has changed. Smoking is now forbidden in restaurants, bars, cafes, hotel public areas, and most hotel rooms. Exceptions are in separate enclosed areas for smokers, in which staff is not allowed to provide drinks, meals, or other services. Smoking tobacco in "coffeeshops" is likewise forbidden, but smoking the pot that is their stock in trade is allowed—don't ask me to explain it! Trams, buses, and Metro trains are smoke-free.

TAXES There's a value-added tax (BTW) in Holland of 6% on hotel and restaurant bills (19% on beer, wine, and liquor), and 6% or 19% (depending on the product) on purchases. This tax is always included in the price. Visitors coming from outside the European Union can shop tax-free in Amsterdam. Stores that offer tax-free shopping advertise with a HOLLAND TAX-FREE SHOPPING sign in the window, and provide the form you need to recover taxes when you leave the European Union. Refunds are available only when you spend more than 50€ ($80) in a participating store. See "The Shopping Scene," in chapter 9 for more details.

TELEPHONES See "Staying Connected" in chapter 3 for info.

TIME Amsterdam is on Western European Time (WET), which is Coordinated Universal Time (UTC), or Greenwich Mean Time (GMT), plus 1 hour. Clocks are moved ahead 1 hour for daylight-saving Western European Summer Time (WEST) between the last Sunday in March and the last Sunday in October. For example, when it's 6pm in Amsterdam, it's 9am in Los Angeles (PST), 7am in Honolulu (HST), 10am in Denver (MST), 11am in Chicago (CST), noon in New York City (EST), 5pm in London (GMT), and 2am the next day in Sydney.

For the exact local time from a "speaking clock," dial © **0900/8002.**

TIPPING The Dutch government requires that all taxes and service charges be included in the published prices of hotels, restaurants, cafes, nightclubs, salons, and sightseeing companies. Even taxi fare includes taxes and a standard 15% service charge. To be absolutely sure if a restaurant is including tax and service, look for the words *inclusief BTW en service* (BTW is the abbreviation for the Dutch words that mean value-added tax) on the bill, or ask the waiter.

Dutch waiters and hotel staff often "forget" that a service charge and a tip are in effect the same thing. If you query them, they'll likely tell you that the tip isn't included in the bill—slightly true, since it's not called a tip but a service charge. Customers pay a standard 15% whether they liked the service or not. The VVV tourist office's advice is: "Tips for extra service are always appreciated but not necessary."

To tip like the Dutch in a cafe or snack bar, leave some small change on the counter or table. In a restaurant, leave 1€ to 2€ ($1.60–$3.20) per person, or to generously reward good service, 5€ ($8) per person or 10% of the tab. Since service can tend toward the lackadaisical, you may need to make due allowance for what constitutes "good." If another staffer took the payment, give the tip to your waitperson directly.

In a hotel, tip if you wish for a long stay or extra service, but don't worry about not tipping—you're unlikely to be hassled by a bellboy who lights every lamp in your room until he hears the rattle of spare change.

Should you feel an irrational compulsion to tip taxi drivers, round up the fare by a euro or two, or splash out 5% to 10%.

TOILETS Maybe you better sit down for this one. The most important thing to remember about public toilets in Amsterdam—apart from calling them *toiletten* (twa-*lett*-en) or "WC" (*vay say*) and not restrooms—is not the usual male/female (*heren/dames*) distinction (important though that is), but to pay the person who sits at the entrance to many such places of relief. He or she has a saucer in which you're supposed to deposit your payment.

If you don't, you may have a vexed visitor in the inner sanctum while you transact your business. It's tiresome, but toilets usually cost only about .30€ (40¢), and the attendant makes sure they're clean.

If you have a toilet emergency in the Center, a good place to find relief is the NH Grand Hotel Krasnapolsky (see "The Old Center," in chapter 5). Just breeze in as if you own the "Kras," swing left past the front desk and along the corridor, past the Winter Garden restaurant, then up some steps. Another option: The restrooms at the University of Amsterdam's Atrium cafeteria (see "The Old Center," in chapter 6) are clean and open to all. Restrooms in department stores (see "Shopping A to Z," in chapter 9) are also useful. Try to avoid visiting a *urinoir* (or *pissoir*— these malodorous, open-air, male-only "comfort stations" are a standing provocation to feminists.

TRANSIT INFO For information regarding tram, bus, Metro, and train services in Amsterdam and around the Netherlands, call ✆ **0900/9292,** or visit www. 9292ov.

WATER Faucet water in Amsterdam is safe to drink—it's referred to locally as *gemeente pils* (municipal beer). Many people drink bottled mineral water, generically called *spa* even though it's not all from the Belgian Spa brand.

WEATHER For weather information, call ✆ **0900/8003** or visit www.weather. com.

2 TOLL-FREE NUMBERS & WEBSITES

MAJOR U.S. AIRLINES
(*flies internationally as well)

Continental Airlines*
✆ 800/523-3273 (in U.S. or Canada)
✆ 084/5607-6760 (in U.K.)
www.continental.com

Delta Air Lines*
✆ 800/221-1212 (in U.S. or Canada)
✆ 084/5600-0950 (in U.K.)
www.delta.com

Northwest Airlines
✆ 800/225-2525 (in U.S.)
✆ 870/0507-4074 (in U.K.)
www.flynaa.com

United Airlines*
✆ 800/864-8331 (in U.S. or Canada)
✆ 084/5844-4777 (in U.K.)
www.united.com

MAJOR INTERNATIONAL AIRLINES

Air New Zealand
✆ 800/262-1234 (in U.S.)
✆ 800/663-5494 (in Canada)
✆ 0800/028-4149 (in U.K.)
www.airnewzealand.com

British Airways
✆ 800/247-9297 (in U.S. or Canada)
✆ 087/0850-9850 (in U.K.)
www.british-airways.com

Continental Airlines
✆ 800/523-3273 (in U.S. or Canada)
✆ 084/5607-6760 (in U.K.)
www.continental.com

Delta Air Lines
✆ 800/221-1212 (in U.S. or Canada)
✆ 084/5600-0950 (in U.K.)
www.delta.com

Qantas Airways
✆ 800/227-4500 (in U.S.)
✆ 084/5774-7767 (in U.K. or Canada)
✆ 13 13 13 (in Australia)
www.qantas.com

South African Airways
✆ 271/1978-5313 (international)
✆ 0861 FLYSAA (086/135-9122)
  (in South Africa)
www.flysaa.com

United Airlines*
✆ 800/864-8331 (in U.S. or Canada)
✆ 084/5844-4777 (in U.K.)
www.united.com

US Airways*
✆ 800/428-4322 (in U.S. or Canada)
✆ 084/5600-3300 (in U.K.)
www.usairways.com

BUDGET AIRLINES

Aer Lingus
✆ 800/474-7424 (in U.S. or Canada)
✆ 087/0876-5000 (in U.K.)
www.aerlingus.com

BMI Baby
✆ 087/1224-0224 (in U.K.)
✆ 870/126-6726 (in U.S.)
www.bmibaby.com

easyJet
✆ 870/600-0000 (in U.S.)
✆ 090/5560-7777 (in U.K.)
www.easyjet.com

CAR-RENTAL AGENCIES

Alamo
✆ 800/GO-ALAMO (800/462-5266)
www.alamo.com

Auto Europe
✆ 888/223-5555 (in U.S. or Canada)
✆ 0800/2235-5555 (in U.K.)
www.autoeurope.com

Avis
✆ 800/331-1212 (in U.S. or Canada)
✆ 084/4581-8181 (in U.K.)
www.avis.com

Budget
✆ 800/527-0700 (in U.S.)
✆ 087/0156-5656 (in U.K.)
✆ 800/268-8900 (in Canada)
www.budget.com

Dollar
- ☎ 800/800-4000 (in U.S.)
- ☎ 800/848-8268 (in Canada)
- ☎ 080/8234-7524 (in U.K.)
- www.dollar.com

Hertz
- ☎ 800/645-3131
- ☎ 800/654-3001 (for international reservations)
- www.hertz.com

National
- ☎ 800/CAR-RENT (800/227-7368)
- www.nationalcar.com

Thrifty
- ☎ 800/367-2277
- ☎ 918/669-2168 (international)
- www.thrifty.com

MAJOR HOTEL & MOTEL CHAINS

Best Western International
- ☎ 800/780-7234 (in U.S. or Canada)
- ☎ 0800/393-130 (in U.K.)
- www.bestwestern.com

Comfort Inns
- ☎ 800/228-5150
- ☎ 0800/444-444 (in U.K.)
- www.ComfortInnChoiceHotels.com

Courtyard by Marriott
- ☎ 888/236-2427 (in U.S.)
- ☎ 0800/221-222 (in U.K.)
- www.marriott.com/courtyard

Crowne Plaza Hotels
- ☎ 888/303-1746
- www.ichotelsgroup.com/crowneplaza

Hilton Hotels
- ☎ 800/445-8667 (in U.S. or Canada)
- ☎ 087/0590-9090 (in U.K.)
- www.hilton.com

Holiday Inn
- ☎ 800/315-2621 (in U.S. or Canada)
- ☎ 0800/405-060 (in U.K.)
- www.holidayinn.com

InterContinental Hotels & Resorts
- ☎ 800/424-6835 (in U.S. or Canada)
- ☎ 0800/1800-1800 (in U.K.)
- www.ichotelsgroup.com

Marriott
- ☎ 877/236-2427 (in U.S. or Canada)
- ☎ 0800/221-222 (in U.K.)
- www.marriott.com

Radisson Hotels & Resorts
- ☎ 888/201-1718 (in U.S. or Canada)
- ☎ 0800/374-411 (in U.K.)
- www.radisson.com

Residence Inn by Marriott
- ☎ 800/331-3131
- ☎ 800/221-222 (in U.K.)
- www.marriott.com/residenceinn

Sheraton Hotels & Resorts
- ☎ 800/325-3535 (in U.S.)
- ☎ 800/543-4300 (in Canada)
- ☎ 0800/3253-5353 (in U.K.)
- www.starwoodhotels.com/sheraton

Westin Hotels & Resorts
- ☎ 800-937-8461 (in U.S. or Canada)
- ☎ 0800/3259-5959 (in U.K.)
- www.starwoodhotels.com/westin

Appendix B:
Useful Terms & Phrases

The Dutch people you encounter will likely speak English every bit as well as you do—some of them, annoyingly, even better. That said, no Amsterdammer will fault you for having a go at Dutch. In fact, they'll hugely appreciate any effort you make in their tongue-twister of a *taal* (language). An occasional *alstublieft* (please) and *dank U wel* (thank you) can take you a long way. These words and phrases should get you started—and help in the rare situation of dealing with people who don't speak English.

1 BASIC VOCABULARY

USEFUL ENGLISH & DUTCH PHRASES

English	Dutch	Pronunciation
Hello	**Dag/Hallo**	dakh/*ha*-loh
Good morning	**Goedenmorgen**	*khoo*-yuh-*mor*-khun
Good afternoon/evening	**Goedenavond**	*khoo*-yuhn-*af*-ond
How are you?	**Hoe gaat het met U?**	hoo *khaht* et met oo?
Very well	**Uitstekend**	out-*stayk*-end
Thank you	**Dank U wel**	*dahnk* oo wel
Goodbye	**Dag/Tot Ziens**	dakh/tot zeenss
Good night	**Goedenacht**	*khoo*-duh-nakht
See you later	**Tot straks**	Tot strahkss
Please	**Alstublieft**	*ahl*-stoo-bleeft
Yes	**Ja**	yah
No	**Neen/nee**	Nay
Excuse me	**Pardon**	par-*dawn*
Sorry	**Sorry**	*so*-ree
Do you speak English?	**Spreekt U Engels?**	spraykt oo *eng*-els
Can you help me?	**Kunt U mij helpen?**	koont oo *may*-ee *hel*-pen?
Give me . . .	**Geeft U mij . . .**	*khayft* oo may . . .
Where is . . . ?	**Waar is . . . ?**	*vahr* iz . . . ?
the station	**het station**	het *stah*-ssyonh
the post office	**het postkantoor**	het *post*-kan-tohr
a bank	**een bank**	ayn bank
a hotel	**een hotel**	ayn *ho*-tel
a restaurant	**een restaurant**	ayn res-to-*rahng*
a pharmacy/chemist	**een apotheek**	ayn a-po-*tayk*
the toilet	**het toilet**	het *twah*-let

English	Dutch	Pronunciation
To the right	**Rechts**	rekhts
To the left	**Links**	links
Straight ahead	**Rechtdoor**	rekht-*doar*
I would like . . .	**Ik zou graag . . .**	ik zow khrakh . . .
to eat	**eten**	*ay*-ten
a room for 1 night	**een kamer voor een nacht**	ayn *kah*-mer voor ayn nakht
How much is it?	**Hoe veel kost het?**	hoo fayl kawst het
The check	**De rekening**	duh *ray*-ken-ing
When?	**Wanneer?**	vah-*neer*
Yesterday	**Gisteren**	*khis*-ter-en
Today	**Vandaag**	van-*dahkh*
Tomorrow	**Morgen**	*mor*-khen
Breakfast	**Ontbijt**	*ohnt*-bayt
Lunch	**Lunch**	lunch
Dinner	**Diner**	*dee*-nay

NUMBERS

1	**een** (ayn)		16	**zestien** (*zes*-teen)
2	**twee** (tway)		17	**zeventien** (*zay*-vun-teen)
3	**drie** (dree)		18	**achttien** (*akh*-teen)
4	**vier** (veer)		19	**negentien** (*nay*-khun-teen)
5	**vijf** (vayf)		20	**twintig** (*twin*-tikh)
6	**zes** (zes)		30	**dertig** (*der*-tukh)
7	**zeven** (*zay*-vun)		40	**veertig** (*vayr*-tukh)
8	**acht** (akht)		50	**vijftig** (*vayf*-tukh)
9	**negen** (*nay*-khen)		60	**zestig** (*zes*-tukh)
10	**tien** (teen)		70	**zeventig** (*zay*-vun-tukh)
11	**elf** (elf)		80	**tachtig** (*takh*-tukh)
12	**twaalf** (tvahlf)		90	**negentig** (*nay*-khen-tukh)
13	**dertien** (*dayr*-teen)		100	**honderd** (*hon*-dayrt)
14	**veertien** (*vayr*-teen)		1,000	**duizend** (*douw*-zend)
15	**vijftien** (*vayf*-teen)			

DAYS OF THE WEEK

Monday	**Maandag** (*mahn*-dakh)		Friday	**Vrijdag** (*vray*-dakh)
Tuesday	**Dinsdag** (*deens*-dakh)		Saturday	**Zaterdag** (*zahter*-dakh)
Wednesday	**Woensdag** (*voohns*-dakh)		Sunday	**Zondag** (*zohn*-dakh)
Thursday	**Donderdag** (*donder*-dakh)			

MONTHS

January	**Januari** (*yahn*-oo-aree)		May	**Mai** (*mah*-eey)
February	**Februari** (*fayhb*-roo-aree)		June	**Juni** (yoo-*nee*)
March	**Maart** (mahrt)		July	**Juli** (yoo-*lee*)
April	**April** (ah-*pril*)		August	**August** (awh-*khoost*)

September **September** (sep-*tem*-buhr)
October **Oktober** (oct-*oah*-buhr)

November **November** (noa-*vem*-buhr)
December **December** (day-*sem*-buhr)

SEASONS

Spring **Lente** (*len*-tuh)
Summer **Zomer** (*zoh*-muhr)

Fall/Autumn **Herfst** (herfsst)
Winter **Winter** (*vin*-tuhr)

SIGNS

Doorgaand Verkeer Through Traffic
Doorgaand Verkeer Gestremd
Road Closed
Geen Doorgaand Verkeer No
Through Traffic

Niet Parkeeren No Parking
Verboden Te Roken No Smoking
Vrije Toegang Admission Free/
Allowed
Wegomlegging Diversion

2 DUTCH MENU TERMS

Basics

ontbijt breakfast
lunch lunch
diner dinner
voorgerechten starters/appetizers
hoofdgerechten main courses
nagerechten main courses
brood bread
stokbrood French bread
boter butter
honing honey

hutspot mashed potatoes and carrots
jam jam
kaas cheese
mosterd mustard
pannekoeken pancakes
peper pepper
saus sauce
suiker sugar
zout salt

SOUPS (SOEPEN)

aardappelsoep potato soup
bonensoep bean soup
erwtensoep pea soup (usually includes bacon or sausage)
groentensoep vegetable soup

kippensoep chicken soup
soep soup
tomatensoep tomato soup
uiensoep onion soup

EGGS (EIEREN)

eier egg
hardgekookte eieren hard-boiled eggs
omelette omelet

roereieren scrambled eggs
spiegeleieren fried eggs
zachtgekookte eieren boiled eggs

FISH (VIS) & SEAFOOD (ZEEBANKET)

forel trout
garnalen prawns
gerookte zalm smoked salmon
haring herring

kabeljauw cod
kreeft lobster
makreel mackerel
mosselen mussels

oesters   oysters
paling   eel
sardienen   sardines

schelvis   haddock
tong   sole
zalm   salmon

MEATS (VLEES)

bief   beef
biefstuk   steak
eend   duck
fricandeau   roast pork
gans   goose
gehakt   minced meat
haasbiefstuk   filet steak
ham   ham
kalfsvlees   veal
kalkoen   turkey
kip   chicken

konijn   rabbit
koude schotel   cold cuts
lamscotelet   lamb chops
lamsvlees   lamb
lever   liver
ragout   beef stew
rookvlees   smoked meat
runder   beef
spek   bacon
worst   sausage

VEGETABLES (GROENTEN) & SALADS (SLA)

aardappelen   potatoes
asperges   asparagus
augurken   pickles
bieten   beets
bloemkool   cauliflower
bonen   beans
champignons   mushrooms
erwten   peas
groenten   vegetables
knoflook   garlic
komkommer   cucumber
komkommersla   cucumber salad
kool   cabbage

patates frites   french fries
prei   leek
prinsesseboonen   green beans
purée   mashed potatoes
radijsen   radishes
rapen   turnips
rijst   rice
sla   lettuce, salad
spinazie   spinach
tomaten   tomatoes
uien   onions
wortelen   carrots
zuurkool   sauerkraut

DESSERTS (NAGERECHTEN)

appelgebak   apple pie
appelmoes   applesauce
cake   cake
compòte   stewed fruits
gebak   pastry
ijs   ice cream
jonge kaas   young cheese (mild)

koekjes   cookies
oliebollen   doughnuts
oude kaas   old cheese (strong)
room   cream
slagroom   whipped cream
smeerkaas   cheese spread
speculaas   spiced cookies

FRUITS (VRUCHTEN)

aapel   apple
aardbei   strawberry

ananas   pineapple
citroen   lemon

druiven   grapes
framboos   raspberry
kersen   cherries

peer   pear
perzik   peach
pruimen   plums

BEVERAGES (DRANKEN)

bier (or pils)   beer
cognac   brandy
fles   bottle
glas   glass
jenever   gin
koffie   coffee

melk   milk
rode wijn   red wine
thee   tea
water   water
witte wijn   white wine

COOKING TERMS

doorbaken   cooked
gebakken   baked, fried
gebraden   roast
gegrild   grilled
gekookt   boiled/cooked
gerookt   smoked
geroosteerd   boiled

gestoofd   stewed
goed doorbakken   well-done
half doorbakken   rare
koud   cold
niet doorbakken   rare
warm   hot

INDEX

See also Accommodations and Restaurant indexes, below.

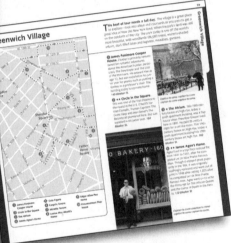

A Guide for Every Type of Traveler

Frommer's Complete Guides

For those who value complete coverage, candid advice, and lots of choices in all price ranges.

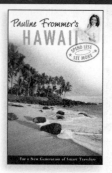

Pauline Frommer's Guides

For those who want to experience a culture, meet locals, and save money along the way.

MTV Guides

For hip, youthful travelers who want a fresh perspective on today's hottest cities and destinations.

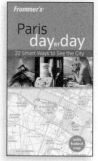

Day by Day Guides

For leisure or business travelers who want to organize their time to get the most out of a trip.

Frommer's With Kids Guides

For families traveling with children ages 2 to 14 seeking kid-friendly hotels, restaurants, and activities.

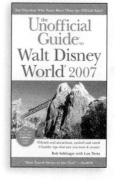

Unofficial Guides

For honeymooners, families, business travelers, and others who value no-nonsense, *Consumer Reports*–style advice.

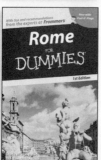

For Dummies Travel Guides

For curious, independent travelers looking for a fun and easy way to plan a trip.

Visit Frommers.com

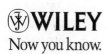